The People in Arms
Military Myth and National Mobilization
since the French Revolution

The People in Arms is concerned with the mass mobilization of society for war. It takes as its starting point the French *levée en masse* of 1793, which replaced former theories and regulations concerning the obligation of military service with a universal concept more encompassing in its moral claims than any that had prevailed under the Old Regime. The *levée en masse* would go down in history as a spontaneous, free expression of the French people's ideals and enthusiasm, and became a crucial source for one of the most powerful organizing myths of modern politics: that compulsory, mass social mobilizations merely express, and give effective form to, the wishes or higher values of society and its members. The papers presented here seek to analyze and trace the historical memory and influence of the original *levée* and, more generally, compare episodes in which the distinctive ideological configuration that it typified plays a leading role.

Daniel Moran teaches international and military history in the Department of National Security Affairs at the Naval Postgraduate School. He is also a Fellow of the Hoover Institution at Stanford University. His most recent book is *Wars of National Liberation*, a volume for the *Cassell History of Warfare* (2001).

Arthur Waldron is Lauder Professor of International Relations in the Department of History at the University of Pennsylvania and Director of Asian Studies at the American Enterprise Institute. His most recent book is *From War to Nationalism: China's Turning Point, 1924–1925* (Cambridge 1995).

The People in Arms

*Military Myth and National Mobilization
since the French Revolution*

Edited by

DANIEL MORAN

and

ARTHUR WALDRON

CAMBRIDGE
UNIVERSITY PRESS

CAMBRIDGE UNIVERSITY PRESS
Cambridge, New York, Melbourne, Madrid, Cape Town, Singapore, São Paulo

Cambridge University Press
The Edinburgh Building, Cambridge CB2 2RU, UK

Published in the United States of America by Cambridge University Press, New York

www.cambridge.org
Information on this title: www.cambridge.org/9780521814324

First published 2003
This digitally printed first paperback version 2006

A catalogue record for this publication is available from the British Library

Library of Congress Cataloguing in Publication data

Seminar on Force in History (Institute for Advanced Study (Princeton, N.J.))
People in arms : military myth and national mobilization since the French Revolution /
edited by Daniel Moran, Arthur Waldron.
p. cm.
Papers presented at the Seminar on Force in History, which was held at the Institute for
Advanced Study, Princeton, N.J.
Includes bibliographical references and index.
Contents: The legend of the levée en masse / Daniel Moran – La patrie en danger : the French
Revolution and the first levée en masse / Alan Forrest – The historiography of the levée en
masse of 1793 / Owen Connelly – Arms and the concert : the nation in arms and the dilemmas
of German liberalism / Daniel Moran – American views of conscription and the German
nation in arms in the Franco-Prussian War / John Whiteclay Chambers II – Defining the
enemy : war, law, and the levée en masse from 1870 to 1945 / John Horne – People's
war: the German debate about a levée en masse in October 1918 / Michael Geyer – The
levée en masse from Russian empire to Soviet Union, 1874–1938 / Mark von Hagen – From
Jaurès to Mao : the levée en masse in China / Arthur Waldron – In lieu of the levée en masse:
mass mobilization in modern Vietnam / Greg Lockhart – The Algerian war (1954–1962): the
inversion of the levée en masse / Douglas Porch – Looking backward : the people in arms and
the transformation of war / Arthur Waldron.
ISBN 0-521-81432-4
1. Nationalism – Europe – History.   2. War and Society – Europe – History.   3. France –
Military Policy.   4. Germany – Military Policy.   5. Soviet Union – Military History.
6. China – Military History.   I. Moran, Daniel.   II. Waldron, Arthur.   III. Title.
UB340 .S45   2002
306.2′7–dc21   2002020178

ISBN-13 978-0-521-81432-4 hardback
ISBN-10 0-521-81432-4 hardback

ISBN-13 978-0-521-03025-0 paperback
ISBN-10 0-521-03025-0 paperback

Contents

Illustrations

Contributors

John Whiteclay Chambers II, Rutgers University

Owen Connelly, University of South Carolina

Alan Forrest, University of York

Michael Geyer, University of Chicago

John Horne, Trinity College

Greg Lockhart, Australian National University

Daniel Moran, Naval Postgraduate School

Douglas Porch, Naval Postgraduate School

Mark Von Hagen, Columbia University

Arthur Waldron, University of Pennsylvania

Acknowledgments

The chapters in this volume originated as contributions to the Seminar on Force in History at the Institute for Advanced Study at Princeton. The Seminar was sponsored by the Harry Frank Guggenheim Foundation and J. Richardson Dilworth, and the editors are grateful for the opportunity to thank them for their generous support. We would also like to acknowledge the special efforts of two seminar participants, Alan Forrest and John Horne, whose assistance in putting this volume together went well beyond what we were reasonably entitled to ask of them. Finally, we wish to offer our special thanks to Professor Peter Paret of the Institute for Advanced Study faculty, who arranged for the Institute to host the seminar and provided indispensable intellectual inspiration and organizational support for its work.

Introduction: The Legend of the *Levée en masse*

Daniel Moran

The chapters presented here are concerned with the mass mobilization of society for war and with the cultural and ideological constructions that surround and arise from such events. The aim of this introduction is not to summarize the chapters that follow, nor to impose an unduly restrictive gloss on the range of historical episodes they survey, but simply to highlight the organizing themes and threads of shared historical memory that bind those episodes together and make it worthwhile to consider them between the covers of a single book. That the book in question might have been longer goes without saying. Our goal, however, was not to exhaust our subject – an impossibility, as we hope our efforts illustrate – but simply to demonstrate the enduring significance of some basic patterns of thought and action, rooted in the experience of Revolutionary France, but spreading from there to a wide variety of other contexts.

Our book takes as its point of departure a decisive moment in the history of the French Revolution: the *levée en masse* of August 1793. The *levée* marked a major step in the radicalization of the Revolution and in the escalation of the war between France and its neighbors. Alan Forrest's chapter describes the circumstances that gave rise to it and analyzes its military and political effects. Without reproducing that discussion here, a few preliminary comments on the *levée* are in order.

The *levée en masse* introduced military conscription into the new French Republic. Under its terms "the French people" [*tous les Français*] were placed at the disposal of the armed forces. Young men were to serve in battle, while married men, women, children, and the elderly were to provide various kinds of economic, logistical, and moral support. At a stroke, the *levée* replaced former theories and regulations concerning the obligation of military service with a universal concept far more encompassing in its moral claims, and in its coercive implications, than any that had prevailed under the Old Regime. That such a measure should have been the work of a revolutionary republic made it all the more startling.

When war broke out between France and the Habsburg Empire in 1792, nearly all French republicans regarded compulsory military service as tyrannical. Its introduction a little over a year later was justified, in official and public rhetoric, by a new ideology of revolutionary patriotism and social mobilization, undertaken to defend the nation against invasion. Although the *levée* was obviously compulsory in character – having been adopted because of the short-falls of earlier, voluntary recruitment measures – its prescriptive core was obscured by its proclaimed ability to give voice to correct attitudes and opinions. Since patriotism and republicanism had acquired supreme moral value, the coercive nature of revolutionary military recruitment was rendered, or at least declared to be, invisible. The power of the state to conscript people into the army was represented, with some success, as an expression of individual freedom, an internalized social obligation linked to the new ideal of citizenship that the Revolution had also advanced. As a number of the chapters that follow note, the French Republic never referred to its soldiers as conscripts, always as volunteers – a distinction that, however implausible on its face, would prove surprisingly robust.

The Republic's effort to compel military service by idealizing it as a form of personal virtue was an attempt to legislate a kind of psychological adaptation that in the past had only existed as a social process. It was, in other words, a quintessentially revolutionary act. The goal was to create, within the mass of French citizens, a moral and social dynamic that bears some comparison (although it was not made at the time) to the aristocratic conception of honor. Honor, too, depends upon an internalization of social norms, which come to be represented, and to some extent subjectively felt by those concerned, as authentic expressions of the individual personality. The aristocrat's honor is a set of external prescriptions and expectations expressed in the form of a personal code, a transference from society to individual that is reinforced by a complex symbology, and a variety of privileges and sanctions. The nameless state of mind rhetorically imputed to the citizen-soldier by proponents and memorialists of the *levée en masse* is the same. The distinctive element in the revolutionary summer of 1793 was not that France's leaders sought to square the circle of compulsory service and freely accepted obligation, but that they did so as a direct expression of the state's power to shape society according to its requirements.

The *levée en masse* might have been remembered simply as an emergency wartime measure, under which the rights of individuals were temporarily but reasonably abridged. Instead, it has gone down in history as a spontaneous, voluntary expression of the French people's ideals and enthusiasm, to which a revolutionary regime had merely given practical effect. This is the root and essence of what the contributors to this volume have referred to as the "legend" of the *levée en masse*. That legend's credibility was reinforced by the striking accomplishments of the armed forces the *levée* created, whose power far exceeded the requirements of national self-defense.

The decree proclaiming the *levée* presented it as a purely reactive measure. Those called up were supposed to serve only until foreign troops were expelled from France, a provision that was later ignored. Like the Reign of Terror, to which it was linked, the *levée en masse* was not merely a response to impending danger but an open-ended process of mobilization designed to make revolutionary change all-encompassing and irreversible. It sought to expand the French army but also to transform it by instilling it with revolutionary energy and values. Its success would be measured not by the speed with which its victorious citizen-soldiers would be free to return to their homes, but by their swift assumption of the strategic offensive, and the subsequent rapid expansion of French power in Europe.[1] Nevertheless, to observe that the *levée en masse* represented an expression of state power does not make it an expression of the state's strength. On the contrary, both the *levée* of 1793 and all the other examples discussed in this volume were undertaken by regimes or revolutionary movements in the throes of dissolution or reconstruction, who sought to bolster their limited moral energies by appropriating those of society at large.

The *levée en masse* of 1793 was a historical event with significant consequences and a source for one of the most powerful organizing myths of modern politics: that compulsory, mass social mobilizations merely express, and give effective form to, the wishes or higher values of the community and its members. It is the latter phenomenon – the social mythology, rather than the institutional mechanics, of national mobilization – this is our chief interest, though the two can never be treated in complete isolation from each other. A number of our authors trace the historical memory of the French Revolutionary *levée*, whose continued saliency for the history of France and its empire is explored in the chapters by Owen Connelly, John Horne, and Doug Porch. Still, no general claim is intended about the motivating influence of such ideas, compared to the other, more proximate forces that may be at work at any given time and place. Our general claim is rather that the distinctive ideological configuration exemplified by the *levée* has proven adaptable to a wide range of circumstances and has accordingly become one of the vital, recurring structures of modern politics and modern war.

One adaptation that proved particularly consequential was achieved by Prussia, the enemy of France that went the farthest in attempting to reconcile revolutionary military methods with the requirements of a conservative social order. In 1813 the Prussian state threw off its imposed alliance with France and embarked upon a military mobilization that, for the first time, extended the obligation, and opportunity, to serve in war through all

---

[1] The case for interpreting the *levée en masse* as something other than a purely defensive measure was first made by Peter Paret in a seminal article, oft cited in the chapters that follow, and recently reprinted. See his "Conscription and the End of the Ancien Régime in France and Prussia," *Understanding War* (Princeton, 1992), 53–74.

levels of Prussian society. Within the framework of the Revolutionary and Napoleonic eras, the Prussian *Erhebung* (a term that, like the French *levée*, combines the meaning of the English words "uprising" and "levy") was the movement that came closest to capturing the dynamism (not to mention the military effectiveness) of the French effort twenty years before. It also demonstrated that the pieces of the puzzle carved out and assembled by the Jacobins of the Year II could be put together in ways that deprived them of their revolutionary import. Like the *levée en masse*, Prussia's *Erhebung* would become the object of an intricate and by no means self-consistent mythology. For some, it would testify to the civic virtue of the educated middle class, whose retrospectively exaggerated willingness to defend the nation weapon in hand would become a token of their rightful claim to greater political influence. Others, however, would portray Prussia's mobilization as an affirmation of dynastic authority, in which a somewhat belated royal call to arms becomes the key moment in the national awakening. In either case, the common note is one not of revolutionary ferment, but of social discipline: a *levée en masse* rendered safe for the consumption of liberals and conservatives alike.

The *levée en masse* in all its forms is distinguished by the scale of its claims upon society, and by the character of the moral and political arguments employed to legitimize it. These rest on complex linkages between citizenship – in some circumstances a purely imaginary phenomenon in itself – military service, political authority, and transforming social action. Such linkages have often been asserted without reference to the example of 1793, nor necessarily in precisely identical terms. Similar episodes have been justified as policies initiated by the people, and then carried out by the state, or as government measures that respond to the sentiments of a saving remnant of loyal, right-thinking people, in the midst of social crisis. In all cases, however, one finds a characteristic tension between the coercive requirements of collective military action and the legitimizing rhetoric of freedom, spontaneity, and popular approval.

The legend of the *levée en masse* provided a compelling ideological justification for universal military service and for the dramatic expansion of state power in wartime. It helped foster the belief that popular forces, raised in an atmosphere of heightened ideological pressure, were exceptionally powerful or even invincible, particularly against armies of professionals, mercenaries, or ordinary conscripts. The present volume includes cases in which the spirit of the *levée* is embraced by revolutionary movements or resistance organizations, so that the element of state authority may be missing, or oriented toward a postrevolutionary future that did not yet exist. Conversely, there are a number of examples in which explicit claims of revolutionary action are absent. The Prussian *Erhebung* is one – though it included a heightened expectation that popular military exertion would be matched by political concessions in the future. As John Chambers shows, American admiration for the Prussian nation in arms was detached from America's own revolutionary tradition, whose iconic figure, the Minute Man, bears closer resemblance to the *franc-tireur* of the new-born Third Republic than to the conscripted *Landwehrman* of Bismarck's Germany – a resemblance that made scant impression on American journalists at the time. Mark Von Hagen's chapter on Russia and Arthur Waldron's on China are both concerned with conditions in which the issue is not necessarily how to effect radical change but also how to promote reform and consolidate revolutionary achievement. That the ideal of the people in arms may even serve the cause of reaction is demonstrated in Doug Porch's chapter on Algeria, where the OAS, a rightist conspiracy with no appreciable social base, sought to graft the rhetoric of the *levée en masse* onto a campaign of counterrevolution. That the OAS should have imputed a great capacity for mass mobilization to its almost equally isolated Algerian opponents only heightens one's sense of the legend's power.

Whatever else one may say about the people in arms, there can be no question that it has enjoyed a formidable military reputation, which often becomes a force in itself. That force is usually described as "people's war," the prospect of which has become one of the imposing strategic realities of modern times. The chapters by John Horne and Michael Geyer provide contrasting examples of its power, if not to vanquish the nation's enemies, then at least to focus the minds of its professional soldiers.

In the aftermath of the Napoleonic Wars, the idea of the *levée en masse* was inevitably submerged beneath the practice of normal politics. It became a kind of underground spring, from which, as my chapter later in the book seeks to show, liberals in particular attempted to draw some sustenance, but without releasing, or even acknowledging, its latent energy. In the last months of the Franco-Prussian War, however, the people in arms were recalled to life by the defeat of the French Empire, and the appearance in its place of a new republican regime, whose first act was to proclaim a new *levée en masse* to drive out the invader. As John Horne's chapter demonstrates, the psychological impact of this effort far exceeded its military achievements. The *franc-tireur* of 1870 became a crucial legitimizing prop to the French Third Republic, while instilling its sibling and hereditary opponent, the Second German Empire, with an obsessive fear of partisans and irregular warriors, whose murderous consequences would become fully apparent in the opening months of World War One.

What, exactly, were Germany's (and not just Germany's) soldiers so afraid of? One is inclined to answer "total war," of which "people's war" is an important expression – the seminal one, indeed, which the annihilatory technologies of the twentieth century have amplified. Yet war on the largest possible scale, entailing the systematic militarization of society and its subordination to the needs of the armed forces – both explicit elements of the French *levée* of 1793 – could scarcely be regarded as anathema to Europe's military elite. The specter of "people's war" invoked by the nascent Third

Republic, however, was not merely one of unbounded violence, but one of violence that had slipped the leash of state control and taken on a life of its own.

Its unnerving appearance in Berlin during the last weeks of the First World War is the subject of Michael Geyer's chapter. As Geyer shows, when confronted with imminent defeat, significant elements of Germany's civilian leadership were prepared to contemplate a *levée en masse* of their own, despite a clear recognition that, in military terms, the result would be not national salvation but certain and catastrophic defeat. For them, the myth of the citizen-soldier's invincibility, at least, had lost its hold. Yet they longed for his appearance just the same, if only as a means of affirming the nation's honor in extremis. For the German officer corps, however, such desperate measures were repellant, not just because they lacked any underlying strategic rationality but also because their adoption would threaten the institutional integrity of the regular army. That, in the end, Germany's leadership turned away from the *levée en masse* as an instrument of self-slaughter was undoubtedly a capital moral accomplishment. Yet the fact that such a prospect should have been so plainly visible testifies to how far Europe's military possibilities had progressed over the course of the nineteenth century.

In the twentieth century they would be projected onto a still larger stage, as the colonized world caught up with the West's capacity to mobilize social energies for war. A preliminary example on the fringe of Europe occurs in Russia, where, as Mark Von Hagen shows, the new Bolshevik regime was compelled to wrestle repeatedly with the problem of how to salvage the logic of revolutionary mobilization while jettisoning what had always been its essential basis: the idea of the nation. Farther afield, as Greg Lockhart's account of the genesis of the People's Liberation Army of Vietnam shows, the persistence of traditional forms of social organization, coupled with the inevitable weakness of anticolonial, liberationist states, normally required that a revolutionary vanguard stand in for the *masse*, while justifying its enforced ascendancy on the grounds that it merely expressed universal values, and the still-inchoate desires of the people as a whole. In China, the subject of Arthur Waldron's chapter, the ideal of the nation in arms appealed to military intellectuals for reasons directly analogous to those that moved Prussia's reformers to seize upon the French Revolutionary model: because, properly domesticated, a citizen army would contribute simultaneously to the integration of society, the strengthening and modernization of the state, and the defense of the nation against outsiders.

The idea of the people in arms is one of the foundational elements of modern war. Its interaction with the other constituent elements of military modernity – professional officers, strong bureaucratic states, diversified industrial economies, and increasingly lethal weapons – has been exceptionally complex, if not paradoxical, a point that is further explored in Arthur Waldron's concluding remarks. In the West at least, the organizing power of the state and the productive capacity of national economies have generally kept up with society's capacity to mobilize its citizens for war. Yet the citizen-soldier's chances of survival on a modern battlefield have been subject to deep discounting since at least the 1840s, when the introduction of rifled weapons transformed the training and command requirements of large armies, by compelling soldiers to disperse across an ever-expanding battlefield.

By the eve of the First World War, European military experts were convinced that the impending clash of arms, while intensely violent, would also necessarily be brief, because no belligerent could sustain the effort of modern war for long. The mass armies required to absorb the impact of new weapons were seen as incorporating a self-limiting social dynamic into war itself, whereby societies, once fully mobilized, would rapidly expend their energy, while losing cohesion in the process. It was without question the most calamitous strategic miscalculation of modern times: one based entirely upon social presumption rather than any real military calculation.

Yet it remains strangely liable to repetition. Although the legend of the *levée en masse* has, to all appearances, lost its grip upon the Western imagination, which invented it, its continued saliency for much of the rest of the world can scarcely be doubted. It is, as has been proposed, the characteristic resort of weak states and revolutionary regimes, with which the human community remains very well supplied. The chapters presented here describe its genesis and initial maturity. But they most certainly do not describe the full extent of its career, for the simple reason that its career is not over.

2

La patrie en danger

The French Revolution and the First Levée en masse

Alan Forrest

When the French decreed the *levée en masse* on 23 August 1793, they were well aware that they were breaking with centuries of tradition and creating a new form of legitimacy for the military demands of the state. The *levée* was based on the simple principle that the nation was the sovereign authority in the French Republic, and that the nation had the right to demand the performance of military service as one of the fundamental duties implicit in the enjoyment of citizenship. No precedent that posited citizenship as the basis for recruitment in this way could be cited – neither in the American Revolution nor in Cromwell's England nor in the Roman republic so lauded in the writings of the Enlightenment and in the speeches of Maximilien Robespierre.[1]

The revolutionaries were here venturing into the unknown, breaking new ground in pursuit of liberty and idealism. Their revolution freed people from the constraints imposed on them during the *ancien régime*, doing so by a process of civic and political empowerment. In 1790 a patriotic society composed of shopkeepers and artisans had been founded in Bordeaux to educate the mass of the population in their new rights and duties, arguing that "since every man is a member of the state, the new order of things can call anyone to the public administration."[2] This was a heady notion in a society where public offices had been widely bought and sold, and where great swathes of government service had been the preserve of privilege and venality.[3] The *levée en masse* would take the principle of universality further

---

[1] Many of the revolutionaries, including Robespierre, were highly selective in the inspiration they chose to draw from historical precedents. Cromwell was for many Frenchmen the epitome of the revolutionary leader corrupted by power and military ambition. See David Jordan, *The Revolutionary Career of Maximilien Robespierre* (New York, 1985), 3.

[2] Pierre Bécamps, "La Société patriotique de Bordeaux, 1790–92," in *Actes du 82e Congrès National des Sociétés Savantes, 1957* (Paris, 1958), 257; quoted in Lynn Hunt, *Politics, Culture and Class in the French Revolution* (Berkeley, 1984), 72.

[3] William Doyle, *Venality: The Sale of Offices in Eighteenth-Century France* (Oxford, 1996), 6.

and apply it to the defense of the state. It must be seen as an experimental device operated against the background of *la patrie en danger*, of threatened invasion and national emergency, and in the face of much popular bitterness and suspicion about the soldier and his lot.

The revolutionaries were acknowledging that they could no longer rely on traditional mechanisms to produce an army of the size and quality that were needed, mechanisms that had served successive kings well, at least until the time of Louis XV. Old Regime armies had seldom lacked men, though the social status of soldiering was low, and the incentive to become an infantryman in the royal service was poor. Those who made a career in the armies knew that there were few opportunities for promotion, officers' batons being reserved for those with aristocratic credentials, and that when their careers were over, often cut short by wounds and fevers, there would be no pension to offer them some security in their declining years. The image of the old soldier who returned to his village broken by war, with no family or smallholding, reduced to begging and petty crime, was a familiar one in the eighteenth-century French countryside. It helps explain the many demands made in the *cahiers de doléances* for an immediate improvement in the conditions of military service – an end to social privilege in the army, a guarantee that soldiers receive their pay on time, a desire that French troops should not be forced to beg and plunder to keep themselves alive.[4]

Many had no alternative but to serve. Indeed, André Corvisier calculated that, at the peak of Louis XIV's wars, around one Frenchman in six was called on to bear arms at some time during his life, though not necessarily to participate in actual warfare. An outbreak of banditry or the appearance of wolves in a rural area could equally result in a call to arms.[5] But few rushed to offer their services. The armies relied heavily on the poor, among them beggars and vagabonds consigned to the public infirmaries and poor houses by a state increasingly concerned with the needs of internal order.[6] Such men were often prepared to enlist in return for the recruitment bounty and the promise of a livelihood. Others were recruited by methods reminiscent of the press-gang, as recruiting officers toured provincial fairs and markets, first banging drums and hoisting flags at local *fêtes* and then seizing drunken revellers before they sobered up sufficiently to realize what was happening to them.[7] The armies also depended on foreign mercenaries to a degree that the nationalist ideology of the Revolution could not accept. For Louis XIV, mercenaries had been a welcome additional source of manpower that presented him with neither practical nor moral dilemmas; indeed, between

---

[4] E.-G. Léonard, *L'armée et ses problèmes au dix-huitième siècle* (Paris, 1958), 298.

[5] André Corvisier, *Armies and Societies in Europe, 1494–1789* (Bloomington, Ind., 1979), 8.

[6] Jean Imbert, *Le droit hospitalier de l'Ancien Régime* (Paris, 1993), 87–90.

[7] Lee Kennett, *The French Armies in the Seven Years' War: A Study in Military Organization and Administration* (Durham, N.C., 1967), 72–3.

the Dutch Wars and the Peace of Ryswick there had never been fewer than
25 percent of mercenary troops in the French infantry, and 22 percent in the
army as a whole.[8] Even in 1789 there were still twenty-three foreign regiments serving Louis XVI, recruited from among the traditional mercenaries
of the European continent, the Swiss, the Germans, and the Irish.[9]

In times of grave peril, the government supplemented military numbers
by levying militia service on the population at large – a highly unpopular practice that routinely dragged young men away from their farms and
workshops for six years at a time. The militia system was seen as unfair and
divisive, a kind of lottery in which an individual's future and self-respect
were callously gambled away, and one, moreover, from which the rich and
privileged, along with their servants and lackeys, were usually exempt.[10]
Such institutions cried out for reform, as Joseph Servan noted in a memorable pamphlet published in 1780, prophetically entitled *Le Soldat-citoyen*,
in which he offered solutions to the abuses he saw all around him. In Servan's
view, it was simply too easy to claim, as many did in the eighteenth century,
that the quality of French troops must always be high because of the inherent excellence of French national character, education, and government.
Nor was it realistic to assert that the country's history and traditions had
always served it well in military matters. In reality, Servan argued, France
had seen a real militia, based upon principles of communal self-defense, give
way first to a feudal levy, and finally to a system of paid vigilantism, "the
least good of the three."[11] While the resulting system might have passed for
a deeply ingrained part of French military culture under the *ancien régime*,
it was incontestably unwieldy and inefficient militarily. After 1789, it would
prove incompatible with the needs of a revolutionary nation that believed
itself to be under threat of extinction.

If the revolutionaries had to devise new ways of recruiting soldiers, they
also had to resolve what they saw as damaging contradictions in the internal
structures of the army. The command structure was steeped in the ideology
of the old order, strongly hierarchical and obsessed with petty differences
of rank. Discipline was pitiless and relied heavily on savage corporal punishments that humiliated the troops and denied them any vestige of civic
rights or human dignity. Ordinary soldiers (though not officers) caught in

---

[8] André Corvisier, "Louis XIV, la guerre et la naissance de l'armée moderne," in Philippe
    Contamine (ed.), *Histoire militaire de la France*, volume 1: *Des origins à 1715* (Paris, 1992),
    395.
[9] Peter Paret, "Conscription and the End of the Ancien Régime in France and Prussia," in
    Paret, *Understanding War* (Princeton, 1992), 54.
[10] Claude Achard, "Le recrutement de la milice royale à Pézenas de 1689 à 1788," in
    *Recrutement, Mentalités, Sociétés: colloque international d'histoire militaire, septembre
    1974* (Montpellier, 1974), 45–56.
[11] Joseph Servan, *Le Soldat-citoyen, ou vues patriotiques sur la manière la plus avantageuse de
    pourvoir à la défense du Royaume* (Paris, 1780), 25.

serious offenses were liable to be put to death, either by hanging or breaking on the wheel. Revolutionary principles sat uneasily alongside an officer
corps that was still defined by its nobility: David Bien has shown that even
before the Ségur Ordinance of 1781 only around 5 percent of officers were
nonnobles.[12] To make matters worse, their sworn loyalty was to the person
of the king, not to France. Many military offices throughout the eighteenth
century had been venal, the object of sale and purchase like so many other
offices under the crown – though Louis XVI had succeeded in reducing the
scale of venality in the infantry during his reign.[13]

By 1793, faced with the reality of a European war and with the frontiers
of France itself at risk, the Revolution desperately needed a new system of recruitment for officers as well as for the ranks, one that would guarantee both
a sufficient pool of manpower and a force loyal to the cause of the French
people. The emigration of large numbers of noble officers and the king's
dependence on his Swiss Guard at the Tuileries in 1792 were just two of
the circumstances that persuaded the new leadership that root-and-branch
reforms were unavoidable. In part, these considerations were political. It
was natural for outsiders, new to power, to fear an army that functioned
as an independent estate and that might easily be turned against the executive authority. Many of France's revolutionaries were inclined, in any case,
to see plots and conspiracies on all sides. But the political aspect was not
exclusive nor necessarily predominant. The *levée en masse* was also born
out of pragmatic considerations at a time when the existing line army was
performing badly in the field and was racked by self-doubt, mass defection,
and treason.[14]

The *levée en masse* was not the first innovatory recruitment measure taken
by the revolutionaries, though it was the first distinctively Jacobin one. The
draining away of men from the line regiments and the prestige that attached
to the new, more patriotic National Guard units had begun to alter the image of soldiering as early as 1789, even though the mutinies at Nancy and
elsewhere during 1790 had cast doubt on the old system of discipline in
a world where soldiers, too, could claim civic rights and even privileges.[15]

---

[12] The Ségur Ordinance of 1781 decreed that army officers would in future be required to prove
four degrees of nobility. It was a measure principally designed to reserve military service for
the poorer nobles, a group without other skills or resources, whose families often had a long
and honorable military tradition. See David Bien, "La réaction aristocratique avant 1789:
l'exemple de l'armée," *Annales: Economies, Sociétés, Civilisations* 29 (1974), 35.

[13] Doyle, *Venality*, 134–6.

[14] Samuel F. Scott, *The Response of the Royal Army to the French Revolution: The Role and
Development of the Line Army, 1787–93* (Oxford, 1978), 182–90.

[15] In the summer of 1790, the line army was rent by a series of mutinies by troops demanding better pay and more humane discipline, partly in response to the ideas of liberty and
citizenship that were circulating and partly in response to the much better conditions that
prevailed in National Guard units. The most serious mutiny, at Nancy, involved both French

In garrison towns along the northern frontier, for instance, troops were already denouncing unpopular officers and forging links with patriots and popular societies in the local population,[16] and in Cherbourg the club demanded the dismissal of the entire general staff and the replacement of all nobles who still held military commands.[17]

Faced with the rapid extension of the war in March 1793, the government could not but seek new methods of recruitment to boost numbers and morale. The call for volunteers and the creation of new volunteer regiments – the preferred solution in 1791 and 1792 – was no longer seen as adequate to the scale of the crisis; and while a major call-up in the spring of 1793 (known as the *levée des 300.000*) eventually produced the numbers required, it also gave rise to bitter resentments. For the first time, the government introduced quotas to reflect local population figures, demanding that each department, each district, eventually each town or village should produce an appropriate number of men for the army. But the method of choosing them was not laid down by law. Some communities used a form of balloting, which at least seemed fair. Regardless of method, however, the choice often fell on men regarded as marginal to village life – shepherds working on isolated hillsides, the indigent from the local poorhouses, and even migrant workers who had the misfortune to pass through when the levy was being raised. There were too many exemptions, too many privileged jobs in the civil administration, and too many opportunities for the rich to buy themselves out of serving in person. Desertion and draft-evasion followed, often with the open connivance of parents, mayors, and entire communities.[18] The Jacobins' demand that all must be equally liable for service had a practical, as well as an ideological, justification.

That the policy was largely successful can be seen in the results achieved by French arms in the months that followed, when the war along the northern and eastern frontiers was effectively turned around, and foreign forces were pushed back from French soil. It was reflected also in the size of the force assembled, which, if it never reached the figure of three quarters of a million that was intended, produced an army of over 600,000 men, far larger than the forces disposed of by France's enemies at that time. This enormous army was at the heart of all France's military successes for the rest of the decade and was not properly replenished until full-blown annual conscription was introduced under the Jourdan Law of September 1798.[19] There were, it is

---

soldiers and a regiment of Swiss mercenaries. It was brutally suppressed on the orders of the National Assembly. See Jean-Paul Bertaud, *La Révolution armée: les soldats-citoyens et la Révolution française* (Paris, 1979), 47–8.

[16] Edmond Leleu, *La Société Populaire de Lille* (Lille, 1919), 77–8.

[17] Pierre Dufay, *Les sociétés populaires et l'armée, 1791–94* (Paris, 1913), 24–5.

[18] Alan Forrest, *The Soldiers of the French Revolution* (Durham, N.C., 1990), 72–5.

[19] The Jourdan Law of 19 Fructidor VI (5 September 1798) introduced compulsory military service for men aged between 20 and 25, except those who were already married before

true, some small, partial levies in the intervening years, especially for the cavalry, but they were half-hearted affairs, announced as exceptional and deeply resented by large parts of the population. Essentially it would be the army of the Year II,[20] weakened by casualties, sickness, and desertion, that would go on to fight the military campaigns of the Directory, conquer Italy, set up "sister republics" in Holland and Switzerland, and carry Bonaparte to the banks of the Nile. Its successes in battle, and the wholly unprecedented glamour that accrued to the army as a result, go far to explain the mystique that the ideal of a citizen-army came to command, not just in France but among the Revolution's many enemies as well.[21]

Nevertheless, the myth of the *levée en masse* cannot be explained in military terms alone. The success of the recruitment campaign and the victories registered by the armies it produced might inspire respect and admiration, mingled with some astonishment from those who had warned that such drastic restructuring could not work in an institution that was critically dependent on discipline and obedience. Other armies had dazzled before in the history of European warfare, without leaving such a deeply engrained cultural legacy. It was the boldness of the patriotic vision of August 1793, not just the tactical proficiency of the army it engendered, that explains the power of the myth and its durability. The clarion call was nationalism and the obligation of every citizen to render service to the nation, a principle welcomed for its own sake by revolutionary militants, especially the leadership of the Paris sections and the Jacobin Club, where it immediately acquired far-reaching ideological significance. The *levée en masse*, in contrast to the partial levies that preceded it, did not base itself upon traditional categories of social distinction. All, in theory at least, had a duty to perform, one that they owed to their country and their fellow-citizens rather than to the person of the king or to any local *seigneur*. The *patrie* had been declared *en danger*, and the whole people of France were mobilized for their own defense. While age, gender, or marital status might excuse most Frenchmen from front-line service, all had a role to play. This is captured in the resonance of the first words of the decree, which spelled out that

12 January of that year. Those liable for service were to be enrolled in five classes by age, with the youngest called up first. Exemptions granted since 1793 were annulled, and, for the first and only time since the *levée en masse*, all those designated had to serve personally, since there was no provision for paid substitutes. See Gustave Vallée, *La conscription dans le département de la Charente, 1798–1807* (Paris, 1936), 10–15; also Georges Lefebvre, *The French Revolution*, 2 volumes (London, 1964), 2: 236.

20   The "Year II" was the second year of the French Republic, strictly from 22 September 1793 to 21 September 1794. More colloquially, the expression is used to refer to the Revolution's most radical phase, which coincided with the period of office of the Committee of Public Safety (6 April 1793 to 28 July 1794).

21   On the conduct of French troops on German soil, see T. C. W. Blanning, *The French Revolution in Germany: Occupation and Resistance in the Rhineland, 1792–1802* (Oxford, 1983), Chapter 3.

henceforth, until the enemies have been driven from the territory of the Republic, the French people [*tous les Français*] are in permanent requisition for army service. The young men shall go to battle; the married men shall forge arms and transport provisions; the women shall make tents and clothes, and shall serve in the hospitals; the children shall turn old linen into lint; the old men shall repair to the public places, to stimulate the courage of the warriors and preach the unity of the Republic and the hatred of kings.[22]

The Republic itself was compared to a city under siege, and the territory of France to a huge military camp, where national property and the abandoned houses of those who had emigrated should be turned into barracks, with public squares reconstituted as public workshops, all in the cause of the war and victory.[23]

In short, war was to be a total effort, in which all members of the community had a role. All were to be mobilized in the common good until such time as France's enemies had been driven off and defeated. This effort was consistent with the principle laid down in the Jacobin constitution of 24 June 1793, which declared that all were equally at the service of the state: "the general force of the Republic is composed of the entire people" (clause 107), or again, "all Frenchmen are soldiers: all have training in handling arms" (clause 109).[24] The fact that the rich could no longer buy themselves out of serving in person was a powerful element in the *levée*'s appeal. Personal circumstance, not status or income level, determined who should march first. "Unmarried citizens or childless widowers from eighteen to twenty-five years shall go first," proclaimed the law. Public officials were allowed to remain at their posts, a provision that occasioned some bitterness among those called to the colors. But otherwise all were equal before the recruiting-sergeant, even if all were not wanted for active service. This was what the ordinary people of France understood by "the nation in arms," the slogan emblazoned on a banner carried by each new battalion, which proclaimed it the representative of "the French people risen against tyrants."

Of course the language of the decree, like that used by the Representatives on Mission sent to the departments to see that it was enforced, was deliberately emotive. The *levée* was proclaimed in tones of high moral fervor and revolutionary nationalism, and the Jacobins took full advantage of the benefits such emotions could bring. The apparent equality of all was a major selling point to the young and to communities that had never previously shown much commitment to military service. Local communities had ways of resisting recruitment measures that they saw as contrary to tradition and natural justice. They could hide the recruits, feeding them in the *bocage* or in

---

[22] Decree of 23 August 1793, in John Hall Stewart, *A Documentary Survey of the French Revolution* (New York, 1951), 473.

[23] *Réimpression de l'Ancien Moniteur*, 31 volumes (Paris, 1858) 17: 475.

[24] Jacques Godechot (ed.), *Les constitutions de la France depuis 1789* (Paris, 1970), 90.

caves in nearby mountainsides; they could call on mayors and local doctors to conceal real identities or invent medical barriers to service; they could provide employment to young men on the run; they could even block roads, riot, and physically resist the gendarmes sent to arrest their sons, brothers, and friends. They had done so when faced with militia service under the *ancien régime* and again in response to the *levée des 300.000*. They would continue to do so throughout the Consulate and Empire, restrained only by the increasingly effective police power of the state.[25]

Even the *levée en masse* was not greeted with unmuted enthusiasm. Localized rioting in recalcitrant villages showed that not all were blinded by revolutionary rhetoric. At Montréal in the Aude the young men sang the *carmagnole* in a collective act of defiance; and at Saint-Dié in the Vosges one of the more violent antirecruitment riots of the period resulted in seventy-five arrests and left two people dead.[26] Yet overall the *levée en masse*, to judge by the testimony of local mayors and municipal officials, met with far less resistance than either the preceding *levée des 300.000* or the more bureaucratically routinized conscriptions of the Napoleonic years. In part, this may be explained by the administrative simplicity of the *levée* and the increased efficiency of local officials, who had grown more accustomed to the new regime. But in the main it can be ascribed to one simple cause: the *levée en masse* was perceived as equitable and fair, even by the young men who were most concerned.

In reality, of course, the *levée en masse* was not intended to be a universal levy, and the Committee of Public Safety was forced to backtrack quickly to play down unrealistic expectations. As one of the Representatives on Mission serving in the Pyrenees made clear, a mass of men compelled by law to serve, with no aptitude for soldiering and (at best) a somewhat abstract enthusiasm for their new calling, would hinder, rather than aid, the army in the field.[27] Besides, a call-up of all the young men in France would leave agriculture so bereft of workers as to pose a threat of famine. There was also an important political consideration, as even Hébert, one of the foremost champions of the *levée en masse*, realized. If mass recruitment emptied Paris of staunch republicans, what might the political consequences be? In the climate of fear and suspicion that prevailed in the autumn of 1793, few radicals doubted that it would be the patriots who would repair to the front, leaving the capital at the mercy of counterrevolutionaries.[28] This was a prospect grave enough

---

[25] Alan Forrest, *Conscripts and Deserters: The Army and French Society during the Revolution and Empire* (New York, 1989), 233–7.

[26] Ibid., 33–4. Singing and dancing the *carmagnole* became a symbol of the more extreme radical activism of the Parisian popular movement at the height of the Jacobin terror. For the text of the song, see Laura Mason, *Singing the French Revolution: Popular Culture and Politics, 1787–99* (Ithaca, N.Y., 1996), 173.

[27] Bertaud, *La Révolution armée*, 115.

[28] Paret, "Conscription and the End of the Ancien Régime," 65.

to take the shine off the *enragés*' dream of sending everyone, however well born and well connected, to fight in the name of the French people.

Yet equality would remain one of the principal forms of legitimation to which the revolutionaries appealed, as speeches in the Convention make clear. The deputies were well aware that they were doing more than raising troops to supply manpower. They were also creating an army worthy of the Republic, an army composed of soldiers with civic rights and political views, an army fit to represent a free people. This was a basic issue in the summer of 1793, one elevated far above the level of propaganda or persuasion. Bertrand Barère, who headed the government's Military Committee, was particularly insistent that all must bear their share. Even children should have a role in the defense of their country, since "it is for them that we are fighting: the children, those who are destined to reap all the fruits of Revolution."[29] There must be no social or economic distinctions among patriots, since all had skills to bring to the defense of the state.

In a republic, Barère insisted, all stood shoulder to shoulder, "the metalworker and the legislator, the physician and the blacksmith, the man of letters and the manual labourer," townsmen and country-dwellers, rich and poor. All were brothers in the national cause, and all should be equally honored by a grateful nation.[30] Not all would be called upon to serve with weapon in hand, however. From the outset Barère was eager to lay down the order in which Frenchmen would march to the front. But all were at the disposal of the state. That, in Jacobin eyes, was the crucial difference between the *levée en masse* and previous exercises in recruitment, which had called for quotas from districts and departments and had left the mechanisms for raising the required numbers to local initiative. Further recruitment along the same lines, pressed forward without a firm and explicit moral basis, could only play into the hands of counterrevolutionaries.[31]

The impact of the *levée* was not restricted to those called up to serve in the army, though it was on them that most official propaganda focused. An army also required arms and provisions, and for these, too, the population had to be mobilized. The 1790s were not yet an age of large-scale factory production, and for many essentials the military found itself dependent upon local craft production, in direct competition with the needs of local people. In around thirty of France's eighty-six departments, those lying closest to war zones, foodstuffs were requisitioned for the armies, and carters and wagoners (along with their horses and carts) were recruited for army service. The spirit of the *levée en masse* was thus extended to include civilian laborers whose exertions were deemed essential for the war effort. There is evidence,

---

[29] *Réimpression de l'Ancien Moniteur*, 17: 475.
[30] Ibid., 475.
[31] Ibid., 474.

indeed, that many workers sought jobs in military supply as a less unpleasant alternative to active soldiering.[32]

The task of finding enough uniforms to clothe the troops proved especially difficult, since there were no large-scale clothiers whose production could be diverted to war use. Rather, the clothing industry remained the preserve of small artisanal firms and individual seamstresses, who were notoriously difficult to organize. When the Jacobin Jean-Baptiste Bouchotte was war minister in 1793, much of this work was channeled through public workshops established in the sections of Paris, a solution that may have had more to do with politics than efficacy. The supply of footwear for the armies was even more problematic, as soldiers were reduced to wearing clogs or going barefoot. Bouchotte's remedy was draconian. In the fall of the Year II, he ordered every shoemaker in France to supply his town council every ten days with five pairs of boots for each journeyman in his employ, the boots to be paid for at a price set by the government. Then, during the (normally slow) winter months, he demanded that cobblers work only for the army, devoting their entire capacity to the needs of war.[33] Seamstresses and shoemakers thus joined carters and watermen in the service of the military.

An even greater dilemma, given the unprecedented size of the armies recruited under the *levée en masse*, was how to provide them with sufficient weapons, a problem that only became worse after the enemy had destroyed the armory at Maubeuge, and the Lyon federalists had captured Saint-Etienne.[34] Again, large-scale mobilization was required if the soldiers were not to be left defending themselves with pikes and shotguns against the much superior weaponry of the Austrians and Prussians. The decree had, of course, allowed for this: "the married men shall forge arms and transport provisions." In Paris, in particular, the Committee of Public Safety enforced this aspect of the *levée* energetically to provide France with the forges and foundries the military required. The Committee brought the best scientific minds of France to bear on the problem, notably the chemist and armaments expert Gaspard Monge. The aim was to produce a thousand muskets per

---

[32] The Convention's decree of 14 March 1793 exempted from service all carters and drivers who could show they were engaged in military provisioning.

[33] Forrest, *Soldiers*, 140–1.

[34] The summer of 1793 was marked by a number of revolts by Republican authorities in provincial France against Jacobin rule, either nationally or locally. Though there is no evidence that they intended to break away from the Republic – indeed, they repeatedly insisted on their loyalty to the constitution – their opponents branded them "federalists" and turned the might of the state against them. The most serious revolt was in Lyon, where the anti-Jacobin faction seized power on 29 May, some days before the Jacobin coup in Paris. The new government sent troops to besiege Lyon, and the Lyonnais in turn prepared the defense of their city, turning federalism into civil war. In the process they sent troops to nearby Saint-Etienne and took over the armory there. See W. D. Edmonds, *Jacobinism and the Revolt of Lyon, 1789–93* (Oxford, 1990).

day, a goal that could not be attained simply by doubling the number of locksmiths, nor by demanding huge increases in productivity, as had first been imagined. Instead, armaments manufacturers were urged to pursue active programs of mechanization and division of labor. A new "innovation workshop" [*atelier de perfectionnement*] was set up to make machine tools to new and much higher technical specifications.[35] The resulting industrial mobilization was a massive one, without which the simultaneous military recruitment effort would have availed little. Munitions workers were requisitioned into service, both in Paris and in provincial centers; the Convention spent over 1.8 million *livres* on manufacturing facilities in Paris, and a further 2 million in the provinces. Peak production reached over 600 gun barrels per day, and the Paris armory, which had produced 9,000 muskets per year before September 1793, turned out over 145,000 in the thirteen months that followed.[36]

The manufacture of guns is well illustrated by Lesueur's famous watercolor (Figure 1), one of a series he produced on the war effort in the capital and one that tellingly illustrates the extent of civilian mobilization. He could have gone even further in showing the ever-extending tentacles of the state war machine. The problem of producing sufficient guns and uniforms could at least be tackled in the relatively structured and disciplined context of the workshop. The production of sufficient gunpowder presented a more general challenge, which could only be met by the population at large. After France found itself at war with England, it was no longer able to import supplies of saltpeter – a critical component of gunpowder – from outside France. An act of national mobilization was called for. New natural deposits were sought out and exploited, and individual householders were urged to search their cellars and outhouses for supplementary supplies – saltpeter being a natural product of oxidizing organic material, especially compost and dung. Once again the Jacobins relied heavily on the patriotism of Paris, where some sixty sectional workshops were established, capable of producing 5,000 pounds of saltpeter every day.[37] It was an impressive achievement, which mobilized not just specific skills and particular categories of workers, but the entire civilian population, anyone capable of scraping the floor of their cellar or their shed.

The hunt for saltpeter was every patriot's contribution to the cause of total war, every citizen's duty in the face of military threat. It was also a duty that might reasonably fall on women, a group whose role in the *levée* as a whole was necessarily somewhat limited. Indeed, given the heavy emphasis placed on the central issue of raising enough men for the battalions, it is

---

[35] Ken Alder, *Engineering the Revolution: Arms and Enlightenment in France, 1763–1815* (Princeton, 1997), 276–7.
[36] Ibid., 288.
[37] Albert Soboul, *Les soldats de l'an II* (Paris, 1959), 144–53.

hardly surprising that the imagery of the *levée en masse* was often highly gendered. The young man offering himself to the recruiting-sergeant, signing away his youth to the military, is the principal actor in the paintings and etchings that the *levée* inspired. Women occupied the wings or played a secondary role in the action. They were there to encourage their sons and brothers, husbands and lovers, to urge them to put their love for the Republic above such feelings as they had for the women in their lives. They also represented the spirit of self-denial and sacrifice in the face of a greater good (Figure 2). Their inclusion in Revolutionary imagery underscored the unity of civil society responding to the call to arms, the commitment of the whole people to save and defend *la patrie en danger*. Female figures became powerful symbols of sacrifice and self-abasement, of quiet fortitude and personal heroism.[38]

Some women, of course, supported the armies more directly, as harvesters in the fields, seamstresses in public workshops, or activists in sections and radical clubs. Or they accompanied the armies in an ancillary capacity, notably as laundresses, often trailing young children in their wake. Dozens of die-hard Republican women sought to conceal their gender and fight alongside their husbands in the Republican cause. One of these, Elizabeth Dubois, became famous as *citoyenne* Favre. She fought in the Nord in 1793, was captured, and would have been shot with the other prisoners had not the enemy commander become aware of her sex. In her statement to the authorities back in Paris, she explained that "having learned that her husband, as well as other defenders of the frontiers, were totally without underwear, clothing, and shoes, she made up her mind to make the greatest sacrifices to assist her husband."[39]

The language of citizenship, of rights and duties and moral legitimation, sets the *levée en masse* apart from the other recruitment exercises of the Revolutionary and Napoleonic years, and plays an important role in the creation of the Republican myth. It should be seen as part of a broader process through which the revolutionaries sought to identify themselves with the future and to deny continuities with the past. It contributes to what Keith Baker has described as "the creation of the *ancien régime*," the invention of an "other" against which the Revolutionary achievement must at all times be judged, a dialectic of the present and the past, of the real and the imaginary, in order to legitimize political power.[40] Mona Ozouf has talked of this process as the creation of *"l'homme nouveau,"* as the self-conscious denial of the

---

[38] This role is well portrayed in an anonymous painting of "Le départ du volontaire," in the Musée Carnavalet in Paris, reproduced in Michel Vovelle (ed.), *La Révolution Française: Images et récit*, 5 volumes (Paris, 1986), 3: 51.

[39] Darline Gay Levy, Harriet Branson Applewhite, and Mary Durham Johnson (eds.), *Women in Revolutionary Paris, 1789–95* (Urbana, Ill., 1979), 225.

[40] Keith Michael Baker, *Inventing the French Revolution* (Cambridge, 1990), 7; François Furet, *Penser la Révolution Française* (Paris, 1978), 73.

Fabrication de Fusils.

Les quatorze armées qu'on oblige d'avoir sur pied exigent une grande quantité d'armes, aussi les autorités de la république maintiennent les ateliers. Dans cinq quartier de Paris, étaient tous le Roi, et les deux ateliers d'armes du Luxembourg et de la place qu'ils ravient à notre comte de ce qu'ils sont en quatre considérable d'ouvriers en fabriquèrent au plus nombre qu'on ne compte plus les marquer.

past, and the assertion that with the Revolution, and more particularly with the Republic, a new era had begun in which subjects had become citizens and men were for the first time endowed with inalienable rights.[41]

The importance of images of regeneration and renewal is reflected in revolutionary discourse and symbolism, but also in the calendar, in festivals, in art and sculpture. Military symbolism played a significant part, especially when that symbolism was so painstakingly integrated into that of the nation, and when military service was portrayed as a vital element in citizenship. The involvement of soldiers in so many of the Revolution's public festivals emphasized the generic links between the people and the army that fought in its name. It is scarcely an accident that the national anthem that emerged during this period, the *Marseillaise*, began as a marching song for the Army of the Rhine, composed at Strasbourg in April 1792.[42] That song, like the National Guardsmen who bellowed its refrain as they marched from Marseille to Paris, became one of the stock images of the Revolution. Later on a painting by Pils of the composer of the *Marseillaise*, Rouget de Lisle, performing before the Mayor of Strasbourg, became

FIGURE 1. Pierre-Etienne Lesueur, *Fabrication de Fusils* (Watercolor, 1793). Musée Carnavalet, Paris. Photograph courtesy of the Photothèque des musées de la ville de Paris/Degraces.

The *levée en masse* of 1793 included explicit provisions for mobilizing the French economy in support of the armed forces. A major success of this effort was the new workshops created in Paris to manufacture firearms, a commodity well suited to the adoption of then still relatively new, assembly-line methods of manufacture. Lesueur's watercolor does not attempt to capture the scale of this effort nor the new techniques and machine tools that were brought to bear. Rather, it renders the process of mass production intimate and familiar. The image shows five artisans – themselves subject to a form of conscription – working harmoniously with traditional tools, while a supervisor, portrayed as a colleague at their side, checks the precision of their musket barrels. The caption, which was evidently added later, describes where the workshops were located (along the Avenue des Invalides and around the former Place Royale) and assures the viewer that any possibility of shortages in the army was quickly alleviated. The image affirms that national service and solidarity extended beyond those in uniform and seeks to distribute some of the credit for the new army's success to broader elements of the society that produced and supported it. The fact that the workshops were a Parisian phenomenon, based upon skilled urban workers – two of whom wear national cockades – quietly illustrates the Revolutionary pedigree of France's military success.

---

[41] Mona Ozouf, "La Révolution française et l'idée de l'homme nouveau," in Keith Baker, François Furet, and Colin Lucas (eds.), *The French Revolution and the Creation of Modern Political Culture*, volume 2: *The Political Culture of the French Revolution* (Oxford, 1988), 213–15.

[42] Michel Vovelle, "La Marseillaise: la guerre ou la paix," in Pierre Nora (ed.), *Les lieux de mémoire: 1 – La République* (Paris, 1984), 85–136; Mason, *Singing the French Revolution*, 94–7.

a commonplace image of political commitment in the textbooks of the Third Republic.[43]

The enthusiasm of the French people for war, the apparent willingness of all classes and conditions to defend the common cause, was integral to this image of regeneration. As such, the *levée en masse* can be seen as a central part of the revolutionary process. It was fundamentally different from the recruitment campaigns of the *ancien régime*, with their press-gangs and their unconcealed reliance on the poor and disadvantaged. But it was

FIGURE 2. Guillaume Guillon-Lethière, *La patrie en danger* (Oil, 1799). Musée de la Révolution Française, Vizille (MRF 1985–14).

In the spring of 1799 France faced a brief but intense military crisis, brought on by the alliance of Britain, Austria, and Russia to form the Second Coalition. The Directory responded by renewing the appeal for a patriotic national defense, and a number of artists responded by reviving the iconography of 1793–94. Guillon-Lethière's *La patrie en danger* is one such work, first exhibited at the Salon of 1799. In it, classical and contemporary motifs combine in a confusing but undeniably dynamic fashion to capture something of the moral complexity inherent in the idea of the *levée en masse*.

The composition revolves around two groups. At the center is a mass of recruits, who salute the seated Statue of Liberty with raised swords. One, wearing the Revolutionary cockade designed by Jacques-Louis David in 1794, is caught at the moment of an impassioned farewell kiss. To the left, a maid holds up his child, while on the right another woman steps forward, bearing an armload of weapons. Where previous depictions of soldiers leaving for war had usually portrayed feminine anxiety and grief, as a counterpoint to male courage and duty, the image here is one of shared sacrifice, willingly borne – a theme that would remain central to the iconography of patriotic recruitment down through the two world wars. It is the women, and not just the state, who send men to war, where the obligations to defend family and fatherland become one. At the same time, the image reaffirms a highly traditional division of labor, by which the sharply gendered nature of military service would be carried forward and expanded. As military service and citizenship came increasingly to define each other, the latter too would become an exclusively male preserve.

The ideal convergence of public and private virtue that lay at the heart of the *levée's* mythology is reinforced by the painting's second focal group, at the left beneath the seated Liberty, where a clerk inscribes the names of those called up in the official role. Behind him a magistrate, in the uniform of a Director, gently restrains two older men wearing the laurels of earlier victories, who again offer their services to the Republic. A young boy carries their weapons. The official presence, however, does not detract from the impression that what we are seeing is an act of generalized civic virtue. Rather, the unity of the painting resides in the official call to arms – embodied in the trumpets at the far left – and the unstinting response of all of society, whose various elements are united by a single emotion.

43 The original Pils painting, "Rouget de Lisle chantant *La Marseillaise* chez le maire de Strasbourg, Dietrich," is in the Musée Historique de Strasbourg. See also Christian Amalvi, *Les héros de l'histoire de France: recherche iconographique sur le Panthéon scolaire de la Troisième République* (Paris, 1979), 80–6.

different, too, from the spirit of voluntarism that had characterized the early Revolution, a voluntarism that might have given the generals young men brimming with enthusiasm for the national cause but that had too often resulted in the sacrifice of committed revolutionaries, while the uninterested and the self-interested had stayed safely in their villages. The *levée en masse*, as we have seen, placed unprecedented emphasis on the equality of sacrifice demanded of the young especially. This was a new element. No longer did the Revolution limit itself to preaching the Rights of Man, without spelling out the extent of civic obligation.[44] The *levée* stated baldly, and for the first time in the Revolution's official discourse, the bleak and startling message that citizenship entailed potentially unlimited obligations.

The cause for which the young men of France were asked to sacrifice themselves was that of the sovereign people of France and of the new nation-state that was in the process of being born. In the 1790s this was, without question, a novel way of interpreting an individual's collective identity and a highly ideological stance that helped define the direction of the Revolution itself. It implied a state built upon consensus and the willing participation of the people, even as it required the destruction of the system of social privilege that had been the organic construct and central pillar of the *ancien régime*. Indeed, it implied more than that. The Revolutionary elevation of the nation as the sovereign unit also meant the curtailment or destruction of other foci for popular loyalty, such as guilds and corporations, voluntary societies, and local or regional identities. In the process the nation became more clearly identified with the power of the centralized state, as the revolutionaries codified the rights and duties contingent upon citizenship.[45] What we are witnessing during this period is an extension of state power and of state legitimacy, which concentrated authority in Paris and reduced those liberties that had previously been enjoyed by the French provinces. Under the Jacobins, this was carried to such extremes that Barère – who hailed from the decidedly peripheral city of Tarbes in the Hautes-Pyrénées – could implicitly equate the periphery with treason, fanatical Catholicism, and a general lack of commitment to the Republic. He saw no contradiction in stating, before the Convention, that federalism spoke Breton or fanaticism Basque. The experience of the summer of 1793 had demonstrated, he felt sure, that the hydra of counterrevolution was always ready to stir in France's most far-flung provinces, and that it was in the center, in Paris and its people, that the passion for the Republic was most assured. To destroy counterrevolution, it was necessary to cement the national identity and replace the

---

44 Godechot, *Les constitutions*, 33–5. For a discussion of Thouret's presentation of the Constitution to the Assembly, and of the limited aspirations of the deputies, see Michael P. Fitzsimmons, *The Remaking of France: The National Assembly and the Constitution of 1791* (Cambridge, 1994), especially 129–35.
45 Reinhard Bendix, *Nation-Building and Citizenship* (Berkeley, 1977), 89–90.

last vestiges of provincial loyalty with a new and unitary commitment to the Nation.[46]

The institution of the *levée en masse* must be seen as part of that process, a key element in the creation of a single national identity in France. It was, of course, only one part, even in the military sphere, where reforms to army discipline and military administration proved equally indispensable.[47] But its impact was crucial in expanding the scale of army recruitment and in heightening the sense of "mass" that shaped both the methods and the morale of the Revolutionary armies. Though the individual retained many of his political rights while he was in uniform, he was increasingly sublimated to the whole, as the theory and practice of warfare on an unprecedented scale continued to evolve, both tactically and ideologically.

For a while the revolutionaries were quite explicit about their desire to use military service as an opportunity to indoctrinate a generation of young men with a sense of national belonging: they were to be separated from their fellow villagers and forced to speak French in a bid to tie them more firmly to the pole of loyalty that was the state. This is one reason for the break-up of the old, regionally recruited regiments in favor of the *demi-brigades*, in which boys from Normandy mingled with those from the Franche-Comté, Bretons with Burgundians. New military formations were intended to forge new loyalties, but as the generals soon realized, they only worsened the perennial problems of homesickness and desertion, so much so that the policy was soon rethought and reversed.[48] Nevertheless, the image of a powerful army drawn from every corner of France, rallying to the Republic to drive out the armies of tyrants, entered the mythology of the nation, to be retrieved and refurbished by nineteenth-century radicals and republicans who sought to ground their politics in the Revolutionary tradition.[49] For them it was living proof of Albitte's dictum that France had to nationalize the spirit of its people, since only that spirit could guide the nation to victory.[50]

---

[46] Michel de Certeau, Dominique Julia, and Jacques Revel, *Une politique de la langue: la Révolution Française et les patois* (Paris, 1975), 295.

[47] The passage of time brought a marked lessening of democratic procedures in the Revolutionary armies, with greater authority left to generals in the field, while the centralization and nationalization of military administration produced radical changes in supply procedures and in troop pay. See Howard G. Brown, *War, Revolution and the Bureaucratic State: Politics and Army Administration in France, 1791–1799* (Oxford, 1995), 119–21.

[48] Marcel Reinhard, "Nostalgie et service militaire pendant la Révolution," *Annales historiques de la Révolution Française* 30 (1958), 1–15.

[49] See, for instance, Maurice Agulhon's *Marianne into Battle: Republican Imagery and Symbolism in France, 1789–1880* (Cambridge, 1981).

[50] Antoine-Louis Albitte, Deputy for the Seine-Inférieure, was a committed Jacobin and regicide with a strong interest in military affairs. He sat on the Military Committee under the Legislative Assembly and served for some years as Representative on Mission to the Army of the Alps. See Albert Soboul, *Dictionnaire historique de la Révolution Française* (Paris, 1989), 13–14.

The emotive image of the *levée en masse* was used by the revolutionaries as part of their own propaganda effort, both to win over the people of France to the sacrifice of war and to create their own legitimizing mythology in the eyes of posterity. They were well aware of the power of legend and of the importance of securing their place in history. The resulting iconography was highly complex. The people in arms, mobilized and deployed by the French state against its enemies, could easily be confused with the revolutionary populations of Paris and other large towns, risen against the injustices of the past. This conflation of the organized power of the revolutionary army and the vernacular power of the revolutionary crowd was deliberate. At the same time, the newly insistent claims of the nation, and indeed of the "mass," on the individual, took second place to portrayals of personal self-sacrifice. The young men recruited in the autumn of 1793 were not volunteers. They were obliged to serve, or at least to make themselves available for service. Yet in the stereotyped language of revolutionary speeches they continued to be referred to as "volunteers," men imbued with the most generous instincts of the people of France.

Some of the most memorable images of the period, in etchings, paintings and cartoons, focus on the moment when the volunteer leaves his family, caught in one last embrace, before marching off to offer his service, and if necessary his life, in war. It is surely no accident that "Le départ du volontaire" became one of the staple themes of contemporary artists, from the well-known *gouache* of Lesueur to the etchings of Guyard and Coqueret, all of whom offered a highly romantic and emotionally charged vision of this seminal moment in the lives of so many families.[51] Other moments in the operation of the *levée*, the process of drawing lots or participating in the recruitment ballot, for instance, were in practice no less central to it. But these had no resonance of voluntary self-sacrifice and were seldom portrayed in works of art of the period.

If the image of the *levée en masse* that was fostered by the revolutionaries and passed down to nineteenth-century republicans was confounded by the competing image of the volunteer, so the National Guard added a further source of obfuscation. The National Guard is best understood in a civic rather than a military context. Its role in the defense of France's frontiers was modest. The first guard units were formed during the spring of 1789, before the assault on the Bastille, and were created by local initiative to defend urban communities from rioting peasants. In Rennes, for instance, a bourgeois militia was recruited as early as 3 February, in Marseille by 23 March, and in Montpellier on 18 April.[52] Soon their ambitions extended to the defense of their communities against any attempt at counterrevolution. By 1790, when

---

[51] Vovelle, *La Révolution Française*, 3: 50–5.
[52] Gilbert Bodinier, "La Révolution et l'Armée," in Jean Delmas (ed.), *Histoire Militaire de la France*, volume 2: *de 1715 à 1871* (Paris, 1992), 196.

National Guard units were at the forefront of the movement for provincial federations that culminated in the great national Federation on the Champ de Mars, their reputation for patriotic commitment was assured.[53] The "active" citizens who formed the first Guard units – men who paid sufficient tax to have earned the right to vote under the law of 29 October 1789 – were proud of their patriotic views and of the blue uniforms that symbolized them; that pride was admirably caught in a number of excellent paintings of the period.[54] In parts of Brittany and the Loire valley, where local communities were sharply divided between royalists and revolutionaries, patriots could define themselves by their membership in local Guard units.[55] By the time war broke out in 1792, the National Guard had already achieved a heroic status as one of the key symbols of the young revolution.[56] But its role was, and remained, largely one of keeping order and defending their own communities against attack. The only significant exception was the Parisian Guard, much of which would be despatched to the frontiers and integrated with other volunteer units.

The myth of the *levée* would also contain a strong dose of spontaneity – the notion that, once the *patrie* was declared to be *en danger*, young men rushed, without coaxing or organization, to offer themselves in its defense. In the words of politicians, they surged to sign on and eagerly assumed their appointed role on the frontiers. There was no reluctance, no time-wasting; the young soldiers would become impatient with the weeks spent in training because they were "burning" to see action and to defend the Revolution. In the propaganda of the nineteenth century, the soldiers of the *levée en masse* were already *francs-tireurs* on the model of those who would fight for the Paris Commune in 1871.

Again, competing images are being confused here to create a single, heroic Revolutionary soldier. There were in fact volunteer *corps francs* in the 1790s, often recruited by individual officers in their locality or department, and styled "legions" or "free companies." These were raised on a somewhat haphazard basis and subsequently aggregated into battalion-sized formations for active service. Often they were recruited in regions with no strong

---

53 Although "federalism" would become synonymous with counterrevolutionary provincialism in 1793 (see note 34), that had not always been the case. The Fête de la Féderation, held in Paris on 14 July 1790 to celebrate revolutionary unity, was the first of the great revolutionary festivals. In subsequent years there were also regional festivals in the principal town of each department, to which local communities were encouraged to send delegates, often National Guardsmen. In 1792 there would even be federations of Jacobin clubs, meeting in Lille and in Valence. For the early federations and the role of the National Guard within them, see Mona Ozouf, *La Fête révolutionnaire, 1789–99* (Paris, 1976), 44–74.

54 Vovelle, *La Révolution Française*, 2: 160, 167.

55 Roger Dupuy, *La Garde Nationale et les débuts de la Révolution en Ille-et-Vilaine, 1789–mars 1793* (Paris, 1972), 263.

56 Georges Carrot, "Une institution de la Nation: la Garde Nationale, 1789–1871," Ph.D. dissertation, University of Nice, (1979), 107.

military tradition, in mountainous areas where the sense of national identity was underdeveloped, or in frontier zones where local people could not
be persuaded to leave their villages but where they were easily galvanized
into defending their own communities. There were *corps francs* in most
parts of Brittany, in the Vendée and the Deux-Sèvres, just as the warriors of
the Pyrenees and the Alps were formed into irregular units whose members
were known variously as *barbets* and *miquelets, chasseurs des montagnes*
and *chasseurs francs*.[57] But their presence in the French armies was less a
sign of spontaneous initiative than a symptom of the recruiting problems
some regions were experiencing. Quite different were the partisans raised in
1814 as part of the last-ditch effort to save the failing Empire. They were unofficial soldiers who took up arms as acts of private faith and initiative, and
the government was accordingly unsure whether to grant them recognition.
For the most part, they remained unpaid irregulars, whose loyalty was to
individual commanders. The government recognized that they fought partly
out of patriotism and partly from opportunism and a belief that there might
be rich pickings for the victors.[58] These partisans did, indeed, demonstrate
a self-organizing spontaneity; but they had little in common with the men
recruited as regular soldiers in 1793.

The idealization of the Revolutionary soldier as a common man fighting
for a cause he believed in, while bearing liberation and human rights to a
continent oppressed by kings, served to legitimize the defense, and later the
expansion, of the Republic. That this idealized soldier bore scant relation
to his real-life counterpart is not surprising: we know that French soldiers,
like nearly all others, burned, raped, and pillaged when they had the chance
and that gathering booty was punished precisely because it was sufficiently
widespread to pose a threat to French military and political ambitions. Nor
is it surprising that the French cultivated an equally mythologized view of
their Prussian and Austrian opponents, who were imagined to be men whose
natural love of liberty had been crushed by tyranny and blinded by super-
stition. Yet even the most ardent revolutionaries were sometimes forced to
admit that such creatures could make brave and resourceful soldiers.

The peasant rebels in Brittany and the West were quite another matter.
They were considered irreconcilable counterrevolutionaries, whipped into a
frenzy by the ambition of their nobles and the intolerance of their clergy. On
the few occasions when there was an attempt at understanding by the Republicans, they simply ascribed the insurrection to the misery or the ignorance
of local people. In the words of three of the Representatives on Mission to

---

[57] Archives de la Guerre, Vincennes, inventory of series Xk. A *barbet* is a breed of spaniel; a
miquelet was an early type of Spanish flintlock musket. The association of partisans (and
skirmishers in regular armies) with hunters (*chasseurs*) was, of course, proverbial in many
languages.

[58] A. G. Vincennes, carton Xk 53, "Les partisans de 1814."

the west, it was "ignorance" that had brought about the war in the Vendée, and it was so deeply engrained in the region that new sparks of insurrection might catch fire at any time.[59] Some of those fighting in the west were more restrained in their condemnation – among them General Turreau, dispatched to the Vendée by the Convention at the start of 1794. Although Turreau's orders called for a scorched-earth policy of exemplary brutality and resulted in the execution of thousands of prisoners, his assessment of the context that produced the conflict was often judicious and measured. He understood the difficulty of fighting in the terrain of the west, knew how news spread through fairs and markets, and appreciated that his troops were at war with the culture of the whole community.[60] For many of the soldiers sent to the Vendée, however, such nuances were unnecessary. They preferred to echo the ideology of the moment, ascribing every evil and savagery to the peasant armies they encountered. Such opponents were not deemed worthy of respect or decent treatment. It was only right that their villages should be destroyed and their warriors executed. As one Republican soldier wrote in a letter to his father in the Gironde, there could be no compassion. Executions had become a daily routine, and rightly so. "We shoot them every day, in batches of fifteen hundred."[61]

With the passage of time the Revolutionary armies lost much of their ideological commitment. They no longer listened to speeches from Representatives on Mission on the eve of battle; they no longer cared about the antimonarchist legends on their uniform badges and buckles. Officers were no longer promoted in recognition of their Jacobin sympathies or their republican virtue. The generals and the politicians were agreed that what mattered was victory, defined as success in the field, and that where virtue and technical competence were in conflict, competence counted more. In other words, the army was slowly becoming professionalized, and its leadership was increasingly composed of professional cadres.[62] This process of professionalization was a gradual one that did not have to wait upon the overthrow of Robespierre. It was already coming to pass under the Jacobins, whose fear of royalism and treachery was counterbalanced by their thirst for

59 Report of Jacques Garnier de Saintes, Narcisse Trullard, and Julien Mazade, *Commissaires à l'Armée des Côtes de la Rochelle*, 4 June 1793, in Alphonse Aulard (ed.), *Recueil des Actes du Comité du Salut Public avec la correspondance officielle des représentants en mission* (Paris, 1885), 4: 445. For a good example of the language used by Republican officers when discussing their Vendean opponents, see J. J. M. Savary, *Guerres des Vendéens et des Chouans contre la République Française* (Paris, 1824).

60 Louis-Marie Turreau, *Mémoires pour servir à l'histoire de la Guerre de la Vendée* (Paris, 1824), 33–6.

61 G. Pages, "Lettres de requis et volontaires de Coutras en Vendée et en Bretagne," *Revue historique et archéologique du Libournais* 190 (1983), 157.

62 Albert Meynier, "L'armée en France sous la Révolution et le Premier Empire," *Revue d'études militaires* (1932), 17–22.

victory. It would become the dominant theme under the Thermidorians and the Directory. These governments still wanted a mass army that would identify with the nation: it is not the case that the main planks of Jacobin policy were simply abandoned. But France's post-Terror governments cared little about a man's politics if his military prowess was assured – hence the large number of radicals and ex-Jacobins whom Isser Woloch found in positions of command under the Directory and the Consulate[63] and the seemingly smooth transformation of the army of the Year II into that of the Empire, a transition that occurred without evident political qualms or internal crises. Under the Directory, the only concerns that arose about the loyalty of the army or its officers were instigated by royalists such as Pichegru.[64]

The explanation for this transition is found in the mentality of the soldiers themselves, as their letters and diaries often reveal. For the most part, they remained loyal to the national cause, even if the focal points of attachment – the *patrie*, the *nation*, eventually the person of the Emperor – might seem curiously unideological compared to the passionate republicanism of the Year II. Even soldiers who had been recruited under the *levée en masse* found themselves increasingly drawn to the institution of the army itself, which became a focus for loyalty every bit as strong as the nation, and stronger than any particular regime.

The practice of military service gradually changed the mentalities of those who turned aside the temptations of desertion. Unlike conventional conscripts, soldiers raised by the *levée en masse* were not liable for a fixed period of service, and many of those recruited in 1793 were still fighting in the armies of Napoleon. A few even struggled through to the final debacle of 1814. Many admitted that they felt increasingly alienated from civilian life, and that they saw no niche for themselves back in the village or on the family farm. After a few campaigns and some limited promotion, they came to see their future as firmly embedded in the military culture that surrounded them, with friends made around the campfire or in the face of shared danger. They ceased to dream of demobilization and a return to their *pays* and looked instead to making a career of soldiering.[65] In the process, much of the ideology of the *levée* inevitably disappeared. Yet the slow professionalization of an army raised by the tide of revolution was in no way incompatible with the spirit of the Revolution itself, which had always preached its commitment to meritocracy.[66] In any case, the reforms of 1793 were not all discarded, even if military discipline was considerably tightened after 1795, and much

---

[63] Isser Woloch, *Jacobin Legacy: The Democratic Movement under the Directory* (Princeton, 1970), 165–9.

[64] See, for instance, Georges Caudrillier, *La trahison de Pichegru et les intrigues royalistes dans l'Est avant Fructidor* (Paris, 1908).

[65] François Vermale, "Lettres inédites d'un sous-lieutenant de l'Armée des Alpes," *Annales historiques de la Révolution Française*, 6 (1929), 56.

[66] Stewart, *Documentary Survey*, 114.

of the traditional authority of the officers reimposed. The army continued to use the tactics of the mass assault and to take pride in its maneuverability, speed, and *élan*.[67] Politicians continued to identify the new mass army with the qualities of republicanism, and to idealize war by resorting to allegorical figures such as Hercules.[68] The very scale of the warfare that attended the Revolution, of the physical and human destruction in which it became enmeshed, became an aspect of the heroic ideal. And the continued success of French arms, widely commemorated in music and in some of the most glorious canvases of the age,[69] helped ensure that the myth of the *levée en masse* survived to inspire the generations that followed.

If, in France itself, that myth was largely confined to the left of the political spectrum, it would be a corollary of the context that produced it. It rapidly merged into a myth of popular insurrection, linked to the image of the French people rising to throw off the chains of tyranny and foreign invasion. As such it would continue to be cited in moments of national danger – by the Communards in 1871, by the Resistance under Vichy, in Algeria in 1962. In all these instances, the motive power of the *levée en masse* meant much more than a simple call to patriotism. It included a direct appeal to civic virtue and public responsibility, just as it had in the 1790s, and it would recreate the image of the sovereign people, properly distrustful of its leaders, ready to rise and sacrifice itself in defense of what it believed to be right.

Underlying this image is an inherited distrust of officially constituted political and military power that also had its roots in the Revolution, a fear of plots and conspiracies on the one hand, and of Caesarism on the other. Throughout the nineteenth and twentieth centuries, these themes recur in French political life, particularly among republicans whose fear of aristocratic, Catholic, and royalist plots was never far below the surface. The propensity of nineteenth-century French liberals to fall back upon conspiracy theories, especially involving the Jesuits, served to systemize their distrust.[70] And even though twentieth-century republicans gradually abandoned the revolutionary implications of a full-blown *levée en masse*, they showed little confidence in a wholly professional army, preferring to maintain some form of conscription even after its military usefulness appeared to have been outlived.

For five decades after the end of the Second World War a consensus prevailed among French politicians that some form of conscription had to be maintained, not only as training in citizenship for the young (an argument

---

[67] John Lynn, *The Bayonets of the Republic: Motivation and Tactics in the Army of Revolutionary France, 1791–94* (Urbana, 1984), 192, 214.

[68] Hunt, *Politics, Culture and Class*, 94–116.

[69] Vovelle, *La Révolution Française*, 5: 60–89.

[70] Geoffrey Cubitt, *The Jesuit Myth: Conspiracy Theory and Politics in Nineteenth-century France* (Oxford, 1993), 309–14.

particularly attractive to Gaullists and other conservative republicans), but also because many politicians (and not just those in the Communist Party) remained distrustful of the political ambitions of army officers and feared some form of right-wing coup. Conscripts, citizens in uniform whose main loyalty was to the nation, to the Republic, to civil authority, seemed a healthy, and some would say a necessary, antidote to the dangers of Caesarism. Only in 1996, when Jacques Chirac's government decided to end conscription and consign France's defense to a professional force, was this delicate nettle grasped, and one strand of the legacy of the *levée en masse* finally laid to rest.

3

The Historiography of the *Levée en masse* of 1793

Owen Connelly

This chapter surveys the history of historical writing about the *levée en masse* of 1793 and the myths that came to surround it. Almost as soon as the Napoleonic wars were over, French republicans and their opponents began to look to the history of the recent past, in order to understand what their predecessors had achieved and where they had gone wrong, and also to support their on-going pursuit of political power. For the former, the enforced mass mobilization of the Year II became the military equivalent of the Rights of Man: young men were now obligated to serve because they were citizens, and they fought with a new morale and self-confidence, enthusiasm and élan, as a consequence. Such ideas were extended almost effortlessly to include Napoleon's soldiers as well and were henceforth taken up without fail at moments of national crisis – in 1848, for instance, and during the Franco-Prussian War, in 1914, and again in 1940 (Figures 3 and 4). They were found in both high and popular culture and were cited in a thousand political speeches.

They also became one of the recurring themes of republican historiography – both the works of major historians and the popularized texts that were studied in the classrooms of Jules Ferry. The heroic soldier of the Year II exemplified republican virtue and French national identity, combining valor and spontaneity, generosity of spirit and a very Gallic virility. That the myth proved to be so enduring is due in no small measure to the efforts of succeeding generations of French historians, most of them committed republicans, who lavished their affection as well as their analytical skills on the soldiers who had fought to defend the Revolution.

The writers with whom we are concerned for the most part exemplify a distinctly republican approach to an aspect of Revolutionary history that, viewed on its face, must give pause to any friend of peace and liberty. Despite reservations about the *levée*'s moral basis and militarizing impact, almost all praised the process of mass mobilization for providing France with an army that not only was energized by the Revolutionary cause but also had

FIGURES 3 AND 4. Left, François Rude, *Le départ des volontaires en 1792*. Sculpture on the Arc de Triomphe de l'Etoile, Paris (1833–6). Right, *Pour le triomphe souscrivez à l'emprunt national*. War Loan Poster for the Banque Nationale de Crédit, by Sem (1916). Photograph courtesy of the Hoover Institution Archives.

François Rude's sculpture for the Arc de Triomphe, often called "La Marseillaise," exemplifies the assimilation of the Revolutionary military experience to the Napoleonic tradition and the transmission of both to future generations. Rude's panel is one of four on the Arc de Triomphe. The others portray Napoleon's victory at Wagram in 1809 (the apogee of his military career), French resistance in 1814, and the peace of 1815. In time, however, Rude's Sculpture has come to stand for the whole structure – the greatest of all Napoleonic monuments, summarized in an image of Revolutionary voluntarism done in the highest Romantic style.

In contrast to the classical motifs that prevailed during the Revolutionary era, Rude's departing warriors are clothed in Celtic garb, a reference to the now-forgotten pseudo-medieval epic "Ossian," with which the Napoleonic legend was once associated. Jacques-Louis David, the preeminent artist of the Revolution, disliked Rude's work

pour le triomphe
souscrivez à l'emprunt national

LES SOUSCRIPTIONS SONT REÇUES À PARIS ET EN PROVINCE
À LA
BANQUE NATIONALE DE CRÉDIT

FIGURES 3 AND 4. *(continued)* for its stylistic extravagance and emotional extremism; a portrait, he felt, not of noble patriotism, but of "passion grimacing in the moment of maximum energy" (T. J. Clarke, *The Absolute Bourgeois: Artists and Politics in France, 1848–51* [London, 1973], 60). Yet, despite a certain aesthetic parochialism, the enduring power of Rude's work to symbolize the feelings of a nation mobilized for war cannot be doubted, as is evident in the victory loan poster published by the Banque Nationale de Crédit in 1916. The poster – one of many to include Rude's sculpture as a central element – shows French soldiers of the past streaming through the Arc, called forth once more by the galvanizing image of the Revolutionary volunteers, and so reincarnated as the French army of World War I. The historical continuity of the nation is thus affirmed as a way of heightening the obligation to defend it in the present. In Sem's poster, the ideal of the nation in arms acquires a fourth dimension, extending not simply through the full height, breadth, and depth of society, but across time to generations past, whose sacrifices must be continuously redeemed to safeguard the futures of those not yet born.

characteristics that ennobled it in the eyes of all nations and all ages. The *levée* was, in these terms, voluntary, defensive, noble, just, and popular, and these would all prove to be powerful elements in its representation by historians.

It was perhaps inevitable that, for those who had experienced the Revolution and its Napoleonic aftermath as adults, the Emperor's career became a kind of lens through which earlier events had to be viewed. Madame Germaine de Staël, the most prolific *litterateur* of the time, did her part to idealize the *levée en masse* in the process of damning her nemesis Napoleon. "The conduct of the French Army during the Terror," she wrote, "was truly patriotic. . . . The soldiers gave their loyalty not to this or that chief, but to France"; whereas Napoleon used the "poor brave conscripts" to tyrannize Europeans and make them hate the French.[1] The might of the Revolutionary and Napoleonic armies exercised other contemporaries. Benjamin Constant stood in awe of the people's power: "Liberty supplies the forces for her defense, common interest produces all the necessary resources."[2] Not all, however, shared an enthusiasm for the idea of the people in arms. Chateaubriand was one who saw it as a veiled threat to liberty, writing that most Frenchmen, after living through the wars of the First Republic and the First Empire, believed conscription to be an evil, whether it was the policy of a democracy or of a despot.[3]

After 1815, the first historians to rise to prominence through accounts of the Revolution were François Mignet (1796–1884) and Adolphe Thiers (1797–1877). Both the same age and from the south of France, they came to Paris at about the same time to work on *Le Courrier Français* and *Constitutionnel*, respectively. "Beau Mignet" and short, plain Thiers became fast friends.[4] Both were induced by large advances to write on the Revolution, and produced classics.

Mignet's *Révolution* (1824) was short, liberal in tone, and popular. He was the son of a *Montagnard* who had suffered after 1793–4, and positively favored the *levée* as a measure necessary to preserve the Republic. "The Mountain," he wrote, "needed dictatorship to establish democracy."[5] Thiers' *Révolution* (1823–7) was even more impassioned, romantic, and popular, a bestseller despite its length (ten volumes in all). It praised the *levée* as the "great impulsion" by which "everything became possible." Thiers credited the Terror's Representatives on Mission with helping to make soldiers of

---

[1] A.-L.-Germaine de Staël, *Considérations sur les principaux événemens de la Révolution française* (London, 1818), 129, 356–357, 359.

[2] Benjamin Constant, *Benjamin Constant: Recueil d'articles, 1795–1817* (Geneva, 1978), 51.

[3] Paraphrased in Richard D. Challener, *The French Theory of the Nation in Arms, 1866–1939* (New York, 1965), 12.

[4] Jacques Leon Godechot, *Un jury pour la Révolution* (Paris, 1974), 35.

[5] François Mignet, *La Révolution française* (Paris, 1824), translated as *History of the French Revolution* (London, 1826), 14–15.

terrified, ignorant, homesick peasants, thus instilling "extraordinary audacity and will" into the army.[6] The losing generals who went to the guillotine got short shrift.[7] He praised the "great and salutary" Jourdan Law of September 1798, which introduced systematic annual conscription, as "one of the most important creations of the Revolution."[8]

Thiers himself was destined for a revolutionary career. His book and his newspaper *National* helped launch the Revolution of 1830, an event that only heightened interest in its great predecessor, and not just in France. Thomas Carlyle's *The French Revolution* (1837) was both a paean to the French People, and a comment on the extremes of human nature.[9] Although Carlyle's work is best remembered for its pathos-filled portraits of the Terror in action, his attitude toward the *levée en masse* was entirely positive: "from every hamlet toward the seat of war . . . the Sons of Freedom shall march; their banner is to bear: *Le peuple français debout contre les tyrans*."[10] That the Law of Suspects was part of the process was understood: "All prisons . . . in the French land are getting crowded to the ridge-tile." But in the end "fourteen armies are got on foot; patriotism, with all that it has in heart or in head, in soul or body . . . dashing to the frontiers, to prevail or die."[11] In 1912, Alphonse Aulard, *doyen* of historians of the Revolution, translated Carlyle's work into French.[12]

In 1836, Sir Walter Scott's *The Life of Napoleon* was published posthumously. Although misleading and ill-informed on its principal subject, the author's unparalleled popularity as a novelist guaranteed that it would be widely read.[13] In a background section on the French Revolution, he glorified the *levée*, presenting it with a wild romantic flourish to a generation that was content with nothing less. Men rushed to the front, he wrote, and among the peasants "youth of spirit [were] glad to . . . take with gayety the chance of death or promotion."[14] Exhilarating stuff, of exactly the sort that Scott's readers had come to expect from him, and it served to stoke the legend still further.

---

[6] Louis-Adolphe Thiers, *Histoire de la Révolution française*, 13th ed., 10 volumes (Paris, 1854), 4: 254–6.

[7] Ibid., 5: 99. He wrote that many generals "perished or retired," ignoring the skilled and loyal men who were guillotined because they were aristocrats.

[8] Thiers, *Révolution*, 10: 98–100.

[9] Thomas Carlyle, *The French Revolution* (London, 1837; reprinted New York, 1942).

[10] Carlyle, *French Revolution* (New York, 1942), 623.

[11] Ibid., 624, 655.

[12] Thomas Carlyle, *Histoire de la Révolution française*, 3 volumes (Paris, 1912). Aulard also wrote the introduction to this "good book." Carlyle coined a number of phrases that have eluded the French, while becoming proverbial in English (e.g., Napoleon's "whiff of grapeshot").

[13] Sir Walter Scott, *The Life of Napoleon, Emperor of the French: With a Preliminary View of the French Revolution*, 2 volumes (Exeter, 1836).

[14] Ibid., 1: 191–3.

The preeminent mid-century account of the Revolution, and the only one of enduring scholarly influence, was that of Jules Michelet (1798–1874) whose *Révolution* (1847–53) was more popular than any account written before or since.[15] It was lauded by republicans of all stripes (including Marxists), had an almost iconic status during the Third Republic, and is still cited.[16] The son of a Paris printer, Michelet was born the year before the Revolution ended and grew up listening to the tales of its veterans. Despite a distinguished career that included prestigious positions at the Ecole Normale, the Sorbonne, the Collège de France, and the Archives Nationales, he remained a *sans-culotte* in spirit. His book *Le Peuple* (1844) is widely credited with helping foment popular unrest in 1848.[17] As intensely romantic, in his way, as Scott or Carlyle, Michelet never let documents overrule the instincts he had developed during his boyhood on the Paris streets. His hero was "the people," undefined; he understood Robespierre but revered the people's scruffy idol, Jacques Danton, a key proponent of the *levée en masse*:

Danton was an intellect too acute to believe that [the *levée*] would have immediate effect. But the *Réquisition* contributed no less to victory.... In those memorable battles [in 1793] our soldiers caught the spirit of an entire nation that had risen to support them; they did not have the people with them, but [had] their force, their soul...the divinity of France.

The Foreigner realized that it was not an army that struck: by the might of the blows, he recognized God.[18]

Where Michelet appealed to radicals and those who reveled in the legacy of the French Revolution, Hippolyte Taine was both more cautious and more conservative. By 1870 he was already famous as a philosopher, critic, and author.[19] It was the rout of the once-mighty French army by the Prussians that inspired him to begin a history of France.[20] He never finished it, but the two volumes on the Revolution were runaway best sellers before World War I (26 French editions), and into the 1930s. His was to be one of the most influential voices in defining the Third Republic's response to the

[15] Jules Michelet, *Histoire de la Révolution française*, 7 volumes (Paris, 1847–53).
[16] See Albert Soboul, *Précis d'histoire de la Révolution française* (Paris, 1962), 29; Simon Schama, *Citizens: A Chronicle of the French Revolution* (New York, 1989), 5, 8, 718; Owen Connelly, *The French Revolution and Napoleonic Era*, 3rd ed. (Fort Worth, Tex., 1999), 72.
[17] See Jeremy Rabkin, "Revolutionary Visions and Legal Imagery," in R. C. Hancock and G. L. Lambert (eds.), *The Legacy of the French Revolution* (Lanham, Md., 1996), 252.
[18] Michelet, *Histoire de la Révolution française* (Paris, 1952), 2: 548, 554–5.
[19] His works included *L'Idéalisme Anglais* (Paris, 1864), *Histoire de la littérature Anglais* (Paris, 1865) and *Philosophie de l'Art* (Paris, 1866). Oxford gave him an honorary L.L.D. in 1871.
[20] *Origines de la France contemporaine*, 6 volumes (Paris, 1875–94; reprinted in 12 volumes, 1906–9).

Revolution, one that refused to accept the legitimacy of everything the Revolution had done and, in particular, declined to serve as an apologist for the Terror. He also predicted that the *levée en masse* would breed catastrophe in time:

> From war to war, the institution gets worse; like a contagion, it is propagated from state to state; at present it has conquered all of continental Europe, and reigns there with universal suffrage, [each] drawing on the other, . . . both the blind and formidable regulators of future history, one putting into the hands of every adult a ballot, the other putting a soldier's pack on every adult; with what promises of massacre and bankruptcy for the 20th century.[21]

In the introduction to the *Révolution* volumes, Taine stated that his purpose was to enlighten the French, who had been misinformed about the Revolution since around 1825–30, when the last adult eyewitnesses had died.[22] Taine reminded his readers that the Terrorists had demanded obedience or death, paraphrasing a famous line of Rousseau's *Social Contract*: "We force them to be free."[23] He tied the ideas of the Terror to socialism, which he saw as a great evil.

With the victory of the Radicals in 1879, republican attitudes regarding the Revolution again became more partisan, as many radicals argued that the legitimacy of the Third Republic implied an acceptance of the entire achievement of the First. During the celebration of the centenary of the French Revolution in 1889, the radicals were instrumental in creating a Chair of the History of the French Revolution at the Sorbonne. The first occupant was Alphonse Aulard (1849–1928), who was too professional to give them exactly what they wanted, but his successors would.

Aulard was the most eminent historian of the French Revolution of his era. Born the son of a professor of philosophy in Montbron (Charente), he climbed the academic ladder from Aix-en-Provence to the Sorbonne. In the Chair of the History of the French Revolution, he was a champion of archival research and trained a generation of historians who dominated Revolutionary studies – Philippe Sagnac, Frédéric Braesch, Raymond Guyot, Albert Pingaud, Jacques Rambaud, and Albert Mathiez. He was also a journalist and active in the Radical and Radical Socialist Parties. Aulard's major work, *L'Histoire politique*, focused mainly on the domestic politics of the First

---

[21] Taine, *Origines* (1906–9), 10: 121. Godechot paired Heinrich von Sybel with Taine but admitted that the German historian saw the Revolution mainly as a "movement that failed to destroy Germany." It destroyed feudalism, Sybel said, but paved the way for communism. Heinrich von Sybel, *Geschichte der Revolutionszeit, 1789–1800* (Stuttgart, 1853–70); Godechot, *Un jury pour la Révolution*, 190–3.

[22] Taine, *Origines* (1906–9), 7: iv.

[23] Ibid., 100.

Republic.[24] He regarded the *levée en masse* as a measure adopted mainly to pacify the Paris crowds – a judgment he also applied to the Law of Suspects; the enactment of price controls under the "Maximum"; and the authorization of "people's armies" to strip the countryside of food. He called the Terror's institutions "provisional" and "socialistic."[25] Aulard's documentary collection, *La Société des Jacobins*, has a transcript of the debate of the *levée* bill, with Danton for it and Robespierre arguing that the Republic needed loyal generals more.[26] And there, more or less, Aulard's scholarly interest terminated. He was not particularly concerned with the war and was too dispassionate in his scholarship to fall into what he would have seen as the error of enthusiasm.

Aulard's personal and journalistic involvement with war as such was nevertheless considerable and revealed the difficulties and ambiguities the whole issue posed for men of the left. His great-grandfather had been a member of the Army of the Rhine, and Aulard himself volunteered in 1870 and fought at Sedan. During World War I, he taught at the Sorbonne and often drew links to the past, for instance comparing the Battle of the Marne to Valmy. His sense of the deep continuities of French patriotism is evident in a small volume he wrote after the war, entitled *Le Patriotisme française de la Renaissance à la Révolution* (1921). Aulard exemplified the characteristic republican fear that the shadow of militarism might fall across even the "just" wars of 1792 and 1914, and sought to portray the Revolutionary message as one of peace. In 1929 he collaborated with an exiled Menshevik, Boris Mirkine-Guetzévitch, on an address entitled "La Révolution française et la renonciation à la guerre," which endorsed the Kellogg-Briand Pact "outlawing" war.

Jean Jaurès was similarly conflicted. His *Histoire socialiste*, the first Marxist history of France, celebrated "the offensive by great masses" that the *levée* unleashed, pushed forward by a tide of "patriotism, of vigor, of courage and of genius." France, he felt, "was worth a world.... She deserved to conquer humanity!"[27] For Jaurès, however, the *levée* was a measure required to win a war that had better not have been fought. Thus he criticized Robespierre, an opponent of the *levée*, for not fighting harder to avoid war in the first place.

Jaurès made a connection between the *levée* of 1793, the Tricolor, and Marxism that would remain a staple of Revolutionary historiography in

---

[24] F.-V.-Alphonse Aulard, *L'Histoire politique de la Révolution française: Origines et developpement de la démocratie et de la républic, 1789–1804*, 4 volumes (Paris, 1901). He also blasted his rival in *Taine: Historien de la Révolution française* (1907). He edited *La Société des Jacobins: Recueil de documents pour l'histoire de Club des Jacobins de Paris* (Paris, 1898–1902) and began the *Receuil des actes du Comité du Salut Public*, (Paris, 1889–1956), finished by others, amounting to twenty-seven volumes in all.

[25] Aulard, *Histoire politique*, 2: 279–80, 292–3.

[26] *Société des Jocobins...Documents*, 5: 357–61, 370–83.

[27] Jean Jaurès, *Histoire socialiste, 1789–1900*, 12 volumes (Paris, 1901–8), 4: 644–6.

France throughout the Third Republic and into our own times. A hyperactive politician and journalist, Jaurès was a founder of the United Socialist Party, which he headed from 1905 until his death in 1914; editor of *L'Humanité*; and author of a book on army reform, *L'Armée nouvelle* (1910), in which he sought to give practical shape to the lessons of the *levée* by promoting a reorganized national army, based upon universal service, deep reserves of manpower, and a bare minimum of professional strategizing.

Before 1914, as war approached, Jaurès stood for conscription despite the socialist dogma that the *levée* was a tool of the *bourgeois* government for exploiting the masses. He argued that "the people" would never gain power unless they did military service and learned to use weapons.[28] At the same time, however, and with an ambivalence characteristic of the left, he sought to organize an international general strike against war – an effort that inspired a right-wing fanatic to murder him a few days before war broke out in August, 1914.

The conservative followers of Taine also had dark forebodings about the precedent set by the *levée en masse* and (far more than the left) loathed the Terror root and branch, so they were less willing to excuse it as an emergency measure. Yet they too backed heavier conscription before the First World War. Among them were Louis Madelin (*La Révolution*, 1911), Jacques Bainville (*Le 18 brumaire*, 1926), and Pierre Gaxotte (*La Révolution française*, 1928).[29] After the Boulanger Affair, Republicans of all shades tended to distrust a professional army and to suspect its officers of political ambitions. Taine's disciples created a surprising degree of consensus on conscription within the French academy, where it became generally accepted that the *levée* was integral to the success of French arms.

After the restoration of peace in 1919 the Republic was in no mood for compromise, and it is not surprising that historians of the classical republican school dominated the historical profession in France. At the Sorbonne, Aulard was succeeded in 1925 by his pupil, Albert Mathiez, though the Chair of the History of the French Revolution went to Philippe Sagnac, an eminent scholar but more Positivist than Socialist. Of the two, it was Mathiez who left the more lasting impression on Revolutionary scholarship.

World War I inevitably shaped Mathiez's approach to the Revolution. His *Victoire de l'An II* (1916), derived from lectures to potential draftees, extolled the *levée en masse* and the citizen soldiers it produced.[30] A note of ambiguity crept in after the Russian Revolution, however. Mathiez supported

[28] Jean Jaurès, *L'Armée nouvelle* (Paris, 1918), 357. Quoted in Challener, *French Nation in Arms*, 70n.

[29] Godechot, *Jury*, 226. Gaxotte's work has been reprinted as recently as 1988.

[30] See the historiographical introduction to Jean-Paul Bertaud, *La Révolution Armée: Les soldats-citoyens et la Révolution française* (Paris, 1979); translated by R. R. Palmer as *The Army of the French Revolution: From Citizen Soldiers to Instrument of Power* (Princeton, 1988), 8–9.

the Bolsheviks as an internationalist party opposed to war (in contrast to
other communist sympathizers, who sought to legitimize the violence of
the Russian Revolution by linking it to that of France, and reinterpreting
the wars of the latter along class lines). Mathiez's communist and pacifist
sympathies caused him to avoid the question of war in his later writings, at
a time when many on the left were finding that their fear of militarism was
outweighed by the need to fight fascism. In an article published four years
after his death in 1932, he regretted the loss of a pacific and cosmopolitan
Europe in the upheaval of the Revolution and its wars.[31]

Mathiez's work was distinguished by an appreciation of the economic
effort necessary to support a major war. The result was his most acclaimed
book, *La vie chère et le mouvement social sous la terreur* (1927), which
subordinated the *levée en masse* to the Terror's economic laws and their
brutal enforcement.[32] Mathiez laid out his case neatly in his conclusion:

On 9 August [1793] granaries were instituted.... The granaries had to be filled.
How? The case was more pressing than the law to draft all men 18 to 25 years
old, ... 500,000 recruits who had to be fed.... On 14 August the workers for thresh-
ing were requisitioned; on 15 August, the grain to feed the capital. On 17 August
a general inventory [was called for]. On 19 August ... the maximum price on com-
bustibles [was fixed]; on 20 and 23 August the maximum on [grains]. On 23 August,
the decree on the *levée en masse*, which [also] ordered payment of taxes in kind [i.e.,
in grain].[33]

On the *levée* proper, he noted with approval the comment of Sébastien
Lacroix, who proposed mobilization during the *Fête du 10 Août* (celebrating
King Louis XVI's overthrow), that "eight days of enthusiasm can do more
for the nation than eight years of combat."[34] As to the architect of the
Terror: "Robespierre considered ... that the war was an evil, but ... a necessary evil."[35] Mathiez, mixing superb scholarship with Marxist predilections,
helped make the socialist version of the Revolution "standard" until the late
1970s. In doing so, he perpetuated the myth of the *levée en masse*, which
had come to be regarded as integral to the Revolution.[36]

---

[31] Albert Mathiez, "Pacifisme et nationalisme au milieu de XVIIIe siècle," *Annales historique
de la Révolution française* 12 (1936), 1–17.

[32] Mathiez sympathized with peasants and workers whose goods were seized by the
Réprentants and the "armies" of rabble mobilized to feed Paris. See Richard Cobb's *Les
armées révolutionnaires: Instrument de la Terreur dans les départements, avril 1793-floréal
An II* (Paris, 1961–3).

[33] Albert Mathiez, *La Vie chère et le mouvement social sous la terreur* (Paris, 1927), 314–15.

[34] Ibid., 303.

[35] Albert Mathiez, *Etudes sur Robespierre* (Paris, 1973), 99.

[36] Mathiez presented the Russian Revolution as having causes in common with the French in *Le
Bolchévism et le Jacobinism* (Paris, 1920). François Furet disagreed in his *Pensée la Révolution*
(Paris, 1981), translated as *Interpreting the French Revolution* (New York, 1981). On the

Georges Lefebvre (1874–1959) succeeded Mathiez at the Sorbonne (1935) and was appointed to the Chair of the History of the French Revolution in 1937. He produced the twentieth century's most famous syntheses of Revolutionary history: *La Révolution française* (1930), and *Napoléon* (1936). Lefebvre was born in northern France to working-class parents. He won the *agrégation* and taught in lycées until he was fifty years old. In 1924, he finally finished and published his doctoral dissertation, *Les paysans du Nord pendant la Révolution française*[37] and received provincial university appointments until called to Paris in 1935.

Lefebvre wrote a score of books. His monographs pioneered in "history from below," but his opinions on the *levée* were expressed elsewhere. In his classic *Révolution*, he praised the army created by the Jacobin government of 1793–4: "The will to conquer was unanimous.... The Army of the Year II was the symbol of national unity."[38] But without much familiarity with the military, or great interest in it, he gave more space to measures for supporting the army than to the *levée en masse*. In his *Etudes sur la Révolution française* (1954), he wrote that the *levée* hurt workers and cut production in mines and factories[39] and called the *Maximum* incompatible with liberty. But he justified both as essential to the defense of the Republic, which he characterized as a true social democracy.[40]

Historians worldwide came to admire Lefebvre's scholarship, if not always his interpretations. Among English-speaking historians, Crane Brinton, of Harvard, wrote a *Revolution* clearly influenced by Lefebvre, which repeated the myth of the *levée*.[41] His colleague Franklin Ford, more realistically, called the *levée* "one of the greatest symbolic acts of the Revolution."[42] Leo Gershoy, of New York University, produced an admiring biography of *Barère*, who introduced the *levée* bill in the Convention.[43] In Britain, J. M. Thompson published a book about the Revolution and another about Napoleon that were rivaled only by Lefebvre's.[44]

---

general issue of linkage between the French and Russian Revolutions, see Furet's *Le passé d'une illusion: Essai sur l'idée communiste au XXe siècle* (Paris, 1995), esp. 117–20.

[37] Paris, 1924; reprinted 1972.

[38] Lefebvre, *La Révolution française* (Paris, 1930), 393–4.

[39] The peasantry suffered as well. See *Paysans du Nord*, 738–40; cited in A. Cobban, *Social Interpretation of the French Revolution* (London, 1968), 171. Cobban wanted to show that Lefebvre knew that conditions for the lower classes were miserable, but that he was determined to praise the Terror government.

[40] Georges Lefebvre, *Etudes sur la Révolution française* (Paris, 1954), 123, 185, 197, 326.

[41] Crane Brinton, *A Decade of Revolution, 1789–1799* (New York, 1934; reprinted 1963), 128–30.

[42] Franklin L. Ford, *Europe, 1780–1830* (Harlow, 1970), 122.

[43] Leo Gershoy, *Bertrand Barère: A Reluctant Terrorist* (Princeton, 1962).

[44] J. M. Thompson, *The French Revolution* (London, 1943) and *Napoleon Bonaparte: His Rise and Fall* (London, 1936).

Norman Hampson's *A Social History of the French Revolution* did not ignore the darker side of the *levée*. Because of it, he said:

The State became the controlling force behind most economic activity ... [As] in the political field coercion took the place of consent. ... In September 1793 the illusion of national unity was replaced by the ruthless extermination of enemies.[45]

Another realist was Robert R. Palmer of Princeton, the leading American French Revolutionist for decades after World War II. His masterwork, *Twelve Who Ruled* (1941), studied the Committee of Public Safety of 1793–4.[46] He was impressed by the Jacobins' war effort and admired their civil aims in education and so on, but he was skeptical about the myth of the *levée* as a spontaneous act of revolutionary enthusiasm:

For the first time the world saw a nation in arms – or [rather] it was carried through on that principle, for in sober fact the whole people was hardly more eager to go to war in the France of 1793 than in the Europe of 1914 or 1939.[47]

After World War II, the French discovered Palmer, and his *1789* (1967) was published first in France, then in America.[48] It said of the *levée*: "Thanks largely to Lazare Carnot, the paroxysm of the *levée en masse* was converted into the discipline of an organized army."[49]

On Lefebvre's death in 1959, Marcel Reinhard succeeded him in the Chair of the History of the French Revolution. Reinhard, among other things, had written a laudatory biography of Lazare Carnot, the Terror's "organizer of victory," praising his reform of the officer corps and his successful reconciliation of Revolutionary egalitarianism and the requirements of military efficiency.[50]

In 1967, Reinhard was in turn succeeded by Albert Soboul (1914–82). Born in Algeria to (he insisted) a French peasant family, he lost both parents as an infant and was reared by an aunt in Nîmes. Since his father was killed in World War I, he had free schooling as a *pupille de la nation*. While at university he joined the Communist Party and never

---

[45] Norman Hampson, *A Social History of the French Revolution* (London, 1963), 193, 187–98.

[46] R. R. Palmer, *Twelve Who Ruled: The Year of the Terror in the French Revolution* (Princeton, 1941; reprinted 2001).

[47] Ibid., 60.

[48] R. R. Palmer, *1789: Les Révolutions de la liberté et de l'Egalité.* (Paris, 1967), translated as *The World of the French Revolution* (New York, 1971). The French publish few foreign works on the Revolution. Before this, an exception had been Richard Cobb's *Les armées révolutionnaires*. More recently, the French have published several of Alan Forrest's books, including *Déserteurs et insoumis* (Paris, 1988); in English *Conscripts and Deserters* (London and New York, 1989).

[49] Palmer, *The World of the French Revolution*, 118.

[50] Marcel Reinhard, *Le grand Carnot* (Paris, 1950–2).

left it.[51] During World War II he taught at Clermont-Ferrand, but he had scrapes with the Vichy police and arranged to disappear. He emerged in Paris after its liberation (1944) to study with Lefebvre.

Soboul's dissertation, *Les Sans-Culottes parisiens de l'An II* (1958), made his reputation. In this and his other works he extolled the Terror and held that conscription was only successful when it was closely linked to Jacobin ideology. In *Les soldats de l'An II* (1959) and *Paysans, sans culottes et Jacobines* (1966), he wrote emotionally of the fighters for "home and country" of 1793–4. In *La Révolution française* he said, "the *levée en masse* was in harmony with the Revolutionary mentality of the *sans-culottes.*"[52] In *Comprendre la Révolution*, he summed up:

In the Year II the war was charged with national and social significance.... The army had been nationalized by the *amalgame* of 1793; the war was nationalized in turn.... In the ranks of the Army of the Year II, national fervor and revolutionary spirit were one and the same.[53]

Soboul's view of the Revolution remained largely that of his Communist youth, though his understanding of popular aspirations, and especially of the peasantry, had become more nuanced in his later years. Central to that understanding was the notion of a "bourgeois revolution" playing its prescribed Marxist role in the development of European society. Implicit in that Marxist model was the idea that the *levée en masse* truly represented the people of France, that the young rose spontaneously to drive out France's enemies, to defend their country and their Revolution. As long as the Marxist interpretation of the Revolution retained its credibility, so did the myth of the *levée.*

After Soboul's death in 1982, the citadel of the "classical" interpretation was increasingly assailed. As the bicentennial of the Revolution (1989) approached, it seemed that the Marxist interpretation was mortally wounded, and the myth of the *levée* with it. The French left, of course, did not think so. Michel Vovelle, who succeeded Soboul at the Sorbonne, published a new, multivolume *Révolution française.*[54] His approach to the particular issue of the *levée* could be described as soft but positive. "[The *levée en masse*] put in motion a complete reorganization of an army making it that of the nation."[55] Whatever its limitations in practice, "the army of the Revolution," he argued,

---

[51] After his death in 1982, the party conducted an elaborate funeral for him after a march to an unfinished monument to his memory. According to Richard Cobb, who knew him well, Soboul's family later reburied him with a religious ceremony in Nîmes.

[52] Albert Soboul, *La Révolution française*, 2 volumes (Paris, 1962), 2: 27, 116.

[53] Albert Soboul, *Comprendre la Révolution: Problèmes politiques de la Révolution française (1789–1797)* (Paris, 1981), 275–6.

[54] Michel Vovelle, *Révolution française: Images et récit* (Paris, 1986); an abridged edition entitled *La Révolution française, 1789–99* was published in Paris in 1992.

[55] Michel Vovelle, *Révolution française*, 108.

was a national army of a people mobilized to defend the Revolution and the nation. The resistance to the *levée* ... by a part of France should not mask the collective enthusiasm and élan. The volunteers and soldiers of the Year II knew why they fought: at Jamappes, in November 1792, they sang the *Marseillaise* while mounting an assault on the enemy lines.[56]

Notwithstanding, some of the "best sellers" in France were histories that roundly damned the Revolution. Reynauld Secher accused the Terror government of inflicting "genocide" on the God-fearing peasants in the Vendée, with increased bloodshed as "*les levées en masse*" replaced regulars.[57] René Sédillot wrote that the cost of the Revolution was far too high.[58] Bernard Deschard touted the virtues of the Royal Army.[59]

Outside France, most of the histories published around the Bicentennial were conservative, but recognized the positive legacies of the Revolution. The *levée*, however, was not one of them. Simon Schama considered the *levée en masse* "by far the most important" innovation of 1793, but for entirely negative reasons: "no sooner had a hypothetically free person been invented than his liberties were circumscribed by the police power of the state. ... Militarized nationalism was not, in some accidental way, the unintended consequence of the French Revolution: it was its heart and soul."[60]

Emmet Kennedy in his *A Cultural History of the French Revolution* said that the *amalgame* created an effective army that won victories. But the *levée en masse* "brought in thousands of peasants who had no desire to march hundreds of miles ... to risk their lives for a republic that was requisitioning their crops and livestock. Desertions were easy and numerous."[61] He quoted Jean-Paul Bertaud on soldiers' letters showing that some were inspired, but more complained of the lack of food and supplies, and some hoped a wound would send them home.[62]

Bertaud's *La Révolution Armée* (1979) is ambivalent regarding the *levée*.[63] In his view the *levée* intensified class conflict, since peasants (85 percent of the French population) were certain that the bourgeoisie was protecting its sons from the draft. In fact, he said, the law was applied

---

[56] Ibid., 108–9.
[57] Reynauld Secher in *La genocide franco-français: La Vendée-vengé* (Paris, 1986) makes reference to statistics in O. Festy, "Les mouvements de la population française du début de la Révolution au Consulat," *Annales historiques de la Révolution française*, 141 (1955), 26–49; also Gaxotte, *Révolution* (Paris, reprinted 1988), 427–8.
[58] René Sédillot, *Le Coût de la Révolution française* (Paris, 1987).
[59] Bernard Deschard, *L'Armée et la Révolution: du service du roi au service de la nation* (Paris, 1989).
[60] Schama, *Citizens*, 760, 858. See also J. F. Bosher, *The French Revolution* (New York, 1988) and William Doyle, *Oxford History of the French Revolution* (Oxford and New York, 1989).
[61] Emmet Kennedy, *A Cultural History of the French Revolution* (New Haven, 1989), 370.
[62] Kennedy, *Cultural History*, 372–3.
[63] Bertaud, *The Army of the French Revolution*, 219–26.

unevenly, and conscription was resisted in rural areas, although the cities and larger towns were enthusiastic. The Committee of Public Safety tried persuasion and propaganda to get compliance but in the end used force and vicious punishments.[64]

In Bertaud's opinion, the Jourdan Law of 1798, which formalized conscription, was sponsored by the Directory to support its policy of expansion.[65] He gives statistics to show that conscription was more efficient under Napoleon, until the last years. However, he believes that it served the interest of democracy and nationalism by mixing Frenchmen of all regions in the ranks, and, with the democratization of the officer corps, served to unite classes and parties. The Army became a factor in politics, and it remains so to this day.[66]

Among the works of Americans, those of Samuel Scott and Isser Woloch eroded the myth of the *levée* by examining the real experience of regulars in the changing French Army of the Revolution.[67] John Lynn, however, upheld the myth in *Bayonets of the Republic* (1984).[68] He studied the *Armée du Nord* (on the Belgian front), where troops of the *levée* were close to home and could believe they were defending their homes and families. The *Nord* won battles, he wrote, with spirited men who flung themselves into the fight. Despite many caveats, he held that the *Armée du Nord* exemplified the "tactics and motivation" of the French Revolutionary army.[69]

Marc Bouloiseau had written (twenty years earlier) that "near the frontiers there was less [draft evasion] because of realization of a common peril";[70] also that "rural France protected the draft evader.... The laws were revolutionary; those who executed them were not.... Sly by temperament, the peasant duped the Republic."[71] Much earlier, Camille Rousset in *Les Volontaires* (1870) observed variations in resistance to service in the Nord and other departments. *Réprésentants*, he said, often made self-serving reports of (imaginary) thousands rushing to serve.[72]

Michel Auvray's *Objecteurs, insoumis, déserteurs* was more blunt and cutting. He called the *levée en masse* "Le Légend des 'volontaires de l'An II'"

---

[64] Ibid., 104, 105–11, 111–17.

[65] Ibid., 344. John English has offered a more prosaic reason: the French fought to "shore up finances," and Napoleon continued the policy. John A. English, *Marching through Chaos: The Descent of Armies in Theory and Practice* (Westport, Conn., 1997), 34.

[66] Bertaud, *The Army of the French Revolution*, 345–6, 352–3.

[67] Samuel F. Scott, *The Response of the Royal Army to the French Revolution: The Role and Development of the Line Army, 1787–93* (Oxford, 1978); Isser Woloch, *The French Veteran from the Revolution to the Restoration* (Chapel Hill, N.C., 1979).

[68] John A. Lynn, *The Bayonets of the Republic: Motivation and Tactics of the Army of Revolutionary France, 1791–94* (Urbana, Ill., and Chicago, 1984).

[69] Lynn, *Bayonets of the Republic*, 278–85, especially 285.

[70] Marc Bouloiseau, *La République jacobine (1792–94)* (Paris, 1972), 150.

[71] Ibid., 149, 173.

[72] Camille F.-M. Rousset, *Les Volontaires, 1791–95* (Paris, 1870), 233–45.

and disputed that there was an alliance between the Jacobin bourgeoisie and "the people." The nobles of the Old Regime, he said, were willing to fight and die for France, but the bourgeoisie sent the sons of the poor to war.[73] In his *The French Revolutionary Wars*, T. C. W. Blanning expresses doubt about the "constant" qualities assigned to the French soldier of 1793–4.[74] But there are more sophisticated studies, notably Alan Forrest's *Conscripts and Deserters* and other works.[75]

So what are we to conclude? As Jacques Godechot and others have noted, and Benedetto Croce said best, "All history is contemporary." This is doubly true of the history of the French Revolution, including the *levée en masse* and its myth. The story was politicized while the Revolution was in progress, in that writers' opinions reflected their ideology, personal relationships, and interests. Since the Revolution, authors have depicted it according to the Revolutionary phase, faction, or personality with which they identified, often for political reasons.

It is clear, however, that, despite persistent apprehensions about war and the dangers of militarism,[76] leftist historians (especially socialists and communists) have supported the myth consistently, while opposing conscription in their own time – the most notable exception being Jaurès. The arch-conservative Hippolyte Taine was the first to see the possible long-range evils that had originated in the *levée*, and derided the myth. His school (Madelin, Bainville, Gaxotte, et al.) echoed his ideas; but all favored conscription when wars came, as did conservatives generally. Finally, the scholarship of the last thirty years (Auvray, Sam Scott, Woloch, Forrest, et al.) has tended to explode the myth of the *levée* – or, more precisely, to provide a framework within which the myths present in earlier historical scholarship can be seen and examined. Only die-hard leftists – and rare birds who trust the self-representation of those who made the Terror – still cling to the vision of men rushing to the front to die for *La Patrie*.

---

[73] Michel Auvray, *Objecteurs, insoumis, déserteurs: Histoire des réfractaires en France* (Paris, 1983), 75–7, 80, 88.

[74] T. C. W. Blanning, *The French Revolutionary Wars, 1787–1802* (London and New York, 1996), 118–9.

[75] Alan Forrest, *Conscripts and Deserters* (New York, 1989); *The Soldiers of the French Revolution* (Durham, N.C., 1990); "Citizenship and Military Service," in Renée Waldinger, Philip Dawson, and Isser Woloch (eds.), *The French Revolution and the Meaning of Citizenship*, (Westport, Conn., 1993), 164–5.

[76] On this general theme see Sergio Luzzatto, *L'Impôt du sang: La gauche française à l'épreuve de la guerre mondiale (1900–45)* (Lyon, 1996).

4

Arms and the Concert

The Nation in Arms and the Dilemmas of German Liberalism

Daniel Moran

An unwritten rule of historical scholarship says that, in the final analysis, nothing ever happens for the first time. Thus it is probably wrong to claim that the idea of the nation in arms is an invention of the Revolutionary era. As an abstract proposition, the right of the community to compel everyone to serve in war is as old as Western Civilization. The revolutionaries who mobilized French society acted in a spirit of radical innovation, but even they were prepared, for symbolic purposes, to find precedents in the armies of the Greek cities and ancient Rome. The monarchs of the Old Regime had good reason to employ foreign troops in preference to their own subjects when possible. Yet they were aware that native levies were their ultimate military resort. Some, like Frederick the Great, also believed that men fighting for their own country made better soldiers. "With such troops," he wrote, "one might defeat the entire world, were not victories as fatal to them as to their enemies."[1] Once pressed by grievous necessity, however, neither he nor any of his fellow princes accepted any theoretical limitation upon their right, as God's lieutenants, to shed the blood of their subjects. The regulations establishing Prussia's cantonal recruiting districts in the early eighteenth century were typical in erecting a labyrinth of corporate exclusions and exemptions – which in practice limited military service to the aristocratic elite and the rural and urban poor – upon a foundation of unlimited military obligation comparable in principle to anything put forward by the Revolution. In time of war, the life and treasure of every inhabitant were held unreservedly at the disposal of the crown.[2]

---

[1] *Principes générraux de la guerre* (1746) , in *Oeuvres de Frédéric le Grand*, 30 volumes in 27 (Berlin, 1845–56), 28: 7. The proposition that European armies would fight better if they were composed less exclusively of what the Comte de Guibert called "the vilest and most wretched parts of the citizenry" (*Essai Générale de Tactique* [Paris, 1772], 147) was widespread among writers concerned with military efficiency at the end of the Old Regime.

[2] Eugen von Frauenholz, *Entwicklungsgeschichte des Deutschen Heerwesens*, 5 volumes (Munich, 1935–41), 4: 225, cited in Peter Paret, *Understanding War* (Princeton, 1992), 55.

Nevertheless, Europeans contemplating the wars of the Revolution were not wrong to conclude that their world possessed military possibilities unsuspected by their ancestors. The hidden hand of providence, which theorists of absolutism had credited with maintaining a naturally ordained balance of power,[3] had been banished from the battlefield in shocking fashion by the revolutionary mobilization in France. Looking back from this new vantage point, it seemed clear that whatever margin of stability the continent had enjoyed in the past had had more to do with the modest capabilities of its military institutions than with any inherent feature of the international system. No serious person imagined that the genie of the *levée en masse* could be put back in the bottle of strategic realism through the simple expedient of marooning Napoleon on a rock in the Atlantic Ocean. He could be dismissed easily enough as a freak of nature. The general mobilization of society for war, upon which his career had depended, could not. Like gun powder or nuclear weapons, the specter of the people in arms could never be banished for good because it was impossible to forget how to make it appear. Those who had experienced it thought they knew the secret of total war.

The Concert of Europe, as the post-Napoleonic international order came to be called, was a bulwark against this latent power. Hostility to the nation in arms was a unifying principle far more significant in practice than the ideological construction of "monarchical legitimacy" devised by the Concert's founders. In its absence, the international congresses and ministerial conferences by which the Concert functioned diplomatically would have made little difference to the peace of Europe. At bottom, the relative stability achieved in the aftermath of Waterloo rested upon a strategic consensus that tacitly ruled out any repetition of the *levée en masse*.

After Napoleon had been safely dispatched, enormous armies like the one he marched into Russia in 1812 held little appeal to the victors. Slow-moving, expensive, difficult to command – and, it was felt, politically dangerous in the bargain – such forces were thought ill-suited to conduct the compact, decisive campaigns that modern theories of war identified as the acme of military excellence. This judgment was reinforced by other considerations, not least a desire to preserve the social exclusivity and prestige of the officer corps – or, where this had become impossible, as in France, to instill it with a professional ethos strong enough to isolate it from the grievances of the larger society. The goals of the Concert were to avoid revolution on the one hand, and general war on the other. As far as anyone in authority could see, neither of these tasks could be accomplished except by relatively modest armed

---

[3] Wilhelm Leibnitz, *Bedenken Welchergestalt Securitas publica interna et externa und Status praesens im Reich iezigen Umständen noch auf festen Fuß zu stellen* (Leipzig, 1670, reprinted 1931), esp. 133–7; cf. Werner Hahlweg, "Barriere – Gleichgewicht – Sicherheit: Eine Studie über die Gleichgewichtspolitik und die Strukturwandlung des Staatensystems Europa, 1646–1715," *Historische Zeitschrift* 187 (1959), 54–98.

forces, composed of tactically proficient, politically deferential, long-serving troops and commanded by officers with a strong personal stake in the status quo. As long as such armies remained the norm among the Great Powers, one might have some confidence that the mob could be held at bay, and that the limited wars and punitive expeditions required to adjust the system from time to time would not escalate into the kind of all-in conflagration the French had ignited in the 1790s.

The resulting international environment is sometimes characterized as a "Restoration," which may be fair enough if you were a king set back on an empty throne. For everyone else, however, the expression suggests a kind of amnesia that was neither possible nor much desired. Even if Talleyrand really believed, as he is supposed to have said, that no one who had not grown up before the Revolution could know the sweetness of life, there is little evidence that he and his colleagues wished to restore pre-Revolutionary conditions within the international system, or that, like their antediluvian predecessors, they valued the freedom of the state above all else. What they valued was security, in a recognizably modern sense that took explicit account, on the margins perhaps, but nevertheless for the first time, of the international system's collective character and interests.

The contrast between the political patterns that developed within the Concert and those that preceded the Revolution is apparent. As Paul Schroeder has observed, no state threatened with war in the decades before 1789 ever succeeded in avoiding it, even if it tried hard to do so.[4] This was certainly not the case after 1815, though one should not overstate the magnitude of the change. A willingness to balance the security of the state and its freedom of action on more equal terms than in the past did not imply a desire for peace at any price. All countries continued to maintain armed forces with a view to using them against each other. Yet war was no longer so readily indulged, or indulged in, as it once had been, and a countervailing obligation to consult the common interest became a recognized component of responsible political behavior. When Lord Palmerston declared in 1846 that it was impossible for anyone to alter territorial arrangements in Europe "without the concurrence of the other Powers who were party to [the Treaty of Vienna],"[5] he was voicing a principle of Great Power condominium that, however imperfectly maintained, would have been quite alien to statesmen a century before, for whom the anarchy of the international order was a given.

Among ideas conducive to international anarchy, none rated higher, on recent evidence, than that of the nation in arms. This chapter seeks to trace its transmission across the inhospitable ideological and institutional terrain the Concert helped to create and, in so doing, to appraise its significance

---

4 Paul Schroeder, *The Transformation of European Politics, 1763–1848* (Oxford, 1994), 52.
5 F. R. Bridge and Roger Bullen, *The Great Powers and the European States System, 1815–1914* (London and New York, 1980), 4.

for German and, by extension, European liberalism, during the period when
liberal politics was reaching the first flush of maturity. The German case is an
inviting one for a number of reasons. Germany's initial encounter with the
nation in arms was especially complex, including experiences of conquest
and subjugation, and also of appropriation, victory, and revenge. German
liberals were also aware, particularly after 1848, of how far their fortunes
were bound up with the international system as a whole. Their credibility
and prospects depended absolutely on their ability to address the security
concerns of the exposed and mostly weak German states, in which military
values and institutions always lay close to the center of politics. Under such
circumstances it is not surprising that the idea of the nation in arms should
have achieved a heightened significance, even among those temperamentally
disposed to underrate the inherent violence of international life.

II

The *levée en masse* transformed the idea of an armed citizenry from an
abstract postulate derived from the Divine Right of Kings into something
like a force of nature. But the enormity of its consequences meant that it
attracted few fully committed advocates among serious contestants for political influence after 1815. No one concerned with international affairs could
be indifferent to its implications, but scarcely anyone was prepared to embrace all of them. Germany's liberals took inspiration from some elements
of the recent past, while fearing and deprecating others – but then so did the
conservatives, revolutionaries, and military experts with whom they had to
contend.

The legacy and meaning of the *levée en masse* were especially contested
in Central Europe because it was there, and specifically in Prussia, that the
Revolutionary mobilization of the 1790s inspired its most institutionally
significant response: the Prussian *Erhebung*, or uprising, that fueled the War
of Liberation in 1813. Like the *levée* of 1793, Prussia's mobilization turned
upon the interaction of official coercion and popular emotions, and gave rise
to a retrospective mythology that was, if anything, even more complex than
that engendered by the French experience.

The conditions that produced the *Erhebung* of 1813 were a product, on
the one hand, of the reform of the Prussian army that followed Prussia's
defeat by France in 1806 and, on the other, of the miseries and humiliations
of the French occupation, which kindled popular resentment against an otherwise somewhat remote foe. The goal of Prussia's military reforms was to
strengthen the regular army. Even among the reformers, only a minority were
prepared to consider more radical measures, along the lines of the *guerrilla*
then building in Spain. Although the need for a much larger army was recognized, the king and most of those around him regarded universal military
service as a unwarranted revolutionary step, whose social costs would render

any subsequent victory empty.[6] The terms of the peace with France made practical action impossible in any case. As long as Prussia remained a subordinate ally of France, only a few surreptitious measures to expand the country's supply of trained men were possible. Toward the end of 1812, however, as the scale of Napoleon's defeat in Russia became apparent, that alliance began to unravel in a way that provided scope for radical measures.

At the end of December the Prussian corps guarding Napoleon's northern flank was neutralized by its commanding general. In early February a program to mobilize East Prussia was begun at the instigation of Prussian armed forces present in the province. Its most storied aspect was the creation of Volunteer Rifle Detachments, called *Jäger* ["hunters"], composed of young men previously exempt from service, who were sufficiently well-off to provide their own equipment.[7] The East Prussian estates also called for the creation of a general militia or *Landwehr*, based on universal service, with individual localities responsible for raising recruits. As the French retreat continued, similar measures became general. On March 16, Prussia finally declared war on France. The next day the Prussian *Landwehr* was formally established, with compulsory service for men between seventeen and forty.[8] This measure was accompanied by two royal decrees, one "To my People," the other "To my Army," calling upon both to rise to the challenge that history had presented. Even the king, on this occasion, felt able to characterize the emerging popular mobilization as an act of "free will," as distinct from the professional obligation of regular soldiers.[9]

---

[6] The first general statement of postwar recruitment policy asserted that all Prussian subjects were liable to military service "under conditions yet to be determined"; but such language had been common enough during the Old Regime, and was viewed with equanimity by the French. "Kriegs-Artikel für die Unter-Officiere und gemeinen Soldaten," August 3, 1808, in Eugen von Frauenholz, *Entwicklungsgeschichte des Deutschen Heerwesens* (Munich, 1941), 101.

[7] An incentive to volunteer was provided in the form of a promise of preferential treatment for future appointments in the state administration (which included the schools and universities), a significant spur given that there was little other employment for those with university degrees. Those who failed to serve at least a year in the volunteers or the regular army were threatened with exclusion for such careers in the future. Neither element of this policy was seriously enforced once the dust of war had settled. Volunteers enjoyed a variety of privileges – including exemption from corporal punishment and most routine military tasks – unknown to either the line army or to the *Landwehr* whose creation would shortly follow. See Dennis E. Showalter, "The Prussian *Landwehr* and Its Critics, 1813–1819," *Central European History* 4/1 (1971), 11.

[8] "Verordnung über die Organisation der Landwehr," *Gesetz-Sammlung für die Königlichen Preussischen Staaten* (Berlin, 1813), 36–7, 109–19.

[9] Bernard Schwertfeger (ed.), *Das Preussische Heer im Jahre 1813*, 2 volumes (Berlin, 1914), 2: 403–4. I am grateful to Peter Paret for bringing this reference to my attention. The Prussian *Landwehr*, it must be emphasized, was never a volunteer organization, though it was possible for individuals to present themselves freely to their local recruitment boards. As in the original *levée en masse* of 1793, considerable coercion was sometimes necessary to fill local quotas, and the resulting units often had rates of desertion, straggling, and illness much higher than those of the line army.

The *Landwehr*, volunteer *Jäger*, and assorted "free corps" created in the winter and spring of 1813 represented a considerable expansion of Prussian military strength. By August, such forces had a total strength exceeding 120,000 men – approximately half of all those then under arms in Prussia. Although many imagined at the outset that Prussia's irregulars would fight as partisans, like those in Spain, the speed with which the French departed made such fighting rare. Getting the *Landwehr* in contact with the enemy thus required organized cooperation with the line army, a challenge in itself, and one with important political and psychological resonance. Those who had initially resisted the *Landwehr*'s formation feared not just the loss of fighting discipline that would result from mixing *Landwehr* and line, but also the consequences of creating large, independent formations of irregular soldiers.[10] As might be expected, a variety of extemporaneous organizational approaches were attempted, and this rough-and-ready wartime integration of *Landwehr*, *Jäger*, and line makes any definitive judgment about the military effectiveness of the new units difficult[11] – a fact of some importance in shaping the way events would later be remembered. Few today would dissent from the conclusions of the General Staff history, which attributed Prussia's military revival chiefly to the reorganization, rapid expansion, and improved performance of the regular army – the result, in other words, of the steady, professional work of reform begun after 1806.[12] Yet the presence at the army's side – or even at its back – of a mass of mobilized civilians, an appreciable number of whom were volunteers from social groups previously exempt from, and indifferent to, military service, was by any reckoning a striking development.

Both the numbers and the social backgrounds of the men who volunteered in 1813–14 were subject to distortion in retrospect. In all about 30,000 men volunteered to serve against France in 1813–14, roughly 10 percent of all those under arms and a figure dwarfed by the conscripted peasantry who filled the ranks of the *Landwehr* and the line army.[13] Even among genuine

[10] Showalter, "The Prussian *Landwehr*," 12–14.
[11] It was only following the Peace of Paris in 1814 that relations between *Landwehr*, *Jäger*, and line were put on a firm organizational footing – firm for a while, at least. The Defense Law promulgated on September 8 of that year established the *Landwehr* as a permanent force separate from the line army, with its own administration and officer corps, whose junior members might be elected from the ranks. All men not conscripted into the regular army were subject to three years' service, except those who met the educational and property qualifications required for one-year volunteers, an important concession to middle-class interests and sensibilities that survived until the First World War. The *Landwehr*'s institutional independence did not, however. In 1819 it was reorganized as a ready-reserve for the line army, a step that deprived it of much of its social significance as a counterweight to traditional military values.
[12] Schwertfeger (ed.), *Das Preussische Heer*, passim; cf. Rudolf Ibbeken, *Preussen, 1807–1813: Staat und Volk als Idee und in Wirklichkeit* (Cologne and Berlin, 1970), 422–39.
[13] The decisive work on this subject is Ibbeken, *Preussen*, 393–433, and the statistical appendix, 442–50. Ibbeken began his work in the 1930s, using archival records that were later destroyed in the Second World War. His data are thus the best that are ever likely to be available.

volunteers, the majority were artisans, shopkeepers, servants, laborers, and so on. Only about 12 percent came from the professions, estate owners, and the senior civil service; of these, over half were students. The retrospective image of the student-warrior, long cherished by educated Germans who imagined the paradigmatic soldier of the War of Liberation was someone much like themselves, was thus seriously at odds with reality.

Pinpointing the exact moral and political forces that brought so many Prussian civilians to the battlefield was likewise subject to divergent memories, though in this case ground truth is less easily established. The chain of actions by which Prussia mobilized for war depended upon the interaction of popular enthusiasm – if not usually an eagerness to serve, then at least a willingness to be called – independent, decentralized initiatives of soldiers and other servants of the state, and government action backed by the force of law. Which of these elements was accorded pride of place in retrospect varied with political interest and social location. On the left, the *Erhebung* was seen as an act of revolutionary spontaneity on the part of the masses, by which the government was finally brought to its duty. What might be called "official" memory – as codified, for instance, in Prussian school books[14] – emphasized (correctly) that most of those who fought did so under sometimes stern legal compulsion; and (less plausibly) portrayed the king's grudging and belated call to arms as the spark that set events in motion. The German bourgeoisie, as has been suggested, overrated both the degree of voluntary action inspired by the war and also the role of the well-educated and well-off. Doing so served to validate the claims of these groups to greater political influence. By the same token, however, German liberals were at pains to represent the *Erhebung* as both a spontaneous popular movement and a demonstration of discipline and loyalty – a *levée en masse* from which the revolutionary energies had somehow been drained.

From the point of view of postwar liberal politics, two sets of issues arose from these events, and from those of 1793 in France, by no means forgotten in the flush of victory. The first turned upon the psychological freedom of the modern soldier, whose ideal type was conceived by liberals as a citizen, acting from a sense of shared obligation, and also as a volunteer. As will be seen, however, the image of the volunteer proved to be difficult for liberals to control in cultural terms. The second set of issues involved the rights and obligations entailed by military service and raised questions about the connections, if any, between the citizen-soldier's political status, the military effectiveness of a citizen army, and the kinds of strategic objectives such an army could support. In this context, the soldier's moral status took on practical significance and impinged upon the interests of military professionals.

---

[14] Christopher Clark, "The Wars of Liberation in Prussian Memory: Reflections on the Memorialization of War in Early Nineteenth-Century Germany," *Journal of Modern History* 68 (1996), 553.

The citizen-soldier's sense of obligation was an essential compliment to his exercise of freedom: the fighting man of the liberal imagination was not a professional, who also freely accepted risks he might legally have avoided, after all, but for private reasons that were thought to render his conduct base. Nor was the citizen-soldier a conscript dragged to the colors by force of law. This distinction raised some difficult questions in application. Yet on the whole it caused liberal proponents of the nation in arms less difficulty than those that arose around what George Mosse called "the myth of the war experience."[15] The essential elements of that mythology had nothing to do with the connection between political rights and military service and everything to do with camaraderie, personal heroism, a hard and manly spirit, and the transcendent nature of death in battle. It was an idea erected in opposition to the perceived regimentation and banality of bourgeois existence, and it became an essential resource to the citizen-soldier's illiberal opponents.

Politically, moreover, the voluntary principle required some interpretation. It was not meant to imply that armed forces should arise like mushrooms from the earth – an element of the mythology surrounding both the original *levée* of 1793 and the Prussian *Ehrhebung* twenty years later, but also a proposition implausible to all but the most hard-bitten radicals after the struggle with France had ended. The liberal conception of voluntary service was roughly akin to the idea that government's just powers derived from the consent of the governed. Justice did not require that an individual's free consent be obtained for all actions that concerned him. It was enough if the state's powers and legal basis were sufficiently rational and fair that subordination to them could be represented as a freely internalized social obligation. Ideally, Germany's defense might rest in the hands of a genuinely volunteer force like the U.S. Army, which liberals vainly hoped would provide the model for the so-called German Federal Army created after the Vienna settlement.[16] Failing that, they were prepared to admire institutions like the Prussian *Landwehr*, which was not a volunteer force but was organized and manned in ways expressive of social equality.

It remained a question whether such a force could fight well enough to secure the existences of continental states, whose exposed frontiers required a level of readiness and tactical proficiency that remote outposts of civilization like the United States could safely ignore. Military professionals doubted whether the loyalty and commitment that liberals imputed to their idealized

---

[15] George L. Mosse, *Fallen Soldiers: Reshaping the Memory of the World Wars* (Oxford, 1990), especially 15–33.

[16] The German Federal Army existed as a real force for only a few weeks in 1866, before being dispersed by its erstwhile Prussian contingent. It was created on paper in 1818 as an instrument of the German Federation. Member states were supposed to provide men on a pro rata basis equal to 2 percent of the total population – a figure on the high end of what had been achieved by strong states under the Old Regime.

man at arms could make up for a lack of discipline and training. Liberals, for their part, pointed to the voluntary, or at any rate consensual, nature of the citizen-soldier's service as an obstacle to aggressive war. Yet a dilemma remained: once begun, a war based upon the mobilization of society as a whole would become manifestly more dangerous than any other kind. If the idea of the nation in arms relieved liberals of the debilitating effects of a doctrinaire pacifism, it did so at the price of perching the security of Europe atop armed forces of known volcanic potential.[17]

III

German states before the French Revolution had generally excluded middle-class men from military service. This had not been a serious grievance for those concerned. Although the eclipse of urban militias and other *ständish* formations by regular armies had been a recurring source of political friction between German princes and local elites, the princely monopoly on military power and the aristocratic monopoly on military commissions that had characterized the Old Regime had served mainly to reinforce the *Bürgertum*'s disinterest in military affairs. That the call to arms issued by Prussia's king in March of 1813 should have resonated at all among men whose social status had previously been bound up with exemption from soldiering was a genuinely new phenomenon, far more limited in scope than the myths that arose around it would suggest, but nevertheless indicative of the fact that the moral significance of service in war was beginning to change.

One of those who captured this change in a particularly compelling way was the poet Theodor Körner, whose hymns to the risen people helped shape the historical memory of the War of Liberation as a genuine national uprising. Körner was a member of the volunteer *Freikorps* commanded by Adolf von Lützow, and he contributed to the unit's fame by writing a stirring poem, "Lützow's Wild Chase," that memorialized its exploits. In a conflict in which most volunteers were necessarily Prussian, Lützow's *Freikorps* became especially celebrated because it included men from all over Germany,

---

[17] The idea that the nation in arms was prone to spontaneous combustion was accepted by even the most astute observers. Its influence can be seen, for instance, in the famous passage in *On War*, in which Clausewitz describes war as a "remarkable Trinity" composed of three elements: "primordial violence, hatred, and enmity"; "the play of chance"; and an "element of subordination, as an instrument of policy, which makes it subject to reason alone" (*On War*, edited and translated by Michael Howard and Peter Paret [Princeton, 1976], 89). It goes without saying that this is an insight of some importance. Yet the sentence that follows, in which the first of these elements is associated with "the people," is more revealing of the times in which it was written than of military reality. Any reader of Clausewitz's histories of Napoleon's campaigns will recognize this at once. There the motive forces propelling French armies across Europe clearly arise within the national leadership, if not, indeed, within Napoleon's personal psychology, rather than among the conscript soldiers who would become the chief instruments of French policy.

FIGURE 5. Georg Friedrich Kersting, *Auf Vorposten* [On Outpost Duty] (Oil on linen, 1815). Staatliche Museen zu Berlin – Preussischer Kulturbesitz, Nationalgalerie.

Georg Friedrich Kersting's *On Outpost Duty* exemplifies, and contributed to, the valorization of middle-class youth as the backbone of the Prussian *Erhebung* of 1813–14. The painting shows three student volunteers – Theodor Körner, Ferdinand Hartmann, and Karl Friedrich Friesen – who served with Kersting in Lützow's *Freicorps*, and were killed in action against the French. The exaggerated role ascribed to such men – a small but highly articulate minority – in prosecuting the War of Liberation bolstered the liberal claim that people of property and education deserved more say in the life of the state. Kersting's painting also illustrates the ambiguous nature of the war's legacy. Its subtext is

who pledged allegiance not to the King of Prussia, but to the German Fatherland.[18] The unit thus qualified as a genuinely national symbol in a conflict in which Germans, awkwardly, had fought on both sides. The army of Körner's native Saxony, like those of the other members of the Confederation of the Rhine, stood alongside the French at the Battle of Leipzig, and commemorations of that famous victory's anniversary were accordingly long banned in the South.

To judge from a letter that Körner wrote to his father, he went to war in a complicated frame of mind. Körner had come to believe that no life was too precious to sacrifice to the nation. But he also feared that only a few men were worthy to make such an offering. Victory, he concluded, would come not from mundane military achievements, but from the self-willed heroism of a natural elite, whose sacrifice would inspire God to save the nation.[19] Körner's own death would be memorialized in turn in a fine painting by one of his fellow volunteers, Georg Friedrich Kersting. Kersting's *Auf Vorposten* [On Outpost Duty](Figure 5) shows Körner resting on one arm in a sun-lit oak forest, in the company of two of his fallen companions. It is not an image of heroism that would have made sense to the military establishment of the day. The oak forest, a familiar symbol of the ancient Germanic past, is calm and welcoming. The mood is elegiac, with no hint of violence or aggressive emotions. The title reinforces the impression of disciplined watchfulness and includes the implication – reinforced by Körner's direct, personal gaze – that those portrayed are the vanguard, the ones who have gone before.[20]

The only distinctly political symbol – if one excepts the uniforms in which the men are dressed – is the Iron Cross around Körner's neck. Its designer, Karl Friedrich Schinkel, modeled it on the square Gothic cross of the Teutonic Knights, and like the forest it linked the heroes of the last war to the feudal warriors of the past. Yet it was also a symbol of equality and shared sacrifice:

FIGURE 5. (*continued*) cultural rather than political: its sensibility romantic and idealistic rather than insurgent. Although intended as a monument to a risen people – a force vigorously extolled in Körner's poetry – Kersting's work drains the uprising of its revolutionary energy and substitutes a calm submission to duty as the essence of the warrior's ethos. *On Outpost Duty* is less a call to arms than an epitaph – an interpretation reinforced by its companion piece, *The Wreath Weaver* (1815), which shows a young woman sitting in the same sun-lit oak wood, weaving funeral wreathes for those who have fallen, and whose names are now inscribed upon the trees.

[18] Ibbeken, *Preussen*, 448–9, estimates the strength of Lützow's forces at just under 4,000, of whom 56 percent hailed from outside Prussia. Ibbeken notes that a persistent "overvaluing" of the military significance and performance of Lützow's *Freikorps* contributed to a general public overestimation of the role of social elites, and especially students, as fighters in the war (ibid., 417).

[19] Körner to his father, 10 March 1813, in Friedrich Donath and Walter Markow (eds.), *Kampf um Freiheit: Dokumente zur Zeit der Nationalen Erhebung* (Berlin, 1954), 283.

[20] Cf. Clark, "Wars of Liberation," 567.

unique among military decorations at the time, the first two classes of the Iron Cross were awarded without regard to rank, to honor "service in actual combat with the enemy, or in other forms on the battlefield or at home, in support of [our] great struggle for freedom and independence."[21]

Could Körner's personal conduct, the attitudes he affirmed, and the images and emotions that attached to him be regarded as conducive to liberty in politics? Körner's commitment to freedom as a personal value, and the disdain that he and his comrades displayed for the routine deference normally accorded the state, were certainly radical enough in a general way. Yet the free act of the volunteer was essentially a personal, rather than a political, gesture, and one intended to signify the volunteer's separation from the mass of society – those unworthy to offer the kind of sacrifice vouched safe to a few. Körner's posthumous volume of verse, *Lyre and Sword*, described by Thomas Nipperdy as the "definitive war book" of 1813,[22] portrayed war not as an instrument of politics, but as a scene of daring and adventure, a crusade for sacred causes, and a vehicle for self-realization: the soldier not as citizen, but as artist.

It took some years for these matters to become clear, in part because discussion about them was inhibited by the pale of political repression that settled over Germany a few years after the war ended. For more than a decade thereafter, efforts to promote or idealize military service on any terms whatever were officially discouraged. Friedrich Karl von Müffling, Chief of the Prussian General Staff in the 1820s, did his best to prevent commemorations of the war, or the formation of veterans associations, which he thought smacked of "the arrogance of young men brought too soon into the world by the War of Liberation."[23] It was a point of view intolerant of subtle

---

[21] Royal decree of 10 March 1813, in Oberstlieutnant Freiherr von Brand, "Das Eiserne Kreuz," *Deutsches Soldatenjahrbuch 1963: Elfter deutscher Soldatenkalender* (Munich, 1963), 50. Shinkel's medievalizing and egalitarian impulses were equally in evidence in his design for the Kreuzberg Memorial, built in Berlin in 1821 as a memorial to the War of Liberation. It resembled a Gothic church tower and honored all who died for Prussia, irrespective of social position. George Mosse (*Fallen Soldiers*, 47) argued that the Kreuzberg Memorial helped establish the Gothic style as "a shorthand for German unity"; also, one might add, for a paternalistic, dynastic interpretation of the *Erhebung*. The dedicatory tablet of Shinkel's memorial described it as a gift "from the king to the people who, at his call, nobly sacrificed their blood and chattels to the Fatherland." The identification of the king with the nation quickly became standard on Prussian war memorials, nearly all of which bore the legend "for King and Fatherland." Cf. Clark, "Wars of Liberation," 558–9; and H. Börsch-Supan and L. Griesebach (eds.), *Karl Friedrich Schinkel: Architektur, Malerei, Kunstgewerbe* (Berlin, 1981), 140–5.

[22] Thomas Nipperdey, *Germany from Napoleon to Bismarck, 1800–1866*, trans. by Daniel Nolan (New York, 1996), 68. I am indebted to John Horne for this reference.

[23] Cited in Max Jähns, "Das *Militair-Wochenblatt* von 1816 bis 1876: Vortrag gehalten bei dem Jubiläum des *Militair-Wochenblattes* am 1. Juli 1876," *Beihefte zum Militair-Wochenblatt 6* (1876), 292.

distinctions, but based upon real experiences, like, for instance, the celebration held on the Wartburg in 1817. This gathering of students, many of whom were veterans of the war, had been organized to celebrate the fifth anniversary of the Battle of Leipzig and also the three-hundredth anniversary of the Lutheran Reformation. It featured a climactic bonfire onto which robed figures, marching behind the Black-Red-Gold banner of Lützow's volunteers, threw sheets of paper inscribed with the names of books deemed hostile to the national cause. Some Prussian and Austrian military paraphernalia also went into the flames, to protest the failure of those states to support a strong German Federation.[24] To a man of Müffling's traditional outlook, and indeed to most observers, there was no need to decipher the precise meaning of such puzzling behavior to see that it counted as evidence against any immediate expansion of political participation. Episodes like the Warburg Festival registered as blows to the liberal cause in the eyes of those responsible for public order and were invoked to explain the need for repressive measures at the federal level.

The general deregulation of public life that followed the revolutions of 1830 allowed the illiberal and apolitical qualities of the war's mythology to clarify themselves, chiefly in response to the rising tide of demands for constitutional reform set free by the lapsing of the Carlsbad Decrees in 1832. German liberals in the 1830s considered themselves heirs to the constitutional promises that had been made in the heat of the *Erhebung*, and regarded the repression of the 1820s as a hiatus in the natural progress of public life toward greater freedom and equality, which was about to resume. Their opponents enjoyed the same new freedom, however, and they organized themselves to contest the idea that the war experience had anything to do with political rights.

On the conservative side, the chief contestants in the struggle to define the war's iconography were veterans groups, which German governments began to tolerate in the 1830s and tacitly encouraged in the 1840s. There were fifty-five such organizations in Prussia in 1848, only four of which had existed twenty years before.[25] All of them identified themselves with the War of Liberation, though only three limited their membership to real volunteers.[26] Some, like the "Trier Association of Retired Patriotic Fighters," included veterans who had served in the armies of Napoleon, an unmistakable sign

---

[24] The complex symbolism of the Wartburg Festival is analyzed in Wolfgang Hardtwig, "Studentische Mentalität – politische Jugendbewegung – Nationalismus: Die Anfänge der deutschen Burschenschaft," *Historische Zeitschrift* 243/3 (1986), 581–628.

[25] Eckhard Trox, *Militärische Konservatismus: Kriegervereine und 'Militärpartei' in Preußen zwischen 1815 und 1848/49* (Stuttgart, 1990), 44, 50–3. Of the four earlier associations, two were burial societies founded in the eighteenth century, and two others were established in 1815–16.

[26] Ibid., 44.

that these were men who considered themselves bound together by an ethos of service and sacrifice that transcended politics.[27] Most included significant numbers of pensioned noble officers, who had presumably embarked upon military service in the relatively sober state of mind characteristic of those fulfilling an established social role. That they should have found themselves banding together with their bourgeois brethren and adopting the rhetoric of military romance was surely a consequence of that role's coming under pressure.

One of the major activities of veterans' associations was to organize public commemorations of the War of Liberation, usually on the 17th of March, the anniversary of Frederick William's proclamation "To My People," or (outside Prussia) on the anniversary of Waterloo. The latter became the feast day for the surviving members of Lützow's volunteers, who gathered every year at the oak tree where Theodor Körner was buried, to renew acquaintance and recall shared triumphs and fallen comrades.[28] At moments like these, an astute observer might have felt the psychological resonance of the war slipping through the fingers of German liberals. There was, after all, no plausible way to appropriate the ultimate equality of death as a symbol for the rights and obligations of the citizen. In the end, liberals managed to retain their grip on Lützow's Black-Red-Gold banner, which the students had brandished on the Wartburg. Yet the most powerful and personal symbol of the war, the Iron Cross, found its way onto the masthead of the most conservative newspaper in Berlin.[29]

1848 was the crisis, and it produced something like a national mobilization of veterans against the idea of the nation in arms. Over the next four years, veterans groups multiplied fourfold, invariably as bastions of counter-revolution.[30] Their satisfaction at having done their share to beat back the threat is apparent in a retrospective account in the *Deutsche Wehr-Zeitung*, which concludes:

We have fought with the sharp weapon of words against the citizen army; against the subordination of the army to the constitution; against any political role for the army; against the right of those in it to assemble or vote; against all calls to adopt the utopian [universal service] law promulgated at Frankfurt, whether delivered behind a glass of sugar-water on the assembly dais, or behind that patented symbol of freedom – the barricade; against the people's army; against the election of officers; against the

---

[27] *Der National-Dank. Herausgegeben vom Comitee der Veteranen zu Berlin*, 1/2 (1852), 3. The Trier society was founded in 1842 and included about 200 veterans of the French army. This article was written to support the proposition that veterans groups that included Napoleonic veterans should be included without prejudice in an all-Prussian umbrella organization.

[28] *Vossische Zeitung*, 5 June 1845, and 27 June 1847.

[29] The *Neue Preussische Zeitung*, founded by Otto von Bismarck and Leopold von Gerlach in the summer of 1848, was popularly known as the *Kreuzzeitung* by virtue of this device.

[30] Trox, *Militärische Konservatismus*, 190–207, 289, lists over two hundred new groups created between 1848 and 1852, with a total membership of about 50,000.

abolition of the cadet schools, or their reform at the expense of military goals; and against absolutely everything that the Revolution sought to achieve in the military sphere.[31]

To those who conceived military service in terms of idealized personal loyalty, citizen-soldiers were anathema: "the hangmen of revolution" and "hirelings [*Söldner*] of tyranny," in the words of one veterans' magazine.[32] Also, revealingly, "the king's lackeys" [*Königsknechte*], an epithet suggestive of the social anxiety at the root of the veterans movement, and a reminder that there were still plenty of conservatives in Germany who regarded absolutism as the real revolution. They wished to assert the continued saliency of aristocratic military values – honor, personal courage, fealty, and so on – against the leveling implications of "the people's army," but also against the abstract, dehumanizing authority of the state and the increasingly discouraging realities of modern war. The latter in particular assured that, in practice, the persistence of aristocratic ideals in the military sphere could have only limited, and inverted, political significance. By refurbishing and reorienting the claims of a traditional elite to positions of military leadership and distinction, the myth of the volunteer helped reconcile its conservative adherents to their real future task, which would be to lead a mass army onto an industrialized battlefield. But it held no answer to the security requirements of the German states, which the deteriorating international politics of the 1850s suggested could only be met by a mass army.

This was a problem, it must be emphasized, before which liberals did not flinch. Although they sought to limit the moral authority of the state over its subjects, they also sought partnership with it on terms that they believed would increase its inherent military strength and place that strength on a more secure social footing, without endangering the stability of the international system. The army of their imaginations might not be a band of brothers, but neither would it depend for its success upon the moral excellence of a few individuals, supported, as Theodor Körner hoped, by the grace of God. It was an army of potentially unlimited size, under whose aegis they believed an orderly society could rest secure.

IV

It was J. R. Seeley – who lived, not coincidentally, on an island – who proposed that the domestic liberty of a state was inversely proportional to the

[31] In Helmut Schnitter, *Militärwesen und Militärpublizistic: Die militärische Zeitschriftenpublizistik in der Geschichte des bürgerlichen Militärwesens in Deutschland* (East Berlin, 1967), 60. The article appeared in 1852.

[32] *Mitteilungen der verbündeten Kriegervereine in der Provinz Sachsen*, Beilage 16 (22 December 1848), 125.

military pressure on its borders.[33] That being so, it would be difficult to overstate the importance of the citizen-soldier for the development of liberal internationalism in Europe. Absent the idea of the people in arms, it is hard to see how liberals could ever have addressed the perfectly obvious security problems of continental states. One of the first to register the theoretical significance of the new Revolutionary army was Immanuel Kant, whose pamphlet *On Perpetual Peace* appeared shortly after the signing of the Treaty of Basle, in April 1795.[34] Kant's brilliant speculation that the spread of republicanism would mean an end to war challenged the basic pattern of Enlightenment thinking about war and peace, and reshaped the way future generations of liberals would think about international relations.[35]

Throughout the eighteenth century, political theorists who favored limited government and political liberty sought to finesse their way past mankind's endless capacity for strife by making social violence a tool of progress. In the same way that even the nastiest individuals must at some point have grown weary of life in the state of nature, so, it was hypothesized, even aggressive states would eventually see that their interests were best served by subordinating themselves to a lawful international order, usually a league of nations with functions akin to those created by the primordial social contract among individuals. Kant's pre-Revolutionary writings adhered to this pattern. Although he believed that a future free from war was the natural goal of history, he also accepted that the way forward included an indefinite period of increasingly destructive conflict, among states whose constitutional make-up and military methods were irrelevant. In the end, all would come around in dialectical fashion to the advantages of a federative peace:

Thus Nature uses the inevitable friction and conflict that is characteristic of men . . . as a means of establishing conditions of peace and security. It is by means of war, by means of the unending taxation and accumulation of arms that it requires, and the privation and distress that all states must feel because of it even in peacetime, that Nature forces them to make their first hesitant, inadequate attempts; until finally,

---

[33] John Robert Seeley, *The Expansion of England* (London, 1895). Seeley's suggestion was intended to help explain why political patterns on the continent differed from those in England. The contrast he draws is not between different kinds of armies but between the political consequences of armies compared to navies. For a more recent discussion, see Bernard Semmel, *Liberalism and Naval Strategy: Ideology, Interest, and Sea Power during the Pax Britannica* (Boston, 1986).

[34] *Zum ewigen Frieden* (Königsberg, 1795), in Ernst Cassirer et al. (eds.), *Immanuel Kants Werke* (Berlin and Leipzig, 1912–18), 8: 341–86.

[35] Kant's argument has since been expanded into the claim that "democracy" is conducive to peace, and additionally that democratic states do not go to war against each other; it has recently enjoyed an enormous vogue in the latter form. See for instance Michael E. Brown, Sean M. Lynn-Jones, and Steven E. Miller (eds.), *Debating the Democratic Peace* (Cambridge, Mass., 1996). The most compelling recent work on this line is John Rawls, *The Law of Peoples* (Cambridge, Mass., 1999).

after much devastation, upheaval, and even total exhaustion, they are driven to do what reason alone could have dictated at the start, with far less sad experience, namely to leave the lawless state of nature and enter into a federation of states. In such a federation, even the smallest member can expect security and justice.[36]

Here was a proposition so utopian and so discouraging as to be utterly delegitimizing in the eyes of anyone concerned with real politics. The military success of the Revolutionary armies seems to have inspired Kant to reconsider, and eventually to reverse, his bleak logic. Perhaps peace was not "prerequisite to a rightful civil constitution," as he had earlier argued,[37] but a consequence of it. The recent treaty between France and Prussia had brought an end to a conflict whose earliest auspices had recalled the wars of religion. Perhaps, Kant now proposed, it was a special characteristic of republics that they need not exhaust themselves in battle to see the futility of war. Because they were founded upon universal values and the consent of the governed, they could respond directly to mankind's natural preference for peace and prosperity over war and penury. As to how this sort of rationality could be expressed in practice, however, Kant says virtually nothing – there is, conspicuously, no mention in *Perpetual Peace* of representative government or the separation of legislative and executive authority – except in one particular: lasting peace required the replacement of regular armies, which were "mere machines," with armed forces composed of "citizens, whose periodic and voluntary military efforts will win security from aggression for themselves and their country."[38]

Kant's essay anticipated the centrality of the citizen-soldier to the liberal agenda of the nineteenth century, as well as his essential characteristics as a fighter: he was a volunteer who responded to periodic, defensive emergencies. That he might also be a harbinger of unparalleled escalation was unsuspected. When Kant wrote *Perpetual Peace*, neither he nor anyone else had any inkling of the military potential then building within the armies of the French Republic. If the *levée en masse* made the Peace of Basle possible, it also ensured that it would be a false dawn. Twenty years later, the ideal of "perpetual peace" had become sufficiently familiar to warrant its own entry in the new Brockhaus encyclopedia – a scant half page, in which the

---

[36] "Idee zu einer allgemeinen Geschichte in weltbürgerlicher Absicht," *Berlinische Montasschrift* (Nov., 1784), in *Werke* 8: 20–21. The idea that a federation of states was the key to peace was a recurring theme of eighteenth-century writing on the subject. The best-known example is probably the Abbé de Saint-Pierre's *Projet de paix perpétuelle* (Utrecht, 1713), which originated as a scheme for ending the War of the Spanish Succession. A similar line is adopted in Jeremy Bentham, *A Plan for a Universal and Perpetual Peace* (London, 1789). An exception is Jean-Jacques Rousseau, *Jugement sur la paix perpétuelle* (Geneva, 1782) which criticizes Saint-Pierre's argument as impractical and claims instead (having perhaps forgotten the question of practicality) that only a complete dissolution of the state can lead to peace.

[37] Kant, "Idee zu einer allgemeinen Geschichte," 19.

[38] Kant, *Zum ewigen Frieden*, 343.

word "republic" does not appear, concluding with a cross reference to "Holy Alliance."[39] "Soldiers," on the other hand, got sixteen pages all to themselves, more than "Freedom of the Press" and "Parliament" combined.[40]

In contrast to Kant, whose chief interest lay in the connection between constitutional citizenship and international stability, Brockhaus's anonymous author was mainly concerned with its relationship to military success. Much of his entry is devoted to exploring the martial characteristics of the modern soldier in comparison with a variety of earlier types, including "craftsmen," who fought under compulsion or for a fee (the *Sold* that gives the man-at-arms his name in both German and English), and privileged elites drawn to the battlefield by a thirst for personal glory. Like the latter, the "national warrior" served of his own free will, but also in response to "a universal and natural obligation, as an element of citizenship deriving from the very bonds of society."[41] Such men fought well in the wars of the Revolution because of the superior morale that came with social solidarity, and because they possessed the psychological independence required by up-to-date, open-order tactics. Once enthusiasm flagged, however, "terror and the guillotine took its place," so that in the end, victory had gone to the side with the most guns.

Thus one arrives, somewhat unexpectedly, at the true center of strength in the liberal position: only by embracing the citizen-soldier could the twin problems of mass and morale be solved simultaneously. There was no other way to be sure of having enough guns in the hands of people willing to use them. That forces raised on liberal principles would also be conducive to peace was still affirmed – but as an inference rather than as the starting point of the analysis. The real issue was security, which could no longer be left exclusively in the hands of a standing army. Doing so, it was claimed, made cowards of the general population, and once such forces were defeated, society would be left defenseless. A standing army engorged by "conscription or compulsory service" was not the answer, either, because it exacted too high a price economically for every new increment of military strength

---

[39] "Ewiger Friede," *Allgemeine deutsche Real-Encyclopädie für die gebildeten Stände (Conversations-Lexicon)* (Leipzig, 1818–19), 3: 571.

[40] "Soldaten," *Allgemeine deutsche Real-Encyclopädie*, 9: 217–32; cf. "Pressfreiheit," 7: 792–4, and "Ständeversammlung," 9: 449–59. Brockhaus aimed his encyclopedia at a broader, more middle-brow audience than was typical for similar works at the time. It was intended less as a scholarly reference than as a concise compendium of information useful in polite society – hence the unusual subtitle, "Conversation-Lexicon." Almost without exception, the longer articles in the 1818 edition are about political or military subjects. Relatively numerous, short entries remain a trademark of Brockhaus encyclopedias to this day. See Arthur Hübscher, *Hundertfünfzig Jahre F. A. Brockhaus, 1805–1955* (Wiesbaden, 1955), 70–8.

[41] "Soldaten," *Allgemeine deutsche Real-Encyclopädie*, 9: 224. Much effort is expended, not entirely successfully, in distinguishing this sort of obligation from ordinary conscription, which is derided for "turning all citizens into military laborers [*Kriegsknechten*]."

and demoralized those young men who were obliged to serve while others remained free.

Let the standing army be done away with, then, or cut back to the barest stems and buds; and do not let those required to serve be separated from society! Then the nations will be assured flourishing prosperity, and princes the love of their subjects. All cabinet wars of political convenience – wars of partition, succession, and conquest – will cease; for the people will only bear arms voluntarily to defend the state. The cabinets of Europe thus need not fear for the balance of power.... For this purpose a militia is to be maintained even in times of peace, from which no one may be exempted.[42]

Viewed in just the right way, the citizen-soldier was supposed to be a figure capable of astonishing feats of arms, who somehow posed no danger to others – a rhetorical trick of some kind, surely. The new-model armies raised by the *levée en masse* were but one possible expression of the nation in arms, after all. The Revolutionary era had also included vivid examples of genuinely vernacular warfare – in the Vendée, Spain, the Balkans, Calabria, the Tyrol, Russia, and elsewhere – and the socially corrosive effects that followed recalled nothing so much as the Thirty Years War, the last major European conflict in which forces other than standing armies had played a prominent part. In an era of "small wars and big riots,"[43] one did not need to be an utter reactionary to wonder whether it was prudent to distribute weapons and military training throughout society. However tightly the case for the citizen-soldier might be made in logical terms, it proved impossible for liberals to purge him of all traces of fanaticism in the eyes of his critics.

V

The prospect that arms and a knowledge of their use might become more widely distributed was the only aspect of the liberal agenda that appealed to real revolutionaries. European radicals after 1815 drew a general kind of reassurance from the *levée en masse*, the Spanish *guerrilla*, the Prussian *Erhebung*, and other episodes testifying, as it seemed, to the latent power of the people. But it was difficult to know how to tap into it and survive. Those who envisioned a revolution brought about by the direct and violent exercise of popular will, exemplified by the Blanquists in France and the Italian Carbonari, quickly concluded that only conspiratorial methods could keep the revolutionary vanguard alive long enough to prepare the ground for widespread violence.[44] Others, like Karl Marx and Friedrich Engels, rejected

---

[42] Ibid., 9: 227.

[43] Paddy Griffith, *Military Thought in the French Army, 1815–51* (Manchester, 1989), 21–51.

[44] There were exceptions. One was August Willich, a Prussian lieutenant whose experiences in 1848–9 convinced him that popular forces might be instruments of revolution. He later served in the Union army during the American Civil War and concluded that its difficulties

what became known as the "force theory,"[45] and looked to the maturation of
objective material conditions to prepare the downfall of the existing order.
The extension of military service to ever-wider social groups was part of
that maturation process, which both supported because it injected military
skill into the revolutionary classes and infiltrated subversive social elements
into the armed forces of the state. It also seemed possible that the general
adoption of the Prussian *Landwehr* system by other European states, which
Marx and Engels anticipated would be one consequence of Prussia's victory
in the Franco-Prussian War, would create "a military burden which must
bring them to ruin within a few years."[46] But whether this point of view
represented a genuine revolutionary tactic, and an analytical attempt to make
a virtue of historical necessity, is difficult to say. From the 1850s on, Marx
and Engels doubted that the forces of order could be defeated in a direct
military confrontation and regarded efforts to prepare for such a thing as a
waste of time. In revolutionary terms, the chief virtue of the nation in arms
was that, once a state's armed forces reflected the class character of society,
the regime those forces were supposed to sustain would become critically
vulnerable to the pressures of class conflict.

   In the meantime, the kinds of incremental reforms that liberals favored
were judged to be instruments not of revolution but of social control, and
masks for bourgeois pacifism. Engels, a genuine military expert, proved himself an astute observer of such matters. He took a great interest, for example,
in the English Rifle Volunteer Corps, a kind of territorial guard created in
one of the less-heralded of the military reforms inspired by the resurgence of
French power in the 1850s.[47] In 1860–2 he published a total of twenty-nine

   stemmed from an excess of military professionalism (*The Army, Standing Army, or National
   Army? An Essay* [Cincinnati, 1866], esp. 12–23). Willich was a rare example of someone
   who really did believe that peace-time armies were unnecessary. Engels, who briefly served
   with him, heaped scorn on his scheme to "revolutionize the world through the Prussian
   Landwehr" (Engels to Marx, 23 Sept. 1851, *Karl Marx-Friedrich Engels Werke*, 41 vols.
   [East Berlin, 1960–74], 27: 343).
[45] So called from the relevant chapters attacking it in the "Anti-Dühring" (*Herr Eugen Dührings
   Umwälzung der Wissenschaft* [Leipzig, 1878], Part II, chapters 2–4).
[46] Ibid., 192. Whatever skepticism Engels may have felt about the *Landwehr*'s revolutionary
   potential, he was not immune to the mythology that surrounded its creation in the War of
   Liberation. The "highest achievement of those years," he once wrote, lay in the fact that
   "we armed ourselves, without waiting for the gracious permission of the princes, and even
   forced those in power to lead us, in short that for one moment we stepped forth as the source
   of power in the state, as a sovereign people." Friedrich Engels, "Ernst Moritz Arndt," in
   Karl Marx and Friedrich Engels, *Werke: Ergänzungsband* (East Berlin, 1973), Part 2, p. 122;
   cited in Clark, "Wars of Liberation," 554.
[47] The Rifle Volunteer Corps was created in 1859 by order of the Secretary of State for War
   under an Act passed during the last great invasion scare, in 1804. The call to arms met an
   enthusiastic public response, and within six months the corps had about 120,000 members,
   about a third the size of the fully mobilized French army of this period. It goes without saying
   that the British army was itself a "volunteer" – which is to say a fully professional – force,

articles for the *Volunteer Journal of Lancashire and Cheshire*, seeking to instruct readers in the characteristics of their eponymous weapon – the new, breech-loading rifle – and on the methods that would be required to defeat an invasion by regular French forces.[48] He also reported on the early stages of the American Civil War, whose appalling muddle he attributed to the presence, on both sides, of "nothing but volunteers."[49] In the aftermath, as he later wrote to Marx, the lessons seemed clear:

> The American war proves nothing except that the militia system requires unheard-of sacrifices of money and men, simply because the organization exists only on paper. How would it have gone for the Yankees if, instead of the southern militias, they had had a standing army of a couple hundred thousand men against them. Before the North got itself organized, it would have been in New York and Boston, dictating terms with the help of the [Peace] Democrats.... The main thing is good officers, and the trust of the people in the officers, neither of which the militia system is capable of providing! Only a society established and *educated* on communist principles can come close to a militia system.[50]

It was a judgment worthy of Moltke himself, not excluding the final sentence. Nevertheless, on its face, the liberal version of the nation in arms, embodied in a structure of territorial forces and local militia, perhaps with some modest professional stiffening, was neither pacifist nor revolutionary. It sought to confound opposition mainly by turning two damaging sets of objections against each other. For if it were true, as most military professionals contended, that popular forces and short-service militia could never achieve the discipline and technique necessary to deliver an effective attack – without which decisive battlefield results were impossible – this should at least comfort those who feared that recourse to the nation in arms would destabilize Europe. Like the conservative architects of the Concert of Europe, in other words, liberals envisioned an international system whose irreducible violence would be managed via a multilateral balance of power.

It is worth asking why this sort of argument made so little headway as a means of bolstering the consensual politics of the Concert. As Richard Langhorne noted, the Concert's functioning depended almost entirely on "attitudes of mind" and "the instinctive responses of statesmen," whose insubstantiality became disconcertingly apparent after mid-century – not least in response to new military possibilities created by thirty years of peaceful

deployed mainly overseas. On the continuing significance of the movement thus begun, see Ian F. W. Beckett, *Riflemen Form: A Study of the Rifle Volunteer Movement, 1859–1908* (Aldershot, 1982); and, on British auxiliary forces generally, see idem., *The Amateur Military Tradition, 1558–1945* (Manchester, 1991).

48 The series has been collected by W. H. Chaloner and W. O. Henderson (eds.), *Engels as Military Critic* (Manchester, 1959).

49 *Volunteer Journal* 3/66 (6 December 1861), reprinted ibid., 109.

50 Engels to Marx, 16 January 1868, in Ernst Drahn, *Fr. Engels als Kriegswissenschaftler* (Leipzig, 1915), 18.

economic and industrial development.[51] Unlike the Concert, the liberal conception did not depend upon some mysterious ideological consensus, nor upon mutual self-restraint achieved by the (entirely revocable) adoption of "small but good"[52] armies and conservative operational methods. The vision is rather one of muscular deterrence, based upon a force structure that was supposed to be inherently defensive in character and, most important, transparently so to potential adversaries.

The strongest part of the answer is perhaps too obvious: until the issue is forced by the pressure of technological change, the social costs of embracing the nation in arms were always perceived as so high that questions about its strategic rationality could scarcely be addressed. Once an international consensus that reduced external threats to manageable levels had been achieved, social questions, most especially those involving the prestige of the officer corps, could safely be allowed to prevail. This was, indeed, an important motive for diplomatic prudence and conciliation.

These issues came to a head in a paradigmatic civil–military crisis inspired by a new round of military reforms in Prussia in the 1860s, generally known as the Roon Reforms after the Minister of Defense, Albrecht von Roon, who brought them forward. The immediate impetus for the reforms was a series of poorly accomplished mobilizations, intended to sustain the deterrent posture of armed neutrality that Prussia had adopted during the Crimean War. The deeper motive was to create a force structure capable of supporting a more independent foreign policy, one less reliant upon the compromising habits of the Vienna system and more assertive of Prussia's own interests.

In military terms, the main value of the Roon Reforms was that they promised a much larger army, better suited to offensive operations.[53] But it was not on military grounds that the proposed reforms were resisted by the liberal majority in the Prussian Diet. Their opposition, which culminated in a constitutional crisis of the first order, did not unfold as a conflict over strategy or even "national security," though the reforms were directly linked to doubts about the fighting power of the regular army and had clear strategic implications. The sticking point was neither the dramatic expansion of the army, nor its increased cost, but structural changes that diminished the status of *Landwehr* formations and the middle-class officers who commanded them.[54]

---

[51] On the elusiveness of the Concert's ideological basis, see Richard Langhorne, *The Collapse of the Concert of Europe* (London, 1989), quotations from pages 11–12, and C. J. Bartlett, *Peace, War, and the European Powers, 1814–1914* (London, 1996).

[52] Griffith, *Military Thought*, 7.

[53] Albrecht von Roon, *Denkwürdigkeiten aus dem Leben des General-Feldmarschalls Kriegsministers Grafen von Roon*, 2 volumes (Breslau, 1897), 2: 521–35.

[54] The proposed reform increased the annual intake of new recruits from 40,000 to 63,000 and extended the initial period of service from two to three years. It also altered the relationship between *Landwehr* and the first echelon of reserves, into which soldiers passed once their

When Bismarck assumed the Chancellorship of Prussia in 1862, he was intent on employing this issue to break the resistance of the Diet (and the king) to a more assertive foreign policy, designed to settle the question of who rules in Germany, in all probability by force of arms. It was a major strategic inflection point for Europe, but one that is scarcely visible in the debate surrounding the creation of the army that would, in a matter of a few years, alter for good the balance of power on the continent. Bismarck, without personal military experience or institutional loyalty to the army, cared nothing about the tactical substance of the military issues in dispute. He assumed that *Landwehr* units would fight well enough on average, as they had in 1815, and as they would later on as well. Roon obviously did care. His liberal opponents insisted that the details of his plan were colored by social animus, and it would be difficult to conclude they were wrong. Nevertheless, to the extent that successful offensive operations required rapid and massive initial deployments, the integration of *Landwehr* and line cannot be regarded as a purely social issue, even though it was largely contested as such at the time.[55]

To which it must be added that, once a military instrument hypothetically consistent with liberal values had been envisioned, new uses for it had begun to arise in any case. Even before 1848, liberalism had ceased to be synonymous with pacifism in Germany, though this fact was not widely understood. Part of Bismarck's genius lay in his early recognition that liberals would in the end accept a nation-state built by war, a judgment that appeared decidedly eccentric to most of his fellow conservatives, whose disdain for bourgeois pacifism obscured its limits in their eyes.

It is instructive, in this respect, to compare the entries on political and military affairs in the 1818 Brockhaus, which are consistent in their treatment of war as justifiable only in self-defense, with those published a quarter century later in the *Staatslexikon* of Carl Theodor Welcker and Carl von Rotteck. Here, too, standing armies are condemned as instruments of "aggressive war." But such a war is no longer identified with offensive warfare per se, which might be necessary and acceptable for a state with a reasonable grievance against its neighbors – reasonable meaning, in this

---

regular service was up. In future, the four most recent annual classes of *Landwehr* were to be transferred into reserve battalions commanded by regular officers, while all remaining auxiliary formations would serve in the interior of the country.

55 Among many scholarly treatments of this crisis, see especially Rolf Helfert, *Der preussischer Liberalismus und die Heeresreform von 1860* (Bonn, 1988), and Frank Becker, *Bilder von Krieg und Nation: Die Einigungskriege in der bürgerlichen Öffentlichkeit Deutschlands, 1864–1913* (Munich, 2001). Bismarck's attitudes are summed up in lapidary fashion by A. J. P. Taylor, *Bismarck* (London, 1955), 46–8, and more discursively in Lothar Gall, *Bismarck: The White Revolutionary*, 2 volumes (London, 1986), 1: 154–96. Gall's account leaves little doubt that Roon's efforts were shaped by social preferences to which Bismarck was personally indifferent.

context, any course of action endorsed by the community, in the absence of clear evidence that it was morally wrong.[56] The latter criterion was elastic. Although what the Brockhaus *Conversations-Lexicon* had called "wars of convenience" were still despised if they arose from dynastic vanity, *casus belli* deriving from middle-class interests were a different matter. It was proposed, for instance, that a nation might reasonably use force to control the mouths of rivers running through it, on which its commerce might depend, and it was noted with satisfaction that the recent American war with Mexico had proved that "militias" were capable of offensive operations.[57] The myth of the citizen-solider may have been oppositional in intent, but its deeper effect, like that of the blood-brotherhood of the war experience for conservatives, undoubtedly helped reconcile its liberal proponents to awkward truths; in this case to the proposition that, in some circumstances, deliberate war might be the only way forward. There were certainly liberals in the Prussian Diet who would have supported a warlike policy toward Austria and France, long before Bismarck left them no choice. It was just that the socially confrontational character of the Roon Reforms made it difficult for them to make themselves heard.[58]

VI

Perhaps the most compelling explanation for the Concert of Europe's endurance as a system, despite its evanescent ideological basis, was that it allowed social considerations like those that dominated the debate on the Roon Reforms to retain their traditional weight in the strategic calculus of the Great Powers. German liberals were unable to overcome this structural fact with arguments about the strategic superiority of a system based upon a balance of forces tailored to defensive war. Their difficulties were compounded by the contradictory impacts of the legend of the *levée en masse*. In reality, the historical record made nonsense of the liberal claim that popular forces could be raised and employed only for defensive purposes. Yet this false historical judgment was reinforced by the equally implausible views of military experts, whose exaggerated disdain for popular forces led them to accept, or at any rate to assert (for purposes of rebutting liberal claims) an inverted version of the same legend: that the people in arms could not fight.

---

[56] Carl von Rotteck, "Krieg, Privat- und Öffentlicher Krieg, Bürgerkrieg; Kriegsrecht, natürliches und positives; Kriegsmanier, Kriegsraison; Kriegsgefangene; Kriegskunst," in Carl von Rotteck and Carl Theodor Welcker (eds.), *Staats-Lexicon, oder Encyklopädie der Staatswissenschaften*, 1st ed. (Altona, 1834–43), 9: 491–508.

[57] "Nationalökonomie," in Carl von Rotteck and Carl Theodor Welcker (eds.), *Das Staatslexicon: Encyklopädie der sämmtlichen Staatswissenschaften für alle Stände*, 2nd ed., rev. (Altona, 1845–48), 9: 360.

[58] Rolf Helfert, "Die Taktik preussischer Liberaler von 1858 bis 1862," *Militärgeschichtliche Mitteilungen* 52 (1993), 34, 36.

One unusually realistic writer who found his way to the intersection of these competing mythologies was Alexis de Tocqueville. His observations about the army most admired by German liberals – that of the United States – might have alerted them to the nature of their dilemma. A democratic army, Tocqueville concluded, will always find two things very difficult: to begin a war, and to end one.[59] On the whole, liberal proponents of the citizen-soldier took too much comfort from the first of these propositions and paid insufficient attention to the second.

The essence of the strategic consensus on which the Concert of Europe rested was not that peace be preserved at the expense of national interests but that all national interests were equally served by the avoidance, not necessarily of war, but of escalation – a military phenomenon unrecognized by strategic theorists under the Old Regime.[60] This goal was sustained by consultative diplomatic methods designed, within limits, to avoid small wars, lest they grow into big ones, and to dissuade third and fourth parties from intervening in bilateral conflicts. It was also supported by armed forces whose characteristics were the opposite of those Tocqueville imputed to a democratic army. Professional standing armies might respond too readily to the casual aggressiveness of their masters, as liberals always feared. But their necessarily modest size, the difficulty of replacing significant losses, and the cautious fighting doctrine that derived from these facts meant that they did not contain the seeds of escalation within themselves. The same could not be said of a citizen army with a moral stake in the decision to fight in the first place. Even if one accepted the claim that wars between such armies would be rare, there was nothing to prevent them from going on forever.

Nothing, that is, except rapid defeat. The constitutional crisis of the 1860s in Prussia was brought about less by a desire to put paid to liberal pretensions in military affairs – though that was certainly a factor – than by the need to take account of the implications of rapidly increasing firepower for regular armies. The emerging combination of rifled weapons wielded by men brought to the field rapidly by rail made new demands on the soldier, whose survival would depend upon a combination of skill and personal commitment that neither the undisciplined enthusiasm of the citizen, nor the corpse-like obedience of the regular, seemed fully adequate to provide. Even well-conducted operations were now perceived as incurring casualties on a scale that no standing army could tolerate. Yet higher quality, more lethal weapons also increased the advantages afforded by training, and forced a

---

[59] Alexis de Tocqueville, *De la démocratie en Amérique* (Paris, 1835), 2, chapter 22, "Why Democratic Nations Naturally Desire Peace, and Democratic Armies War."

[60] The first theorist of war to take analytic account of war's escalatory nature was Clausewitz. His famous proposition, put forth in Book One of *On War*, that the violence of war knows no natural limit but will always tend to expand unless checked by the effects of policy and "friction," is now so familiar that its originality is no longer noticed.

dramatic discounting of the value of popular forces, even when fighting on the defensive. Engels' proposal that a swiftly mobilized regular army could have cut its way to Washington in the early weeks of the American Civil War was fully in accord with the views of professional observers, whose outlook, even if rooted in social prejudice, was also supported by concrete facts that made reliance on an army slow to anger look increasingly perilous.

In the final analysis, the liberal vision of the nation in arms succumbed as much to the cult of the offensive as it did to the resentments of the social conservatives in whose interests the Concert of Europe was established. The "small but good" armies on which the Concert depended during its early years, and the endless trainloads of conscripts that its members flung against each other at the end, were equally attempts to solve the same problem: how can modern societies go to war without arousing the ghost of the *levée en masse*. Both answers were reflective of a deep strategic pessimism, rooted in the Revolutionary era and the escalatory violence that it engendered. Neither proved convincing. Yet it would be difficult to conclude that the underlying pessimism was not justified.

5

American Views of Conscription and the German Nation in Arms in the Franco-Prussian War

John Whiteclay Chambers II

The American Revolution, like the French, succeeded in part because it was able to channel the energy of popular rebellion into military forms that were tactically effective and consonant with the values the revolution espoused.[1] Like their French counterparts, the Americans fought, as they believed and said, to throw off an unjust tyranny, to affirm the dignity and rights of the individual, and to create a government respectful of, and answerable to, the people. Because the political conditions and military requirements of the war for America were different from those in France, however, the ideological construction of "the people in arms" that the American Revolution engendered was also different.[2]

The loose, mutually suspicious federation of colonies that rose against the English crown in 1776 could not have employed the radically centralizing methods of the Jacobins in the Year II, even had it wished to. Numerically, military recruitment in the American Revolution was overwhelmingly a concern of state and local governments, whose part-time forces, organized as militia, served mainly to suppress Loyalist opposition in their own regions. Alongside these stood the Continental Army, a national force composed of state units paid and directed by the fledgling national government. These "regulars" were intended to resist, as far as they could, the British and mercenary forces sent to suppress the rebellion. They seldom numbered more

---

[1] The author wishes to thank Peter Paret, School of Historical Studies, Institute for Advanced Studies, Princeton, for invaluable discussion of the topic; Jörg Nagler, director of the Kennedy Haus Kiel, Deutsch-Amerikanisches Institut, Kiel, Germany, for his useful bibliographical suggestions; and Daniel Moran, U.S. Naval Postgraduate School and editor of this volume, for his most helpful advice.

[2] On the evolution of American ideas concerning voluntary and compulsory military recruitment, see John Whiteclay Chambers II, *To Raise an Army: The Draft Comes to Modern America* (New York, 1987); and John Whiteclay Chambers II (ed.), *Draftees or Volunteers: A Documentary History of the Debate over Military Conscription in the United States, 1787–1973* (New York, 1975).

than 25,000 soldiers, an insignificant force by European standards, but in the end sufficient, with French assistance, to win independence.[3]

Coercive methods, along with positive incentives like recruitment bonuses, were not unknown in the raising of America's Revolutionary War forces. Compulsory service was limited primarily to the state militias into which local officers could, if necessary, draft citizens for short-term service within the state. Yet in the Continental Army, nearly all who served were volunteers in the most straightforward sense: they had taken up arms of their own free will, and (New Englanders most famously) sometimes saw fit to return home on the same basis.[4]

Although the rhetoric of republican virtue and communal self-defense played its part, the central idea that held all together was less "the nation" than "liberty," a concept that included a pronounced distrust for central governments on the European model and for the large, permanent military establishments on which they relied. The "Minute Man," who came to personify the American myth of the citizen-soldier, was both a voluntary and a temporary warrior, whose loyalties were by no means focused on the state. America's first national government lacked clear authority to maintain a standing army, or to impose the taxes necessary to pay one. And while the U.S. Constitution ratified in 1789 remedied these omissions – the new Federal government was given the power to "raise" an army and "maintain" a navy – it nowhere spoke of a citizen's military obligation. The outlook of most Americans on the eve of the French Revolution was the same as that of French republicans, who regarded national compulsory military service as an expression of tyranny.

America's military institutions were largely shaped in opposition to the standing armies and professionalized soldiery of Europe. Its experience of citizen-soldiers and revolutionary war also inoculated American opinion against the mythology that came to surround the wars of the French Revolution and Napoleon. As viewed from the United States, neither the *levée en masse* of 1793 nor the more regularized forms of conscription that succeeded it appeared to be a free expression of the French people's ideals and enthusiasm. To the majority of Americans such methods represented the extreme coercion of the individual by the nation state. The radical measures

---

[3] See Fred Anderson, *The Crucible of War: The Seven Years' War and the Fate of Empire in British North America, 1754–1766* (New York, 2000); Lawrence D. Cress, *Citizens in Arms: The Army and the Militia in American Society to the War of 1812* (Chapel Hill, N.C., 1982); Charles Royster, *A Revolutionary People at War* (Chapel Hill, N.C., 1979); and Richard Kohn, *Eagle and Sword: The Federalists and the Creation of the Military Establishment in America, 1783–1802* (New York, 1975).

[4] James Kirby Martin and Mark E. Lender, *A Respectable Army: The Military Origins of the Republic, 1763–1789* (Arlington Heights, Ill., 1982); for the origins of the New Englanders' view and practice, see Fred Anderson, *A People's Army: Massachusetts Soldiers and Society in the Seven Years' War* (Chapel Hill, N.C., 1984).

of mass mobilization adopted by the French Republic in extremis did nothing to legitimize compulsory national service in American eyes. When the (Democratic-Republican) Madison administration found itself desperate for soldiers toward the end of the War of 1812, and proposed a temporary national draft (primarily as a means of prodding volunteers), the Federalist orator Daniel Webster declared in Congress that conscription was a tyrannical instrument of Napoleonic despotism, and branded the administration's emergency measure "a horrible lottery" based upon the throw of "the dice of blood."[5]

Nevertheless, half a century later, one European army did for a time become an object of public esteem in the United States: that of Prussia, whose victory over France in 1870-1 was widely hailed in the American press. The majority of editors and other northern commentators applauded the Prussian victory over the France of Napoleon III, and they attributed that victory in large part to the moral superiority, as well as the military efficiency, of the Prussian army. A number of influential commentators celebrated the Prussian military system as the triumph of the "citizen-soldier" and the "nation in arms" over the forces of despotism. As the most respected weekly opinion magazine in America, the *Nation*, put it early in the war:

The Prussian system is now clearly to be the system of the future everywhere, and this, too, will be a gain for civilization. If fighting is to be the only mode of terminating international controversy, the world is interested in having it done by citizens, and not by hired men.[6]

It goes without saying that such attitudes contrast sharply with those that prevailed toward the turn of the century, when American opinion became increasingly hostile to what it perceived as German militarism and expansionism.[7] It is also true that the American press in 1870-1 was not especially well informed about the details of the Prussian military system, which arose from reforms that followed Prussia's defeat by Napoleon in 1806. Those reforms had drawn upon the concept of the *levée en masse*, to the extent of incorporating the basic principle of universal, compulsory military training and service. During the war against Austria in 1866, and against France in

---

[5] Daniel Webster, speech of December 9, 1814, reprinted in C. H. van Tyne (ed.), *Letters of Daniel Webster* (New York, 1902), 56–68. The administration's proposal was not enacted.

[6] "The Transfer of Power in Europe," *Nation* 11 (August 25, 1870), 117–18.

[7] See, for example, William R. Thayer (ed.), *The Life and Letters of John Hay*, 2 volumes (Boston, 1915), 2: 269–95; Mark Sullivan, *Our Times: The United States, 1900–1925*, 6 volumes (New York, 1927–35), 1: 326–29, 557–58; Frederick L. Paxon, *American Democracy and the World War* (Boston, 1936), 1: 163–79; Alfred Vagts, *Deutschland und die Vereinigten Staaten in der Weltpolitik* (New York, 1935); Lester B. Shippee, "German-American Relations, 1890-1914," *Journal of Modern History* 8/4 (1936), 479–88; Alfred Vagts, *A History of Militarism* (New York, 1937, rev. ed. 1959), 186–228; and Arthur A. Ekirch, Jr., *The Civilian and the Military: A History of the American Antimilitarist Tradition* (New York, 1956), 121, 157.

1870–1, the Prussian system, progressively modified to insure its political
reliability and military effectiveness, provided the basis for the mobilization
and utilization, for conservative rather than revolutionary purposes, of the
mass enthusiasm of the "people in arms."

There had been little on the Prussian army in American newspapers and
magazines prior to its astonishing victories in France in the summer and fall
of 1870. When the French army, previously considered the most powerful in
Europe, crumbled so quickly, the press scrambled to understand the reasons.
Editors often presented simplified summaries of events for public consumption, based on relatively limited information, some of it misconstrued or
inaccurate. Many accounts of the Prussian military system simply reported
the formal military structure provided by law, rather than exploring the way
it actually operated, much less the nuances of social and political conditions
in Prussia. There was little if anything in the mainstream American press
about the political controversies of the 1860s, in which the decentralized,
"popular" elements of the Prussian military system were brought more firmly
under state control, over the fierce opposition of Prussian liberals. It would
not be possible to write a sound account of Prussia's military system, nor of
its success against France, based on the coverage in the American press, and
the present chapter makes no attempt to do so. Rather, it seeks to understand the ways in which the Prussian military system was represented and
interpreted to readers of leading American newspapers and periodicals.[8] It

---

[8] The present study is based on editorials, articles, and illustrations about the war and
the Prussian military system in fifteen daily newspapers and ten opinion magazines pub-
lished in the United States in 1870–1. Those surveyed included: in Boston, the *Herald*,
Journal, and *Post*; in Chicago, the *Tribune*; in Cincinnati, the *Gazette* and *Enquirer*; in
Louisville, the *Courier-Journal*; in New York City, the *Herald*, *Post*, *Times*, *Tribune*, and
World; in Philadelphia, the *Inquirer*; in Providence, Rhode Island, the *Press*; in Springfield,
Massachusetts, the *Republican*; and in San Francisco, two weekly papers, the *Alta*, a general
circulation newspaper, and the *Elevator*, an African-American newspaper. Among the periodi-
cals consulted were *Atlantic Monthly*, *Harper's Monthly*, *Harper's Weekly*, *The Independent*,
Leslie's Illustrated Weekly, *Lippincott's Magazine*, *Littell's Living Age*, *Nation*, *North
American Review*, and *Old and New*.

For the position of the German-language press in the United States, I drew upon Carl
Wittke, *The German Language Press in America* (Lexington, 1957), 164–8. The Washington,
D.C., press was not included because its reputation had deteriorated so greatly by the mid-
nineteenth century that it had little influence in the national debate. Since my emphasis is
on civilian public opinion, I did not survey the American professional military journals on
this issue. That work has been done by Jay Luvaas, "The Influence of the German Wars of
Unification upon the United States," in Stig Förster and Jörge Nagler (eds.), *On the Road to
Total War: The American Civil War and the German Wars of Unification, 1861–1871* (New
York, 1997), 597–620, an essay that deals solely with the impact of those wars on the U.S.
Army.

Press opinion is not the same as public opinion, of course, although the press and what it
prints help to frame public debate. Public opinion on any complex issue in nineteenth-century
America is virtually impossible to determine with certainty. Yet press opinion still counts as
directly relevant evidence. Although newspapers and other popular periodicals cannot be

is a study of the initial, decidedly favorable American image of the Prussian citizen-soldier, at the time when he was being employed to create the German nation-state.[9]

That image was shaped above all by the American experience of military mobilization during the Civil War, the first and only occasion when armies on a European scale were employed in North America. The Union and the Confederacy both faced the task of raising mass armies for national purposes, and both employed methods that tested the limits of Americans' attitudes toward compulsory military service. In general, it was not compulsory service per se, but its imposition by the central government, that many argued violated American traditions of localism, states' rights, and individual liberty. Even at the time of the Revolution, training for state militia service was often compulsory, and remained so in much of the North until the 1830s (albeit with increasing provisions for exemptions and the payment of fines in lieu of service). Service in Southern militias was still compulsory for white males when the Civil War began in 1861. In limited conflicts such as the War of 1812 against Britain or the war with Mexico in 1846–8, the United States' forces were composed overwhelmingly of ad hoc units of locally raised and officered, if nationally financed, U.S. Volunteers, many composed of former militiamen. These forces, combined with a small regular army, met (if sometimes just barely) the nation's military requirements, and so reinforced the myth of the volunteer soldier, the Minute Man, responding to the country's call in times of need.

When the Civil War began, both sides raised units of U.S. Volunteers (called the Confederate States Volunteers in the South) for their main armies.

---

naively identified with their customers, they exist because they echo, as well as influence, the ideas of their readers. If they do not, they quickly shrink or disappear. Although this dynamic reciprocity is difficult for historians to investigate, let alone define, its existence seems beyond dispute.

    The present chapter shows how information and interpretation about the war and the military systems involved were presented by editors and by the writers and illustrators whose work they printed. Particular emphasis is placed on periodicals whose coverage and opinions were most respected by influential Americans at the time and thus played an important role in the public policy debate. I also examined published editions of the letters of several influential American political, diplomatic, and cultural figures to ascertain their own views and their sense of where American opinion stood on the war and the Prussian military system.

9 Previous studies of American attitudes toward nineteenth-century Prussia have recognized that American public opinion supported German unification and favored Prussia over France in the war, but these works give little if any notice to American attitudes toward Prussia's military system based on the nation in arms. See, for example, Clara Eve Schieber, *The Transformation of American Sentiment Toward Germany, 1870–1914* (Boston, 1923; reprinted New York, 1973), 3–38; John G. Gazley, *American Opinion of German Unification, 1848–1871* (New York, 1926); Otto Stolberg-Wernigerode, *Deutschland und die Vereinigten Staaten von Amerika im Zeitalter Bismarcks* (Berlin, 1933), 121–46; Henry M. Adams, *Prussian-American Relations, 1775–1871* (Cleveland, 1960), 101–5; Detlef Junker, *The Manichean Trap: American Perceptions of the German Empire, 1871–1945*, German Historical Institute, Occasional Paper No. 12 (Washington, D.C., 1995), 11–16.

But they soon augmented such recruitment with compulsion, first through state drafts and then national drafts. Although both sides drew upon European methods, including the acceptance of hired substitutes and the use of national military officers to implement the system, each side publicly differentiated its draft from European-style conscription, which they portrayed as designed for conquest. Both North and South justified national service as a supplement to voluntarism and as a defensive measure – defense of the Union in the case of the North and of the new Confederacy in the case of the South.

The South, with less than half the population of the North, was more hard pressed for troops, and its slave-owning elites were more willing to employ direct coercion, initially at the level of state militia service, and subsequently to raise national forces. The Confederate Congress adopted a Conscription Act in the second year of the war, one that exempted specific occupations (including, controversially, overseers of twenty or more slaves). Despite substantial opposition to conscription in the South, Jefferson Davis's government ultimately mobilized nearly half of all adult white males into the army, a feat seldom equaled in any nation. Although only 21 percent of the one million Confederate soldiers were obtained through the draft, the Conscription Acts included a provision that allowed the other 79 percent, who had joined up as volunteers, to be compelled to serve for the duration of the war.[10]

The North, with greater resources and an active political opposition, moved more cautiously with regard to conscription. When the need for greater manpower became evident in the second year of the war, the U.S. Congress first created a federal program that encouraged the states to draft men to fill their quotas. Only in 1863 did a divided Congress adopt a national draft law. Despite much bold rhetoric about demonstrating the political will to preserve the Union, the actual statute provided considerable opportunity to avoid personal service. The so-called Enrollment Act – the North, like the first French Republic, balked at the word "conscription" – exempted those who provided a substitute or paid a "commutation" fee of $300 (an amount equal to a skilled worker's annual wage).

The law was written in consultation with Francis Lieber, a Berlin-born Columbia College professor who had fought in the Prussian Army at Waterloo and was familiar with European systems of conscription.[11] Congress, however, facing a variety of conflicting political, military, and

---

[10] Of the 21 percent of Confederate soldiers obtained by the draft, 11 percent were actual draftees, and 10 percent were substitutes for men who had been drafted. The Confederacy enlisted 87 percent of its white males of military age. See Albert B. Moore, *Conscription and Conflict in the Confederacy* (New York, 1924), 356–61. George Wythe, the third man to become secretary of war of the Confederacy, introduced a manpower procurement system in Virginia that was obviously inspired by that of Prussia. See Herman Hattaway and Archer Jones, *How the North Won: A Military History of the Civil War* (Urbana, Ill., 1983), 113.

[11] Frank Freidel, *Francis Lieber: Nineteenth-Century Liberal* (Baton Rouge, La., 1947).

economic pressures, designed its legislation primarily to reassure the army and to prod enlistment rather than to obtain large numbers of conscripts, who were considered unreliable and prone to desert. The Enrollment Act's sponsors also wanted to avoid disrupting industrial production in the North. Unlike the South, the Northern armies were aided by an influx of immigrants (25 percent of recruits) and recruitment of black soldiers (10 percent), primarily slaves freed as Union armies marched into the South. When first implemented, the draft produced much evasion and, in New York City in July 1863, the worst riot in American history, with dozens, perhaps scores, of people killed.

In the course of the war, the Northern draft provided only 6 percent of the Union Army; 94 percent of the two million Union soldiers were volunteers, although after the initial surge many were encouraged to serve by the prospect of being drafted, coupled with rising enlistment bonuses.[12] In later years military planners assumed privately that in any war against a major power, the U.S. government would have to employ some form of national conscription; nevertheless, the myth of the volunteer citizen-soldier remained fixed in the American public mind, strengthened now by virtue of his patriotism and endurance during the Civil War.

The Civil War shaped American attitudes toward events in Europe in other ways as well. When the Franco-Prussian War began in July 1870, the Northern press was already overwhelmingly hostile to the French Second Empire. Earlier American gratitude for French assistance in achieving independence from Great Britain had been eroded by conflicting interests and cultural differences.[13] These were exacerbated by Napoleon III's imperial manner, which recalled the dangerous arrogance of his uncle, and by his restless and provocative foreign policy. The French exploitation of U.S. distraction during the Civil War, when Napoleon III intervened militarily in Mexico,[14] and Paris' generally benevolent attitude toward the Confederacy, were especially resented in the North.

Napoleon, in any case, ruled (to all appearances) as a despot, a fact sufficient in itself to brand him as an aggressor in the eyes of a majority of the

---

[12] Hattaway and Jones, *How the North Won*, 113–17, 273–7, 437–40. The Union army included 6 percent substitutes and 2 percent conscripts held to actual personal service (U.S. Provost Marshal General, *Final Report* [Washington, D.C., 1866], 1: 95). See also Eugene C. Murdock, *Patriotism Limited, 1862–1865: The Civil War Draft and the Bounty System* (Kent, Ohio, 1967).

[13] On Franco-American tensions, see Henry Blumenthal, *A Reappraisal of Franco-American Relations, 1830–1871* (Chapel Hill, N.C., 1959) and his more extensive *France and the United States: Their Diplomatic Relations, 1789–1914* (Chapel Hill, N.C., 1970).

[14] French troops were sent to Mexico in 1861 at the invitation of Mexican conservatives. They helped to overthrow the liberal government of Benito Juarez and establish a Habsburg prince, Maximillian, as emperor of Mexico. They withdrew in 1867 as a result of pressure from the United States and from a Mexican uprising led by Juarez.

American press and to produce heightened sympathy for Prussia, a regime about which most journalists knew far less. Napoleon's claim to have declared war because the Prussian king refused to renounce his family's candidacy for the Spanish throne was dismissed by American commentators as a flimsy pretence. They attributed the French emperor's motives to fear of increasing Prussian power and leadership in Europe and to a desire to prop up his increasingly shaky regime through military victories whose real purpose was to gain territory east of the Rhine.[15]

Although the Grant Administration declared the United States officially neutral, the President and the U.S. ambassadors in Europe sympathized with Prussia's North German Confederation and admired its army of citizen-soldiers. Grant personally reminded the French ambassador that "the Germans sympathized with the Union and took its [revenue] bonds freely during the [Civil] war."[16] In late August, as the fighting turned sharply against the French, Grant confided to his envoy in Paris that "the Prussian military system is so perfect however that I believed, single-handed, they would be too much for the French in the end."[17]

Germany was supported in similar terms by the great majority of the American press, as well as many leading figures in American politics and culture, who contrasted Napoleonic despotism and imperialism with, if not republicanism (Prussia being, of course, a monarchy), then at least with what many influential Americans viewed as continued respect for local rights and liberties that prevailed in Germany, and also (however inconsistently) with Germany's laudable desire for national unity.[18] The U.S. minister to Berlin, George Bancroft, a leading historian of American democracy and a personal friend of Bismarck, cheered the German victories, writing that "a people in

---

[15] For condemnation of France and support for Prussia, see *New York Times* (July 28, 1870); *New York Herald* (July 11, 1870); *Cincinnati Daily Gazette* (July 13, 1870); *New York Tribune* (July 12, 1870); *Chicago Tribune* (July 20, 1870); and *Springfield Republican* (July 12 and 16, 1870). Most newspapers of this period were only a few pages in length, often without page numbers. For magazines, see *Harper's Weekly* (August 13, September 3, and September 10, 1870; March 18, 1871); and *Living Age* (August 13, 1870).

[16] Journal of Assistant Secretary of State J. C. Bancroft Davis, entry of August 5, 1870, reprinted in Jeannette Keim, *Forty Years of German-American Political Relations* (Philadelphia, 1919), 8.

[17] Ulysses S. Grant to Elihu B. Washburne, August 22, 1870, in John Y. Simon (ed.), *The Papers of Ulysses S. Grant*, 24 volumes to date (Carbondale, Ill., 1967–), 20: 254. The proclamation of neutrality is reprinted in ibid., 235–40; also in the *New York Post* (August 22, 1870).

[18] James Russell Lowell to Charles Eliot Norton, August 28, 1870, in Charles Eliot Norton (ed.), *Letters of James Russell Lowell*, 2 volumes (New York, 1894), 2: 62–63; Ralph Waldo Emerson to Hermann Grimm, January 5, 1871, in Frederick William Hollis (ed.), *Correspondence between Ralph Waldo Emerson and Hermann Grimm* (Boston, 1903), 85; Louisa May Alcott to her mother, August 11, 1870, in Ednah Dow Cheney (ed.), *Louisa May Alcott: Her Life, Letters, and Journals* (Boston, 1900), 244; Andrew D. White, *Autobiography* (New York, 1905), 2: 154. White was later U.S. minister (1879–81) and ambassador (1897–1902) to Germany.

arms crushes the degenerate hosts of despotism." Later he told Secretary of State Hamilton Fish: "If we need the solid, trusty good will of any government in Europe, we can have it best with Germany; because German institutions and ours most nearly resemble each other."[19] A number of pro-German influentials believed that the new German Empire, proclaimed at Versailles in January 1871, represented a unification process similar to that of the original American states in their movement toward a strong republican union. President Grant emphasized the similarities between the American and German nation-states in a special message to Congress in February 1871.[20]

Although some of America's support for Prussia in 1870 reflected hostility to the regime of Napoleon III, much of it derived from attitudes toward Germany that were positive, if not very deep. The dominant view in America was that Germany was a land of intelligent, industrious people.[21] It was seen as a country of religious freedom,[22] and of high learning, with a culture that emphasized literature, music, philosophy, and science.[23] The Prussian military heritage was often viewed in terms of individual leaders working for the good: Frederick the Great protecting and expanding a small nation against overwhelming odds, "Baron" von Steuben aiding the American Revolution, Friedrich von Bülow helping Wellington defeat Napoleon at Waterloo.

The American press also recalled that the German Federation and its individual members had supported the North during the Civil War, and that German investors had helped finance the Union cause. Current Prussian leaders were portrayed as forging their own national union, like the one for which Northerners had just fought. The *New York Herald*, with its typical hyperbole, asserted: "America sees in King William and Bismarck instruments of Providence to bring about political and commercial unity of a grand

---

[19] George Bancroft to Mrs. J. C. Bancroft Davis, September 4, 1870, and to Hamilton Fish, October 18, 1870, reprinted in M. A. De Wolfe Howe, *Life and Letters of George Bancroft*, 2 volumes (New York, 1908), 2: 236, 246–7. Similar expressions came from the U.S. ministers in Paris and London. See Dale Clifford, "Elihu Benjamin Washburne: An American Diplomat in Paris, 1870–1871," *Prologue* 2/3 (1970), 161–74; John Lothrop Motley to Otto von Bismarck, September 9, 1870, in Susan and Herbert St. John Mildmay (eds.), *John Lothrop Motley and His Family: Further Letters and Records* (London, 1910), 288–93.

[20] Message to Congress, February 7, 1871, reprinted in Simon (ed.), *Papers of Ulysses S. Grant*, 21: 163–4.

[21] See James Cruikshank, *Geography* (New York, 1867), the primary geography book used in the nation's schools at the time, quoted in Sullivan, *Our Times*, 2: 63; also the editorial by William Cullen Bryant in the *New York Post* (August 12, 1870); and his article, "A Yankee among the Germans," ibid. (August 5, 1870).

[22] Legal religious freedom, which applied to Protestants, Catholics, and Jews, was not the whole story, of course. Thousands of German Jews, particularly those from southern and eastern Germany, emigrated to the United States in the late 1830s to escape social and economic discrimination.

[23] See, for example, the editorial in the *New York Post* (July 10, 1870); and George Bancroft, U.S. minister to Germany, to Secretary of State Hamilton Fish in September 1870, reprinted in Keim, *Forty Years of German-American Political Relations*, 14.

people hitherto divided and discordant."[24] There was some criticism of the dominance in Prussia of the conservative, land-owning *Junkers*, but there was also much hope and belief that political liberalization would follow the social, cultural, and economic progress being made in Germany.[25] "Germany is far more inclined towards free institutions than France," a leading Rhode Island paper declared, "and the tendency of her people is towards increased liberty."[26]

Part of the sympathy toward Germany came from the fact that Germans formed the largest single group of European immigrants in nineteenth-century America, comprising 30 percent of foreign-born Americans in 1870.[27] By the 1860s, the majority of German Americans were affiliated with the Republican Party, which meant that they were vigorous opponents of slavery and ardent champions of the Union.[28] In 1870 virtually the entire German language press, the largest foreign language press in America, was united in applauding the defeat of France and celebrating the German army and the new German empire.[29] Liberal German émigrés to the United States were divided over the Prussian military system. Karl Heinzen, who had been embittered by a year of Prussian military service, and who came to the United States after the failed revolutions of 1848, continued to attack Prussian militarism despite the victory over France and the unification of Germany. Friedrich Hecker, a leading figure in Baden's revolution in 1848, who had fled to America after his movement had been crushed by Prussian arms, took a more popular position. As the main speaker at a victory celebration in St. Louis in 1871, he hailed Germany's recent military success, attributing it to compulsory education and universal military training, and what he called the true *égalité* of the German army.[30]

---

[24] *New York Herald* (July 25, 1870; see also August 29, 1870). James Gordon Bennett's editorials, while entertainingly provocative, were often so erratic and flippant as to be discounted by serious readers. On Germany's role in the Civil War, see *New York Tribune* (July 22, 1870); *Cincinnati Enquirer* (September 2, 1870); *New York Post* (July 21 and August 12, 1870); San Francisco *Elevator* (October 18, 1871).

[25] Some hoped the war would bring political progress as well, including reduced influence by the *Junkers*, in a unified Germany. H. W. Hemans, "Prussia and Germany," *North American Review* 112 (January 1871), 158.

[26] *Providence* [Rhode Island] *Press* (September 2, 1870).

[27] U.S. Bureau of the Census, *Historical Statistics of the United States from Colonial Times to 1970* (Washington, D.C., 1975), 105–6, 116–18.

[28] Carl Wittke, *Refugees from Revolution: The German Forty-Eighters in America* (Philadelphia, 1952); and Carl Wittke, *The German Language Press in America* (Lexington, Ky., 1957); Frederick C. Luebke (ed.), *Ethnic Voters and the Election of Lincoln* (Lincoln, 1971); Mack Walker, *Germany and the Emigration, 1816–1885* (Cambridge, Mass., 1964); Philip Gleason, *The Conservative Reformers: German-American Catholics and the Social Order* (Notre Dame, Ind., 1968); Kathleen Neils Conzen, "Germans," in Stephen Thernstrom (ed.), *Harvard Encyclopedia of American Ethnic Groups* (Cambridge, Mass., 1980), 405–25.

[29] Wittke, *German Language Press in America*, 164–8.

[30] See Carl Wittke, *Against the Current: The Life of Karl Heinzen* (Chicago, 1945), 50–1, 253–4; and Friedrich Hecker, "Hecker's Festrede zur St. Louis Friedensfeier," in

In France, Napoleon III relied primarily upon a regular army that would be loyal to his regime. He had accordingly reduced short-term conscription of a kind that tended to strengthen direct links between the army and the citizenry and to ensure social diversity within the ranks. France's army in 1870 was composed disproportionately of long-service professionals drawn from the peasantry, the urban poor, and French territories in North Africa (the so-called Zouaves and Turcos). Although French forces were armed with a rifle superior in range and rate of fire to that of the Germans, this advantage was more than offset by the superior training, enthusiasm, and leadership of the Prussian army (which also possessed superior artillery). At the battle of Sedan, on September 1, less than a month after fighting had begun, the French emperor himself was forced to surrender, along with 100,000 of his troops. Three days later, a popular uprising in Paris overthrew the Imperial government and proclaimed France a republic. The new government immediately began to improvise a defense of Paris, and organize new armies south of the Loire.

In the aftermath of Napoleon III's capture, American press sentiment shifted somewhat toward France. Yet the French effort to raise popular forces by means of a new *levée en masse*, which might have been expected to inspire sympathy in the land of the Minute Man, did not do so (Figures 6 and 7). Most American editors continued to favor Prussia, judging that further French resistance would lead to a useless prolongation of the war. Although virtually all American papers hailed the downfall of "Napoleonic despotism," few had much confidence in the ability of the French to establish a true republic.[31] American public opinion became genuinely critical of the Germans only when the German army began bombarding Paris on January 5, 1871, using new long-range cannons.[32] Paris surrendered on January 26, however, and formal hostilities soon ended.

From the beginning of the war, most major American newspapers and periodicals attributed the German victories in large part to the Prussian military system and the superiority of what the majority of them considered a representative, well-trained, educated, and dedicated citizen-army. This outlook mirrored the long-standing admiration of many Americans for the Prussian system of compulsory education, to which its military system seemed to present an obvious parallel. Reportedly, many Americans believed that Prussia's armed forces, based on compulsory service, were both democratic and

Deutsch-Americanisher Heckerdenkmal-Verein, *Friedrich Hecker und sein Antheil an der Geschichte Deutschlands und Amerikas* (Cincinnati, 1881), 49–62.

[31] "What we talk of as the French Republic is in reality nothing more than a number of men trying to establish one," declared the *Nation* (October 27, 1870); see also *Harper's Weekly* (December 31, 1870); and "France Delivered!," *The Independent* 23 (February 2, 1871), 6.

[32] Condemnation of the German shelling of Paris came not simply from the few pro-French papers like the *New York World* (January 30, 1871) and the *Boston Post* (January 16 and 18, 1871) but also from some pro-German publications, such as *Harper's New Monthly Magazine* 42 (March 1871), 633–4.

FIGURES 6 (TOP) AND 7 (BOTTOM). *Irregular French Troops* and *Prussian Soldiers Cooking in the Trenches Before Paris.* Lithographs for *Harper's Weekly* (November 19, 1870). Courtesy of Stanford University Library.

At the start of the Franco-Prussian War, the majority of the American press hailed Germany as a nation of intelligent, industrious people and praised the Prussian military system as morally and militarily superior to that of France. In contrast, Napoleon III was denounced as an imperialistic despot, and French forces were denigrated as a ragged and repressed band of peasants and proletarians.

The two illustrations shown here capture this contrast with exceptional precision. They originally appeared together on a single page of *Harper's Weekly,* along with a third sketch showing three hooded, grim-faced, dark-skinned men identified as "Turcos," "wild people brought over from Algeria" to thicken the French ranks, who could scarcely be expected to stand up to a modern army like that of the Germans.

nonaggressive.[33] Certainly many hailed Prussia's victory as a moral as well as a military one. The *Independent*, an influential Protestant, reformist magazine, was typical in declaring that "Prussia has shown . . . the superiority of a force consisting of the nation itself – industrious, educated, civilized – over a body of hirelings who do their work for 'pay and provant.'"[34]

Romanticizing the spirit of the citizen-soldiers of the Prussian army, some of the American press compared them with the victorious volunteers of the Union army in the Civil War.[35] The basis of German progress and greatness, said the *New York Post*, lay in the German character, as well as Germany's vast internal commerce, its system of compulsory education, and what the editor called

the democratic system of militia [sic] training, whereby all, regardless of rank, wealth or position, were required, as part of the duty of citizenship, to acquire a military education. If the German soldier is to-day a better man than his French antagonist, it is not that he is braver, but that he is better educated; it is because he is like our own northern volunteer, a man, a citizen, defending his home, and knowing and caring wherefore he fights.[36]

FIGURES 6 AND 7 *(continued)* The essential contrast between the two images is that of the self-organizing energy of the Prussians, compared to the passive indifference of the French. The latter are portrayed as listless civilians awaiting instructions from high authority, while the Prussians, all in uniform, exert themselves cooking and improving their trench, despite no officer being present.

The significance of the image is heightened by the fact that it appeared relatively late in the war, after the defeat of the French regular armies had given risen to a general mobilization of precisely the kind with which Americans might have been expected to identify. Yet the American press remained almost entirely immune to the notion that the French irregulars of 1870 were the rightful heirs to the Minute Men of 1776. In the wake of the American Civil War, the American media had learned to admire well-trained, disciplined, and efficient troops, so long as their appearance on the battlefield could somehow be reconciled with democratic processes, as seemed (at least from a distance) to be true in Prussia. Even with Louis Napoleon gone, the French desire to continue the war attracted little support and was portrayed not as a patriotic demonstration in the face of overwhelming odds but as a capricious and unjustified waste of life.

---

33 Gazley, *American Opinion of German Unification*, 351, 377.

34 "Standing Armies Doomed," *The Independent* 22 (October 20, 1870), 4.

35 On the reported enthusiasm of German citizen-soldiers, see for example the Associated Press dispatch from Berlin, "Further War News from Europe; Great Enthusiasm in Germany; The Whole Male Population Demanding Arms," in the *New York Post* (July 19, 1870), 1, and "Germany in War Time: An American's Impressions and Experiences," ibid. (September 15, 1870).

36 "The German Empire," *New York Post* (August 12, 1870). In July, an American correspondent came across a group of French soldiers at Rouen and reported: "They were mostly quite young men and full of fire, yet they did not carry with them the appearance of calm, settled military loyalty, such as marks the English or American or German soldier." Samuel Osgood,

Published descriptions of the Prussian military manpower system ranged from brief summaries to detailed explanations. The basic elements presented to American readers emphasized that virtually all able-bodied Prussian males were required at age twenty to serve two or three years in the regular army, then two years in the reserves, and finally half a dozen to a dozen years in the *Landwehr*, a long-term, inactive reserve. Thus Prussian men spent nearly twenty years of their lives in active or reserve military service. They were trained, organized, had their uniforms, and could be called up, mobilized, and put into the field within a few weeks.[37] The system was described as representative of all socio-economic classes and was hailed as not only militarily efficient but equitable and, some even said, democratic. Compulsory military training, it was argued, had turned the Prussian army into a school of civic as well as military virtue, through which the men of the nation passed in turn.[38]

Emphasizing that Prussia owed her rapid growth and strength to compulsory education and compulsory military training and service, some admirers of the system, such as a writer in the prestigious *North American Review*, explained: "Both are obviously and essentially democratic." Compulsory national military service might seem draconian, the author said, but although the service might be hard, it was not unjust.

The absence of all privilege, the disregard of rank and wealth, with which the liability to military service is enforced, deprives this institution of all that might render it heinous and unjust.... The terrible tribute of blood cannot fairly be exacted from anybody, unless it is extracted from all and paid by all.[39]

It was the alleged (and exaggerated) universality of the Prussian military system, as well as the spirit of nationalism and self-sacrifice that seemed to infuse the Prussian soldiers, that appealed to so many writers in the American press.

E. L. Godkin, British-born founder and editor of the *Nation*, the most respected opinion weekly in the United States at the time, continually touted

---

"Napoleon and Prussia," *New York Post* (July 20, 1870), 1. See also "France Delivered!" *The Independent* 23 (February 2, 1871), 6. "This is not the victory of Bismarck, the diplomatist, or of von Moltke, the strategist," the anonymous author declared, "half so much as it is the triumph of Pestalozzi, the pedagogue. It is only the old lesson over again. To the illiterate Breton peasant, Germany opposed the intelligent student; against the savage Turco was pitted the Berlin Sanskrit scholar."

[37] The most extensive description of the Prussian system and its evolution was written by the leading instructor at West Point, Dennis Hart Mahan. See D. H. M., "Notes on the War," *Nation* 11 (September 11, 1870), 167–9. Even Mahan, an undisputed authority, insisted that under the laws and decrees of 1814 and 1815, every Prussian subject was called upon to bear arms for the defense of the state.

[38] H. W. Hemans, "Prussia and Germany," *North American Review* 112 (January 1871), 115.

[39] Ernst Gryzanovski, "On the Origin and Growth of Public Opinion in Germany," *North American Review* 112 (April 1871), 294.

the Prussian system as offering a valuable lesson for modern society. Godkin saw the Prussian system as a model, not simply in preparing for war but, more importantly, in industrializing America, for the more efficient mobilization of society for economic and political progress. "The feeling of amazement with which the world is looking on at the Prussian campaigns comes not so much from the tremendous display of physical force they afford," he declared in September 1870, "as from the consciousness which everybody begins to have, that to put such an engine of destruction as the German army into operation, there must be a new kind of motive power."[40]

"We are not witnessing simply a levy *en masse*, nor yet the mere maintenance of an immense force by military monarchy, but the application to military affairs of the whole intelligence of a nation of extraordinary mental and moral culture," Godkin concluded. "The peculiarity of the Prussian system does not lie in the size of its armies or the perfection of its armament, but in the character of the men who compose it." All modern armies, he said, except Cromwell's "New Model Army" in the English Civil War and the Union and Confederate armies in the American Civil War, were "composed almost entirely of ignorant peasants drilled into passive obedience to a small body of professional soldiers. The Prussian army is the first, however, to be a perfect reproduction of the society which sends it to the field."[41] A number of newspapers concluded that the German military system was invincible. The *New York Times* editorialized: "The war proves that no army or combination of armies can stand against the German nation, every man in which is a well-trained soldier."[42]

Not all the American press accepted the idea that the Prussian military system was equitable and desirable, or even that Prussia was the victim of French aggression. Two important northern newspapers, the *New York World* and the *Boston Post*, challenged that dominant view. The *World* denounced the Prussian government as "the most autocratic in Europe," and warned against the "militarism of the North German Caesar."[43] In July 1870, declaring that Napoleon III's government was becoming liberalized, the two newspapers portrayed the conflict as one of French liberalism against Prussian despotism. "Prussia is a military government in the strictest sense," the *Boston Post* declared. "The king lays his iron hand on his people in their very cradles, and keeps it there with a tight grip 'til they go to their graves. . . . The Prussian soldier fights for his king, not for his country."[44]

While denunciations of Prussian autocracy and militarism would become commonplace in America after the turn of the century, in 1870 they were

[40] [E. L. Godkin] "Culture and War," *Nation* 11 (September 8, 1870), 151–2.
[41] Ibid.
[42] *New York Times* (January 30, 1871).
[43] *New York World* (July 16 and 20, and August 25, 1870).
[44] *Boston Post* (July 14 and 18, 1870).

distinctly a minority view. Such accusations were generally ignored in the majority of newspapers and magazines at that time, but some did respond to them. While acknowledging that the popular form of government was lacking in the Prussian monarchy, *Harper's Weekly* declared that a true popular spirit existed in that country and would present a major obstacle to militarism and aggressive war.[45]

Prussia's champion, Godkin's *Nation*, responded most directly and fully to criticism of the Prussian military system. On October 13, 1870, it declared that "Prussia to-day counts among her soldiers nearly all of her leading men in every walk of life, whether statesmen, financiers, men of science or scholars. Her laws compel every subject, from her premier down to the meanest inhabitant, to defend his home."[46] A week later, however, the magazine published a letter to the editor, rejecting that assertion. The letter writer, identified only as "A.T.," cited an article in the *Pall Mall Gazette*, a leading English publication, denying press reports that all able-bodied young Prussian men were really taken into service at age twenty. "A.T." suggested instead that the bulk of the Prussian army was probably composed, like most other armies, of "loafers, roughs, restless, reckless, shiftless, dissatisfied, unsuccessful men." If the *Nation* really believed the Prussian army was representative of the population, "A.T." asked for proof.[47]

Godkin published his own, somewhat qualified, rebuttal. He declared that no nation mobilized a greater proportion of its population than Prussia. The important point, he asserted, was that in Prussia's military system, every able-bodied man between twenty and thirty-nine "is either called to the field, or *liable to be called if wanted.*"[48] Prussia called into the field whatever size force it found necessary. Godkin termed "a wild mistake" the view that the army was composed primarily of "loafers" and other alienated men. The Prussian army, Godkin said, was unlike all other armies for two reasons: because "in no other country is *every man* liable to military duty, and *actually enrolled*," and because conscripted men were not allowed to purchase their way out by hiring substitutes. "It is strictly and literally true," Godkin insisted, that "'nearly all her leading men in every walk of life are soldiers.'" He noted that another article in the same issue referred to six Sanskrit scholars, one a Berlin judge, who were serving in the Prussian army, and he promised more evidence as soon as it could be obtained.

---

[45] "Bismarck's Master," *Harper's Weekly* 14 (October 22, 1870), 674; see also the *New York Post* (September 10, 1870).

[46] "Military Resources of Prussia and France," *Nation* 11 (October 13, 1870), 239–40.

[47] A.T., "Correspondence: The Prussian Military System," *Nation* 11 (October 20, 1870), 258.

[48] Editor's response, *Nation* 11 (October 20, 1870), 258–9; emphasis throughout this paragraph is in the original.

That evidence appeared in a long, detailed and highly favorable evaluation of the Prussian military system published in the *Nation* a month later under the title, "What the Prussian army is composed of."[49] It took the form of a 4,300-word letter to the editor written from Berlin on November 5. The author was Friedrich Kapp, one of the best-known leaders of the German-American community, who had returned to Germany in the spring of 1870 to reside there permanently. A native Westphalian, Kapp, like Hecker, had fled to the United States after the suppression of the 1848 revolution. In New York City he had become a successful lawyer, journalist, and political activist, second only to Carl Schurz in obtaining German-American support for the Republican Party and the cause of the Union during the Civil War. He had been appointed to New York's commission of immigration, but in 1870 he was perhaps best known for his liberal writings in both the German-language and mainstream American press, as well as for a number of historical works. The latter included biographies of German-born generals in the American Revolutionary War, Friedrich von Steuben and Johann Kalb, and a history of German immigration to America. Kapp was in Germany when the Franco-Prussian War broke out, and he contributed articles to a number of leading American newspapers and magazines explaining and justifying German conduct.[50] These included glowing reports of German enthusiasm for a war of national defense and unity. He enthusiastically certified the fairness of the Prussian military system.

Although containing some valuable details of the Prussian law and its operation, Kapp's essay, ostensibly a report on the wartime mobilization, contained a number of exaggerations, distortions, and errors. Kapp sought, incorrectly, to link Prussia's Napoleonic-era military reforms to the American Revolutionary War, by claiming that it was service in North America that gave one of Prussia's leading reformers, Count Neidhardt von Gneisenau,

---

[49] Friedrich Kapp, from Berlin, November 5, 1870, "What the Prussian army is composed of," *Nation* 11 (November 24, 1870), 348–50.

[50] Friedrich Kapp was naturalized as a Prussian subject in 1870 and then elected to the Reichstag as a National Liberal in 1871, serving with only a three-year interruption until his death in 1884. In 1870 Kapp was writing to American newspapers to justify Germany's position. See Kapp to E. Cohen, September 13, 1870, reprinted in Hans-Ulrich Wehler, *Friedrich Kapp: Vom radikalen Früsozialisten des Vormärz zum liberalen Parteipolitiker des Bismarck-reichs, Briefe, 1843–1884* (Frankfurt am Main, 1969), 66–7; also see his letter to the *Nation* (November 5, 1870), and references in the *New York Post* (August 12, 1870), and *Harper's Weekly* (September 10, 1870), 578. For more on Kapp's life, see the biography by his great-granddaughter, Edith Lenel, *Friedrich Kapp* (Leipzig, 1935); F. Monaghan, "Friedrich Kapp," *Dictionary of American Biography*, 22 volumes (New York, 1928–44), 10: 259–60; and Adolf E. Zucker (ed.), *The Forty-Eighters: Political Refugees of the German Revolution of 1848* (New York, 1950), 307–8. Fifty years later Kapp's son, Wolfgang, became the leader of the rightist "Kapp Putsch" that sought to overthrow the new Weimar Republic in 1920. See Wehler, *Friedrich Kapp*, 7.

his insight into "the power of a popular army against mercenaries."[51] He was on slightly firmer ground, however, when describing changes made in Prussia's military organization in the years leading up to the Franco-Prussian War. Every recruit, Kapp reported, served for three years in the army starting at the age of twenty; then four years in the reserves, and five years in the *Landwehr*. An exception was made for young men with a higher education – he cited students, artists, and merchants as examples. They could enter the army as volunteers when they were seventeen years old, serve only one year on active duty, and have a chance of later becoming junior officers in the *Landwehr*.[52]

Kapp's defense of the proposition that the Prussian military system was socially equitable was more measured. Of course not everyone served, Kapp admitted, but the reason for this did not negate the equity of the system. The population of North Germany was about 30 million, he explained, of which 1 percent, or 300,000 men, were in the active army in peacetime. Even such a large force as this could not contain all the male population that became liable each year. Rather, only about 100,000 were called each year, out of between 320,000 and 380,000 men who were legally liable. The remaining two-thirds were free from service. There were also exemptions, Kapp said, for convicted criminals, and for "cripples, invalids, young men not fully developed or too small"[53]; clergy and teachers, who were obligated to serve only six weeks; the only sons of widows or aged parents who could not support themselves; foreign nationals or other people excluded under treaties; and finally the volunteers who served only one year "on account of their higher standard of education."[54]

---

[51] Kapp, "What the Prussian army is composed of," 348. Gneisenau served briefly in Canada as a lieutenant toward the end of the American Revolution. There is no question, however, that the roots of his military thinking, like that of his colleagues, were entirely continental.

[52] The measures that Kapp described were the Roon Reforms (see pp. 70–2, above). They had the effect of more firmly subordinating the *Landwehr* to the line army and were opposed by Prussian liberals. Under the old system, a young man of twenty was theoretically obligated for three years of regular service but in practice usually served only one-and-a-half or two years. After that he spent two years in the reserves, seven years in the first echelon of the *Landwehr*, and finally five years in the second echelon. The new laws kept each soldier in a regiment from age twenty to twenty-three. Reserve service was reduced to four years, plus five years in the *Landwehr*, so that, as Kapp said, a man was free of military duty at thirty-two, instead of at thirty-eight. From ages twenty-three to thirty-two, the average male citizen was called up once for six weeks as a reservist, and twice for two weeks as a *Landwehrman*, making in all ten weeks training in nine years. In wartime, however, as Kapp noted, those who were called up served either until they reached age thirty-two or until the war ended.

[53] The German minimum height for military service was just over five feet, Kapp reported, compared to the French minimum of four feet ten inches. "What the Prussian army is composed of," 349.

[54] All these exemptions left about 120,000 young men per year, from whom about 100,000 were taken into the army. The 20,000 who were left out (nearly 17 percent) were determined

Addressing the charge of class bias, Kapp conceded that although the agricultural population of North Germany amounted to 72 percent of the nation, it made up 80 percent of the army, but he explained the difference by asserting that farmers were generally healthier than factory workers, so that more passed the physical examination. More importantly, Kapp declared:

the difference is partly made up by the wealthier classes, who consider it an honor to serve, and are ambitious of being promoted as officers in the *Landwehr*. On the whole it can be said that about 90 per cent of able-bodied men are really taken into the service of the army at the age of 20 or sooner, while about 10 per cent are free.

Kapp concluded that the *Nation* magazine had therefore been justified in stating that "[Prussia's] army, in time of war, absorbs the best part of the male population, and that it contains men of all professions and pursuits in about the same proportion in which they are found in civil life."[55]

Knowing his American audience, Kapp placed great emphasis on volunteering. He noted that in a popular war such as the one against France, many young Germans who were not yet subject to compulsory military service eagerly enlisted. He estimated that among the one million men mobilized for the war, more than 15,000 who might have avoided service volunteered anyway, including two of his own nephews, aged 17 and 18. At the University of Berlin, for example, 800 out of 2,000 students had enlisted voluntarily. Students were joined by their teachers, large numbers of whom volunteered if they were not called up. Two professors who had volunteered, Kapp reported, had already been killed in battle. The entire medical faculty of the Breslau University was in the field along with its students, serving as surgeons, nurses, and soldiers.

Indeed, Kapp said, men from all walks of life had been called up or volunteered: teachers, musicians, dancers, singers, machinists, lawyers, assistant judges, young diplomats, and the sons of bankers and merchants. He reported extensive losses: "More than thirty Prussian judges, who served as privates, sergeants and lieutenants in the army, have thus far been killed in battle."[56] There had been considerable disruption: 35,000 young men in the field were from Berlin alone, 5 percent of the whole population of the city, and their absence had affected the daily life in the capital, although it had not been brought to a standstill. Like the editor of the *Nation*, Kapp concluded that the Prussian army was a people's army, and that it was morally as well as militarily superior to a hired, professional force:

(note 54 *cont.*) by drawing lots in each town. These remained liable in case of need, such as illness or death of those chosen to serve. Ibid., 349.

[55] Ibid., 349.

[56] Ibid., 349.

However burdensome this military system may be in some respects, it is at all events the only one which deserves the honor of being called democratic, and the nation which is raised under and by it will always prefer peace to war, and never be dominated by a conquering spirit. For the very reason that it is interwoven with the nation's greatest and smallest interests, the German army will never be more or less than the people in arms, and ask nothing better than to be sent home at the earliest practicable moment, in order to pursue nobler and more productive callings than marching and killing.[57]

Like Kapp and Godkin, many American editors and writers were capable of considerable exaggeration and inaccuracy in regard to the Prussian military system. Part of this stemmed from political ideology and partisanship. In this period, American newspapers were beginning to demonstrate increasing political independence; however, many of their editorial stances were still directly influenced by their political affiliation.[58] In addition, ideological divisions remained from the Civil War. During the Franco-Prussian War, Germany was supported by northern periodicals that were Republican or pro-Unionist Democrat; France was supported by Southern papers (which were Democratic) and pro-Southern Democratic papers in the North.

Many contemporary observers and even some historians asserted that the American press divided on the Franco-Prussian War strictly on partisan lines – Republican papers for Prussia and the Democratic press for France.[59] The present study indicates that this was not strictly the case. The division of opinion in the American press depended less on party-political loyalty than on the positions papers had taken during the Civil War. Republican newspapers that had supported the Union in 1861–5 were sympathetic to Prussia, perhaps for aiding the Union, but so too were a number of important northern Democratic papers, such as the *New York Herald* and the *New York Sun*. Papers that supported the Confederacy supported France in 1870. Ideologically, Republican newspapers, like the Republican Party, were committed to national unity and strong central government as an instrument of progress. In the Civil War, they had supported the adoption of the national Enrollment Act for reasons of military efficiency and equity and as a demonstration of the North's will to preserve the nation. Some critics claimed in 1870 that the Republicans were simply wooing German-American voters, a charge that most pro-Prussian publications vigorously denied, asserting the justice of the German cause in a war initiated by Napoleon III. Unionist Democratic newspapers had also supported the Lincoln administration's war

---

[57] Ibid., 350.
[58] Frank Luther Mott, *American Journalism: A History of Newspapers in the United States* (New York, 1947), 411–14.
[59] See for example, "The Democrats and the War," *Harper's Weekly* 14 (September 24, 1870), 610–11; Keim, *Forty Years of German-American Political Relations*, 9; Gazley, *American Opinion of German Unification*, 323–48.

effort, although dissenting from some of its other actions. In 1870–1, they too supported Prussia.[60]

Support for Napoleon III came almost exclusively from newspapers that had supported the Confederacy – Democratic papers in the South and the few prominent Peace Democratic papers in the North. During the Civil War, the derisively labeled "Copperhead" papers in the North had opposed the Lincoln administration, contested the use of force against the South, opposed the end of slavery, and resisted the adoption of national conscription and other war measures. The most influential Northern papers favoring France in 1870–1 were the two largest Copperhead papers during the Civil War – the *Boston Post*, the leading Democratic paper in Republican New England, and the *New York World*, a voice of Tammany Hall, the city's ethnic-Irish-based Democratic machine.[61] In both the North and the South, the Democratic party favored state's rights and a vigorous defense of local autonomy and individual liberty (at least for whites) against interference from the national government. Its electoral strength lay primarily among urban ethnic groups like the Irish in the North, and among whites in the predominantly rural South.

Democratic papers in the former Confederacy, some of them still in states with federally protected Republican Reconstruction governments, retained their hostility to the nationalizing tendencies of the Republican Party and the Civil War. In an 1870 editorial about the Franco-Prussian War, states' rights Democrat Henry Watterson of the *Louisville* [Kentucky] *Courier-Journal*, linked Prussia and the U.S. government:

Like Prussia in her views of consolidation, the ruling powers of the United States have sought, and still seek, to obliterate all State lines and to create a strong government. Hence we are not surprised to learn that the sympathies of the United States Government are all for Prussia, and that the vital services of France in securing the independence of this country are forgotten and overlooked.[62]

---

[60] In a handwritten note to the U.S. envoy in Paris, President Ulysses S. Grant confided that "The war has developed the fact here that every unreconstructed rebel simpathyses [sic] with France, without exception, while the loyal element is almost universally the other way." Grant to Elihu B. Washburne, August 22, 1870, in Simon (ed.), *Papers of Ulysses S. Grant*, 20: 254. A month later a leading Republican magazine noted the widespread support for France among the Democratic press, attributing it cynically to the influence of Irish-Americans in the North (Fenian Irish independence organizations had declared for France) and even more scathingly to the former slave owners and their allies. The editor declared bitterly: "The former apologists of slavery, and the present enemies of equal political rights at home are instinctively the friends of Caesarism and the empire abroad." "The Democrats and the War," *Harper's Weekly* 14 (September 24, 1870), 610–11.

For an example of an exchange on whether German-American voters were being wooed, see the pro-Prussian *New York Post* (August 6, 1870); and the pro-French *New York World* (August 12, 1870).

[61] On their party affiliation, see Mott, *American Journalism*, 217, 259, 350–2.

[62] *Louisville* [Kentucky] *Courier-Journal* (July 18, 1870). Watterson subsequently declared that "King William of Prussia is to-day as completely the representative of armed irresponsible kingly power in Europe as was the Czar Nicholas in 1854," ibid. (July 19, 1870).

American opinion also included pacifists and liberal "antimilitarists," who on principle opposed the Prussian military system, indeed any system of widespread military training, as contributing to a martial spirit, authoritarianism, and war. One of the most influential was Senator Charles Sumner, Republican of Massachusetts and head of the Committee on Foreign Relations, who as a committed pacifist attacked both the French standing army and the German nation in arms. "Military citizenship, according to Prussian rule, is military serfdom," Sumner declared in a widely reprinted speech, "and on this is elevated a military despotism of singular grasp and power, operating throughout the whole nation, like martial law or a state of siege." "An army," he continued, "is a despotism; military service is bondage." Sumner warned that unless war were abolished all nations would have to follow the Prussian model of making every citizen become a soldier.[63] Echoing Sumner, the American Peace Society and the Universal Peace Union blamed both Prussia and France for the war, and decried its basic causes, which they declared to be militarism, the balance-of-power system, and nationalistic ambitions by two despotic regimes.[64]

Germany's defeat of France accelerated the transformation of Europe's military institutions away from long-service professional armies, toward a heavier reliance on easily mobilized reserves prepared through national systems of military training.[65] By the turn of the twentieth century, only Great Britain and the United States (among major powers) had failed to adopt the new, mass conscript-reservist military format, because, as maritime powers, neither imagined that land warfare on a large scale could be necessary or desirable for them.[66]

---

[63] Senator Charles Sumner, lecture at the Music Hall, Boston, October 26, 1870, published subsequently as *The Duel between France and Germany with Its Lesson to Civilization* (Boston, 1871), quote on pages 68–9; see also Sumner's remarks in Congress, February 4, 1871, reprinted in Charles Sumner, *Charles Sumner: His Complete Works*, 20 volumes (Boston, 1900), 18: 319–20.

[64] *Advocate of Peace*, n.s. 20 (August 1870), 270–1, 282–4; (September 1870), 279; (December 1870), 316–17; (February 1871), 15; *Bond of Peace* 3 (December 1870), 113; (June 1871), 90; *Herald of Peace* 12 (June 1871), 221. See also Merle Curti, *Peace or War: The American Struggle, 1636–1936* (Boston, 1936; reprinted 1959), 101–3; and Ekirch, *Civilian and the Military*, 120–3.

[65] See Hew Strachan, *European Armies and the Conduct of War* (London, 1983), 90–129; John Gooch, *Armies in Europe* (London, 1980), 109–44; and the essays in Peter Paret (ed.), *Makers of Modern Strategy: From Machiavelli to the Nuclear Age* (Princeton, 1986), 281–407.

[66] For an overview, see John Whiteclay Chambers II, "The American Debate over Modern War, 1871–1914," in Manfred F. Boemeke, Roger Chickering, and Stig Förster (eds.), *Anticipating Total War: The United States and Germany, 1871–1914* (New York, 1999), 241–80. Within the U.S. Army, Brigadier General Emory Upton advocated copying the extended training and mass conscript-reservist army system of the Prussians (Stephen E. Ambrose, *Upton and the Army* [Baton Rouge, La., 1964]). Some officers thought that the United States should prepare to fight a major power, probably Germany, Britain, or

It was at the turn of the twentieth century that important elements of the American policy elite, the public, and the press became increasingly hostile to Germany.[67] Many Americans came to view Germany as dominated by its military, giving rise to a martial spirit within society, and an aggressive, bellicose foreign policy. German "militarism" came to be seen as antithetical to the ideals and principles of American democracy, which included civilian control of the military, individual initiative, representative government, and the search for a just, stable, and peaceful world order.

But as this survey of the American press has shown, the dominant twentieth-century American view of "militaristic" Prussia was not the dominant American view of 1870–1. The majority of writers in mainstream American publications of that era was not inherently opposed to Prussia and its military system. They supported German unification and looked favorably upon universal military training and service in Prussia as an equitable and efficient system of mobilizing the citizenry in a war for unity and national defense.

When the United States was faced in World War I with raising a mass army for use against Germany, it finally turned to effective national conscription. By then the American national government had begun to emerge as a modern and more centralized state.[68] Its model, however, would not be the German system of permanent, widespread, adult male military training and longtime reserve duty. On the contrary, following the U.S. declaration of war in 1917, Woodrow Wilson, a progressive and reputed "antimilitarist," pressed a divided Congress to adopt a distinctly American version of the *levée en masse*, employing temporary wartime "selective service" – the word "conscription" being avoided yet again.

The administrative machinery of the Selective Service System, although headed by a military bureau in Washington, was highly decentralized and operated through four thousand local draft boards composed of civilian volunteers. Within broad national guidelines, these local draft boards made the actual decisions about which individuals would be drafted and which would remain at home for industrial or domestic reasons. In justifying the selective

---

Japan (James L. Abrahamson, *America Arms for a New Century: The Making of a Great Military Power* [New York, 1981]). However, an alternative to Uptonian conscription was greater emphasis on a volunteer citizen-army, as was proposed by former Union army general and U.S. senator from Illinois, John A. Logan, *The Volunteer Soldier of America* (Chicago, 1887).

[67] On the deterioration of German–American relations between 1870 and 1914, but particularly around the turn of the century, see Schieber, *Transformation of American Sentiment toward Germany, 1870–1914*; Junker, *The Manichean Trap*; Melvin Small, "The American Image of Germany, 1906–1914," Ph.D. dissertation, University of Michigan, 1965; Hans-Jurgen Schroder (ed.), *Confrontation and Cooperation: Germany and the United States in the Era of World War I, 1900–1924* (Oxford, 1993).

[68] See John Whiteclay Chambers II, *The Tyranny of Change: America in the Progressive Era, 1890–1920*, 2nd ed., rev. (New Brunswick, N.J., 2000).

wartime draft, President Wilson rhetorically wove together conscription and America's volunteer tradition when he proclaimed that the new system "is in no sense a conscription of the unwilling. It is rather, selection from a nation which has volunteered in mass."[69] The *levée en masse* had come to the United States, but in its own particular American form. Seventy-two percent of the 3.5 million "doughboys" who served in World War I were raised under its auspices.

Selective service ended with the war, but it was adopted again in virtually the same form in 1940, when the United States rearmed following Hitler's conquest of France. During World War II, although four million Americans served voluntarily, ten million servicemen were drafted. That experience reinforced the success of the twentieth-century American political-military formula of mass recruitment. Yet Americans continued to view even a selective draft as at most a temporary expedient during time of war, and as augmenting voluntarism. Peacetime selective service was renewed during the Cold War to enhance voluntary enlistment. But when it was employed to raise forces for limited, expeditionary wars in Korea and Vietnam, public support for it eventually broke down. In 1973, while disengaging from combat in Vietnam, the United States returned to its tradition of voluntary military service, albeit for what, in relative historical terms, was still a large army.

The citizen-soldier has been a legitimizing image in the raising of America's wartime armies since the origin of the Republic. Indeed, that image is rooted in the local militias supported by most of the original English colonies. The idea of the virtuous republican citizen-soldier, and of the people in arms, emerged in the American Revolution as one of the most powerful myths and icons – the embattled farmer, the Minute Man – of the founding of the nation. Like the legend of the *levée en masse* in France, it has always emphasized the enthusiastic response of citizen-soldiers to the defense of the nation.

Americans have often defined themselves in opposition to Europe. Although many of them could view the Prussian military system as acceptable in Germany in the 1870s, most Americans have viewed permanent systems of universal military service, however equitably administered, as unnecessary and unacceptable in America.[70] The spirit of the *levée en masse* may find an

---

[69] Woodrow Wilson, Statement, May 18, 1917, printed in Arthur S. Link et al. (eds.), *The Papers of Woodrow Wilson*, 69 volumes (Princeton, 1966–94), 41: 181. The World War I draft is analyzed in its historical context in Chambers, *To Raise an Army*; and Chambers (Spring, 2003), "Decision to Draft," *The OAH Magazine of History*, forthcoming.

[70] The one European military system advocated by supporters of an expanded American military in the twentieth century, such as Theodore Roosevelt and Henry Stimson, and Generals Leonard Wood and George Marshall, was that of the Swiss Republic, whose forces were organized as a national militia, with short-term annual military training and long-term service in the reserves. See Chambers, *To Raise an Army*, 79, 97, 104. From 1945 to 1951, the Truman Administration advocated universal military training because of the Cold War, but

American echo in time of war, as it did in Woodrow Wilson's speech in 1917, but the effect has always been fleeting. Without a tradition of strong central government nor a major military threat across its borders, the United States defined its military tradition in terms of the citizen who answered the call when needed by the republic, and then returned to the liberty of civilian life. In America's myth of the citizen-soldier, the second element is as important as the first.

although the legislation of June 1951 was called the Universal Military Training and Service Act, it was merely a continuation of the basic selective service formula first adopted in 1917. See George Q. Flynn, *The Draft, 1940–1973* (Lawrence, Kan., 1993) and, for a comparative analysis in the twentieth century, George Q. Flynn, *Conscription and Democracy: France, Great Britain, and the United States* (Westport, Conn., 2001).

6

Defining the Enemy

War, Law, and the Levée en masse *from 1870 to 1945*

John Horne

The *levée en masse* and comparable myths celebrating popular involvement in the armed forces were central to a fundamental change in the relationship between the political and military spheres in Europe during the long century between the French Revolution and the First World War. In its legendary form, arising from the mass mobilization of French society in 1793, the *levée en masse* presented military recruitment and service as an internalized act of the individual and collective will. With the country and Revolution in danger from invasion, the citizen became a soldier and spontaneously sprang to the defense of both. The state merely confirmed and generalized this act by compulsion.[1] In other cases, too, myths of military service came to revolve around the figure of the volunteer, whether national (as in the German War of Liberation of 1813–5) or revolutionary (the Garabaldini of the Italian war of unification in 1860–1, for instance).[2]

Taken as a whole, these images of armed service were an idealized military expression of a broader transformation in the way state power and national identity were legitimized, in which the claims of dynastic right and social privilege were gradually displaced by growing popular political participation. This process, however bitterly contested, became inexorable during the nineteenth century. By the same token, new forms of political legitimacy

---

[1] Jean-Paul Bertaud, *The Army of the French Revolution: From Citizen-Soldiers to Instruments of Power* (Princeton, 1988); Alan Forrest, *Soldiers of the French Revolution* (Durham, N.C., 1990).

[2] On Germany, see Gordon Craig, *The Politics of the Prussian Army, 1640–1945* (Oxford, 1955; rev. ed., 1978), 53–65; Michael Hughes, *Nationalism and Society: Germany 1800–1945* (London, 1988), 30–54; Thomas Nipperdey, *Germany from Napoleon to Bismarck, 1800–1866* (Dublin, 1996), 67–84; Karen Hagemann, "Nation, Krieg und Geschlechterordnung: Zum kulturellen und politischen Diskurs in der Zeit der antinapoleonischen Erhebung Preußens, 1806–1815," *Geschichte und Gesellschaft* 22 (1996), 564–91. On Italy, see Mario Isnenghi, *Il Mito della grande guerra* (Bologna, 1970; new ed. 1989), 105–8, and idem., *Le Guerre degli italiani fra il 1848 e il 1945* (Rome, 1989).

opened up the possibility of new types of warfare, making the nexus between the two spheres a question of military practicality as well as political
ideology. The increasingly intimate connection between national identity, political legitimacy, and military capacity was one that few states could afford
to ignore.[3]

The military dimension was important for an additional reason. The increasingly absolute secular identities, both national and political, that accompanied the relegitimization of the state through broadened political participation, were established in part through their negative obverse – that is, in
opposition to the idea of the enemy.[4] Almost by definition, military mythology supplied an important source of imagery and language for this binary
formulation of identity and antagonism. Military heroism (whether in the
guise of an ordinary soldier or a popular general) embodied the nation, the
revolution, or the political regime. The enemy was construed in demonized
form as a national, and also sometimes an ideological, foe, and one who
threatened the nation's very existence.

From the start, the *levée en masse* contributed to this definition of the
enemy. The formula of *la patrie en danger*, which antedated it by a year,
underpinned its conception, but so too did the idea of generalized opposition to "tyranny."[5] Indeed, as Peter Paret has argued, the creation of this
ideological antagonism as an instrument of political mobilization was the
preponderant motive for the *levée* of 1793, since there were other solutions
to the strictly military requirements for increased manpower.[6]

This chapter is concerned with the role that the mythology of the *levée en
masse* played in constituting the image of the enemy, and indirectly his reality,
in the reciprocal relations between France, Germany, and other European
powers in the period from the Franco-Prussian War to the Second World
War. This question highlights the way in which different forms of national
political legitimization reacted upon the growing international tension of the
period. It turns on the military experiences of 1870–1 and 1914–18, and also
on the long period of relative peace that separated them, which witnessed the
first attempts to define and regulate combatant status (and hence the enemy)
in international law. First, however, it is necessary to distinguish the various
dimensions of the myth of the *levée en masse*.

---

[3] Michael Howard, *War in European History* (Oxford, 1976), 75–115; Omer Bartov, *Murder in
    our Midst: The Holocaust, Industrial Killing, and Representation* (New York, 1996), 33–50.
[4] This tendency has been recently studied by Michael Jeismann, *Das Vaterland der Feinde:
    Studien zum nationalen Feindbegriff und Selbstverständnis in Deutschland und Frankreich
    1792–1918* (Stuttgart, 1992).
[5] As Alan Forrest described in "*La patrie en danger*: The French Revolution and the First *Levée
    en masse*," this volume, the declaration establishing the *levée en masse* proclaimed that every
    battalion should carry a banner inscribed "The French people risen against tyrants."
[6] Peter Paret, "Conscription and the End of the Ancien Régime in France and Prussia," *Under-
    standing War* (Princeton, 1992), 53–74.

Ambiguities of the Mythology of the *Levée en masse*

The French *levée en masse* of 1793 was and is open to a number of overlapping interpretations, which helps explain the ambiguity as well as the potency of its subsequent mythification. The first such interpretation emphasized the spontaneity and totality of the upsurge (*élan*) of popular support for the defense of the *patrie* and the Revolution. In this form, the idea of the *levée en masse* absorbed that of the Revolutionary volunteer, which had preceded it. Defending the polity and the nation from external menace was considered as elementary a feature of citizenship as political participation. The volunteer spirit was central to the *levée en masse*, despite its coercive nature, since it resolved the contradiction between a duty emanating from citizenship and the need for state compulsion. This feature of the myth was connected to the notion of *la patrie en danger*, so that the *levée en masse* appeared as the appropriate response to an emergency in which national survival was at stake.

The second sense of the *levée en masse* presented it as the equal and universal obligation of male citizens to bear arms and defend the nation, and the corresponding right of the state to organize the nation in arms. Although the decree of 1793 did not summon married men to fight, and was a purely emergency measure, it was perceived to provide an ideological foundation for universal military service as a permanent institution, even if only limited use was subsequently made of systematic conscription by the Revolution or the Napoleonic regime.

A third understanding of the *levée en masse* formulated the idea of mobilizing the whole population – women, children, the old, as well as adult males of military age. It involved the economy as well as the armed forces and had a pronounced ideological dimension, quite apart from the demands of military efficiency. The decree of 1793 not only ordered the young men to go into battle but also envisaged that "the married men shall forge arms and transport provisions; the women shall make tents and clothes, and shall serve in the hospitals; the children shall turn old linen into lint; [and] the old men shall repair to the public places, to stimulate the courage of the warriors and preach the unity of the Republic and hatred of kings." Perhaps not surprisingly, the French Revolution, which sought to create universal male citizenship, also expressed the ideal of an equally universal military mobilization, and thereby intimated the possibility of total war.

For post-Revolutionary French regimes struggling to resolve the legacy of the recent past, the danger of equating citizens with soldiers and political rights with military duties, led to the eclipse of the *levée en masse*, or its absorption into the generalized epic of the Napoleonic wars. It was through the reawakened nationalism of the July Monarchy, and even more through the republicanism that emerged in opposition to it – and went underground during the Second Empire, after the short-lived Second Republic of 1848–51 – that the legend of the *levée en masse* found its definitive form. In the writings of Jules Michelet and Victor Hugo, it became a key component of romantic republicanism, serving to distinguish the Revolutionary wars from their Napoleonic sequel and providing a military basis for the claim that the Revolution created and defended the nation. The *levée en masse* exemplified the general will in its least controversial form, with the response of 1793 seen as the collective apotheosis of the individual revolutionary-patriot.[7]

After the Third Republic was installed in 1870, each of the overlapping meanings of the mythified *levée en masse* outlined earlier shaped different aspects of French military organization and experience. The universal obligation of male citizens to bear arms became the basis for the republican conception of the nation in arms. Initially, this was far from self-evident. Precisely because of its associations with the Revolution, conservatives and even moderate republicans shunned the *levée en masse* as the ideological foundation for conscription. Thiers, still shaken by the Commune, observed that the nation in arms placed a gun on the shoulder of every socialist, and the 1872 military service law represented a compromise between long-term professionals and a highly qualified universal conscription.[8] Generals and the military establishment were even more reluctant to accept a theory of military organization that undermined their professional authority and conservative values.

But for the same reason, the Radical Republic after the Dreyfus Affair invoked the *levée en masse* to underwrite universal military service. The preamble to the crucial 1905 law – which implemented something approaching universal short-service conscription for the fit, adult male population – declared that: "It is from the lofty ideas born of the French Revolution that the military legislation of a great republican democracy must be inspired."[9]

---

[7] Jules Michelet, *Histoire de la révolution française*, 2 volumes (Paris, 1979), 2: 560–6. Michelet's purpose is made quite explicit in the "Légende d'or," the first of whose heroic fables concerns "Nos Armées républicaines" (July 1851) and distinguishes sharply between Napoleon's cavalier attitude toward his men and the revolutionary fraternity that gave birth to the armies of the Republic. "There were no soldiers then, only citizens in arms, who only made war in order to establish peace, to begin building the city of the world. It was the beauty of those times (already ancient and far away): *the polity was the army, the army was the polity [la cité fut l'armée, l'armée fut la cité]*." "Légende d'or," *Oeuvres complètes de Michelet*, 21 volumes (Paris, 1980), 16: 31; italics in the original. Victor Hugo's poem, *Châtiments* (1853), which derides the pretensions of Napoleon III by comparing him unflatteringly with the first Napoleon, and in particular with the Revolution, contains an entire section entitled "Passive obedience" (Book 2, part 7), which contrasts the cowed soldiers who carry out the coup d'état of 2 December 1851 against the Second Republic with the heroic figure of the "Soldier of the Year Two": "The Revolution cried to them: 'Volunteers, / You must die to deliver your brothers, the peoples [of Europe]!'/Content, they answered 'We will.' "

[8] The 1872 law made military service compulsory in principle for the entire adult male population. In reality, many loopholes allowed something approaching a long-service professional army to be approximated. Richard D. Challener, *The French Theory of the Nation in Arms 1866–1939* (New York, 1955), 28–90.

[9] Ibid., 58.

Once introduced, the leveling Jacobinism of the "blood tax" [*impôt du sang*]
gained wide acceptance, which it retained down to the abolition of conscription in 1996.[10] During the First World War, the experience of 1793 was
constantly invoked, not only as the foundation of national defense but as
the yardstick for equality of sacrifice in the trenches. One historian recently
argued that the determination with which French soldiers refused to pursue
suicidal tactics on the western front in 1917 drew upon their sense of being
"citizen-soldiers," with a right to invoke the supreme authority of parliament
and the civil government in deciding how the nation should be defended.[11]

The *levée en masse*, therefore, legitimized universal conscription as a
corollary of citizenship and patriotism, a legitimization that found different
expression in other nations. Like the broader political culture of republicanism, it was associated with, and most readily invoked by, the political left.
But it was a doctrine that met with wider consent than its Jacobin pedigree
might suggest. The idealized view of the original *levée en masse* was an integral part of the official outlook promoted by the Third Republic and its key
supporters, including socialists.[12]

The economic mobilization prefigured by the 1793 decree, which gave
the state sweeping powers of requisition, shaped the republican left's understanding of how to mobilize for an industrial war in 1914–18. The example
of the cannon forgers and pike makers, an important component of the myth
of the original *levée en masse*, was invoked in connection with the munitions
effort, as was the economic Jacobinism of the Convention, in order to justify
state direction of the wartime economy.[13] More generally, it might be argued
that the *levée en masse* in its military, economic and above all its ideological
dimensions, provided the French in 1914–18 with a model for adapting a parliamentary democracy to the requirements of total war. Certainly, this was
how it was seen in retrospect by two critics of the failed German mobilization
in the same conflict. Both Ernst Jünger, in an essay on "total mobilization"
written in 1930, and Erich Ludendorff, in a study of "total war" published
in 1935, considered that the key difference in the performance of the Western

---

[10] Sergio Luzzato, *L'Impôt du sang: La gauche française à l'épreuve de la guerre mondiale,
1900–1945* (Lyon, 1996).

[11] Leonard V. Smith, "Remobilizing the citizen-soldier through the French army mutinies of
1917," in John Horne (ed.), *State, Society and Mobilization in Europe during the First World
War* (Cambridge, 1997), 144–59.

[12] The description of the *levée* by the socialist leader, Jean Jaurès, in his *Histoire socialiste de
la révolution française*, is directly descended from those of Michelet and Hugo, described
earlier in note 7. Jaurès wrote that "the new military tactic of the Revolution [was] the mass
offensive . . . [and] the levy of all citizens. Thus appealed to and organized . . . in all its force,
all its patriotic resources, all its vigor, courage and genius by the Revolution, France was
worth a world. It was worth more than the world of the coalition" (*Histoire socialiste de la
révolution française* [1898; reprinted Paris, 1972], 5: 244).

[13] John Horne, "*L'Impôt du sang*: Republican Rhetoric and Industrial Warfare in France,
1914–1918," *Social History* 14/2 (1989), 201–23.

powers and Germany during the war lay in the formers' ability to mobilize what Ludendorff called the "spiritual and psychic forces of the nation" invented by the French Revolution as the nation in arms.[14] Significantly, the first use of the terms "total war" and "integral war" seems to have occurred in France in 1917–18 to describe the ideological remobilization required by the last phase of the conflict.[15]

It is, however, the first image or sense of the *levée en masse* that will be explored further in this chapter – that is the spontaneous organization of the national defense in a crisis by means of the spirit of volunteer militancy. This goes to the heart of the ideological construction of the *levée en masse*, in which the state calls on the citizen to perform, under threat of compulsion and through state coordination, deeds that he must (by definition) wish to do as an upright individual – that is, resist tyranny and defend the fatherland. This deeply voluntarist impulse, with all its revolutionary associations – being in essence a militarized version of insurrection, directed against the tyrant without rather than within (Figures 8 and 9) – profoundly marked the French experience in 1870–1 and continued to color peoples' understanding of the *levée en masse* down to the Second World War, and beyond. At the same time, however, it was matched by a negative legend (a *mythe noir*) of the insurrectionary citizen, which developed in conservative circles in France, Germany, and elsewhere between 1870 and the 1920s. These antagonistic but reciprocal mythologies – of the citizen-in-arms as law-abiding patriot and as lawless rebel and partisan – in turn helped shape the definition of military enmity more generally, in law, ideology, and practice.

The Franco-Prussian War

The Franco-Prussian War was a pivotal and supremely ironic episode in the crystallization of opposed myths of the *levée en masse*. For the Prussian army, based on an explicitly antirevolutionary variant of universal service (the reforms of 1806–14, as amended by Roon in the 1860s), rapidly demolished the long-service professional army of a Bonapartist regime, only to find itself confronted with an attempted renewal of the *levée en masse* by the nascent Third Republic.

It is important to remember how much the understanding of military events on both sides was shaped by the mythology of the French Revolution. For the men of the new Republic, the precedent of the 1790s was explicit and omnipresent. Even before the final capitulation of Bazaine's army at Metz,

[14] Ernst Jünger, "Die totale Mobilmachung," translated as "La Mobilisation totale," in L. Murard and P. Zylberman (eds.), "Le Soldat du travail: Guerre, fascisme et taylorisme," *Recherches* 32/33 (1978), 35–53; Erich Ludendorff, "The Nature of Totalitarian Warfare," *Der totale Krieg*, translated as *The Nation at War* (London, 1936), 11–24.

[15] John Horne, "Mobilizing for 'total war,'" in Horne, *State, Society and Mobilization*, 4.

FIGURES 8 and 9. Honoré Daumier, *L'appel de leurs réserves* and *La République nous appelle*. Lithographs from *Charivari* (August 31 and September 20, 1870). Photographs courtesy of the Stanford University Art Library.

Honoré Daumier was a mordant critic of the French Second Empire and a bitter opponent of the war that brought it down. Most of the drawings and lithographs he published during or about the Franco-Prussian War portray it as a tragic folly by both sides and as a universal catastrophe for mankind, with death indiscriminately stalking a blasted battlefield. The two lithographs presented here, which appeared three weeks apart in the Parisian magazine *Charivari*, are unusual for their explicit partisanship, and, in the case of the one on the right, for its sympathetic portrayal of the Republican *levée en masse* organized by Léon Gambetta and the Government of National Defense in the fall of 1870. It is the only unambiguously positive image of war or military service to appear in Daumier's work from this period.

Daumier's drawings affirm the moral distinction, advanced by proponents of the nation in arms since the Year II, between the beleaguered draftee and the self-mobilizing citizen-soldier. Both turn upon a central moment in the mobilization process, in which a man leaves his wife and family to go to war (cf. Figure 2). In the German case, however, the man is a reluctant conscript, whose wife holds up their child by way of pleading for mercy

La République nous appelle,
Sachons vaincre ou sachons mourir!

FIGURES 8 and 9. (*continued*) from the press-gang, a gesture that heightens the contrast between pubic and private duty. His French counterpart serves with a glad heart: "The Republic calls us. Let us know how to vanquish, or how to die." Although his wife's posture conveys a realistic degree of anxiety, her resolve is equal to his. The French *franc-tireur*, although fully realized as an individual figure, is shown against a supporting mass of fellow-citizens, including a young boy – another echo of the rhetoric and iconography of the 1790s. The German *Landwehrman* is alone and helpless before the coercive power of the state.

Daumier's Republican soldier also stands as a reproach against the military policies of the recently defunct Second Empire. Although the historical memory of the *levée en masse* was often conflated with that of its Napoleonic sequel (cf. Figures 3 and 4), here the distinction is reinforced. Under the Second Empire, the composite mythology of Revolutionary mobilization and Bonapartist triumphalism came apart, and the two halves confronted each other. The mythologized historiography of the *levée en masse* was the creation chiefly of the Second Empire's republican opponents, who celebrated the soldiers of the Year II not simply as bearers of French historical greatness but as legitimizing symbols of the republican tradition.

in October 1870, irregular Republican units harassed German formations advancing on Paris, with the explicit encouragement of the Republican government.[16] The term by which they immediately became known – "*francs-tireurs*," literally "free-shooters" – went back to 1792.[17] Such units were not envisaged as anything more than a temporary expedient, however, until a new army could be raised on the basis of universal service. Léon Gambetta, a leading member of the Government of National Defense who escaped from Paris in a balloon in October 1870, immediately invoked the memory of 1793 in a renewed call to arms: "The Republic appeals for the support of everyone; its government will make it its duty to utilize everyone's courage, to employ all capacities... *Levons-nous en masse* [let us rise *en masse*] and die rather than submit to the shame of [national] dismemberment."[18] The first decree of the Republican government set up in Tours proposed to create a new army divorced from the professional forces of the Second Empire. It invoked the radical break with the royalist army during the Revolution as a reassuring precedent: "It was by resolutely breaking with tradition that the First Republic was able to realize the prodigious [achievements] of 1792." It went on to formalize the role of the volunteers by creating an "auxiliary army" consisting of "free corps" [*corps francs*] and National Guard units parallel to the regular army; and later decreed a full *levée en masse*, into which the volunteers were incorporated, at the beginning of November.[19]

The resultant reality fell far short of these exalted expectations. Nonetheless, the populations of occupied northern France, Alsace-Lorraine, and the cities, initially responded with a good deal of enthusiasm. The prefect of the Rhône, for example, reported in early September that "the population [appears] to want resistance rather than peace... and many [demand] the *levée en masse*."[20] And while this mood proved unequal in strength and duration in different regions, a heightened feeling of national identity undoubtedly emerged. Together with local measures of self-defense, it allowed a second phase of the war to be opened, one aspect of which was the participation of some 60,000 irregular soldiers outside Paris.[21]

The German response was likewise shaped by the overlapping meanings of the *levée en masse*. The Prussian government accorded legal recognition

---

[16] Stéphane Audoin-Rouzeau, *1870: La France dans la guerre* (Paris, 1989), 195–7.

[17] The *Dictionnaire Littré* of 1878 defines the *francs-tireurs* as "soldiers of certain mobile corps created during the wars of the Revolution." The *Dictionnaire Robert* confirms the Revolutionary origin of the term (1792) which, it states, derives from *corps francs*, a volunteer unit raised in the event of invasion.

[18] Charles de Freycinet, *La Guerre en province pendant le siège de Paris, 1870–1871* (Paris, 1871), 10.

[19] Ibid., 369–468.

[20] Audoin-Rouzeau, *1870: La France dans la guerre*, 205.

[21] Ibid., 198, 210–19.

to the armies levied by the republican government. But the self-recruited volunteers of the *corps francs* were considered illegal and treacherous guer-rillas, necessitating the harshest reprisals against the populations from which they came.[22] The French Ministry of Foreign Affairs was told that *francs-tireurs* would be recognized as soldiers if they were fully incorporated into formal military units and were recognizable as such.[23] But as early as the battle of Bazeilles on 1 September 1870, and before the surrender of nearby Sedan, the First Bavarian Corps engaged in a bitter house-to-house battle with French troops and local civilians, in the course of which the village was burned and a number of civilians (including one woman) were sum-marily executed. During the campaign against the new Republican army on the Loire, collective reprisals for *franc-tireur* actions, directed against local villages and their inhabitants, became common policy in the Twenty-Second Prussian Division as well as in the First Bavarian Corps. On the night of 7–8 October, for example, the town of Ablis, near Orléans, was razed and its male inhabitants killed in reprisal for an attack by *francs-tireurs*.[24] At Varice, also near Orléans, ten *francs-tireurs* of the Lipowski company were summar-ily executed after the latter surrendered after engaging the First Bavarian Corps for three hours. In one of the worst incidents, on 22 January 1871 at Fontenay, four hundred *francs-tireurs* wearing a vestigial uniform attacked a German infantry post and blew up a near-by viaduct, whereupon the out-raged Fifty-Seventh Infantry Regiment burned the village as they retook it, bayoneting the inhabitants and throwing them into the flames.[25] German commanders, at local and senior levels, effectively adopted a doctrine of "military necessity" that condoned whatever severity seemed necessary to repress civilian fighting.

This behavior was partly an operational response to irregular warfare. Although only about a thousand soldiers were lost to *francs-tireurs*, per-haps a quarter of the German troops in France were deployed in protecting the communication lines on which the irregulars preyed.[26] It was also an ideological response to what was understood as a *levée en masse*, in the sense of a spontaneous, emergency mobilization of popular energies. This last was regarded as trebly illegitimate. First, it refused to accept the ver-dict of formal French defeat in conventional battle. Second, it generated

---

[22] Michael Howard, *The Franco-Prussian War: The German Invasion of France, 1870–1871* (London, 1961; new ed., 1979); Audoin-Rouzeau, *1870: La France dans la guerre*, 210–19.

[23] A. Brenet, *La France et l'Allemagne devant le droit international pendant les opérations militaires de la guerre de 1870–71* (Paris, 1902), 10.

[24] M. Stoneman, "The Bavarian Army and French Civilians in the War of 1870–71," *Magis-terarbeit* dissertation, University of Augsburg, 1994, Chapters 4 and 7, for these examples and an illuminating discussion of the questions involved. I should like to thank the author for showing me his work.

[25] Brenet, *La France et l'Allemagne devant le droit international*, 12–15.

[26] Walter Laqueur, *Guerrilla: A Historical Study* (London, 1977), 85.

a "treacherous" [*heimtückisch*] style of combat, including ambush, street-fighting, and barricades, and hence a new and totally negative image of the enemy as an insurrectionary civilian and possibly (by a complete inversion of gendered codes of combat) as a woman.[27] Third, such warfare seemed to be directly inspired by the principles of republicanism and emanated from the Paris revolution. Moltke encapsulated all three objections in a letter to his brother in late October 1870:

> The [Republican] government still tries, by means of lying reports and patriotic phrases, to rouse the unfortunate population of the provinces to a new resistance, to put down which will entail the destruction of whole towns. Then, too, the nagging of the *francs-tireurs* has to be paid for by bloody reprisals, and the war puts on a more violent character. It is bad enough that armies have sometimes to be set to butcher one another; there is no necessity for setting whole nations against each other – that is not progress, but rather a return to barbarism. How little can even the *levée en masse* of a nation, even so brave as this one, do against a never so small but well-trained division of troops![28]

The Franco-Prussian War, in other words, crystallized opposed conceptions of the relationship between nation and military service – that of the risen people improvising an army in its own image to save *la patrie en danger*, on the one side, and that of the army as the School of the Nation explicitly dedicated to resisting revolutionary disorder on the other. Two further distinctions arose from this fundamental divergence of understanding. In the matter of tactics, irregular warfare was seen as patriotic and legitimate to French republicans and as anarchic and treacherous to the Germans. At the level of national stereotypes and the construction of the enemy, 1870 furnished a defining terminology and set of images. Each side accused the other of barbarism and saw itself as, on the French republican side, the defender of civilization against brutal military tyranny and, on the German side, as the upholder of order against lawless insurrection – a view that the repression of the Commune by the *Versaillais* simply confirmed.[29]

These dual contrasting perceptions proved influential and durable. In France, the *levée en masse* of 1870 supplied a rehabilitating myth for the resurgent nationalism of the democratic opposition during the early Third Republic, whose leading figure was Gambetta, and underpinned the left-republican argument for universal military service. Charles de Freycinet,

---

[27] For this new image of warfare, see Stoneman, "The Bavarian Army and French Civilians," 93–7.

[28] Helmuth von Moltke, *Moltke's Letters to His Wife*, 2 volumes (English translation: London, 1896), 2: 231.

[29] On the German side, see Jeismann, *Das Vaterland der Feinde*, and the bibliography in T. Rohrkrämer, *Der Militarismus der "kleinen Leute": Die Kriegervereine im Deutschen Kaiserreich 1871–1914* (Munich, 1990). On the French side, see C. Digeon, *La Crise allemande de la pensée française, 1870–1914* (Paris, 1959); O. Reshef, *Guerres, mythes et caricatures* (Paris, 1984); and Audoin-Rouzeau, *1870: La France dans la guerre*, 261–91.

Gambetta's lieutenant and four times prime minister between 1880 and 1892, argued in 1871 that the collapse of France in 1870 was the fault of the long-service imperial army, and that popular military instruction followed by universal service (which would complete the patriotic education of the citizen) was the proper basis of military recruitment. He concluded by stating the obligation that lay at the heart of the *levée en masse*:

Let us teach our children that to defend the fatherland is not a burden but a duty, a duty like that of defending one's family and home that, in consequence, is close, direct, and personal, the performance of which no one has the right to avoid.[30]

The *franc-tireur* became one of the figures in memoir literature and fiction that incarnated this patriotic will to resist foreign invasion. Epitomizing French individualism and nonchalant courage, he exacted a literary revenge on the overwhelming power and brutal repression of the German enemy in 1870.[31]

Conversely, in a united Germany where the role of the military remained profoundly antirevolutionary and, at the same time, a potent source of political legitimacy for the regime, the *levée en masse* was an anathema. In a revealing incident, the maverick general, Colmar von der Goltz, who had been attached to the General Staff of the Second Army in the 1870 campaign, published a book on Gambetta's armies in 1877, which hazarded the argument that if ever Germany were to suffer a comparable defeat to that of the French at Sedan, it would need to find an equivalent to the French Republican leader and his policies. The professionalization of the Prussian army under Roon's reforms had moved in the opposite direction – even before the experience of revolutionary war in France reinforced everyone's sense of the dangers inherent in the idea of the people in arms divorced from monarchical authority. Von der Goltz found himself exiled for his pains to a small garrison in Thuringia.[32] The significance of the *levée en masse* for the German military after 1870 was better represented in memoirs, regimental histories, and popular literature, in which the *franc-tireur* appears as a demonic figure. Official military thinking about future conflict would henceforth be shaped by a retrospective loathing of irregular and insurrectionary combat, which menaced the conventional understanding of warfare as a professional activity.[33]

---

[30] Freycinet, *La Guerre en province*, 359.

[31] Digeon, *La Crise allemande de la pensée française*, 50–72.

[32] Colmar von der Goltz, *Léon Gambetta und seine Armeen* (Berlin, 1877; translated as *Gambetta et ses armées* [Paris, 1877], esp. 3–6 and 431–65); E. Carrias, *La Pensée militaire allemande* (Paris, 1948), 297.

[33] A. Pingaud, "Impressions de guerre allemandes en 1870," *Revue des Deux Mondes*, 15 September 1915, 371–95; Stoneman, "The Bavarian Army and French Civilian," Chapters 4 and 7.

International Law and the Debate on the *Levée en masse*, 1871–1914

Between 1871 and 1914, the question of the *levée en masse* became part of an international debate over the humanitarian codification of warfare. It is perhaps here that one can best measure how it became a touchstone for different views of legitimate military organization and also for varying constructions of the enemy. The essentially liberal and rational belief that war between "civilized" powers could itself be made more civilized (a belief by no means shared by all parties to the debate) was, ironically, a response to the evidence of war's increasing destructiveness and its tendency to overspill traditional boundaries.[34] Since any attempt at adducing laws of war meant defining legitimate combat, the question of who fought and under what circumstances became a central concern. The Franco-Prussian War overshadowed the entire discussion.

The debate was conducted in three international gatherings, at Brussels in 1874 and at the Hague in 1899 and 1907. It resulted in the Hague Conventions of 1899, which had the status of international law; and in the conventions of 1907, which sought to modify and expand the earlier agreement.[35] The determination of the politically conservative great powers – Russia and Germany – to define legitimate combat in such a way as to exclude (or at least to curb) the *levée en masse* and irregular warfare ran through all three gatherings like a *leitmotiv*. Small powers without a large standing army – Holland, Switzerland, and Belgium, backed by Britain – were equally consistent in their refusal to allow the *levée en masse* to be curtailed in international law.

At the time of the Franco-Prussian War, there was no internationally agreed law that defined the conditions under which civilians might constitute an armed force or the obligations of a hostile army toward them. The only guidance came from the experience of the American Civil War, and notably from article 81 of Francis Lieber's National Enrollment Act, adopted by the Union in 1863,[36] which authorized properly constituted *corps francs* to resist an invasion, although not to rise up against an enemy occupation. At Brussels, the Russian delegation tried both to ban any volunteer force or militia not subject to national military command and – in a veiled reference to 1870 – to place the obligation on the invaded population "to act in conformity with the laws and usages of war, so as to prevent the struggle

---

[34] For the best overview of the subject, see Geoffrey Best, *Humanity in Warfare: The Modern History of the International Law of Armed Conflicts* (London, 1983), at 141 for this particular paradox.

[35] On the Brussels conference of 1874, see J. Lorimer, *The Institutes of the Law of Nations* 2 vols (Edinburgh & London, 1884), 2: 337–402. On the Hague conferences, see J. B. Scott, *The Proceedings of the Hague Peace Conferences: Translation of the Official Texts*, 5 volumes (New York, 1920–1), especially Volumes 1 and 3.

[36] See the discussion of Union and Confederate manpower policies in John Chambers' chapter, "American Views of Conscription and the German Nation in Arms in the Franco-Prussian War," this volume.

becoming cruel and barbarous." In a move that placed the two most compelling interpretations of the *levée en masse* in contrast to each other, the
smaller powers argued that in the absence of universal military service they
had no recourse against aggression other than spontaneous mobilization for
self-defense. They defeated the Russian proposal, replacing it with a new
article (unchanged in the Hague Conventions twenty-five years later) that
stated: "The population of a non-occupied territory who, on the approach
of the enemy, of their own accord take up arms to resist the invading troops,
without having had time to organize themselves, . . . shall be considered belligerents, if they respect the laws and customs of war."[37] The question of
resistance to an occupation remained unregulated.

When the debate was taken up again at the Hague in 1899, the British and
Swiss delegations tried further to strengthen the right of popular resistance
by explicitly endorsing it as a principle and, in the Swiss case, by forbidding
(illegal) retaliation by the invader.[38] In a textbook exposition of popular
mobilization on behalf of *la patrie en danger*, Künzli, the Swiss delegate,
referred to the *levées en masse* in certain parts of Switzerland early in the
century, and to popular Austrian resistance to Napoleon in the Tyrol and
elsewhere.

They fought in open combat; the stragglers were not struck down and the sick and
wounded were not killed. Not only able-bodied men but also old men, children and
women took part in the battles. You will say that this was an excess of patriotism.
Perhaps, but it was an excess which delights the heart and which may occur again.
You will understand that we cannot subscribe to a convention which would subject
part of the population to martial law and courts-martial [i.e., those civilians not part
of an organized unit]. We are of [the] opinion that love of country is a virtue which
should be cultivated and not suppressed.[39]

Such a view was anathema to the German delegate, Colonel Gross von
Schwarzhoff. Revealingly, he considered the tacit basis of the Hague debate to be that "the population shall remain peaceful." Against the right of

---

[37] In Lorimer, *The Institutes of the Law of Nations*. This was article 10 of the Brussels accord,
which became Article 2 of the Hague Conventions of 1899, in which the definition of
the status of belligerent was more logically placed at the head of the accords (Scott, *The
Proceedings of the Hague Peace Conferences*, 1: 53–4, 253–4).

[38] The proposition of the British delegate, Sir John Ardagh, stated: "Nothing in this chapter
shall be considered as tending to lessen or abolish the right belonging to the population of an
invaded country to fulfill its duty of offering by all lawful means, the most energetic patriotic
resistance against the invaders," while that of the Swiss delegation stated more baldly that
"[n]o acts of retaliation shall be exercised against the population of the occupied territory
for having openly taken up arms against the invader" (Scott, *The Proceedings of the Hague
Peace Conferences*, 1: 550). The motivation of the British initiative, coming at the height of
international opprobrium for its conduct of the South African War, which raised just such
issues, requires further investigation.

[39] Scott, *Proceedings of the Hague Peace Conferences*, 1: 551.

civilians to resist, he pitted the rights of the invading soldiers to secure their rear and enjoy peace after open combat. "Since we are speaking of humanity," he stated,

it is time to remember that soldiers are also men, and have a right to be treated with humanity. Soldiers who, exhausted by fatigue after a long march or a battle, come to rest in a village have a right to be sure that the peaceful inhabitants shall not change suddenly into furious enemies.

If the latter resisted, stated Schwarzhoff, they forfeited any claim to be treated as combatants according to the laws of war, since "[a reconciliation of] the interests of large armies, imperiously demand[ing] security for their communications and for their radius of occupation, . . . and those of the invaded peoples, is impossible."

Schwarzhoff declared (with much misgiving) that the Brussels provision already endorsed at the Hague, by which a population openly resisting invasion might enjoy combatant status, marked the extreme limit of German concessions. Despite moral support from the Belgians and French, the British and Swiss, faced with deadlock, withdrew their resolutions.[40] In 1907, the German delegation tried to strengthen its position by requiring irregular forces to communicate their uniforms or distinctive signs to potential enemy powers in advance, again to curb the spontaneous *levée en masse*; but on strenuous French objection the proposal failed, and the 1899 definition of combatant status remained more or less intact.[41]

Most obviously, this international debate turned on the irreconcilable differences between potential invaders with large armies, and smaller powers reliant on an improvised *levée en masse* to deter or resist aggression. But the imaginary and symbolic canvas was larger. The legitimacy of democratic revolution and wars of national liberation had been accepted in principle by liberal states at the end of the nineteenth century. Accordingly, these same powers, including Britain and France, justified the right to civilian participation in national defense, including the self-organizing *levée en masse*, with the full protection of international law. This point of view, it goes without saying, was confined to conflict in Europe. Quite different criteria applied in colonial campaigns. In the German case, on the other hand, the antirevolutionary thrust of the army made any such military participation by civilians deeply suspect, with the *franc-tireur* symbolizing the subversive threat to military authority. Additionally, the doctrine of the key military theorists of the Wilhelmine period, like that of Moltke in 1870, held that law and war were at root incompatible, and that humanitarian considerations that delayed victory (and so prolonged suffering) were counterproductive.

---

[40] Ibid., 1: 552–4.
[41] Ibid., 3: 101–2. The Germans did manage to get accepted an amendment stating that irregular forces had to bear arms openly.

Ironically, as a conservative French military theorist sympathetic to the German position pointed out, the Prussian experience in 1812–13, and especially Frederick-William III's ordinance on the *Landsturm* of the latter year, provided one of the clearest historic statements of the idea of the *levée en masse*. The 1813 order stated that: "Every citizen shall repulse the enemy with the arms at his disposal, whatever these may be" (Article 1). It continued that: "In case of invasion, the *Landsturm* shall fight the enemy in battle and harass his rear and cut his communications" (Article 3). It also stated that "each citizen who is not confronting the enemy or who does not belong to the *Landwehr* shall consider himself to be part of the *Landsturm*, every time that the opportunity presents itself" (Article 5), and that "the *Landsturm* has neither uniform nor special insignia, for these ... would only make it recognized by the enemy and expose it to persecution" (Article 13).

Here was a salutary reminder that there was no exclusive connection between the *levée en masse* and revolution, for it might as easily be associated simply with national defense against a foreign invader, or even with the defense of a conservative polity against a liberal or revolutionary enemy. The notion of a *Volkskrieg*, or "People's War," was indeed bound up with German myths of the 1813 war, as it was with the peasant resistance led by Andreas Hofer in the Austrian Tyrol against Bavarian and Napoleonic forces in 1809. But this was the dark alter ego of Prussian military tradition. Despite the arguments of von der Goltz, Prussian military thinking between 1870 and 1914 preferred offensive, not defensive, strategy. The Schlieffen Plan made the civilian *levée en masse* a purely negative phenomenon, envisaged only as a likely obstacle to German invasion.[42]

The divergence between the German and the Franco-British positions, apparent at the Hague conferences, emerged clearly in the military publications that followed them. Whereas the French, British, and Americans produced military handbooks that simply reproduced the Hague Conventions with a gloss, the Germans proved much more reluctant to communicate the conference results to their troops. The official outlook is indicated by a staff college book, *Kriegsbrauch im Landkriege*, published in 1902, which took a fundamentally skeptical view of the attempt to codify war, warning officers against "excessively humanitarian notions" and arguing that "certain severities are indispensable to war, nay more, ... the only true humanity very often lies in a ruthless application of them."[43] In particular, the German volume came close

---

[42] Gerhard Ritter's classic study, *The Schlieffen Plan: Critique of a Myth* (1956; English translation, London, 1958), has nothing to say on this aspect. But the comportment of the German army in 1914, discussed later, makes it clear that the question had been anticipated, and a systematized application of the response in 1870 envisaged.

[43] Translated into English as J. H. Morgan (ed.), *The German War Book* (London, 1915), 55. For the British manual, see T. E. Holland, *The Laws and Customs of War on Land, as Defined by the Hague Convention of 1899* (London, 1903). For the French manual see Lt. R. Jacomet, *Les Lois de la guerre continentale* (Paris, 1913). For a summary, see G. W. Scott

to denying that the *levée en masse* or *Volkskrieg* (both terms were used) – of which the "horrors" of irregular warfare in 1870 remained the explicit measure – had any valid status in international law. Only if the *levée en masse* was highly organized would it justify the legal protection allowed for by the Hague Conventions of 1899, "a case which is by no means likely to occur often." Assuming that popular insurrection remained an isolated and spontaneous affair, *Kriegsbrauch im Landkriege* considered that no recognition of combatant status could be granted, and that "the disadvantages and severities inherent in such a state of affairs are more insignificant and less inhuman than those which would result from recognition."[44] This was tantamount to justifying the severest repression of civilian resistance.

The Phantom of the *Volkskrieg*, 1914–1918

Not surprisingly, the First World War drew on the myths of military service, and the idealized images of soldiers, that had developed since the French Revolution. In a variety of ways, as has been argued, the *levée en masse* influenced French mobilization for the war and provided one of the legitimizing legends that helped sustain the military effort in the face of unprecedented sacrifice and suffering. In Germany, the myth of a national uprising in 1813 (whose crowning moment, the Battle of Leipzig, had been commemorated in celebration and monument less than a year before the outbreak of hostilities), and the image of the army as the architect of national unity in 1870, contributed in varying degrees to the "ideas of 1914."[45] Military myths thus reinforced the ideological resources of the various wartime powers. One of the difficulties faced by the German, Austro-Hungarian, and Russian armies as the war dragged on lay precisely in the difficulty they faced in infusing the military effort with new, energizing political ideas and symbols, of a kind that had been systematically discounted before the war.[46]

Because military myth and political values were so closely connected, however, the *levée en masse* (understood as a mass civilian uprising) also played a crucial role in defining and demonizing the enemy, via reciprocal "atrocity" allegations. The imaginary construction of the national enemy in

---

and J. W. Garner, *The German War Code Contrasted with the War Manuals of the United States, Great Britain and France* (Washington, D.C., 1918), and J. W. Garner, *International Law and the World War*, 2 volumes (London, 1920), 1: 3–8.

[44] Morgan, *The German War Book*, 63.

[45] Wolfgang J. Mommsen (ed.), "German artists, writers and intellectuals and the meaning of war, 1914–1918," in Horne, *State, Society and Mobilization*, 24–31; George Mosse, *The Nationalization of the Masses: Political Symbolism and Mass Movements in Germany from the Napoleonic Wars through the Third Reich* (Ithaca, N.Y., 1975; new ed., 1991), 64–6.

[46] On the German case, see Wilhelm Deist, "The German army, the authoritarian nation-state and total war," in Horne, *State, Society and Mobilization*, 160–72; for Austria, see Mark Cornwall, "Morale and patriotism in the Austro-Hungarian Army, 1914–1918," in ibid., 173–91.

1914 included, in the German case, the resurgent image of the evil *franc-tireur*. This was grafted onto the military leadership's anticipation that not only France but also small neutral countries like Belgium might engage in a *levée en masse*. Other elements of cultural nationalism, sometimes redirected from the "enemy within" to the external enemy – such as anti-Catholicism and fear of the proletariat – fleshed out the specter of a treacherous insurrection inspired by priests and vaguely reminiscent of the Communards.

The result was deeply paradoxical. In reality, there was no popular resistance of any serious kind in either Belgium or France in August 1914, apart from the mobilization of the rather old-fashioned Belgian bourgeois militia, the *Garde Civique*, including one component that wore only identifying arm bands and hats rather than a full uniform. Even this conformed to the 1907 Hague Conventions. But all seven German armies in the west were swept by a cycle of rumor and self-suggestion, locally turning to hysteria, according to which they were faced with widespread resistance by *francs-tireurs*, often led by priests, who shot, poisoned, and mutilated hapless German soldiers while communicating with the retreating Allied armies.[47]

Immediately, the entire German command structure endorsed and generalized the repression of this phantom enemy with exemplary collective punishments and widespread intimidation of the Belgian and French populations. "Every hostile act of the inhabitants against the German military, every attempt to interrupt their communications with Germany... will be severely punished. All resistance or revolt... will be quelled unmercifully," declared one order by none other than Colmar von der Goltz, who became military governor of Belgium at the end of August 1914.[48] In an eerie echo of the language of *Kriegsbrauch im Landkriege* and other prewar texts, he went on: "It is one of the cruel necessities of war whereby the punishment of hostile acts falls not only upon the guilty but also on the innocent."[49]

---

[47] Ferdinand van Langenhove, *The Growth of a Legend: A Study Based upon the German Accounts of Francs-Tireurs and "Atrocities" in Belgium* (London, 1916). For a full discussion of the "German atrocities" issue, see J. Horne and A. Kramer, *German Atrocities, 1914: A History of Denial* (New Haven, Conn., 2001).

[48] There were other links of personal continuity between senior commanders in 1914 and the young officers of 1870. Generaloberst von Hausen, commander of the Third Army, which was responsible for the single largest slaughter of supposed Belgian *francs-tireurs*, in the taking of Dinant on 23 August 1914 (665 killed), frequently referred to his experiences as a young man in 1870. Karl von Einem, minister of war from 1898 to 1909 and successor to Hausen in command of the Third Army in September 1914, had won the Iron Cross as a seventeen-year-old lieutenant in the Franco-Prussian War, when he was active in combating *francs-tireurs*. M. Kircheisen (ed.), *Des Generalobersten Frhrn. v. Hausen Erinnerungen an den Marnefeldzug 1914: Mit einer einleitenden kritischen Studie* (Leipzig, 1922), passim; Generaloberst von Einem, *Erinnerungen eines Soldaten 1853–1933* (Leipzig, 1933), 12, and passim; and J. Alter (ed.), *Ein Armeeführer erlebt den Weltkrieg: Persönliche Aufzeichnungen des Generalobersten v. Einem* (Leipzig, 1938), 14, and passim.

[49] U.S. National Archives, State Department M 367 763.72/ 1076–1196 (copy of Von der Goltz's declaration, 2 September 1914). See also Colmar von der Goltz, *Denkwürdigkeiten* (Berlin, 1929), passim.

In three months, and principally in ten days from 18 to 28 August, over six thousand civilians were executed, and some twenty thousand buildings deliberately burned down, by the German army in France and Belgium, in defiance of the Hague Conventions, which expressly forbade indiscriminate reprisals.

Since the German army and Supreme Commands took no trouble to hide what they saw as legitimate punishment, the Allied powers, who knew that there had been no civilian resistance (though without necessarily understanding the nature of the German illusion) quickly accused the German army and government of committing "atrocities," and they determined to try those responsible for war crimes.[50] On both sides, the battle of mutual recrimination became a key component of the ideological and cultural mobilization behind the war, with the charge of "atrocities" contributing to the construction of a dehumanized and ferocious image of the enemy. But what matters here is that the *levée en masse*, in the sense of spontaneous, self-organizing popular warfare, lay at the heart of the ensuing war of words.

The Germans portrayed the imaginary *franc-tireur* resistance in Belgium and France as nothing less than a full-scale *Volkskrieg*. The German military's preoccupation with the *levée en masse* turned into a self-fulfilling prophesy: the invading soldiers and military commanders evolved a collective fantasy in which the enemy they had been preprogrammed to find really did appear. When the Belgian government informed the Germans on 8 August of the militarization of the *Garde Civique* and the style of its uniforms (a measure that the Germans had unsuccessfully tried to make compulsory at the Hague in 1907), Wilhelm II raged that the "population of Belgium [had] behaved in a diabolical, not to say bestial manner, not one iota better than the Cossacks."[51] Ten days later, the German Foreign Ministry claimed that "reports from German troops show that contrary to international law a war in which the whole population is involved is being organized in France (and) members of the population in ordinary clothes have treacherously shot at German soldiers."[52] On 7 September 1914, the Foreign Ministry sent a telegram from the Kaiser to Woodrow Wilson formally charging the Belgian government with organizing mass civilian resistance: "The Belgian government has openly encouraged and long since carefully prepared the participation of the Belgian civil population in the fighting. The atrocities committed even by women and priests in this guerrilla warfare, also on wounded soldiers, medical staff and nurses... were such that my generals were finally compelled to take the most drastic measures in order to punish the guilty and to frighten the

---

[50] For the outcome, see J. F. Willis, *Prologue to Nuremberg: The Politics and Diplomacy of Punishing War Criminals of the First World War* (Westport, Conn., 1982).

[51] Politisches Archiv des Auswärtigen Amts, Bonn, R 20880, fol. 8–9, handwritten copy of a pencil-written commentary on the telegram of the Spanish Ambassador in Berlin, received 9 August 1914.

[52] U.S. National Archives, State Department, M 367, 763.72116/ 1–79, note communicated to the French government via the German Embassy in Stockholm, 18 August 1914.

blood-thirsty population from continuing their work of vile murder and horror."[53] German military investigators talked about a rising, or insurrection, by *francs-tireurs*, and when the foreign ministry presented its rebuttal to Allied reports on German "atrocities" in Belgium, it took the form of a large and deliberately falsified report on the supposed Belgian *Volkskrieg*, or *levée en masse*.[54]

The Allies, for their part, did not merely accuse the German army of committing atrocities. They also argued that, although there was no significant civilian resistance, it would have been legitimate, had it occurred, under Article 2 of the 1907 Hague Convention regulating land warfare. In other words, they defended the right of invaded populations to engage in patriotic self-defense and contrasted this with a German doctrine of "military necessity" that rapidly came to exemplify the "barbarism" and naked "militarism" of an authoritarian enemy.

No resolution of these conflicting interpretations of events during the German invasion of France and Belgium was ever reached. This was because of profound disagreement over what had happened, and because an extraordinary case of mass self-suggestion went unrealized and unquestioned by most of those who had been part of it. In addition, the ideological and imaginary frameworks on which meaning was constructed on both sides were so different. The divergent understanding of the laws and customs of war, the opposed legitimacy accorded to the *levée en masse*, and the mutually exclusive visions of the enemy that these helped to create meant that no linguistic or perceptual basis for agreement, let alone reconciliation, existed between the Germans and the Western Allies.

On the contrary, the historical forces that underlay those opposed meanings persisted. Despite the obvious relevance of patriotic self-defense to a partially occupied Weimar Republic – reflected in the postwar agitation of the *Freikorps* and, somewhat differently, in the plans of *Reichswehr* officers like Joachim von Stülpnagel for a *Volkskrieg* – continued condemnation of the imaginary Franco-Belgian *Volkskrieg* of 1914 helped German nationalists close ranks in the wake of what they considered a humiliating defeat.[55]

---

[53] Arthur S. Link (ed.), *The Papers of Woodrow Wilson*, 69 volumes (Princeton, 1979), 31: 17.

[54] Auswärtiges Amt, *Die völkerrechtswidrige Führung des belgischen Volkskrieg* (Berlin, 1915), published in abridged form as *The Belgian People's War: A Violation of International Law. Translations from the Official German White Book, Published by the Imperial Foreign Office* (New York, 1915). On the deliberate suppression and altering of awkward evidence by the Auswärtiges Amt, see P. Schöller, *Le Cas de Louvain et le livre blanc allemand* (Louvain, 1958).

[55] For German military plans for a *Volkskrieg*, see Michael Geyer's "People's War: The German Debate About a *Levée en masse* in October 1918," this volume. For the defense of the intellectual positions of 1914–15 by public servants and nationalist politicians during the Weimar Republic, see Horne and Kramer, *German Atrocities*, 1914, 353–5, 360–5; and Holger H. Herwig, "Clio Deceived: Patriotic Self-Censorship in Germany after the Great War," in S. E. Miller, S. M. Lynn-Jones, and S. Van Evera (eds.), *Military Strategy and the Origins of the First World War* (Princeton, 1991), 262–301.

FIGURE 10. French Resistance Poster, *La Patrie en danger* (1943). Collection D.M.P.A. (Direction de la mémoire, du patrimonie et des archives), French Ministry of Defense.

This poster appeared on the walls of Paris on the night of September 20, 1943, the hundred-and-fifty-first anniversary of the Battle of Valmy. Although that French victory was the work of the remnants of the royal army, stiffened by the volunteers celebrated in François Rude's sculpture (Figures 3 and 4), it is here combined with the memory of the *levée en masse* of the following year to create a composite image of popular resistance to tyranny. The poster is a call for volunteers "like our great ancestors, the volunteers of the *levée en masse*," and takes as its starting point the proclamation of "*la patrie en danger*" (perhaps an understatement, under the circumstances). As in the Guillon-Lethière painting (Figure 2), magistrates in Republican costume enroll a swelling mass of eager citizens with swords held high. The reference to "*francs-tireurs partisans*" recalls the popular resistance of 1870 – the founding myth of the Third Republic; while the call "*en avant et mort aux Boches*" [forward, and death to the Boches] echoes the patriotic rhetoric of World War One, when Germans first became known as "*boches*" [roughly "pigs"]. The poster concludes with a line from Rouget de Lisle's *Marseillaise* (1792): "Let us march, let us march, until an impure blood [of the invader] flows in the furrows [of our fields]."

The young Hitler, among others, made political capital out of the attempt by the Allies in 1919–21 to try the German soldiers deemed responsible for war crimes; in 1927 a massive Reichstag inquiry exonerated the German army for its conduct during the invasion of 1914.[56] During the Second World War, the *Wehrmacht*'s policy toward real or perceived civilian resistance in France (and other countries still covered by international conventions) showed distinct continuity with 1870 and 1914. Hitler, faced with partisan resistance in the East, expressed approval for the conduct of the "old Reich" toward (supposed) Belgian civilian saboteurs in 1914.[57] Irregular warfare was condemned and treated with the same policy of "military necessity" as before, including collective reprisals, punitive arson, and deportations; though of course the scale was far larger and many of the cases related to occupied, as opposed to invaded, territory, on which international deliberations after the First World War (as before) had failed to rule.[58] Conversely, on the French side, a further experience of defeat renewed the relevance of the *levée en masse* as the voluntary and autonomous defense of the Republic. The leading communist military formation took the title "Francs-Tireurs et Partisans,"

FIGURE 10. (*continued*) In reality, of course, the French Resistance was a clandestine organization in which only a small minority of French people participated. The German occupation made mass recruitment of the kind envisioned by the poster impossible. Yet both the rhetorical constructions and the military possibilities of the *levée en masse* retained their power. Charles De Gaulle's externally organized Free French movement called for a "national insurrection" following D-Day in June 1944, an action referred to at the time and since as a *levée en masse*. Although the slow progress of Allied armies led to the insurrection being rapidly countermanded (Jean-Louis Crémieux-Brilhac, *La France libre: De l'appel du 18 juin à la liberation* [Paris, 1996], 772–95), the fact that it was attempted at all illustrates the staying power of the military mythology of the French Revolution for republican France.

---

[56] W. Maser, *Hitler's Letters and Notes* (1973; English translation, London, 1974), 274–5, and on the Allied attempt at trying the German accused, Willis, *Prologue to Nuremberg*; and J. Bell, E. Fischer, and B. Widmann (eds.), *Völkerrecht im Weltkrieg: Dritte Reihe im Werk des Untersuchungsausschusses* (Berlin, 1927).

[57] *Hitler's Table Talk, 1941–44* (1951; English translation, London, 1953), 29. In fact, the person singled out for Hitler's approval was none other than Von der Goltz.

[58] An order by Marshal Keitel of 13 May 1941 stated that *francs-tireurs* should be "liquidated without pity by the combat unit from which they flee," and the Army High Command order of 4 June 1941, anticipating events after the invasion of the Soviet Union, decreed that "agitators, Bolsheviks, *francs-tireurs*, saboteurs, and Jews" should be exterminated (M. Veuthey, "Guerrilla Warfare and Humanitarian Law," in *International Review of the Red Cross* 234 (1983), 115–37, quoted in H. A. Wilson, *International Law and the Use of Force by National Liberation Movements* [Oxford, 1988], 40). Mark Mazower argues that the legacy of 1870 and 1914 was one of the two factors, along with racial views imbibed from the Nazis, that explain the brutality of Wehrmacht antipartisan actions in Greece (*Inside Hitler's Greece: The Experience of Occupation, 1941–1944* [New Haven, Conn., 1993], 157).

and *maquis* leaders declared a *levée en masse* when they moved into open revolt against the Germans (Figure 10).[59]

Conclusion

The *levee en mass* of 1793 set in motion an ideological and political process that would gradually redefine the basis on which European states could demand the military allegiance of their citizen-subjects. This chapter has argued that its impact in the period from 1870 to the era of the world wars, in France and Germany, was twofold. The Third Republic employed the myth of the *levée* to legitimize universal male military service, since it allowed a coercive measure to be presented as an internalized corollary of democratic citizenship, endorsed by the values of Jacobin egalitarianism as well as by historical reference to 1793 and 1870. In Germany, on the other hand, 1870 shifted the military and ideological scales decisively in the other direction. There the prestige of an army composed of short-term conscripts, and officered by aristocratic professionals, provided a different integrative and nationalizing myth for a new regime based on conservative and dynastic principles. The national festival of the Second Reich, *Sedanstag*, celebrated the army's preeminence, both on the battlefield, and as the School of the Nation – not necessarily with equal success.[60] 1870 thus marked the cruelest moment of French self-appraisal in the nineteenth century, while for Germany a comparable hour struck during the First World War, when the Wilhelmine Reich found itself incapable of articulating a vision of the nation – for which its soldiers were fighting and of which the army was ostensibly the School – in terms consonant with the demands of industrialized mass warfare.

The myth of the *levée en masse*, in its several forms, contributed to the identification of the nation as the principal protagonist in European warfare and, by extension, to the definition of the national enemy. Liberal democrats might take a positive view of the citizens rising up to defend the nation by virtue of their own internalization of the state's authority. For more authoritarian regimes, on the other hand, the same phenomenon subverted warfare as an activity firmly controlled by professional soldiers and challenged the values of the conservative elites. In the eyes of the German officer corps, and of Wilhelmine elites generally, the experience of irregular warfare in 1870, personified by the stereotype of the evil *franc-tireur*, revealed the idea of the *levée en masse*, or *Volkskrieg*, to be nothing less than a military expression

---

[59] H. R. Kedward, *In Search of the Maquis: Rural Resistance in Southern France, 1942–1944* (Oxford, 1993), 188.

[60] Mosse, *Nationalization of the Masses*, 90–2. Mosse argues that the conservative and military nature of the celebration ultimately doomed it to failure as a mechanism of enhanced political integration in Wilhelmine Germany, symbolically mirroring the fate of the regime itself.

of the politics of democracy and revolution, to which they remained deeply opposed.

The myth of the *levée en masse* lent new significance to questions of combatant status, and also served as a kind of lens though which the issue could be viewed. By heightening and generalizing the moral basis on which military service was demanded, the ideal of the citizen-soldier inevitably made the distinction of civil and military spheres more difficult. For if the answer to the question "who fights?" was to become "everyone," then questions about the identity and nature of "the enemy" acquired new and disquieting significance. That is why the international debates on the laws of war became so tense and antagonistic, with the Germans in particular anxious that legal protection should not be afforded to the kind of independent citizen-soldier whom they had faced in 1870. The culmination of German anxiety about the people in arms came in the form of the mass delusion that afflicted the German army in 1914, when it found itself confronting an imaginary civilian foe; and in the ensuing dialogue of the deaf over what had occurred, and over the legitimacy of civilian resistance as such. Not surprisingly, the ideological radicalization of relations among European states following the First World War produced further divergence over the legitimacy of popular resistance to invasion and occupation – until the contest of values from which this sprang was closed, in Europe at least, by the outcome of World War II.

7

People's War

The German Debate About a Levée en masse *in October 1918*

Michael Geyer

> The defense of the nation, an insurrection of the people must be initiated....
> There is absolutely no time for delay.
>
> Walther Rathenau, "A Dark Day," October 7, 1918

Insurrectionary warfare is not commonly associated with German military thought or the German way of fighting war.[1] Yet there it is: the call for all-out war in the defense of the nation, for a *levée en masse*, issued on October 7, 1918, and debated at some length by the War Cabinet of Prince Max von Baden, the last imperial government and the first quasi-parliamentary one. To be sure, the appeal referred to a *Volkserhebung* [popular insurrection] rather than a *levée en masse*. But the reference to the French original was used interchangeably at the time. The possibility of "going French" was well understood, with no irony intended.[2]

The appeal was issued by Walther Rathenau, the industrialist and intellectual, against the objections of the guiding spirit of the Supreme Command, General Erich Ludendorff. Rathenau had been involved in the war effort all along, having helped to create a Department of War Raw Materials in 1914. But it is one thing for a leading industrialist to mobilize industry at the beginning of a war. It is an entirely different matter to plead for a popular uprising to continue war in the face of defeat, against Ludendorff, who had come to Berlin to plead for an armistice.

The interest of this chapter is to find out how and to what effect the German government, the military, and a national public came to debate the

---

[1] I would like to thank Karrin Hanshew for research assistance and Miriam Hansen for her careful reading of the manuscript. Dan Moran went far beyond the call of duty in editing this paper, which is based upon a much longer manuscript. A revised version of that additional material has been published under the title "Insurrectionary Warfare" in the *Journal of Modern History* 73 (September 2001).
[2] On the explicit use of the French terminology see Erich Matthias and Rudolf Morsey (eds.), *Die Regierung des Prinzen Max von Baden* (Düsseldorf, 1962), 92, 103.

issue of popular insurrection in 1918, and what this Franco-German hybrid of ideas was about. In the end, Rathenau's call for popular insurrection proves to be as much a matter of coping with defeat as of avoiding it. It also bears upon a debate among historians about the way the First World War ended in Germany. On this issue, most scholars have followed the lead of Gerhard Ritter who considered it an "illusion to believe ... that the German people, half starved and plagued by the influenza virus, 'thinned out' in hundreds of supplementary drafts, would now once again be inflamed in a *furor teutonicus* and would let themselves be formed into a '*levée en masse*.' "[3] This argument is supported by evidence of a "military strike" during the summer of 1918,[4] marked by exhaustion, desperation, and a growing refusal to fight.[5] Nonetheless, it is surprising that Ritter should use such strong language to downplay what he characterizes as mere "ideas of certain literati and publicists,"[6] or that he should refuse to study the "deeply depressing and often chaotic negotiations" that ensued.[7]

A similar reluctance colors the work of Hans-Ulrich Wehler, who has emphasized that the revolution of 1918 was the cumulative effect of long-standing problems.[8] But why should remote causes, which Wehler dates back to the 1890s and before, carry so much weight in explaining 1918, while impending defeat and peace negotiations should matter so little? For Wehler, as for Ritter, a month or two in the calendar of 1918 are missing: the Empire collapses in the face of military defeat sometime between July and September, and history is restarted with the November Revolution.

The most egregious consequence of such neglect is the unwitting perpetuation of the so-called stab-in-the-back legend, according to which the imperial army was sabotaged by civilian politicians, and eventually brought down by unrest and revolution at home.[9] The viciousness of this mythology

---

[3] Gerhard Ritter, *Staatskunst und Kriegshandwerk: Das Problem des "Militarismus" in Deutschland*, 4 volumes (Munich, 1968), 4: 417–18.

[4] Wilhelm Deist, "Der militärische Zusammenbruch des Kaiserreichs. Zur Realität der Dolchstoßlegende," in Wilhelm Deist (ed.), *Militär, Staat und Gesellschaft: Studien zur preußisch-deutschen Militärgeschichte* (Munich, 1991), 211–33; idem., "Verdeckter Militärstreik im Kriegsjahr 1918," in Wolfram Wette (ed.), *Der Krieg des kleinen Mannes: Eine Militärgeschichte von unten* (Munich, 1995), 146–67. Nick Howard, "The German Revolution Defeated and Fascism Deferred: The Servicemen's Revolt and Social Democracy at the End of the First World War, 1918–1920," in Tim Kirk and Anthony McElligott (eds.), *Opposing Fascism: Community, Authority and Resistance in Europe* (Cambridge and New York, 1999), 12–32.

[5] Christoph Jahr, *Gewöhnliche Soldaten: Desertion und Deserteure im deutschen und britischen Heer 1914–1918* (Göttingen, 1998).

[6] Ritter, *Staatskunst*, 4: 418.

[7] Ibid., 425.

[8] Hans-Ulrich Wehler, "Der erste totale Krieg: Woran das deutsche Kaiserreich zugrunde ging – und was darauf folgte," *Die Zeit* (August 20, 1998), 66.

[9] Ulrich Heinemann, *Die verdrängte Niederlage: Politische Öffentlichkeit und Kriegsschuldfrage in der Weimarer Republik* (Göttingen, 1983).

helps to explain the countervailing tendency of historians to overdetermine the causes of the November Revolution and to downplay the fact of defeat. Yet it makes no sense to reject the substance of the stab-in-the-back legend while accepting its logical structure. Interpreting the breakdown of domestic morale as a righteous, politically progressive upheaval, or as a consequence of past injustices, may be closer to the truth than the legend is, but it still garbles and misinterprets the events of October 1918.[10] It also inadvertently slanders all those in Germany who were not on the right, who were desperate about Germany's defeat, and in fact held the right responsible for the disaster. It overlooks the tortured and terrified deliberations that accompanied the single most important event of those weeks – the decision by Max von Baden's government to end the war. The conventional interpretation ignores all those who did not favor peace at any price but, nonetheless, concluded that the war had to end at once if complete social collapse was to be averted. Nor does it account for those who thought that "peace now" was the best thing for Germany, even though they knew that they, rather than the imperial elites, would have to pay the price for German defeat.[11] Finally, the conventional interpretation of how the war ended obscures the deep emotional crisis that ran through German society in the aftermath of defeat.[12]

It is significant, in this last respect, that the idea of popular insurrection, although seriously pressed by its proponents, should have remained a fantasy. Once the decision to end the war had been made, fatigue and resistance precluded all efforts to initiate a national insurrection. Nonetheless, the decision not to pursue real insurrectionary war only enhanced its imaginary hold over the future. Once articulated, the idea of popular insurrection opened a vista of expectations, images, yearnings and desires that would not go away. We discover here not just the repercussions of a lost war but also the contours of a catastrophic nationalism that obliges the citizen to die so the nation might live, articulated as a natural and self-evident reaction to defeat.[13]

Fear of Annihilation

What could possibly have enticed a German War Cabinet to contemplate the idea of "going French" in 1918? This question points simultaneously to concrete events and to the repository of cultural memories that shaped people's reactions to them. The crisis of October 1918 was set in motion by the request of the Supreme Command for an immediate armistice and

[10] Fritz Klein, Willibald Gutsche, and Joachim Petzold, *Deutschland im ersten Weltkrieg* (East Berlin, 1968).
[11] Dieter Riesenberger, *Geschichte der Friedensbewegung in Deutschland von den Anfängen bis 1933* (Göttingen, 1985), 118–23.
[12] An exception is Richard Bessel, *Germany after the First World War* (Oxford, 1993).
[13] See Geyer, "Insurrectionary Warfare," for a more detailed discussion of German expressions of catastrophic nationalism in 1918/19.

peace negotiations and for a more representative government to carry the initiative forward. The request was discussed and accepted at a meeting between Chancellor Count von Hertling, Foreign Minister Paul von Hintze, and the emperor at headquarters in Spa on September 29. A rush of additional meetings followed, leading to the appointment, on October 4, of a new German government under the chancellorship of Prince Max von Baden, including representation of the left-center majority of the Reichstag. A diplomatic note to the American president, Woodrow Wilson, had gone out the night before, initiating a series of diplomatic exchanges that culminated in the armistice of November 11.

The details of what happened on September 29 are, perhaps inevitably, in dispute.[14] At the same time, historians have forgotten something that contemporaries agreed on – that September 29 was the beginning of the end. The stab-in-the-back legend asserts that government officials and members of the Reichstag were shocked by the results of the Spa meeting. The argument continues that whereas Ludendorff, who had previously lost his composure due to the strain of overwork, quickly recovered, the civilians did not. They squandered the last chance of resistance against the Allies and did nothing to stop antiwar propaganda. The result was an armistice that amounted to a capitulation, whereas a continuation of war could have salvaged Germany's position.[15]

The only thing that seems true about this story is that Ludendorff faced the situation of late September with grim resolution and a preternatural calm. His bearing and diction reminded at least one member of his staff of the mythical hero Siegfried.[16] Everyone agreed it was an "overwhelming historical moment."[17] The notion of being overwhelmed is indeed a suitable starting point for unraveling what happened because it appropriately invokes the sublime: on September 29, late in the evening, Ludendorff repeated, in a briefing to his staff officers, something he had apparently said in the War Council – that the field army faced not merely defeat, but imminent annihilation.[18]

---

[14] The two most recent accounts are Joachim Petzold, "Die Entscheidung vom 29. September 1918," *Zeitschrift für Militärgeschichte* 4 (1965), 517–34; and Eberhard Kessel, "Ludendorffs Waffenstillstandsforderung am 29. September 1918," *Militärgeschichtliche Mitteilungen* 4 (1968), 65–86.

[15] Bernhard Schwertfeger, *Das Weltkriegsende: Gedanken über die deutsche Kriegführung* (Potsdam, 1937).

[16] Albrecht von Thaer, *Generalstabsdienst an der Front und in der O. H. L. Aus Briefen und Tagebuchaufzeichnungen, 1915–1919*, edited by Siegfried A. Kaehler (Göttingen, 1958), 234.

[17] Wolfgang Foerster, "Ludendorffs seelische Haltung im Unglück (15. VII. – 26. X. 1918)." Typescript with extensive handwritten revisions. In Bundesarchiv-Militärarchiv Freiburg [hereafter BA-MA], Kriegsgeschichtliches Forschungsanstalt des Heeres, file W10/50723, 90.

[18] Ludendorff later denied having spoken of an impending catastrophe and made it look like an invention of Berlin civilians. He also rejected Paul von Hintze's account of the War Council of September 29. However, Hintze's account is for the most part truthful, and, as far as what happened in Berlin is concerned, Ludendorff plain lied.

The crushing Allied offensive of late September was not the first crisis of 1918. Ludendorff had feared a possible breakthrough of Allied forces since July 18, when French forces counterattacked successfully at Villers-Cotterets. His fears intensified after August 8, when British and Commonwealth formations broke through the German lines at multiple points. The breakthrough of August 8 led the Supreme Command to declare that "the war could no longer be won."[19] This assessment was endorsed by a War Council on August 13–14, an occasion rightly taken as a turning point in German strategic decision making. However, what Ludendorff famously called "the black day of the German Army"[20] should not be allowed to obscure the course of events in late September.

In strategic terms, the crisis involved two very different adversaries – Serbia and the United States. The unraveling of the Serbian front, with Bulgaria suing for peace and Habsburg resistance crumbling, is often regarded as the straw that broke the back of German determination to continue the war.[21] This sounds far-fetched, but a closer look at Germany's strategic situation would suggest otherwise. Altogether more important, though, was the growing role of the American forces. They began to weigh heavily long before they were fully deployed because their presence allowed more effective use of French and British reserves.

The situation was grim. The official briefing of the Supreme Command on September 29 acknowledged that "yesterday our troops in Flanders have suffered a major defeat."[22] Colonel von Thaer, section chief in the Supreme Command, recorded Ludendorff's outlook in his diary:

It can be predicted that the enemy will succeed in the immediate future with a great victory, a breakthrough on an unprecedented scale with the help of the Americans who clamor for battle. Then the western army will loose its last resolve, flood back in dissolution across the Rhine, and carry the revolution into Germany.[23]

Foreign Minister Paul von Hintze later asserted that Ludendorff had previously spoken in the Crown Council to the same effect. On that occasion,

[19] Erich Ludendorff, *Meine Kriegserinnerungen, 1914–1918* (Berlin, 1919), 550–2.

[20] Ibid., 547.

[21] Erich Ludendorff and Hans von Haeften, Notes of General Ludendorff on the events from August 18 to his dismissal [copy of the original] (BA-MA, W10/52066), 8. This was also the assessment of the section chiefs in the Supreme Command. See Foerster, "Ludendorffs seelische Haltung," 90; also Bogdan Krizman, "Der militärische Zusammenbruch auf dem Balkan im Herbst 1918," *Österreichische Osthefte* 10 (1968), 268–93.

[22] The Bavarian military representative at the Supreme Command noted the unusual nature of this admission, which stood in contrast to the habit of "making every set-back into a major German victory" and added that "this unusual veracity makes one think." He concluded that "if they do not find the courage to tell the full truth today, a catastrophe will be inevitable." Königlich bayerischer Militärbevollmächtigter beim Großen Hauptquartier, September 29, 1918; Bayerisches Hauptstaatsarchiv IV [Militärarchiv], Akten Kriegsministerium 1828.

[23] Thaer, *Generalstabsdienst*, 235.

Ludendorff highlighted the possibility of "a breakthrough of the enemy, a decisive defeat at the point of the breakthrough, drawing in neighboring formations, an uncontrolled flooding back of troops and the eventual dissolution of the imperial army with extraordinary losses in men and material."[24] According to Hintze, Supreme Command feared a "catastrophe" on the Russian model, meaning "complete military defeat, capitulation," "*finis Germaniae.*"[25] No wonder some of the assembled staff officers broke down in tears.[26]

Did the Supreme Command actually expect an imminent Allied victory? The question is difficult to answer, not least because the Allies did not actually break through. But the mind-set of Ludendorff and his staff is apparent. Ludendorff reportedly greeted his operations chief, Heye, day after day with a desultory "Now they are through,"[27] and said he wanted an armistice in order "to save his army."[28] Thaer also records Ludendorff saying that "this catastrophe must be prevented at all costs," adding in a curious twist that "for this reason we cannot afford to be beaten anymore."[29] Any tactical defeat, in other words, could trigger collapse. General von Kuhl, a highly esteemed staff officer, reinforces the point with reference to a communication from the Supreme Command on October 3: "The charge is: the armies must be preserved, no catastrophes!"[30] There is thus no doubt that the notion of impending catastrophe was Ludendorff's own. The idea of an "instant armistice" emerged from the frantic attempt to salvage the army in the face of an expected rout and to prevent a Russian-type revolution.

Portrayals of panic in the fall of 1918 normally feature civilian officials and parliamentarians in Berlin, not the senior members of the Supreme Command. This conventional depiction can be traced back to Ludendorff's account of the events of late October, and has become a staple of the stab-in-the-back legend.[31] The civilians, in turn, would subsequently maintain that they had been misled by propaganda and had no idea how serious the

---

[24] The quotation of Ludendorff is by Colonel Heye (chief of Operations Section for the Supreme Command), as represented by Foreign Secretary Paul von Hintze, *Die Ursachen des Deutschen Zusammenbruchs im Jahre 1918*, Volume 2: *Gutachten des Sachverständigen Oberst a.D. Berhard Schwertfeger*, in *Vierte Reihe im Werk des Untersuchungsausschusses der Deutschen Verfassungsgebenenden Nationalversammlung und des Deutschen Reichstages 1919–1926* [hereafter UA 4/2], (Berlin, 1925), 407.

[25] Ludendorff as paraphrased by Hintze, UA 4/2, 408.

[26] Thaer, *Generalstabsdienst*, 235.

[27] Ludendorff quoted by Hintze, UA 4/2, 405, 412.

[28] Hans von Haeften, quoted in Max von Baden, *Erinnerungen und Dokumente* (Berlin and Leipzig, 1928), 340.

[29] Thaer, *Generalstabsdienst*, 235.

[30] Telegram of Supreme Command, October 3, 1918, in the von Kuhl collection (BA-MA, W-10/50652), 194.

[31] Erich Ludendorff, *Urkunden der Obersten Heeresleitung über ihre Tätigkeit 1916–18* (Berlin, 1920), 530.

situation was, a claim that most historians have accepted. Neither version of events corresponds with the facts.

Following the Spa meeting, the Supreme Command sent an emissary, Major von dem Busche, to Berlin to inform the parliamentary representatives of the urgent need for an armistice. Busche lied about the seriousness of the military situation, basing his report upon staff assessments dating from August 13 ("we can no longer impose peace on our enemies") rather than the "catastrophic" appraisal of September 29.[32] Nevertheless, his chief task was to impress on the civilians that they should immediately issue an armistice initiative. Ludendorff wanted an armistice fast and had no patience with civilians haggling over the terms of a new government or, for that matter, the armistice note itself. His relentless demand for haste allowed the Berliners to apprehend what Busche's anachronistically optimistic report had tried to conceal: that the survival of the army depended on getting an armistice "not merely in days, but in hours."[33]

Busche, of course, was not the only one with news from Spa. Paul von Hintze (and Finance Minister Count von Roedern, who had accompanied Hertling to Spa as a potential successor) did not remain silent upon their return and spread the news of impending disaster. As a result, Berlin was abuzz with what Ludendorff only dared to intimate in solemn gestures – that there was an acute danger of the front collapsing and the imperial field army being routed. The civilians knew perfectly well what was going on. The problem was that, at this point in time, they wanted a government of national defense and had to be dragged into armistice negotiations.

Ludendorff's strategic assessment was not shared throughout the army. Some senior officers, like von Gallwitz or von Mudra, strongly rejected the armistice initiative,[34] while others, like von Kuhl and General Wilhelm Groener, Ludendorff's successor at the end of October, thought the strategic assessment was right, but that the decision to initiate negotiations was premature.[35] The most serious opposition came from the army commanded by the crown prince of Prussia, whose chief of staff, von Schulenburg, called the armistice offer a "declaration of bankruptcy."[36] He made no bones, in a private letter, that "a *Feldherr* who has the fate of 70 million people in his hand must have nerve. If he loses his nerve, he must go. To stay without nerve is

---

[32] Ibid., 535–8.

[33] Note of State Secretary Count Roedern on the events leading to the peace and armistice offer of October 4, 1918, in UA 4/2, 418.

[34] Matthias and Morsey, *Max von Baden*, 397–411.

[35] Max von Gallwitz, *Meine Führertätigkeit im Weltkriege 1914/1916: Belgien, Osten, Balkan* (Berlin, 1929), 441. Von Kuhl, diary excerpts, September 30, 1918, von Kuhl collection (BA-MA W10/50652), 194. Letter of Wilhelm Groener to Paul von Hintze, October 28, 1918, in Foerster, "Ludendorffs Seelische Haltung," 102–3.

[36] Undated note by Schulenburg, in BA-MA, Nachlass Schulenburg, file N-58/1, p. 221.

unthinkable."[37] The implacable hostility emanating from the crown prince's staff was one of the reasons Ludendorff was not just relieved, but fired, at the end of October.[38] The deep rift between field army commands and Supreme Command was in any case apparent to everyone. It was papered over only in hindsight.

The Supreme Command regained some of its composure by October 6 (that is, after the armistice note had gone out), when it reported that "after initial successes of the enemy the situation has calmed down.... The planned breakthrough has failed."[39] Nevertheless, its confidence that the army could hold a defensive line was gone.[40] On October 23, Field Marshall Paul von Hindenburg, Ludendorff's formal superior, signed an order declaring that "the forces of the field army do not suffice to guarantee holding fixed positions,"[41] a phrase that Groener would repeat in his retrospective *tour d'horizon* to the Cabinet on November 5.[42] The latter may have been too optimistic: there is evidence that on November 4–5, in the battle of Valenciennes and at the Sambre, German units took flight.[43] This suggests that, in the end, the German field army was saved by the armistice.

Even if, as is likely, the idea of an armistice was the brainchild of the Supreme Command's section chiefs, Ludendorff had made it his own.[44] He was well aware that the "offer" of an armistice was a "grave decision." While he occasionally wavered, he stuck to it for the time being, and only later came to regret it.[45] Hindenburg backed him up in the Crown Council of September 29, although he was apparently more noncommittal when it came to implementing the initiative. Fundamentally, Hindenburg agreed with his staff's assessment.[46] He and Ludendorff had come to the conclusion – and

---

[37] Foerster, "Ludendorffs Seelische Haltung," 104.

[38] Within the framework of the stab-in-the-back debate, there was always another, equally vicious, but entirely internal, debate about the military leadership having lost its nerve and raised "the white flag." This debate resurfaced in earnest in 1942–3 (both among the Nazis and within the military leadership), but by then it had been transformed by the mythical memory of 1918.

[39] Von Tieschowitz, Research Notes for the final volume [of *Der Weltkrieg 1914–1918*], summer 1940 (BA-MA W10/50726), 15.

[40] Ibid., 17.

[41] Instructions to the Armistice Commission, October 23, 1918 (signed by Hindenburg and Ludendorff); *Amtliche Urkunden zur Vorgeschichte des Waffenstillstandes 1918*, 2nd ed. (Berlin, 1924), 191–2.

[42] Meeting of the cabinet with General Groener, November 5, 1918, in Matthias and Morsey, *Max von Baden*, especially 529–32.

[43] J. P. Harris, "Das britische Expeditionsheer in der Hundert Tage Schlacht vom 8. August bis 11. November 1918," in Jörg Dupler and Gerhad P. Groß (eds.), *Kriegsende 1918: Ereignis, Wirkung, Nachwirkung* (Munich, 1999), 116–34, here 133.

[44] Ritter, *Staatskunst*, 4: 415, speaks of a "palace revolution" of the section chiefs.

[45] Ludendorff, *Kriegserinnerungen*, 582.

[46] Paul von Hindenburg, *Aus meinem Leben* (Leipzig, 1934), 306.

the emperor concurred – that the military situation had become untenable. They were prepared to bring the war to an end and, within narrow limits, to accept responsibility for defeat, provided revolution, which they always envisioned as arising from a routed field army, could be averted.

The problem is that the terms the Supreme Command deemed acceptable are difficult to square with an admission of defeat. This has led some historians to suspect that the offer was deceitful.[47] Such a reading, while not implausible, misses an important aspect of the Supreme Command's desperation. The Supreme Command kept open the possibility of a renewal or a continuation of war[48] – but if it came to it, it was to be war in a different key.

Terms of Honor

Ludendorff had old-fashioned ideas about the peace process. He thought that, once Germany's offer of negotiations was accepted, delegates would be sent to Washington while a cease-fire would take effect for the duration of the meetings.[49] This sounds like a fairytale ending for World War I, but it is what the Supreme Command imagined at the end of September. The seriousness of such expectations can be gauged by the fact that Ludendorff condoned concessions that only a month earlier had been unthinkable. He accepted President Wilson's Fourteen Points (some tinkering aside), pushed for a parliamentarization of the German government, and was ready to negotiate about Lorraine. Furthermore, he agreed to a staged, complete withdrawal of German troops from western occupied territories, once an armistice was in place. All this reinforces the sense of absolute urgency. In Ludendorff's mind, however, the desire for quick action combined with a powerful sense of entitlement to equal treatment. Ludendorff repeated like a mantra that "the German people had a right to honorable conditions," if only because they fought so hard for so long. He was thus caught on the horns of a dilemma. Ludendorff felt he had to make peace in order to save a defeated army from revolutionary dissolution. But in order to make peace with a defeated army, he could not back up the claim to equal status that honor demanded.

It was in this atmosphere that ideas about insurrectionary war began to take shape. The issue came up briefly, during a private conversation between Ludendorff and Ernst von Eisenhart-Rothe after the staff briefing on September 29. They began by reminiscing about a more glorious past. At the end, Eisenhart-Rothe brought up the issue of a renewal of hostilities if, "as was to be expected, the allies were to make insufferable demands."

---

[47] Bullitt Lowry, *Armistice 1918* (Kent, Ohio, 1996); Pierre Renouvin, *L'armistice de Rethondes, 11 Novembre 1918: Trent journées qui on fait la France* (Paris, 1968).
[48] Von Tieschowitz, Research Notes, p. 18, in BA-MA W10/50726.
[49] Ludendorff, *Urkunden der Obersten Heeresleitung*, 534.

Then, will Your Excellency not hope with me that a *furor teutonicus* will break out in the entire land, like August 1914 had seen, which will give us the ability to fight on, albeit unto destruction. His [Ludendorff's] eyes started to gleam and he responded with a strong and secure voice: "I count on it and hope for sure."[50]

We should take this effusion as an indication that the Supreme Command always considered a renewal of hostilities possible. But we should also note a change of register. The war to be fought in the aftermath of the army's defeat – there is no other way to describe it – had no particular strategic purpose, not even the defense of Germany's territorial integrity. Renewal of hostilities meant engaging in a war of honor leading to self-destruction.

An assessment of the situation by the Political Section of the Supreme Command on October 6 amplified the notion of war "unto destruction" and suggested that Ludendorff's remark was no mere outburst. It started from the presumption that the "offer" of an armistice would fail. It ended with the explication of what a war unto destruction entailed:

If the Entente does not countenance the armistice and peace offer, but forces us down on our knees, they will find the people and the army ready to defend German honor and German soil to the last. The army's might is not yet broken. Step by step we will retreat toward the borders of the Reich. If the occupied territories are given over to devastation, the Allies will be responsible.[51]

This is war in a new key, set in motion by an expectation of, and readiness for, collective self-destruction. The latter grants the license for devastation without guilt. A dead man can kill with impunity.

The push for an armistice, alongside simultaneous contemplation of renewed hostilities on even more destructive terms, is best understood not as some devious deception, but as a reflection of the disorientation that accompanied the military leadership's recognition of personal failure. In these circumstances, ideas and images of a war *à outrance*, of popular mobilization [*levée en masse*] or insurrection [*Volksaufstand*], a people's war [*Volkskrieg*], came to flourish. The language of October 1918 is the language of the freefall into defeat.

October 1918 was a phantasmagoric moment, in which the extremes of twentieth-century German existence were touched in a month-long controversy over how to obtain an honorable peace by continuing the war, or at least threatening to do so. Whether one considers the story of these days as a descent into capitulation (Ritter) or as marking the ascendancy of popular sovereignty and democracy (Wehler), the missing piece is the political debate on armed resistance to defend the Fatherland. This was the major choice to be made in October 1918 – and it was only after the option of a people's

[50] Ernst von Eisenhart-Rothe, *Im Banne der Persönlichkeit: Aus den Lebenserinnerungen des Generals der Infantrie a.D.* (Berlin, 1931), 122–3.

[51] Von Tieschowitz, Research Notes, p. 17, in BA-MA W10/50726.

war of national defense was rejected that defeat and revolution could take their course.

There were three distinct projects, each with its own proponents. Some sought merely to simulate national defense in order to ease a defeated nation into accepting peace without revolution. Others called for a *levée en masse* to fight for the integrity of the nation. Still others sought a terminal battle [*Endkampf*] to salvage the honor of the German army.

The first initiative to call up a *levée en masse* came from an unexpected quarter, the former admiral turned foreign minister Paul von Hintze.[52] He had gone to Spa on September 28 to present a plan for "the defense of the Fatherland," which he had been pushed to develop by key staff officers in the Supreme Command.[53] At this stage, however, Hitze's conception of what constituted defense was decidedly pessimistic. The challenge, he argued, was "to facilitate the transition from victory to defeat," lest the country be dealt a "shock that the Empire and monarchy might not survive."[54] The example of Russia was clearly on his mind. Defeat itself was no longer at issue. It was a fact one had to work with. But the transition to defeat needed political staging if it was not to end in the nightmare of a "revolution from below." Hintze proposed instead to launch a "revolution from above."[55]

The idea of a revolution from above came straight from a Foreign Office memorandum that advised "[gathering] the forces of the nation on the broadest possible basis in order to make them usable for the defense of the Fatherland."[56] This reflected an ideal of national coalescence that can be traced back to August 1914, and that was what Hintze set out to present in Spa. It was a plan to salvage the monarchy while including the parliamentary majority in government, and directing peace feelers toward the American president, Woodrow Wilson. That plan became the guideline for political action, which Ludendorff adopted as his own.[57] Under the impact of Ludendorff's confession about the threat of imminent annihilation in the War Council of September 29, however, Hintze's rhetoric underwent spontaneous mutation. Overnight the imperial official turned into a Prussian nationalist, issuing an incendiary call for a *Volkskrieg* that would "put the last man onto the front" under the battlecry: "The Fatherland is in danger."[58]

[52] *Aufzeichnung des Auswärtigen Amtes* (September 28, 1918), in *Amtliche Urkunden zur Vorgeschichte des Waffenstillstandes*, 47; also UA 4/2, 405–6.
[53] Johannes Hürter (ed.), *Paul von Hintze, Marineoffizier, Diplomat, Staatssekretär: Dokumente einer Karriere zwischen Militär und Politik, 1903–1918* (Munich, 1998), 103–107; Ritter, *Staatskunst*, 4: 415.
[54] UA 4/2, 401
[55] See UA 4/2, 386–415, 401, 406.
[56] Memorandum, signed by Rosenberg, Bergen, and Stumm, September 28, 1918, in *Amtliche Urkunden zur Vorgeschichte des Waffenstillstandes*, 47. See Hürter, *Paul von Hintze*, 103–5, 639–40.
[57] Ibid., 640–2, 643.
[58] UA 4/2, 406.

Still, Hintze remained the consummate Wilhelmine official. He tapped into a powerful rhetoric but feared the consequences. The new, inclusive parliamentary cabinet would merely appear to be one.[59] Rather than calling for a people's war, the new government was to act *as if* the people were ready to fight:

> The purpose is to generate *an atmosphere* at home and to convey this sentiment to the enemies, *as if* the German people – in a summons to each and every one to dedicate their abilities and their lives to the deliverance of the fatherland – *were united and would want to act* accordingly.[60]

Hintze wanted the "*appearance and sound* of a united front of the German people, prepared to die rather than accept a dishonorable and unbearable peace" in order to finesse his way out of a revolution at home and deceive the Allies abroad.[61] His plan was to simulate a people's war.

That Hintze chose to propose a people's war, and that he did not want to act on the proposal, are of equal importance. In the first place, it is striking how self-evidently compelling the rhetoric of a people's war appeared. Obviously, the idea of popular insurrection was part of a readily available cultural inventory. By the same token, Hintze considered it "an illusion that the German people would go down in an honorable last stand."[62] Nor did he really want the people to rise – because this would have amounted to the very revolution he wished to avert. The fear of revolution outweighed the desire for desperate action. The result was a game of smoke and mirrors meant to deceive both the enemy and the nation.

It was Max von Baden who seemed best suited to play the leading role in this situation. Max wanted to save his patrimony from invasion and revolution and had convinced himself – he had thought differently only a year earlier – that representative government legitimized by the monarchical principle could combine to mobilize people even at this point in the war, provided the initiative was linked to a call for a nonannexationist peace. In his assessment of the military situation, Max relied for the most part on Crown Prince Rupprecht of Bavaria, the commander of one of the armies on the western front. Rupprecht was far more clear-headed than Max, insisting that peace at all cost was the only chance for Germany to survive reasonably intact.[63] Max accepted Rupprecht's military assessments but

---

[59] Hintze speaks explicitly of a "democratic façade." Hürter, *Paul von Hintze*, 666.

[60] Ibid., 406 [emphasis added].

[61] Ibid.

[62] Ibid.

[63] Rupprecht to Max von Baden, August 15, 1918, in Max von Baden, *Erinnerungen*, 288–9. On October 18, Rupprecht wrote to Max again: "Perhaps you are interested to hear something about the military situation. Our soldiers are over-tired and have suffered horrendous losses. I do not expect very much for a *levée en masse* following Carnot's example at the beginning of the French Revolutionary wars. The *levée* was so successful because it occurred at the beginning of the war, but we are in our fifth year of war and our reserves are exhausted to the limit....Ludendorff does not recognize the entire seriousness of the situation. We

disagreed with him on the remedy. He thought that a broadly based, non-partisan government stood a chance to rouse the nation, and if necessary to withstand an invasion, on which basis he hoped to negotiate a mutually agreeable peace with the Allies.[64]

This perspective was widely shared among the Berlin political elite and members of the Reichstag, although by the end of October it was to be abandoned by all concerned, including Max himself. In late September, though, the alliance of majority parties in the Reichstag – the so-called *Interfraktionelle Ausschuß* – agreed to constitute a "strong...government for the organization of national defense and the pursuit of a compromise peace."[65] Max's recollection that "again and again the phrase 'Ministry of National Defense' comes up" is quite to the point.[66] A draft memorandum of the majority parties insisted:

German defensive strength is insurmountable, provided all popular forces are put at the service of an unequivocal political idea. Only the recognition of the insurmountable obstacle of popular resistance will bring the enemy to negotiations and secure for us the benefits of a negotiated peace.[67]

The quest for a compromise peace was tied to the idea that only parliament could mobilize the power of the people [*Volkskraft*] to achieve a negotiated settlement. As keenly as the majority parties were aware of the profound war-weariness of the German population, so were they prepared "to do the utmost in order to defend the vital interests of the nation and the population," as the Social Democratic Party leader Friedrich Ebert put it.[68] Even Philipp Scheidemann, one of the more skeptical Social Democrats, wrote a lead article in *Vorwärts* demanding the organization of a national defense, if a just and equitable peace was not to be had.[69] In the end, the parliamentarians had talked themselves into thinking not only that they could do a better job of governing Germany but that they could deliver a peace in which Germany

---

must have peace under all circumstances, before the enemy forces its way into Germany; or woe is us." Max von Baden, *Erinnerungen*, 466–7.

[64] See Klaus Epstein, "Wrong Man in the Maelstrom: The Government of Max von Baden," *Review of Politics* 26/2 (1962), 215–43. Max's connection to the "ethical imperialism" movement (which informed his stand on peace) has recently resurfaced in Eberhard Demm, "Kurt Hahn's Memorandum on the Subject of Ethical Imperialism 1918," *War in History* 5 (1) (1998), 84–120.

[65] Conrad Haußmann, *Schlaglichter: Reichstagsbriefe und Aufzeichnungen* (Frankfurt am Main, 1924), 227–8. In view of the worsening military situation, the *Interfraktionelle Ausschuß* insisted that defense was no longer a military but rather a "political-moral issue." Erich Matthias and Rudolf Morsey (eds.), *Der Interfraktionelle Ausschuß 1917/1918*, 2 volumes (Düsseldorf, 1959), 2: 653.

[66] Max von Baden, *Erinnerungen*, 319–20.

[67] Matthias and Morsey, *Interfraktioneller Ausschuß*, 2: 653.

[68] *Vossische Zeitung*, no. 489 (September 24, 1918).

[69] *Vorwärts*, September 24, 1918.

would be treated as an equal – perhaps even a bit more than that – among the warring powers.

This conviction of the parliamentary majority is best captured by Konrad Haussmann, a dyed-in-the-wool liberal from Württemberg and state secretary in the new cabinet, who became one of the main champions of a *levée en masse.*

We have starved, suffered want, and fought. We could not gain victory against the superior force of the enemy, but we have gained liberty at home. Much is achieved. Greater things are yet to come. Germany is on its way to become the freest nation of the world.... Onwards German people, defend yourself and your young freedom. We are in for a fight that is as just and sacred as any nation has ever fought. War weariness is a burden on other peoples as well. Now they are the ones who moan under their chauvinist rulers. They will recognize, in the newly found resistance of our regiments, throwing themselves against the enemy out of their own free will, that a free people that fights for its life is invincible.[70]

Max von Baden set out to launch a government of national defense. He insisted, in the draft for his (undelivered) maiden speech before the Reichstag, that it may yet be that "the German people will be called upon to bring into action their devotion and voluntary spirit, in order to fight a battle of life and death."[71] However, he was stopped cold by the Supreme Command and the Foreign Office, which declared that the new government was headed for military disaster if it did not go along with Ludendorff's armistice initiative.[72] While Ludendorff was mortified by the threat of an imminent military collapse, and the Foreign Office was dissimulating, the parliamentarians in Berlin and a chancellor who is generally regarded as weak were prepared to raise the nation in order to avert a "national humiliation."[73] The irony is compounded by the fact that the kind of government the American president wanted to see installed in Germany was the only one, at this point, ready to fight on – for peace, to be sure, but fight all the same. If nothing came of the call for a government of national defense in early October, it was because the Supreme Command wanted an "instant peace" and was desperate enough to squash the faintest trace of national self-assertion in order to avert the breakdown of the army in the field.

---

[70] This particular draft was written on October 19; this draft and those emanating from the War Ministry deserve a more detailed analysis to study their mixture of radical republicanism, racism, and totalitarianism. All reflected an attitude, dating back into the summer of 1918, that was central to the formation of the new government: that domestic liberty was worth fighting for and that the latter was now threatened by the chauvinism of the enemy. Hauptstaatsarchiv Stuttgart, Nachlaß Conrad Haußmann Q1/2/17.

[71] Max von Baden, *Erinnerungen*, 366.

[72] Max von Baden, *Erinnerungen*, 356–9; Matthias and Morsey, *Max von Baden*, 65–82, especially 77–82.

[73] Max von Baden, *Erinnerungen*, 367.

This is where Rathenau intervened, in an act of high drama. He had been stewing over the formation of the new government and the news about the Supreme Command's armistice initiative. He insisted that the desperate military situation demanded a radical departure from older practices. In an initial piece called "The Hour Tolls" he called for "popular resistance, a national defense, the organization of mass insurrection. Not for the purpose of annexation, not for the purpose of prolonging the war, but for peace. For a dignified peace."[74] This unpublished statement circulated widely among Berlin elites, and was presented to the Cabinet on October 6 by Finance Minister Count von Roedern.[75] On October 7, Rathenau's call for a *levée en masse* appeared in a right-of-center bourgeois newspaper, the *Vossische Zeitung*, under the title "A Black Day."[76] Rathenau continued to defend his position into January 1919, when he published a brief essay called "The Darkest Hour."[77] In it he argued that, if only a *levée* had been called in October, a cease-fire could have been achieved sooner, which would have prevented the collapse of the home front and the revolution.

The excitement over Rathenau's action largely focused on his public attack on Ludendorff. The military may surrender if it must, Rathenau insisted, but diplomacy cannot negotiate capitulation. Germany's "black day" had come when Ludendorff lost his composure. The solution was unequivocal: "Those who lost their nerve must be replaced." But Ludendorff was not the only victim of Rathenau's impassioned plea for "mass insurrection" and "people's war." Popular insurrection as he conceived it entailed a call to arms that was "frank and truthful" – which was to say that it should come "not from army bullies, naval enthusiasts, or movie producers; not in the old language, but in a new one." It required volunteers, rather than an extension of conscription and auxiliary service, which was a slap in the face of the War Ministry. And it demanded a total mobilization of resources, for in Rathenau's view "the country is [still] unexhausted." Such mobilization was not going to happen with a mere "parliamentarization of the administrative state."[78]

It goes without saying that the insistence on combing through factories, offices, and public spaces for additional manpower did not exactly endear him to the masses either. For all the shared sentiment and symbolism of the appeal for national defense, it was stunningly bad politics. Nonetheless, Rathenau had pushed the issue of popular insurrection back onto the political agenda. His initiative also entailed elements of political and military thought that have more far-ranging implications. In Rathenau's scheme, voluntarism

---

[74] Walther Rathenau, "Die Stunde drängt," *Nachgelassene Schriften* (Berlin, 1928), 68–9.
[75] Gerhard Hecker, *Walther Rathenau und sein Verhältnis zu Militär und Krieg* (Boppard am Rhein, 1983), 428–44.
[76] Walther Rathenau, "Ein dunkler Tag," *Vossische Zeitung*, October 7, 1918, also in Walther Rathenau, *Gesammelte Schriften*, 7 volumes (Berlin, 1929), 6: 258–61.
[77] Walther Rathenau, "Die dunkelste Stunde," *Die Zukunft* 27/14 (1919); 50–4.
[78] Rathenau, "Die Stunde drängt," 68–9.

was the key to releasing the people's power [*Volkskraft*]. Subjects could be pressed into service, but citizens were ready to give their all, if their "will to self-assertion and self-determination in liberty" was rallied.[79] The spirit of voluntarism could not be had for war aims such as "the usurpation of global hegemony." Above all, it could not be achieved by implanting a "barren and superannuated militarism and feudalism among the new nations of the world."[80] Rather than fighting for territory or material gain, free citizens fought for values that they held dear.

Popular insurrection, as Rathenau envisioned it, was above all war over self-government and self-determination – an act of the nation and also of nationalization. In his view, national wars based on a *levée en masse* had to be fought for subjective aims such as dignity or integrity, and ultimately for survival and its prerequisites – the ability to "work" and the right to "living space." All modern war, Rathenau insisted, was in this sense ideological war or, as he called it, *Gesinnungskrieg*. This was the war he thought the Germans should have fought in the first place. It was the only war they would still fight in 1918.[81]

Ideological, nationalizing war entailed, however paradoxically, a radical increase of state power. Rathenau demanded the creation of a civilian Ministry of Defense, tailored to the needs of a people's state, in contrast to the Wilhelmine class- and caste-state.[82] He reasoned that inasmuch as the people ruled, they ruled over themselves. And since they ruled over themselves, the effect of democratic self-determination consisted in "the overwhelming strengthening of the state in relation to the individual will." Nobody rules more totally than the people themselves. A people's state thrives both on the state's "amplitude of power" [*Machtfülle*] and the "devotion" [*Hingabe*] of individuals.[83] The combination of state power and popular devotion is the very signature of the people's state fighting a people's war. Insurrectionary war is thus a violent *plébiscite de tous les jours* orchestrated by the state.

Rathenau's initiative came to naught. On October 9, two days after its publication, Max von Baden presented Ludendorff with a questionnaire, attempting to nail him down on the issue of national defense. Among other things he asked whether the "*levée en masse* . . . as it has been proposed by Rathenau in the *Vossische Zeitung*" provided a "sufficient improvement of forces." Ludendorff's answer was unequivocal. "No. I do not expect anything from a *levée en masse*. . . . The *levée en masse* would destroy more than

---

[79] Rathenau, "Ein dunkler Tag," *Gesammelte Schriften*, 6: 258–61.

[80] Ibid.

[81] On Rathenau's ideas about ideological war, see Walther Rathenau, *Zeitliches* (Berlin, 1919), 71–82.

[82] Paul Letourneau, *Walther Rathenau ou le Rêve Prométhéen: Pensée Politique et Economique (1867–1922)* (Quebec, 1987).

[83] Walther Rathenau, *Von kommenden Dingen*, in *Walther Rathenau-Gesamtausgabe* (Munich and Heidelberg, 1977), 465.

one can tolerate."[84] This apodictic rejection was not the end of deliberations about national defense or, for that matter, preparations for a *levée en masse*; but it nipped in the bud any further initiative along this line by the new parliamentary government. On October 9, the Supreme Command still wanted to avoid anything that could jeopardize the armistice – and surely did not want the civilians in Berlin and, for that matter, a German Jew, to organize national defense.[85] Rathenau's initiative was too republican for the military, and too much war for the republicans.[86] Rathenau himself stuck to his idea but cut his losses. Within little more than a week after the call for popular insurrection, he demanded the systematic demobilization of Germany. He was enough of a calculating *grand bourgeois* to realize that, if defeat could not be averted and a *levée* could not be raised, one could at least bring home the army without causing a revolution. However genuine his desire to defend the Fatherland, Rathenau's call for popular insurrection was also an attempt to avert domestic disaster – "civil war, military coup, and food strike."[87]

After the Cabinet meeting of October 9 some members expressed their "suspicion that in the end the Supreme Command would yet come out in favor of the Rathenau ideas."[88] They feared it was a trap for the parliamentary majority. Their suspicion proved right, but the trap was sprung later. Ludendorff and his supporters emerged as the defenders of the nation only in the Weimar courtrooms. To be sure, there were quite a few demands in the conservative press that anything and everything should be done to avert defeat.[89] However, the open acknowledgment of impending defeat remained an insurmountable obstacle for conservative groups. Only when the issue of defeat could be displaced into a rejection of President Wilson's and, later on, of Allied demands, could the rally of conservative and radical nationalist groups gain steam.[90]

---

[84] Ludendorff, *Urkunden der Obersten Heeresleitung*, 547–8.

[85] Lothar Burchardt, "Walther Rathenau und die Ursprünge deutsche Rohstoffbewirtschaftung im Ersten Weltkrieg," *Tradition* 15/4 (1970), 169–96.

[86] After the revolution Rathenau was accused of being a "war-monger" [*Kriegsverlängerer*]. Harry Graf Kessler, *Walther Rathenau* (Berlin, 1928), 267.

[87] Rathenau suggested that all three would happen as a result of the "dissolution of the front" – a rather shrewd analysis. Letter to Harden, October 8, 1918, in Hans Dieter Hellige (ed.), *Walther Rathenau – Maximilian Harden: Briefwechsel 1897–1920* (Munich, 1983), 750.

[88] Matthias and Morsey, *Max von Baden*, 127.

[89] Adolf Sturzenberger, *Die Abdankung Kaiser Wilhelms II.: Die Entstehung und Entwicklung der Kaiserfrage und die Haltung der Presse* (Berlin, 1937), 48–78; Karin Herrmann, "Der Zusammenbruch 1918 in der deutschen Tagespresse. Politische Ziele, Reaktionen und Ereignisse und die Versuchung der Meinungsführung, 23. September bis 11. November 1918," Ph.D. dissertation, University of Münster, 1958.

[90] Heinz Hagenlücke, *Deutsche Vaterlandspartei: Die nationale Rechte am Ende des Kaiserreiches* (Düsseldorf, 1997); James Retallack, *Notables of the Right: The Conservative Party and Political Mobilization in Germany, 1876–1918* (Boston, 1988).

The Final Battle

The common denominator of conservative and radical nationalist ideas was the notion of a terminal battle, or *Endkampf*. It remains unclear when the idea first appeared. Hintze mentioned it on September 29. Eisenhart-Rothe talked to Ludendorff about a "battle onto annihilation." Even Max von Baden alluded to it.[91] It was invoked by conservatives and nationalists,[92] who nevertheless could not overcome their *étatist* complacency. When they demanded a call to arms, they never thought of acting themselves. They wanted the state to mobilize the population, which is to say everybody else but them.[93] They produced petitions galore, but no action whatsoever. Nevertheless, by the mid-twenties, radical nationalists had convinced themselves that they had invented the idea of popular insurrection and had pursued it all along (figure 11).[94]

In reality, throughout the first half of October, both the Supreme Command and the War Ministry were embarrassed by the civilian pressure for a national call to arms. From their vantage point, mobilizing the nation boiled down to problems of conscription, meaning the provision of sufficient reserves for the field army (and, indirectly, of women and children for the workforce).[95] After that came propaganda and censorship, which they treated as some sort of *deus ex machina* that could raise the masses.[96] Bureaucratic squabbling over these matters reached an impasse in the spring and summer of 1918, at exactly the moment when German casualties were again reaching an all-time high.[97] The deadlock over propaganda and censorship produced

---

[91] Max von Baden, *Erinnerungen*, 331, speaks of the "determination to fight to the death."

[92] Alfred von Tirpitz, *Deutsche Ohnmachtspolitik im Weltkriege*, 2 volumes (Hamburg and Berlin, 1926), 2: 616–23.

[93] See the October 5 statement of the Deutsche Vaterlandspartei: It is a "sacred duty" to do everything in order "to bring the German people to the recognition of the dangers that are threatening them and, if necessary, to entice them to the strongest possible resistance against the enemy." Karl Wortmann, *Geschichte der Deutschen Vaterlandspartei* (Halle, 1926), 59.

[94] Anneliese Thimme, *Flucht in den Mythos: Die deutschnationale Volkspartei und die Niederlage von 1918* (Göttingen, 1969).

[95] Stig Förster, *Der doppelte Militarismus: Die deutsche Heeresrüstungspolitik zwischen Status-quo-Sicherung und Aggression, 1890–1913* (Stuttgart, 1985); Holger Afflerbach, "Bis zum letzten Mann und letzten Groschen: Die Wehrpflicht im Deutschen reich und ihre Auswirkungen auf das militärische Führungsdenken im Ersten Weltkrieg," in Roland G. Foerster (ed.), *Die Wehrpflicht: Entstehung, Entscheidungsformen und politisch-militärische Wirkung* (Munich, 1994), 71–90.

[96] Dirk Stegmann, "Die deutsche Inlandspropaganda 1917/1918. Zum innenpolitischen Machtkampf zwischen OHL und ziviler Reichsleitung in der Endphase des Kaiserreiches," *Militärgeschichtliche Mitteilungen* 12 (1972): 329–78; Wilhelm Deist, "Zensur und Propaganda in Deutschland während des Ersten Weltkrieges," in Deist, *Militär, Staat und Gesellschaft*, 153–64.

[97] Dr. Diekmann, *Die Ersatzlage im Jahr 1918*, Part 1: *Die Entwicklung bis Ende Juli 1918*, 22–35; and Part 3: *Die Streit um eine Volkserhebung*, 17–18. Bound manuscript in BA-MA W10/51834.

FIGURE 11. Koven, *Wer rettet das Vaterland?* (1919). Hoover Institution Archives.

In the wake of Germany's defeat in World War I, thousands of demobilized or displaced soldiers organized themselves into *Freikorps* and purported to serve as extemporized instruments for the maintenance of public order in a time of revolutionary turmoil. Such forces became bastions of counterrevolution in Germany and elsewhere and posed an important threat to the stability of the fledgling Weimar Republic. Although they failed in their initial purpose, which was to reverse the results of the Revolution of 1918, they became seedbeds for the countless right-wing paramilitary groups that would haunt the new regime throughout its existence.

   The poster shown here invokes the legacy of the War of Liberation to recruit men to a reborn *Freikorps Lützow*, in commemoration of the celebrated volunteer unit that took up arms against the French in 1813. In this instance, however, the question "Who will save

ever more elaborate plans to salvage the nation, but without the "truth and honesty" Rathenau had demanded.

Surprisingly, the first institution to jump over its Wilhelmine shadow was the Prussian War Ministry under its new head, General Heinrich Scheuch. Egged on by Rathenau's insistence that there were enough men ready to serve if disaster beckoned, and savaged by Ludendorff for not providing sufficient reserves, Scheuch promised 200,000 recruits immediately and an additional million men within the next half year.[98] One week later, on October 17, he had revised the Rathenau-inspired numbers and offered a regular monthly quota of 190,000 men into the spring of 1919, or alternatively a one-time allocation of 600,000 to 650,000 men. These supplementary drafts were ordered in a meeting of the department heads of the War Ministry and the military representatives of the German states.[99] Simultaneously, State Secretary Haussmann, together with Captain Colin Ross, an officer in the War Ministry and a well-known writer in civilian life, began drafting an official call for national defense. Altogether, the War Ministry expected to mobilize between 1.5 and 2 million men.[100] Ludendorff was flustered by these figures. The only thing that came to his mind was that "if all these favorable numbers

FIGURE 11. (*continued*) the Fatherland?" is not directed against a foreign foe – the Great War has already been lost, the last opportunities for resistance foregone – but instead against internal enemies on the left. Although liberals and civilians had shown themselves willing to support a last-ditch popular uprising against the advancing Allies a few months before, posters of this kind are a reminder of how thoroughly, over the course of the nineteenth century, the iconography of *Erhebung* in Germany had become the property of the right.

The poster's central image recalls countless recruiting posters produced in Germany and elsewhere during the war, in which a single figure confronts the viewer with a personal call to duty. Here the figure is a ghost, looming up from an imagined past. The poster incorporates one telling concession to conservative sensibility: the uniform of the man offering the viewer a sword is not that of Lützow's *Freikorps* (cf. Figure 5), but of a Prussian hussar. Over time, the familiar soft, loose-fitting "Old German" outfits [*altdeutsche Tracht*] favored by the volunteers of 1813 had become synonymous with student societies and a vaguely liberal idealism and so were not suitable to express the hard spirit needed in a real emergency. The *Freikorps* of 1919 were not an embodiment of state power but a repudiation of it, a movement arising within a dissolving regular army, directed against society and a new republican regime. Yet it was still important, in the construction of a reactionary *levée en masse*, to represent the call to arms as emanating from some kind of higher authority – if not from king to people, then from one "real" soldier to another.

[98] Meeting with the chancellor in the presence of Ludendorff, October 8, 1918, Matthias and Morsey, *Max von Baden*, 122; Diekmann, *Ersatzlage*, Part 3: 36–8; letter to Scheuch, October 9, 1918, in Walther Rathenau, *Politische Briefe* (Dresden, 1929), 188–91.

[99] Kgl. Württ. Militärbevollmächtigter, Nr. 1717/18 geh. to Württemberg War Ministry, October 18, 1918, Hauptstaatsarchiv Stuttgart, Nachlass Gen. Ltn. Theodor von Ströbel, M6601/226. Thanks to Oliver Stein, who pointed me to this file.

[100] Cabinet Meeting of October 17; Matthias and Morsey, *Max von Baden*, 226; Diekmann, *Ersatzlage*, Part 3, 41–2.

had been available, there would not have been a crisis on the Western Front in the first place."[101]

It is one thing to wonder if even 600,000 men would ever have been available.[102] It is another to note that Ludendorff did not understand what was being offered. He thought that the Supreme Command was finally getting what it had demanded all along and accepted the new numbers as a long overdue tribute. But the War Ministry's offer was not business as usual. The proposed levy was meant for a situation in which "the armistice and peace negotiations collapsed due to the harsh conditions imposed on Germany. This requires the use of all forces for the approaching *Endkampf*."[103] The catch was that they could only fight once because, in order to ready two million men for war in spring 1919, every other activity of society would have to be curtailed or shut down.[104]

In order to live up to its promise, the War Ministry considered changing the basic premises that had guided Prussian–German conscription, as codified in the service law passed by the Reichstag.[105] The War Ministry had long held, against the Supreme Command, that expanding the service law to encompass everybody was technically impractical and politically impossible. In their view, "total war" mobilization was literally nonsense.[106] However, emboldened by the idea of a terminal battle, officials of the War Ministry now concluded that the German constitution justified extralegislative emergency measures. They interpreted Article 57 – "every German has the duty to defend the Fatherland" – to mean that "every man who somehow knows how to use a weapon . . . has the duty to fight." These men were to be mobilized in special units attached to regular reserve and field formations.[107]

As a consequence of this totalitarian draft, policing gained a new urgency as well. The War Ministry had been stepping up paramilitary policing for quite some time, and had begun to consider arming local militias against insurrection. Also, a variety of initiatives were under way to increase control of communication and transportation hubs, which suggests preparation for

---

[101] Matthias and Morsey, *Max von Baden*, 227.

[102] Meeting of cabinet with Groener, November 5, 1918, Matthias and Morsey, *Max von Baden*, 529–30.

[103] War Ministry, Order to the Territorial Commands, October 20, in Diekmann, *Ersatzlage*, Part 3, 50–1.

[104] Report of Count Lerchenfeld, October 10, Matthias and Morsey, *Max von Baden*, 132.

[105] Diekmann, *Ersatzlage*, Part 1, 17–33. On the plans of the Supreme Command: Minutes of a meeting concerning reserves, June 18, 1918, in Ludendorff, *Urkunden der obersten Heeresleitung*, 110–16.

[106] Ludendorff, *Urkunden der obersten Heeresleitung*, 110–16; Richard Bessel, "Mobilization and Demobilization in Germany, 1916–1919," in John Horne (ed.), *State, Society, and Mobilization in Europe during the First World War* (Cambridge, 1997), 212–22.

[107] Diekmann, *Ersatzlage*, Part 3, 51–3.

civil war, as opposed to strike-breaking.[108] But the novel and decisive step was to be the introduction of a internal passport that, by abolishing freedom of movement, allowed the identification of malingerers and gave authorities the right to detain them without formal charges.[109] The proposed Pass Law also entailed an expansion and toughening of the military justice system. Instant court-martial, the curtailment of due process, a general stiffening of punishment, as well as the extensive use of penal companies, plus the death penalty for shirkers in the army and the factory, were among the penalties envisioned for those who failed to comply.[110]

The idea of a terminal battle changed the face of the Wilhelmine conscription and mobilization regime. Even though none of these initiatives became reality, they mark a totalitarian turn both in their collective disregard of individual rights and due process, and in their abandonment of any pretense of legality. In the face of defeat, one of the most bureaucratic institutions of the Prussian–German state threw overboard constraints that had heretofore made it a vigorous opponent of the nation in arms. The War Ministry came up not simply with a more encompassing mobilization, but with a totalizing, extra-legal economy of human resources, of a kind that would finally become reality in the middle years of World War II.

There are no indications that the General Staff had prepared plans for continuing the war after the army's defeat. Despite a lack of practical preparations, however, the idea of the terminal battle acquired rhetorical importance within the Supreme Command. In a telegram to Max von Baden on October 14, Hindenburg and Ludendorff proposed a propaganda initiative to mobilize public opinion against "the terrible consequences of a peace *à tout prix.*"[111] They emphasized that the military situation depended on the ability of the government to raise the "despondent spirit" of the people and overcome "inner strife." Without the home front giving full support to the "men in the field," one could not expect victory. As this had been said many times before, the cabinet suspected once again that Ludendorff and Hindenburg were merely attempting to elude responsibility for defeat. Still, another idea had snuck into the telegram, which in retrospect must be considered its main point. The Supreme Command now argued for an *Endkampf,* which they understood as a battle fought for the sake of honor, rather than to deter invasion or as a lever for peace negotiations, which had been the purpose of the civilian proposals for a government of national defense.

---

[108] Peter Holquist, "'Information Is the Alpha and Omega of Our Work': Bolshevik Surveillance in Its Pan-European Context," *Journal of Modern History* 69/3 (1997), 415.

[109] Memorandum of the Reserve Section, War Ministry, 8 October 1918, Diekmann, *Ersatzlage*, Part 3, 37.

[110] Generalquartiermeister, July 18, 1918, Diekmann, *Ersatzlage*, Part 1, appendix 5, n.p.

[111] Ludendorff, *Urkunden der obersten Heeresleitung*, 551–3.

Our enemies gain strength from our inner strife and despondent heart. . . . Hostile and neutral countries no longer view us as a people that joyously sets everything on the defense of its honor. . . . Nobody must doubt the iron-clad will of the people to defend itself to the last extremity against humiliating conditions. Only then will the army find the strength to defy superior force. . . . In all manner of public proclamation we must make clear the will of the German people, who know only two ways: honorable peace or war *à outrance*.[112]

This stance of epic outrage was to become the common language of the terminal battle. It was articulated by the Supreme Command not as a military measure but as an act of defiance against a peace process that in their view had gotten out of control.

For a great many officers in the staffs and the field army, the terminal battle was probably never more than rhetoric. For them the idea of defending military honor amounted to saying that the end of the war should be sought on the battlefield rather than at the conference table – and that they were being kept from defending German honor by an evil and traitorous government. Nevertheless, there is ample reason to believe that the Supreme Command calculated by mid-October that German forces might retreat in order to engage in a final battle along the German border in spring of 1919. It seems that Ludendorff, and especially Hindenburg, thought of this battle as a Verdun-type confrontation in which the Allies would run up against the German border fortresses.[113] But as the idea came to be taken seriously, the metaphorical notion of a sacrificial "last stand" came into play – and with it the question of the sacrificer and his victim. Ludendorff pointed to this issue in a military briefing on October 23 when he emphasized the need for "a continuation of war in a radicalized [*verschärfter*] form," if and when armistice negotiations failed.[114]

Public opinion caught on quickly and developed its own chilling rationale for the *Endkampf*. Bernhard Schwertfeger's opinion in the *Norddeutsche Allgemeine Zeitung* in November 1918 was unusual only in its clarity:

It will be necessary for our enemies to pay for every step ahead with streams of blood. Large areas which so far have been unaffected by war will be wrecked completely. If the enemy wants to push us out of the occupied parts of northern France and if they want to force a retreat from Belgium, they will have to count on an extended period of bloody battles and the completely useless destruction of their own territory.[115]

---

[112] Ludendorff, *Urkunden der obersten Heeresleitung*, 552.

[113] On planning for border defense, see Hermann von Kuhl, *Der Weltkrieg 1914–1918, dem deutschen Volke dargestelt* (Berlin, 1929), 432. Metz was envisioned as the German Verdun.

[114] Chief of General Staff, Situation Report, 23 October 1918; Ruptecht von Bayern, *Mein Kriegstagebuch*, edited by Eugen von Frauenholz, 3 volumes (Munich, 1929), 3: 363.

[115] Schwertfeger, *Das Weltkriegsende*, 197.

The prospect that a war of hostages directed against civilians might be necessary to restrain vastly superior allied forces had been an element of staff analyses as early as May of 1918.[116] Scorched-earth tactics had been used before, for example during the withdrawal to the Hindenburg line, and again during the retreat in August–September 1918.[117] But now Ludendorff insisted "that Germany cannot continue its old restraint in areas to be evacuated, because it harms itself in the process." He considered the destruction of civilian infrastructure self-evidently necessary, and intimated that it would include the wholesale despoilment of shelter and provisions.[118] He envisioned a retreat in which the army lived off the land, left behind a devastated country, and moved toward an all-out war against civilians.[119] This is, of course, a possibility against which President Wilson warned in his second and third notes.[120] The irony of his accusation is that Wilson mostly had in mind earlier episodes like the 1914 war against "partisans" and the submarine campaign. What outraged the president was scattered acts of pillage, destruction, and vengeance of a kind common throughout history. There was little recognition of the possibility of a systematic war of devastation. In the end, the very haste of the retreat, and the new German government's insistence that destruction be curtailed,[121] limited the impact of such actions. Nevertheless, a psychological threshold was crossed in October 1918. The *Endkampf* had evolved from a set-piece battle centered on a chain of border fortresses into a retreat that "necessitated" total devastation of the civil infrastructure and population.

How serious was Ludendorff? Much as with the Busche mission, the Supreme Command attempted to double-talk the cabinet into action without acknowledging it. On the surface, Ludendorff seemed to be condoning wanton destruction, partly as military necessity and partly as an inadvertent consequence of retreat. This outraged the cabinet, which proceeded to outlaw any such action because its members thought that it was a ploy to undermine the armistice negotiations with President Wilson. In reality, however, the cabinet nixed something quite different. The actual background for Ludendorff's comments were preparations for a new defensive line, the

---

[116] Hans Meier-Welcker, "Die deutsche Führung an der Westfront im Frühsommer 1918: Zum Problem der militärischen Lagebeurteilung," *Welt als Geschichte* 21 (1961), 164–84; Peter Graf Kielmannsegg, *Deutschland und der Erste Weltkrieg*, 2nd ed. (Stuttgart, 1980), 642–55.

[117] See, for example, Supreme Command, Retrospective Assessment of the Military Situation, September 15, 1918; *Amtliche Urkunden zur Vorgeschichte des Waffenstillstandes*, Doc. 10c, 39–40.

[118] Ibid.

[119] Meeting of October 17, Mattthias and Morsey, *Max von Baden*, 240–1.

[120] Klaus Schwabe, *Woodrow Wilson, Revolutionary Germany, and Peacemaking, 1918–1919: Missionary Diplomacy and the Realities of Power*, translated by Rita and Robert Kimber (Chapel Hill and London, 1985).

[121] Meeting of October 17, Matthias and Morsey, *Max von Baden*, 241.

Antwerp–Maas, or A-M, line. There has been considerable retrospective comment on this nonexistent defensive line, most of it ill-informed. The A-M line was never meant to be a built-up trench system. Rather, it was more of a free-fire zone in one of the most heavily populated industrial areas of Belgium; urban warfare "amidst the sea of houses and the mines," as Colonel Heye put it in his memoirs. Such tactics were thought to favor German defenders confronting English tanks, long-range guns, and airplanes.[122] If the Supreme Command had had its way, Belgium would have been "essentially destroyed."[123]

This is not quite the end of the story, although we have to cross into the postwar era to complete it. In the summer of 1918 Joachim von Stülpnagel was a youngish major serving as deputy operations officer for the Supreme Command. After the war, he sought to fashion an operational doctrine for *Volkskrieg*, in which the military and political implications of the *Endkampf* would be fully developed.

Stülpnagel asked the question that Ludendorff never dared ask: How to continue fighting if "the army is no longer capable of defending the integrity of German borders."[124] In a lengthy memorandum written in late 1923 and early 1924, entitled "Thoughts on the War of the Future," he argued that, in order to "liberate" Germany in the face of superior forces, the army would have to change the "grand laws of warfare, [because] a desperate situation requires desperate means."

The inequality of the military strength forces us to seek new ways [of waging war]. What is to be new in strategy and tactics must come as surprise and as bewilderment to the French, who will depend on the superiority of their weapons and proceed mechanically. It will have to be supported by the moral force of a popular insurrection to be initiated on a grand scale.[125]

A popular insurrection entailed the preparation for a war in which "any distinction between combatants [and noncombatants] disappears, and all persons and all things become means of war."[126] Total mobilization was to be complemented by systematic evacuation and large-scale devastation. The ground yielded to enemy forces was to be stripped of all useful objects and

---

[122] Lebenserinnerungen des Generaloberst Wilhelm von Heye, Part II: Wie ich den Weltkrieg erlebte (BA-MA Nl Heye N18/5), 79.
[123] Ibid.
[124] Joachim von Stülpnagel to Hasse, June 26, 1925 (BA-MA Nl Stülpnagel N5/20).
[125] The original is in BA-MA, Nl Stülpnagel 5/10; an official copy – that is, a copy that circulated among the staff – can be found in the file named [Zentrale] 153/24 z, February 26, 1924 (BA-MA RH8/v. 911). Stülpnagel also distributed copies widely among former officers, including Hindenburg.
[126] Ibid.

shelter. Germany itself would become ground zero for a war of scorched earth. To this would be added partisan warfare, acts of "sabotage and murder," that Stülpnagel expected would lead to brutal reprisals by the invading forces – the burning of towns, the murder of hostages, concentration camps, and "the shooting of a large number of civilians."[127] In turn, the brutality of the invading enemy would inflame the people, who would rise in desperation. People's war was "area warfare in zones of maximum depth" [*Flächenkrieg in tiefsten Zonen*], which would force the enemy "to slowly eat his way through German territory,"[128] where he would encounter a "popular insurrection" in which "the many who have nothing to lose, fanatically incited and supported by the German hinterland, can do anything."[129] What Stülpnagel sketched was literally a war of self-annihilation: "If victory is at stake, considerations concerning the survival of the population do not matter."[130]

The Stülpnagel memorandum distilled the essence of the evolving military debate about a final battle in late 1918. For a majority of officers the issue was simply one of hanging on into 1919, in order to bring about a climactic encounter along the German border. But this kind of battle-centric view gave way to an emergent doctrine of a war of annihilation, and of self-annihilation at that. It was a war that pitted peoples rather than armies against each other – and not simply in the sense that all citizens were liable to be conscripted or that civilians were subject to attack. Rather, all men, women, and children were meant to be fighting, digging trenches, hauling ammunition, and so on. By 1923–4, this doctrine was the subject of war games, and by 1925–6 mobilization, evacuation, and demolition schemes had been worked out.[131] As the notion of the *Endkampf* became more radical, it moved from the realm of metaphor into that of reality.

October 1918 was a turning point in the history of German military thought and practice. Rathenau's call for popular insurrection stands at the cusp of a seminal transition. Politically, Rathenau's ideas reflected the desire of a good part of the civilian and political elite to rally for the defense of the

---

[127] Draft of summary conclusions for the 1924 war game "People's War and Border Defense," file number 279/24 T1 IB geh. to TA, in BA-MA Nl Stülpnagel N5/20.

[128] Ibid.

[129] Draft of concluding evaluation of the 1925 war game "Battle against Poland," June 1925 (BA-MA Nl Stülpnagel N5/20).

[130] Draft of summary conclusions for the 1924 war game "People's War and Border Defense," file number 279/24 T1 IB geh. to TA, in BA-MA Nl Stülpnagel N5/20. The Operations Section anticipated casualty rates of up to 75 percent among the border defense units.

[131] Michael Geyer, *Aufrüstung oder Sicherheit: Die Reichswehr in der Krise der Machtpolitik, 1924–1936* (Wiesbaden, 1980); Johannes Hürter, *Wilhelm Groener. Reichswehrminister am Ende der Weimarer Republik (1928–1932)* (Munich, 1992), 128–48.

nation. This sentiment emerged not from the right but from the cosmopolitan Berlin elites and the left-center parties of the Reichstag. When the new government yielded to the pressures of the Supreme Command, the damage to itself proved extraordinary. Max von Baden's move to initiate armistice feelers without a call for national defense undermined the unselfconscious sense of legitimacy and integrity that gave the ruling left-center coalition its moral authority to speak for the nation. Had Max prevailed, of course, he might have been swept away like Kerensky in Russia. As it was, his submission to the civil and military experts disastrously undermined the prospects for liberal nationalism in Germany.

At the same time, what was left of the traditional outlook of the Prussian–German military, perennially averse to people's war, was dismantled. Wherever we turn after 1918, we encounter a new way of imagining war, and the first indications of a military/political practice that contemporaries called people's war. Its key feature is a turn away from a class- and caste-based military system, toward one based on plebiscitary mobilization, extralegal organization, and unrestrained violence against enemy populations. What linked republicans like Rathenau and totalitarians like Stülpnagel was the shared presumption that war had become a violent conflagration of everyone and everything. What separated them was that the latter was prepared to wager the collective death of a people in order to avert – or transcend – defeat.

"To Make a Lost War Lost"

It did not come to an *Endkampf* in 1918 because the government of Max von Baden, backed by the Reichstag majority, chose to forego a terminal battle. Its decision set in motion the events that led to revolution in November. There is hardly a more consequential and courageous act in twentieth-century German politics. Yet it is almost completely forgotten. Max von Baden ended the war by political means because the survival of the nation was a higher good than military or even national honor. The lines of the civic conflict that divided Germany thereafter set a democratic camp against a nationalist one, with the former being associated with the Versailles Treaty, but not the decision to forswear national self-destruction; the latter gained prestige in resistance to an unjust peace – while remaining untainted by the apocalyptic vision of the *Endkampf*.[132]

---

[132] The reverberations extend into the historians' debate on the Third Reich during the 1980s. Ernst Nolte's argument about the world wars as European and global civil wars can certainly be traced back to this debate (Ernst Nolte, *Marxism, Fascism, Cold War* [Atlantic Highlands, N.J., 1982]). Nolte's "past that does not go away" (Ernst Nolte, *Das Vergehen der Vergangenheit: Antwort an meine Kritiker im sogenannten Historikerstreit* [Berlin, 1989]) has more to do with 1917 than with 1933. The key link in the post-World War II continuation of this debate is Carl Schmitt, to whom we turn briefly later.

In a long letter to his cousin Fritz (Friedrich II, Archduke of Baden), Max von Baden described the controversy over the *Endkampf* as his "Calvary," where he would "stand and fall." He would have to do the unthinkable: "We are forced to accept Wilson's harsh conditions, if we do not want to see the last flower of German manhood and our hopes for the future bleed to death uselessly on the battlefield." The "military backbone is broken" and the only chance was "to hold out for a peace which gives us life and a glimmer of hope for the future." To this end, he would "sacrifice himself" because this is "the task predestination has in store for me."[133] Here speaks the spirit of piety, and indeed pietism, in contrast to the rhetoric of epic upheaval preferred by the Supreme Command and the manifestos of the nationalist right, which now began to pour in. We also observe the language of sacrifice and salvation. But above all, we note that the agent of salvation is the "self," while its object is neither patrimony nor monarchy, but the nation.

Max von Baden stood up to Ludendorff. In a remarkable *aide mémoire* he sketched out his position a day ahead of the crucial Cabinet meeting on October 17. With the military situation being what it was, he insisted, the political leadership would have to make choices:

Either continuation of the war unto annihilation or the attempt, in the wake of the military collapse, to salvage what can be salvaged economically and politically. The desire to perish with honor surely suggests itself to the individual, but the responsible statesman must recognize that a people in its entirety has the right to demand, with all due sobriety, that they go on living, rather than die in beauty.[134]

The climactic debate over continuing the war took place on the morning of October 17 in the presence of Generals Ludendorff and Hoffmann (East), and the chief operations officer, Colonel Heye. The minutes are less dramatic than the issues at stake might lead one to expect. Its result was that the peace process was allowed to continue, and this was decisive. To be sure, preparations for a supplementary draft and even for a *levée en masse* also continued; but the Supreme Command's attempt to stop the peace process was defeated. The Cabinet, which had been dragged into the armistice initiative at the beginning of the month, now decided that it had to stick with it, even if it amounted to a capitulation. With the decision to continue the peace process, the Cabinet had chosen "to make a lost war lost," as Vice Chancellor Friedrich von Payer put it on October 20.[135]

Was the *Endkampf* a viable alternative? In the midst of the *Angst*-ridden deliberations, Ludendorff appeared in stunningly good spirits. When asked

---

[133] Max von Baden, *Erinnerungen*, 405–7.

[134] *Aide mémoire* of Chancellor Prince Max von Baden, October 16, 1918; Matthias and Morsey, *Max von Baden*, 216–17, here 216.

[135] Payer, at the Cabinet Meeting of October 20, 1918, in Matthias and Morsey, *Max von Baden*, 289. The full quotation is: "One is allowed [in this situation] to think of one's good name. We are the ones to make the lost war lost. We carry the responsibility before history."

if the new reserves would make a difference in determining the outcome of the war, he answered that he could not promise anything: "War is not a mathematical calculation," he said, and while it was likely that Germany would be defeated, one never knew. There was always another chance and, for once, the "soldier's luck might shine on the German side." When pressed by Max von Baden to say if a continuation of war for another six months, at the rate of perhaps 20,000 to 25,000 casualties per month, would make any difference, he cheerfully answered: "Maybe yes, maybe no." In his memoirs, Ludendorff added that he was certain that the German border could be held.[136] But at the time, when challenged by the Chancellor to consider the prospect that the enemy might "break into Germany and devastate the country," he responded, more accurately, that we "are not yet there by any means."[137] What matters here is that Ludendorff refused to consider the implications of his own position – that invasion, devastation, and occupation were a likely outcome of the *Endkampf.*

The government was forced into a decision a week later. Hindenburg and Ludendorff had come to Berlin against the expressed will of Max von Baden in order to convince the emperor to reject the Allies' armistice terms and to continue the war.[138] The emperor rebuffed them and sent them to the apartment of Vice-Chancellor Payer because Max von Baden had fallen ill. According to the chief of the Naval Staff, Levetzow, one of several senior officers who accompanied them, Ludendorff set out to convince Payer "that the honor of the nation and of the soldier demands a rejection of the excessive demands of Wilson," whereupon Payer responded that "he had lost confidence in the capability of the people and the army to resist," adding: "I am a simple *Bürger* and civilian; I only see the starving masses." Ludendorff countered: "Then, your Excellency, I throw the entire shame of the Fatherland into your and your colleagues' faces." Levetzow had a keen cinematic eye for the protagonists. Ludendorff is "a majestic man, a representative of German honor"; Payer is "a small, crappy party hack without a sense of national dignity and honor . . . weighing everything only from a petit bourgeois point of view . . . sitting there cowering, with his beady, hate-filled eyes and clasped hands, under the powerful blows of the general."[139] Here, acted out, is the pivotal scene in the stab-in-the-back legend. Levetzow's recollection became a crucial piece of evidence in the stab-in-the-back trials of the mid-twenties, while the image of the "beady-eyed" Payer inevitably recalls the standard depiction of the dwarf Alberich, beaten into submission by the mighty Siegfried.

[136] Ludendorff, *Kriegserinnerungen*, 570.

[137] Meeting of the Cabinet, October 17, 1918, afternoon; Matthias and Morsey, *Max von Baden*, 246.

[138] Chief of the General Staff of the Field Army, Field Marshal von Hindenburg to the Armies, 24 October 1918, *Amtliche Urkunden zur Vorgeschichte des Waffenstillstandes*, Doc. 76b, 104.

[139] Wilhelm Deist (ed.), *Militär und Innenpolitik im Weltkrieg 1914–1918*, 2 volumes, (Düsseldorf, 1970), 2: 1338–40.

Payer had a very different account of the showdown, which is rarely quoted in full.

The gentlemen of the Supreme Command submitted their opinion that in view of Wilson's last note, which means nothing but capitulation and a shameful peace, the armistice negotiations must be ended. The Emperor, the dynastic heads of the states, the imperial government, the leadership of army and navy and the parliament were to issue a solemn, joint proclamation for a gathering of all forces in order to continue the war with utmost decisiveness.[140]

Payer summarized his response as follows:

I had a great deal of sympathy for the manly and soldierly character of the [Supreme Command's] plan and I did not expect good things to come from armistice negotiations, judged by the way Wilson treated our armistice request. But it was my duty to assess the situation calmly rather than follow my sentiments. An Army Commander with his entourage may well end his illustrious career with a death ride, but a people of seventy million cannot make the decision about life and death according to a single estate's conception of honor. It cannot make its future dependent on potentialities which rest on hopes rather than facts. . . . I could not find that the idea of continuing the war indefinitely . . . would bring us any chance of success.

The Emperor dismissed Ludendorff on October 26. On the night of October 26–27, Levetzow ordered the High Sea Fleet on its suicide mission, triggering a mutiny. Simultaneously, unrest broke out in Berlin and in the Ruhr as a result of the War Ministry's recall of workers to the military. When these protests linked up with pervasive food-riots by women and children in other cities, the stage for the revolution was set. As early as October 17 Phillip Scheidemann had put popular opinion in a nutshell: "Rather an end with horror than horror without end."[141]

People's War

If Walther Rathenau's plea for popular insurrection initially appeared as an aberrant pronouncement by a despairing visionary, the debates and the events of October 1918 suggested otherwise. They point to the profound desire for self-defense among the majority parties of the Reichstag; the relentless pursuit of a terminal battle, an *Endkampf*, in order to salvage, if not a collapsing monarchical regime, then the honor of the military and, indeed, of the nation in arms. The decision to forgo a last call to arms was motivated by concern for the public good but was ultimately driven by an overwhelming desire for peace after four years of relentless war. These debates and the

---

[140] Friedrich Payer, *Von Bethmann Hollweg bis Ebert: Erinnerungen und Bilder* (Frankfurt am Main, 1923), 142–3.

[141] Cabinet Meeting of October 17 with Ludendorff, in Matthias and Morsey, *Max von Baden*, 229.

decisions that they engendered brought the war to a deliberate, political end. If the members of Max von Baden's government started out with hopes for a national defense in order to negotiate an equitable peace, they ended up literally "making a lost war lost." In negotiating the conditions of German defeat, they had little doubt that the ensuing peace would be terrible. The exchange with President Wilson had disabused them of any hope that they might be able to sign an equitable peace agreement. And yet they concluded that these conditions were preferable to continuing or renewing a war effort that could only end in self-destruction – the *Endkampf,* which the Supreme Command had come to endorse. There was nothing, they argued, that could justify this kind of war.

German historiography has done everything to minimize the import of this painful decision. The reasons vary, but the effect is the same. The fact that the war was already lost is sufficient to explain how defeat became effective.[142] Yet in October 1918 we have a dramatic case of a war being deliberately ended, an event that gains added poignancy when compared with 1944/45. Historians do not remember because contemporaries chose to forget. The fact that Germany capitulated rather than destroy itself disappeared in chatter about he German army remaining undefeated and the peace treaty being unjust.

One might turn to Richard Bessel's closely argued study of returning soldiers for an explanation of this reaction. He points out that defeat is not something soldiers remember choosing, although they clearly opted to stop fighting.[143] But why should entire nations and governments act the same way? One might say that they too are only human; but, true as this is, the more convincing answer is not, or not only, psychological. Rather, it has much to do with the idea and practice of *Volkskrieg* as a reaction to crushing defeat, arising from the reality and myth of Prussian–German insurrectionary warfare against Napoleon. An interwar military study picked up on this tradition and defined *Volkskrieg* appropriately enough as "the last best hope of an un-armed or lightly armed state against a superior enemy that has the power to invade the opponent's territory," while adding that "a people of honor would naturally fight . . . even though they would have to have more or less certain destruction before their eyes."[144]

The genealogy of *Volkskrieg* in 1918 is clarified in two texts, by Carl von Clausewitz and by Carl Schmitt, which suggest that the schemes for popular insurrection in 1918 were less of an aberration than we might have thought.

---

[142] Holger H. Herwig, *The First World War: Germany and Austria Hungary 1914–1918* (London and New York, 1998).

[143] Richard Bessel, "Die Heimkehr der Soldaten: Das Bild der Frontsoldaten in der Öffentlichkeit der Weimarer Republik," in Gerhard Hirschfeld and Gerd Krumeich (eds.), *"Keiner fühlt sich hier mehr als Mensch . . .": Erlebnis und Wirkung des Ersten Weltkriegs* (Essen, 1993), 221–39.

[144] Liesner, "Volkskrieg (Hauptabhandlung)" (BA-MA W10/50203), 1 and 9.

On the contrary, both propose, from different vantage points, that the potential for far-reaching popular violence is implicit in the idea of modern war itself.

Contrary to what one might expect, Clausewitz does not identify the people in arms with some regime of universal conscription, but with "war by means of popular uprising."[145] Clausewitz professed uncertainty about this kind of war, which occurred when "conventional barriers have been swept away . . . by the elemental violence of war."[146] Yet he was convinced that popular insurrection would be integral to the war of the future – a form of fighting that was "not as yet very common," distinctly a "phenomenon of the nineteenth century."[147] Although well aware of the deep history of such uprisings, he set *Volkskrieg* apart as a distinctly national and nationalizing kind of war.

According to Clausewitz, the "elemental violence" of the people in arms is set free when "a whole nation renders armed resistance."[148] This turn to generalized resistance is the breaking point of modern war. It is reached when the survival of a people is thrown into the balance by military defeat. At such a moment *raison d'état* may demand peace, but national emotion and popular passion cannot be reconciled with the loss of self-government and liberty. Clausewitz ends his chapter on the people in arms with a rousing invocation of the *Endkampf* as the exemplary gesture that breaks through the conventional barriers of violence:

Even after a defeat, there is always the possibility that a turn of fortune can be brought about by developing new sources of internal strength or through the natural decimation all offensives suffer in the long run or by means of help from abroad. There will always be time enough to die; like a drowning man who will clutch instinctively at a straw, it is the natural law of the moral world that a nation that finds itself on the brink of an abyss will try to save itself by any means.

No matter how small and weak a state may be in comparison with its enemy, it must not forego these last efforts, or one would conclude that its soul is dead. The possibility of avoiding total ruin by paying a high price for peace should not be ruled out, but even this intention will not, in turn, eliminate the usefulness of new measures of defense. . . . A government that, after having lost a major battle, is only interested in letting its people go back to sleep in peace as soon as possible and, overwhelmed by feelings of failure and disappointment, lacks the courage and desire to put forth a final effort, is, because of its weakness, involved in a major inconsistency in any case. It shows that it did not deserve to win, and possibly for that very reason was unable to.[149]

---

[145] Carl von Clausewitz, *On War*, translated by Michael Howard and Peter Paret (Princeton, 1976), 479–83.
[146] Ibid., 479.
[147] Ibid., 485, 479.
[148] Ibid., 479.
[149] Ibid., 483.

The desperate debate of October 1918 was in no sense a spur-of-the-moment affair.

Endkampf is part and parcel of a cultural legacy that was activated in October 1918, against which the sensible and circumspect reasoning of Max von Baden's government had little to offer but common sense. Yet one can go further. Clausewitz's argument proposes that popular resistance against overwhelming odds is an act capable of engendering a new social and communal consciousness. The firebreaks against violence collapse in the struggle for liberty and self-government. *Volkskrieg* is unbridled, existential violence, beyond the legality of the state and the rationality of military organization. It contemplates complete self-destruction, and it is for this reason that it is constitutive of the modern nation. Nations come into their own by wagering their ruin. If it were not for the willingness to die, the nation would indeed be an "imagined community."[150] Collective death is the reality test for national fantasies, and discourse about it is the essence of the German notion of *Volkskrieg*. Clausewitz saw it as the hidden origin of modern war. In eliding the moment of defeat and the passions that it engenders, German historians obscure this legacy.

More than a century later, Carl Schmitt picked up the issue of people's war at just about the time when Gerhard Ritter was putting the entire matter to rest, by declaring *Volkskrieg* a revolutionary-democratic aberration with no place in a world of modern states and professional military institutions.[151] In sharp contrast, Schmitt attempted to resurrect insurrectionary war, at least in political theory, by declaring that its history had barely begun.

Schmitt's theory made the "partisan" into the phenotype of the insurrectionary warrior and established a genealogy of the latter that began with the wars against Napoleon, specifically the Spanish insurrection against the "modern, well-organized, regular army that emerged from the experience of the French revolution."[152] "The Prussian ideal of 1813" engendered its own myth. Russia remained the wild card, an empire that oscillated between aristocratic and popular forms of war. England disappeared from the scene. The result is a deeply mythologized dichotomy between the "localist" guerrilla and the globalizing abstractions of empire (e.g., the Rights of Man), whose instrumental applications of violence are juxtaposed against the checkered map of European self-government.

---

[150] Benedict Anderson, *Imagined Communities: Reflections on the Origin and Spread of Nationalism*, rev. ed. (London and New York, 1991).

[151] Ritter, *Staatskunst*. The post-World War II background for his resolute opposition to *Volkskrieg* was a debate about the lessons of the war against Napoleon that raged in German military historical circles throughout the Third Reich and fed into the *Endkampf* propaganda between 1942 and 1945.

[152] Carl Schmitt, *The Concept of the Political*, translated by George Schwab (Chicago and London, 1996); *Theorie des Partisanen: Zwischenbemerkungen zum Begriff des Politischen* (Berlin, 1963).

Schmitt, it must be noted, is uncompromisingly illiberal. He has no patience for either imperial pieties or multicultural pleasantries. The world is not imagined. It is conquered, and conquest is resisted in bloody upheavals. The experience of France's imperial army was but the first act in an ongoing war of insurrection, whose endgame (as Schmitt proposed in 1963) would pit the United States against a world of partisans.

Schmitt's work points to an alternative genealogy of modern war – a genealogy that leads from Prussia to Algeria; links Clausewitz to Lenin and Mao; and puts community-based upheaval from Spain to Vietnam and Palestine at the center of military history. This analysis – which conspicuously omits the revolutionary history of the United States – is strengthened by a second, historical and legal-constitutional, argument. Schmitt rejects the idea that the "Westphalian" states' system is merely a framework for anarchical competition. Instead, he sees a conservative regime of international order based upon a common system of law, a *ius gentium Europeaum*, that puts a premium on limiting interstate violence. Because Schmitt is never tempted to confuse law with peace, he need not imagine that war is an expression of international "anarchy." On the contrary: in his terms, it is not war as such that destroys international order, but civil war.

People's war is, in theory and practice, all-consuming war, a form of violence defined by its twin practices of self-destruction and extermination. It is a war of civilians against civilians, civil war raised to the level of interstate conflict; always exceptionally cruel, and capable of engendering extraordinary passions. It is not a war that states choose to fight, but one that nations may unleash when faced with subjugation, or for other purposes, such as racial goals, as Germany does in 1939.

Schmitt is rather coy in his treatment of twentieth-century German history. But this much is clear: the phantom of *Endkampf* first appeared there at the very moment when the European *ius gentium* had collapsed for good. It is not just that Germany was faced with the choice of insurrectionary war or surrender. German fantasies of popular insurrection were echoed in the civil wars that swept through central and eastern Europe, Russia, and Turkey at the same time. The Bolshevik revolution in Russia and the nationalist upheavals in the Ottoman Empire marked the onset of a new age.[153] The phantom of the *Endkampf* thus becomes a premonition of the waves of civil and revolutionary violence that swept back and forth across Europe, with ever-increasing momentum, until the final climacteric in 1945. This

---

[153] Whether we accept Schmitt's contention that a new age of civil war was emerging from the ruins of an older order is another matter. The adaptation of this argument by scholars like Eric Hobsbawm and François Furet suggests that Schmitt's conception of history is very seductive indeed. See Eric Hobsbawm, *The Age of Extremes: A History of the World, 1914–1991* (New York, 1996); and François Furet, *The Passing of an Illusion: The Idea of Communism in the Twentieth Century* (Chicago and London, 1999).

European civil war unfolded in a "logic of terror and counter-terror" whose effect consists in the "utter destruction of social structures, . . . insecurity, fear, and a pervasive sense of distrust."[154] Much as with Clausewitz, there is more truth to this pitiless argument than we might like. All the more reason, then, to remember the choice of Germany's last imperial and first parliamentary government, which chose surrender over the seductions of terror.

[154] Schmitt, *Theorie des Partisanen*, 75.

8

The *Levée en masse* from Russian Empire to Soviet Union, 1874–1938

Mark Von Hagen

The idea of the people in arms, and the various legends that have surrounded it, resonated in Russia and the Soviet Union in seemingly contradictory ways. Despite the heroic mythology that attached to popular resistance during the "Fatherland War" against Napoleon in 1812, the autocrat and his military leadership always preferred the model of professional, long-service regular forces to the French example of the *levée en masse*.[1] To the extent that Russia's military and political elites sought inspiration in the Revolutionary era, they found it in the conservative synthesis of popular enthusiasm, institutional egalitarianism, and monarchical legitimacy that they believed had been achieved by the Prussian reforms of 1806–13 (and strengthened in the 1860s). The Prussian–German model of universal military service as the school of the nation was very much on the minds of the enlightened bureaucrats around Emperor Alexander II and his minister of war, Dmitrii Miliutin, when they drafted a new law on military conscription in 1874, one of the most important in a series of social and political innovations – the so-called Great Reforms – whose centerpiece had been the abolition of serfdom thirteen years earlier.

Miliutin and his circle envisioned the army as an institution that would integrate Russia's vast, polyglot peasant majority into local and national institutions of rule, without forsaking the advantages of military professionalism and a large, politically reliable standing army. This reformist model was tentatively repudiated by the Provisional Government and its non-Bolshevik successors during the military emergency of 1917, and decisively

---

[1] See William Fuller, Jr., *Strategy and Power in Russia, 1600–1914* (New York, 1992), Chapter 5, for a thoughtful discussion of the history and myths surrounding the War of 1812. On the myth of a "national war," Fuller writes: "The Emperor Alexander I had a proclamation calling on the people of Russia to rise up in armed struggle with the invaders. The proclamation, however, appears to have had little success in rousing the masses." He also discusses partisan warfare against Napoleon but concludes that the celebratory vision of the War of 1812 had mostly "insidious consequences for the development of Russian strategy" (179).

so by the young Soviet state, which proclaimed a new revolutionary and patriotic *levée en masse* during the Civil War that secured its existence. The new Soviet regime regularly invoked the armed people, the socialist militia, and the *Armée nouvelle* of Jean Jaurès by way of explaining its military outlook.[2] The Red Army eventually adopted more conventional forms of conscription, discipline, and hierarchy, which restored much of the professional ethos of the past, but important elements of revolutionary military rhetoric and organization continued to reflect the original Jauresian inspiration.

At every stage, however, the response of both Russian elites and their Soviet successors to the idea of the nation in arms was hampered by a fundamental ambivalence toward the organizing and legitimizing role of the nation itself. National institutions with any claim to embody popular sovereignty came late to Russia – the Duma that was wrenched from the tsar following the 1905 Revolution was the first, and it did not survive the upheaval of 1917. Although the Great Reforms were partly intended to replace traditional social and confessional categories with a new form of political nation, the new polity the reformers imagined was implicitly based on Russian ethnicity and culture, despite the fact that, by the middle of the nineteenth century, Russians as such made up less than one-half of the Empire's population. The tension between a civic understanding of citizenship, with its abstract and generalized rights and obligations, and the type of ethnic belonging that stressed group distinctiveness and solidarity constrained all projects of democratic reform prior to the Soviet ascendancy.

The Bolshevik elites, for their part, embraced more modern notions of social organization, and elevated one in particular – class – to preeminence in the new constitution. Bolshevik attitudes toward nationality were tempered by the primacy of class as an organizing principle and of a particular (minority) class, the proletariat, within the post-Revolutionary social order. Moscow was likewise committed to an internationalist vision of world revolution so that even its experiments with nation-building (*korenizatsiia*) in the 1920s were pursued in the name of overcoming national differences. Nevertheless, the Soviet state found reason to reinforce and exploit national identities and loyalties, not least in the military sphere. Under Stalin, the Soviet Union effectively returned to the project launched a half century earlier by Miliutin: conscription and military service would again be employed to educate a new Soviet "nation," with the Russian language as the central medium of that effort.

---

[2] Jean Jaurès, *L'Armée nouvelle* (Paris, 1910). Vladimir Lenin regularly called for "the replacement of the police and the army . . . by the direct arming of the whole people." See Lenin's "The Dual Power" and "State and Revolution" in Robert C. Tucker (ed.), *The Lenin Anthology* (New York, 1975), 302 and 338, where Lenin invokes the experience of the Paris Commune of 1871 as a new stage in the revolutionary arming of the masses.

The Russian–Soviet experience of military mobilization and nation building thus resembles that of western Europe, with two differences that, while by no means absolute, are worth highlighting. On the one hand, the strength of antinational and nonnational ideologies – whether deriving from traditional elitism or Marxian internationalism – was relatively greater and more enduring than elsewhere in Europe. On the other hand, and more consequentially in practice, both the Russian Empire and the Soviet Union were multiethnic polities in which the claims of culture, language, and personal identity cut against the universalizing claims of the state. The present chapter surveys Russian and Soviet efforts to grip the nettle of the nation in arms in light of these conditions, from the modernizing reforms of 1874 to the eve of the Second World War.

The Imperial Army and the Miliutin Reforms

Until the early nineteenth century, tsarist military manpower requirements were met by levies chiefly on the Russian peasantry, for whom obligatory military service was an important marker of nonprivileged social status.[3] Military service was a modality of serfdom, in which a small number of young men were called up, for practical purposes, for life. As the Empire extended its frontiers, more and more non-Russian subjects were added to its population and also, somewhat hesitantly, to the ranks of its soldiers. Imperial military authorities incorporated conquered peoples into the armed forces only with great caution, however, because the extension of conscription to non-Russian populations frequently met with resistance and was accordingly understood as a potential security risk in itself.[4] One of the most violent instances of resistance was the Polish rebellion of 1863. Although the Polish national movement and its historic grievances against the violation of Polish autonomy figured as the main causes, Imperial authorities' efforts to extend military recruitment to the Polish population provided the important tinder for the explosion.[5]

---

[3] For English-language summaries of Imperial recruitment policies, see John L. H. Keep, *Soldiers of the Tsar: Army and Society in Russia, 1462–1874* (Oxford, 1985), Chapter 7; and Elise Kimerling Wirtschafter, *From Serf to Russian Soldier* (Princeton, 1990), Chapter 1. In Russian there is M. Zakharov, *Natsional'noe stroitel'stvo v Krasnoi Armii* (Moscow, 1927), Chapter 1.

[4] Land-militiamen were remembered for having sympathized with Pugachev's revolt in the 1780s, while the Don and Dnepr Cossacks rose up in left-bank Ukraine after Catherine the Great stripped them of their privileges. See L. G. Beskrovnyi, *Russkaia armiia i flot v XVIII veke* (Moscow, 1958), 297, 318, 322. In 1819, military settlers raised a mutiny in Slobodskaia Ukraina. And in 1848, as nationalist movements began to stir in the Ukrainian and Polish provinces of the Habsburg and Russian Empires, rebellious Imperial officers were supported by many soldiers.

[5] See A. A. Kersnovskii, *Istoriia russkoi armii*, 4 volumes (Belgrade, 1933–8), 3, part 2: 411–14; and Keep, *Soldiers of the Tsar*, 358–64.

The autocracy was more willing to accept non-Russian elites into the Imperial officer corps, especially if those concerned accepted conversion to Orthodox Christianity. As a consequence, and despite an official policy of Russification energetically pursued under Alexander III (1881–94) and Nicholas II (1894–1917), non-Russians, especially Baltic Germans, Poles, Ukrainians, and Finns, played important roles at the top of the military hierarchy until the end of the Empire.[6]

The Imperial Army that entered the Great War in the summer of 1914 was largely the creation of the Great Reforms. Beginning in 1874, Dmitrii Miliutin and his circle set about modernizing the army in line with the practices of continental European militaries.[7] The reformers' ideal, marrying economic and military motivations, was to reduce the peacetime army to the smallest size possible (thus sparing the overburdened Imperial budget), while creating a system that was capable of rapidly expanding in wartime. An important impetus for innovation was provided by Prussia's stunning victories over Austria and France a few years before, for which the Prussian system of national military service was given much of the credit.[8]

Military reform was also viewed as an integral and logical extension of the broader social and political reforms set in motion with the emancipation of the serfs in 1861. Miliutin believed that all men should be liable to bear arms, and that the gentry should give up their anachronistic privileges in the name of "the genuine good of Russia and the Russian people." He also felt

---

[6] On the officer corps before the Miliutin reforms, see Hans-Peter Stein, "Der Offizier des russischen Heeres im Zeitabschnitt zwischen Reform und Revolution (1861–1905)," *Forschungen zur osteuropaeischen Geschichte* 13 (1967), 351–63. On the Baltic Germans, see John A. Armstrong, "Mobilized Diaspora in Tsarist Russia: The Case of the Baltic Germans," in Jeremy Azrael (ed.), *Soviet Nationality Policies and Practices* (New York, 1978), 63–104. On the Finns, see J. E. O. Screen, "Finnish Officers in the Russian Army and Navy during the Autonomy Period (1809–1917)," *Siirtolaisuus Migration* 4 (1981), 1–7; and his "The Entry of Finnish Officers into Russian Military Service 1809–1917," Ph.D. dissertation, London (1976). The ethnic breakdown of the officer corps differed only slightly from the general troop percentages. At the turn of the century roughly 80 percent of all officers were Russians (including Ukrainians and Belorussians), with the rest, varying from 15 to 21 percent depending on rank, divided among Poles, Germans, Muslims, Armenians, Georgians, and others. See also Petr A. Zaionchkovskii, *Samoderzhavie i russkaia armiia na rubezhe XIX–XX stoletii, 1881–1903* (Moscow, 1973), 196–202. The elite Guards were 90 percent Russians; the remaining 10 percent were mainly Baltic Germans and men from princely Georgian families. Nikolaus Basseches, *The Unknown Army* (New York, 1943), 59; Stein, "Der Offizier," 457–67.

[7] The discussion that follows is based on Forrest A. Miller, *Dmitrii Miliutin and the Reform Era in Russia* (Nashville, Tenn., 1968), 184–230; Keep, *Soldiers of the Tsar*, 351–81; R. F. Baumann, "The Debates Over Universal Military Service in Russia, 1870–1874," Ph.D. dissertation, Yale University (1982); Petr A. Zaionchkovskii, "Podgotovka voennoi reformy 1874 goda," *Istoricheskie zapiski* 27 (1948), 170–201; and Stein, "Der Offizier," 363–73.

[8] On the crucial role of Prussian military victories, see P. A. Zaionchkovskii, *Voennye reformy 1860–1870 godov v Rossii* (Moscow, 1952), 259–60.

strongly that the obligation to serve should fall equally upon all parts of the Empire (excepting only very remote or newly annexed regions, as well as the Cossacks); and that only the younger men should be called up – in practice roughly 25 percent of eligible twenty-one year olds.[9] Hiring substitutes was not allowed. A shorter term of active service was provided for young men with some education.[10]

As one scholar has noted, Miliutin's army reform was "the most radical social measure of the reform era," apart from the Emancipation Act itself.[11] Even so, however, the Miliutin army fell far short of the ideal of universal service, which would have required the army to take in 600,000 men annually (in 1874; the number tripled by 1914). The fact that the soldier's term of service remained very long by European standards – seven years, as against one to three elsewhere – made it doubly impossible for the autocracy to accommodate so many new men each year: there were not enough officers and NCOs, nor barracks, nor money for equipment. As a result, the Miliutin conscription law was whittled down by re-introducing exemptions based on ethnicity and family status, the latter being an especially fruitful source of exemptions. According to official statistics, those claiming to be excused because they were their family's sole or primary breadwinners reached one-half of all draft-age males during peacetime, and between one-quarter and one-fifth during wartime.[12]

Partly as a consequence of this uneven burden of service, military life remained very unpopular among the Empire's populations. Self-mutilation and drunken orgies of new recruits continued to accompany every call-up. Furthermore, there is little evidence that the tsar's subjects ever developed the type of civic or patriotic consciousness that would have made them eager to fight for their nation. In the imaginations of the intelligentsia, at least,

---

[9] The Cossacks were a legally separate estate, whose conscription into military service was conducted through their own host organizations. Cossacks' terms of service were also different because of their distinctive historic relations with the throne. Miliutin's reforms only partly transformed these special institutions. Nevertheless, the Imperial Manifesto that announced the new conscription obligations asserted that "the strength of a state is not only in the numbers of its troops, but primarily in their moral and intellectual qualities, which reach a high level of development only when the cause of defending the fatherland becomes a common cause of the people, when all, without distinction of title or status, unite for this sacred cause." For Miliutin's emphasis on the "welfare of Russia and the Russian people," see his diary entries from 1864–5, in P. A. Zaionchkovskii (ed.), *Dnevnik D. A. Miliutina 1873–82*, 4 volumes (Moscow, 1947–50), 1: 31.

[10] Other exemptions or deferments could be granted for single male breadwinners, those who wished to complete their education, and certain categories of workers deemed vital to the national economy.

[11] Allan Wildman, *The End of the Russian Imperial Army*, 2 volumes (Princeton, 1980), 1: 25.

[12] General Golovin complained that the system of conscription continued to resemble the prereform lottery too much. N. N. Golovin, *Voennye usiliia v mirovoi voine*, 2 volumes (Paris, 1939), 1: Chapters 1 and 2. For a summary of prewar conscription see also Wildman, *The End of the Russian Imperial Army*, 1: 25–31.

the barrier lay in the peasants' "mystical attitudes toward the person of the tsar" so that they did not identify with the goals of educated society or with such abstractions as the nation, the state, or the Empire. For its part, and perhaps understandably, the autocracy did nothing, before the Revolution of 1905–7, to foster the growth of a civic consciousness capable of replacing such traditional loyalties.[13] Imperial policy and considerations of state security also gave rise to discriminatory practices toward the various ethnic groups that made up the Empire. Russia might have been able to do with a much smaller army, Miliutin concluded, if her geographic situation were not so unfortunate. "With our extended borders, with our undefended coastlines, and, finally, with the suspect orientation of the population of certain of our frontier regions, however," a large portion of Imperial troops would always have to be stationed away from the battlefield.[14] In line with his general nation-building ambitions and his personal affinity for Slavophile "nationalism,"[15] Miliutin hoped that extending conscription to previously excluded regions and ethnic groups might be "the best means for the weakening of tribal differences among the people, the correct unification of all the forces of the state."[16]

The military reform extended the service obligation to new ethnic groups among the tsar's subjects. Among the categories made eligible for the first time, several, including German colonists,[17] Tatars, and Greeks, emigrated in large numbers or petitioned to have their former exemptions restored. Here

[13] On the failure to inculcate citizenship through conscription, see Norman Stone, *The Eastern Front, 1914–1917* (London and Sydney, 1975), 212–14 (which is also the source of the quotation about mystical attitudes); and Leonid Heretz, "Russian Apocalypse 1891–1917: Popular Perceptions of Events From the Year of Famine and Cholera to the Fall of the Tsar," Ph.D. Dissertation, Harvard University (1993), Chapter 6.

[14] Zaionchkovskii, *Voennye reformy*, 261.

[15] See Miller, *Miliutin*, 152–68, for Miliutin's views on Poles and Baltic Germans in particular. Miliutin had a characteristic Imperial military career. He took an active part in the Caucasian wars of the mid-century as acting chief-of-staff to Viceroy Bariatinskii. Stein ("Der Offizier," 459n) reminds us that Miliutin's brother Nikolai was one of those who prepared the intellectual grounds for the Russification policy in Poland.

[16] Miliutin, "On the Main Bases of Personal Military Service," as quoted in Robert F. Baumann, "Universal Service Reform and Russia's Imperial Dilemma," *War & Society* 4/2 (September 1986), 31. Joshua Sanborn argues that the principles behind the 1874 statute signaled "a commitment to an inclusive multi-ethnic army that would grow more inclusive over time as ethnicities assimilated to the imperial norm." See his *Drafting the Russian Nation: Military Conscription, Total War, and Modern Identity, 1905–1925* (DeKalb, Ill., forthcoming), 141. Sanborn's discussion of ethnic thinking in conscription policy is the best available and is based on new archival materials.

[17] German agricultural colonists settled in large numbers in Ukraine, Bessarabia, and the middle Volga, at the invitation of Russia's tsars, who hoped to promote better farming practices and populate sparsely inhabited regions. See Detlef Brandes, *Von den Zaren adoptiert: Die deutschen Kolonisten und Balkansiedler in Neurussland und Bessarabia 1751–1914* (Munich, 1993).

too the new law fell short of its ambitions of universality because the war minister deemed that "the diversity of the Empire's population in terms of its civic development" demanded certain local variations. Official statistics estimate the newly eligible ethnic groups at nearly one-ninth of the Empire's population. Inhabitants of the Grand Duchy of Finland remained exempt, thanks to the nominal autonomy of their region within the Empire. So too did certain Muslim minorities in the Caucasus and Turkestan because of their "low level of civic development." Still other Turkic or Muslim populations were encouraged to preserve their tribal armed forces and were singled out to play the role of praetorian guard in the Empire. Finally, inhabitants of Turkestan and parts of Siberia were exempted in order to encourage agricultural colonists from Russia and Ukraine to migrate there.[18]

In the last years before the Great War, and following on the shattering losses in the Russo-Japanese War, the War and Interior Ministries considered reducing such exemptions and reopening the debate on ethnic policy in the army. The accounts of their deliberations, conducted by interministerial commissions, are revealing about prevailing attitudes among the political and military elites. Much of the discussion focused on limiting the family status and educational exemptions. The resulting Law of 23 June 1912 was a serious step toward more truly universal service, but a combination of inertia and the outbreak of war two years later rendered it largely stillborn.[19] The exemptions for ethnic and national groups were also reviewed. Among the questions discussed, answers to the following were particularly revealing of official attitudes. Should national minorities be called up to serve in special units made up only of that nationality? Or should the current practice of distributing them among various service branches and units be preserved? What physical and cultural characteristics made national minorities more or less suitable for military service? Which national groups were likely to serve the autocracy loyally, and which might pose a risk to security?

The formation of special units was rejected as "not corresponding to either the political or domestic situation of Russia. Historical experience has shown that attempts to form native units in the borderlands have led to one

---

[18] Zaionchkovskii, *Voennye reformy*, 304–05, 308, 312; and Aleksandr V. Fedorov, *Russkaia armiia v 50–70-kh godakh XIX veka. Ocherki* (Leningrad, 1959), 256–7, 259. By the end of the century recruitment was extended to the populations of Transcaucasia and the Northern Caucasus, but not to Turkestan, Amur, or Primor'e and distant parts of Siberia, nor to the non-Russian populations in all of Siberia, Astrakhan and Arkhangel'sk provinces, and Turgai and Ural oblasts (Zaionchkovskii, *Samoderzhavie i russkaia armiia*, 115). See also the interesting discussion of the debates about Jews and military obligation in Zaionchkovskii, *Voennye reformy*, 323–4.

[19] In addition to redefining the qualifications for a whole series of exemptions for family status, the new law removed the service exemption for teachers and medical personnel, probably under the influence of German conscription policy. See Sanborn, *Drafting the Russian Nation*, Chapters 1 and 3.

and the same result: these units must be dissolved as soon as the national question becomes exacerbated." Furthermore, the officials concluded that purely native units always performed worse in combat than analogous units of the regular army, which made them a waste of money.

Among non-Russian peoples who remained exempt from military service, the largest were concentrated in Finland, eastern Caucasia, and Turkestan (including Kirghizia). The interministerial commissions declared themselves against removing these exemptions, largely for political reasons.[20] The officials remained convinced that a few years of service in the Imperial Army would not make loyal soldiers out of Kirghizes but would instead teach them how to handle weapons and so fill the ranks of the Empire's enemies. Similar conclusions were reached concerning Uzbeks, Tajiks, and Kara-Kalpaks, all of whom were judged lacking in "a consciousness of their belonging to the Russian fatherland" [*chustva obshchnosti russkogo otechestva*].[21]

Despite all official reluctance, however, the general trend to whittle away exemptions or special conditions for non-Russian subjects persisted, in part, paradoxically, because it coincided with the rise of a right-wing Russian nationalist movement eager to preserve and extend the economic and political power of ethnic Russian elites. Finland's special autonomy was a particular target of the Russian right. Since 1878 Finland had had its own military formations, separate from the Imperial Army. In 1901 Governor General Nikolai Bobrikov unilaterally dissolved these and attempted to impose Russian conscription practices on the Finnish population. The resistance of the Finnish Diet resulted in a standoff. As a compromise, the obligation to perform military service was replaced by an annual payment from the Finnish government amounting to several million rubles per year.[22] Later the Third Duma (1907–12) used this agreement, among other pretexts, to limit the jurisdiction of Finland's provincial Diet and Senate. A similar attitude – which might be called punitive inclusiveness – was manifested toward the Jews, who, it was proposed, should be assigned to special units that would be sent to the front line in the event of war. Though this measure failed, the

---

[20] The Finns were viewed as "separatists," while the Turkic and Muslim peoples were considered "unreliable."

[21] As further evidence of their suspect loyalties, the officials pointed to the mass annual pilgrimages to Mecca, prompting speculation that these peoples viewed faraway Arabia as their real unifying center. In the event of a war with the Ottoman Empire, it was feared they could not be counted upon to serve the Russian cause loyally. Meanwhile, just the opposite conclusions were drawn about the Buriats, Iakuts, and Muslim populations of the Caucasus, who seemed to possess some natural warlike attributes.

[22] Karl Tiander, *Das Erwachen Osteuropas* (Vienna and Leipzig, 1934), 44. The Grand Duchy of Finland had its own troop formations: one guards battalion, one dragoon regiment, and one rifle battalion. All officers were required to be Finns. They were trained in a military gymnasium and were eligible to serve in either Finnish or Russian units. See Stein, "Der Offizier," 458–9. On Bobrikov's conflicts with the Finns, see Tuomo Polvinen, *Imperial Borderland: Bobrikov and the Attempted Russification of Finland, 1898–1904* (London, 1995).

Duma did bar Jewish students from the St. Petersburg Military Academy on the grounds that Jewish doctors had demoralized Russian troops during the recent war with Japan.[23]

The Empire's ambivalent efforts to create a "national" soldier from its polyglot population encouraged the development of new attitudes toward military training, discipline, and morale, which would be inherited more or less intact by its Soviet successor. At stake was the question: What kind of preparation and command climate brought out the best qualities of the modern Russian man at arms? On this matter, the most important voice belonged to General Mikhail Ivanovich Dragomirov, a member of Miliutin's Special Committee on the Structure and Training of Troops, and later head of the General Staff Academy. His textbook on tactics, published in 1879, was the standard work on the subject within the army until after the Revolution. Dragomirov was known as a "fanatical partisan of Suvorov"[24] in his conviction that morale, fighting spirit and commanders' leadership qualities were the primary determinants of an army's strength. These in turn were to some extent rooted in national character. Although Germans, Swedes, and other Nordic types might fire away at each other from a distance, it was in the nature of the Russian soldier (in common with the Latin races of southern Europe) to close with the enemy, and triumph through cold steel: "able to suffer, able to die – this is the foundation of the martial prowess which is peculiar to the Russian soldier in the highest degree."[25]

In some respects, and despite their obscurantist ethnocentrism, Dragomirov's ideas conformed well with the notion that the tsar's soldiers were now free men, no longer serfs. He deprecated parade-ground show, and emphasized the importance of realistic training and combat skills, along with systematic indoctrination designed, as Bruce Menning has said, "to instill devotion to sovereign and country, discipline, belief in the sanctity of orders, courage, determination, and esprit de corps."[26] At the same time, his insistence upon the preeminence of moral factors blinded him to the impact of technological innovation, leading him in his later years to oppose the introduction of machine guns and rapid-fire artillery, lest the infantry's will to conquer be sapped.[27] Dragomirov's legacy included

[23] Tiander, *Das Erwachen Osteuropas*, 47; Sanborn, *Drafting the Russian Nation*, 201–5.

[24] Wildman, *End of the Russian Imperial Army*, 1: 18

[25] M. I. Dragomirov, *Ocherki* (Kiev, 1898), 139; in Fuller, *Strategy and Power in Russia*, 304.

[26] Bruce Menning, *Bayonets before Bullets: The Imperial Russian Army, 1861–1914* (Bloomington, Ind., 1992), 39.

[27] Wildman, *End of the Russian Imperial Army*, 1: 18–19. For more on Dragomirov, see S. Dmitriev, "General Dragomirov," *Istoricheskii zhurnal* 5 (1943), 26–32; Kersnovskii, *Istoriia russkoi armii*, 3: 507; V. A. Sukhomlinov, *Vospominaniia* (Berlin, 1924), 50–60; A. I. Denikin, *Staraia armiia*, 2 volumes (Paris, 1929–1931), 1: 34–6; Menning, *Bayonets before Bullets*, 38–42; and Stein, "Der Offizier," 371–2. Stein argues that after Miliutin and his successor, Petr Vannovskii, Dragomirov probably had the greatest impact on the character of the late Imperial Army.

a new view of the proper relationship of officers and men, which was, Allan Wildman argues, "that officers were encouraged to draw close to their men, to speak to them 'soul to soul', to be their 'older brother,' and to gain their confidence." The Army instructed officers to advise soldiers on their personal problems, to read books to them, and to help them write letters home.[28]

Many of these attitudes, both the antipathy to technological modernization and professionalization, and the idealization of "brotherly relations" between officers and soldiers, found their way into the Red Army of the interwar years. In the meantime, however, the social gulf between officers and educated society, on the one hand, and between officers and soldiers, on the other, continued to deepen, even as the officer corps took in more and more representatives of the nonnoble estates, to cope with the growing number of men under their command.[29]

The Great War and the Russian Army

The Great War politicized issues of military service, and of ethnicity generally. Like never before the autocracy had to mobilize the population of the Empire and improvise new means of managing its mobilized society. As the war became the focus of national attention, it became a testing ground for social privilege, especially that of the gentry, which had lost all vestige of social function. The war was waged with patriotic appeals and calls to national sacrifice very much in the spirit of the *levée en masse*. Exemption from wartime service became a growing source of resentment among those who were serving or who had relatives on the fronts. Despite plenty of evidence to the contrary, however, the High Command and the political elites persisted in their faith that the Russian population would remain loyal to the cause of Russia despite such perceived inequities. They assumed that, forty years after the Great Reforms, the common conscript had learned to identify his interests with those of the Russian nation and state. Characteristically, when General Nikolai Ianushkevich, chief of the Imperial General Staff, made a proposal during the occupation of eastern Galicia to reward particularly valorous soldiers with land confiscated from, or abandoned by, subjects of the Habsburg Empire, the State Council and others denounced the suggestion as unpatriotic and insulting to the honor of the Russian Army.[30]

---

[28] Wildman, *End of the Russian Imperial Army*, 1: 35.

[29] Peter Kenez, "A Profile of the Pre-revolutionary Officer Corps," *California Slavic Studies* 7 (1973), 121–58.

[30] Arkadii N. Iakhontov, *Prologue to Revolution: Notes of A. N. Iakhontov on the Secret Meetings of the Council of Ministers, 1915*, translated and edited by Michael Cherniavsky (Englewood Cliffs, N.J., 1967), 22.

Inevitably, the autocracy's performance in the war became a test of its legitimacy, one that it ultimately failed. Wartime policies had economic and social consequences that dramatically undermined the position of many traditional elites, especially the gentry.[31] (Indeed, when the Provisional Government abolished Imperial estate and rank distinctions in March 1917, it was acknowledging a *fait* largely *déjà accompli*.) The war hastened the reconfiguration of identities that was part of the longer term shift in the way Imperial society was structured, from traditional dynastic, confessional, and estate categories to categories of class and ethnicity. The diminished importance of traditional anchors of social position created space for heightened emphasis on national and ethnic identity, on the one hand, and class identity on the other.

Norman Stone, in his history of the Eastern Front in the Great War, has argued that the war had the effect of accelerating the modernization of the Russian Empire's economy and administrative structure.[32] Although he does not extend the argument to questions of ethnicity, it seems clear that new forms of patriotism and national identities, and new means for their expression, emerged and were provisionally consolidated during the war, both as a consequence (often unintended) of state policies, but also as a consequence of the "unofficial" activities of elites, especially after the abdication of Nicholas II.[33]

The war was a watershed in relations between Russians and non-Russians and among non-Russians. It was not just the war per se, but (1) the character of the regimes waging that war, which in the East included three multi-national, dynastic empires – Austria-Hungary, the Ottomans, and Russia; (2) the destructive character of the war, the first since the Napoleonic invasion to involve the loss, destruction, and occupation of the Empire's densely populated European provinces; and (3) the specific policies pursued by both Russia and its opponents with respect to military recruitment, wartime propaganda,

---

[31] Most scholars have agreed that the heavy losses in the army contributed to a democratization of the officer corps, resulting in a sharp and rapid decline in the weight and power of the gentry in that institution.

[32] "There was, in other words, a burst of economic activity between 1914 and 1917 that brought as much change to Russia as the whole of the previous generation. It was, indeed, the economic 'take-off' that men had been predicting for Russia, that had, in a sense, caused the First World War, since German apprehensions of it had led Germany's leaders into provoking a preventive war. The First World War provoked a crisis of economic modernisation, and the Bolshevik Revolution was the outcome." Stone, *The Eastern Front*, 285. Peter Holquist also makes a persuasive argument that the Great War introduced institutions and practices that modernized the Empire far more rapidly and unpredictably than anything the state had undertaken in the past two decades. See his "'Information Is the Alpha and Omega of Our Work': Bolshevik Surveillance in Its Pan-European Context," *Journal of Modern History* 69 (September 1997), 415–50.

[33] See Hubertus F. Jahn, *Patriotic Culture in Russia during World War I* (Ithaca, N.Y., and London, 1995).

occupation and evacuation, and even refugee aid. The consequences were
nothing less than the internationalization and militarization of the Empire's
"national questions."[34]

Ironically, the Russian Empire's wartime policies contributed in important ways to the emergence of nationalist mass politics and ethnic conflict
by 1917. Those non-Russian national elites who had tried to build their national movements in the brief period between the Revolution of 1905 and
the outbreak of war, through primary schooling, publishing activities, and
cooperative societies, may not have succeeded nearly so well as the Imperial
elites' own politics of occupation and evacuation, however unintended the
consequences may have been. In several instances, the latter policies were all
too clearly intended to pit one ethnic community against another.

War waged among multinational empires comprised of the same, overlapping ethnic groups raised new issues and intensified existing hostilities among
the subject peoples of all the belligerents. Wartime policies dealing with
occupation, evacuation, and resettlement measures provided new grounds
for asserting old grievances. The propaganda of "national liberation" that
became ubiquitous as the war dragged on called the legitimacy of all the
imperial dynasties into question, undermined the transnational pretensions
of their cosmopolitan elites, and exacerbated tensions between the confessional and ethnic communities and those elites. Experiments with national
military units extended those tensions to the soldiers, a major social group
in themselves, and one that had not been a target of most prewar national
movements. Occupation policy, conducted in the name of national security,
changed the stakes of ethnic identity, privileging the "correct" groups and
condoning property confiscation, deportation, arrest, or execution for the
"wrong" ones. Evacuation policy and refugee relief efforts further served to
reinforce the new, "nationalized" politics of the war.[35] Many earlier social
and political tensions had an ethnic element overlaid on them, while ethnicity became a weapon and policy instrument for all the belligerent powers.[36]
When Nicholas II abdicated in early 1917, many educated citizens still expected social and ethnic tensions to abate. In fact, their utopian hopes were
quickly and tragically dashed.

The Revolutions of 1917 and the Provisional Government

The consequences of these wartime expedients were to be seen early in 1917.
The Provisional Government assumed that it would be able to rally the

---

[34] For more on this, see Mark von Hagen, "The Great War and the Mobilization of Ethnicity
in the Russian Empire," in Barnett R. Rubin and Jack Snyder (eds.), *Post-Soviet Political
Order: Conflict and State Building* (London and New York, 1998), 34–57.

[35] Peter Gattrell, *A Whole Empire Walking: Refugees in Russia During World War I* (Bloomington, Ind., 1999).

[36] For more on this, see the unpublished manuscript by Eric Lohr, "Nationalizing the Russian
Empire: The Campaign Against Enemy Minorities during World War I."

demoralized troops, and the citizenry more generally, around the defense of the Revolution, now that the hated autocracy was removed from the scene. But how the Empire's diverse communities understood "revolution" proved to be quite distinct from the understanding of the liberals and moderate socialists in the Provisional Government. Very quickly, the transformation of politics that had begun with the 1905 revolutions and accelerated with the onset of war in 1914 confronted the would-be rulers of democratic Russia with serious challenges. In response to their appeals for national unity, which entailed the continued prosecution of an increasingly unpopular war,[37] they heard in reply a variety of demands – for national autonomy or independence in some quarters, for economic and social concessions in others.

From the start, class and nation threatened to splinter the optimistic social cohesion that the Provisional Government projected onto "society." The class conflicts that shaped so much of the politics of 1917 have been well treated by historians of the Revolutionary year.[38] In the present context, however, it is the appeal of nation that matters most; which is not, however, to downplay the impact that class appeals had in undermining the illusory social harmony that was proclaimed following the fall of the Romanovs.

The liberals and moderate socialists who presumed to rule over the Russian Empire were caught off guard by the virulence and rapid spread of the "national question" throughout the country, in the same way that they were surprised by the ingratitude and impatience of workers, peasants, and soldiers newly emancipated from the tyranny of the autocracy. Within weeks of the February/March Revolution, the Provisional Government found itself confronting Finnish, Polish, and Ukrainian demands for autonomy. The new rulers shared a faith that greater democracy would "solve" the national problem on its own terms, because they believed that the diverse national movements that had formed in the last decades of tsarism were a direct consequence of tsarist oppression.[39] Once that oppression was lifted, and the discriminatory measures of the Old Regime ended, the national question would be resolved with the proclamation of full equality of citizens, regardless of religion, race, or nationality. That being so,

---

[37] The moderate socialist parties, the Socialist Revolutionaries and the Mensheviks, split further apart after February 1917, into revolutionary "defensists" (who supported the war effort), internationalists (who called for an immediate ceasefire and peace negotiations), and outright defeatist factions. Even the Bolsheviks faced these dilemmas, though their most severe trials would come after October and during the negotiations at Brest-Litovsk.

[38] For a good overview of the social history of 1917 see Marc Ferro, *The Russian Revolution of February 1917: The Fall of Tsarism and the Origins of Bolshevik Power*, translated by J. L. Richards and Nicole Stone (London, 1972); and his *October 1917: A Social History of the Russian Revolution*, translated by Norman Stone (London, 1980).

[39] This faith was shared by the leadership of the two most important parties in the Provisional Government coalitions, the Kadets and the Socialist-Revolutionaries; but the Georgian Menshevik Iraklii Tseretelli recalled that this "blindness" on the national question was certainly characteristic of the socialist intelligentsia generally. See I. I. Tseretelli, *Vospominaniia o Fevral'skoi revoliutsii*, 2 volumes (Paris and The Hague, 1963), 2: 69.

the new government concluded that the continuing stridency of Russia's national minorities was a result of the machinations of foreign powers, particularly Germany and Austria-Hungary. In the end, the centripetal demands of national self-determination proved irreconcilable with the more universalizing aspirations of the liberal and socialist leadership, which was unable to envision a new political structure for the multinational state.[40]

Many of the key participants in 1917, whatever their political orientation, were prepared to understand their experience as a replay of the French Revolution more than a century earlier. Aleksandr Kerensky in particular recalled the experience of the first French Republic, whose troops defeated the armies of the coalition of autocratic states that had united against them. In accord with that understanding of history, the Provisional Government chose to prosecute the war, a problem that quickly came to dominate all other concerns and provoked the most profound crises of the new regime. At the same time, the need to keep the army fighting became a reason for the Provisional Government to procrastinate in other areas, while maintaining a formalistic adherence to legal proprieties, which suggested an unwillingness to grasp the nettle of revolutionary change.

Calling for the soldiers to defend "the holy Russian Revolution,"[41] Kerensky ordered a general offensive in June that he hoped would restore the fighting spirit of the Russian army, on the model of the French *levée en masse*. Unfortunately for Kerensky and the Provisional Government, the offensive turned into a rout and helped prepare the way for the final collapse of the new regime. When Kerensky appealed to the soldiers in the name of the Russian Revolution, and less frequently in the name of the nation itself, he was confronted by a rising tide of non-Russian national programs and parties, including a rapidly spreading movement for Ukrainization in the army.[42] Soldiers from the traditionally Ukrainian provinces led the way for other non-Russian nations in demanding permission to form separate Ukrainian national units and to have these serve on the Southwest and Romanian Fronts, so that they could defend their "homelands" against the foreign aggressors. These demands, no less than Kerensky's appeals, were often couched in the familiar rhetoric of the *levée*. They were also tied to the expectation of a general redistribution of the land. Soldiers, still overwhelmingly peasants, wanted to be close to home when that redistribution took place. The demands for national military formations, and national

---

[40] For documentation of the struggles between the central leadership in Petrograd and the competing elites on the imperial peripheries, see Robert P. Browder and Alexander F. Kerensky (eds.), *The Russian Provisional Government 1917*, 3 volumes (Stanford, 1961), 1: 317–433.

[41] Tseretelli, *Vospominaniia*, 1: 41.

[42] See M. S. Frenkin, *Russkaia armiia i revoliutsiia 1917–1918* (Munich, 1978), on national movements among soldiers; and Mark von Hagen, "The Russian Imperial Army and the Ukrainian National Movement in 1917," *The Ukrainian Quarterly* 54/3–4 (Fall–Winter 1998), 220–56.

autonomy more generally, had been limited to minority political parties before 1917, but the experience of the war and the anxieties unleashed by the collapse of the monarchy and the resulting breakdown in authority served to elevate this minority platform into a powerful challenger to the Socialist Revolutionary and Bolshevik appeals of class. As the center's hold over the country slipped, national separatist movements gathered strength in the army,[43] and the very fact of their strength encouraged nonsoldiers to press their demands for national autonomy and self-determination more ardently.

By the middle of 1917 the movement for "nationalization" of the army began to inspire counterdemands from Russians, or those who purported to speak for the Russian nation, either to disallow the non-Russian national formations or to allow the formation of exclusively Russian units. Morale and discipline were in decline, for which the High Command blamed Bolshevik propaganda and agitation (and socialist politics in general). Some of its members concluded that the only way to combat the radical infection was to make concessions to the national parties, in the hope that nationalism would undercut Bolshevization. No one in the military leadership was sanguine about such reforms, but all were increasingly desperate as they saw the army melting away before their eyes.

The Civil War and the *Levée en masse*: Anti-Bolshevik Military Rhetoric and Practice

In the conditions of protracted international and civil war that raged across Eastern Europe and the former Russian Empire until roughly 1923, the fates of political elites everywhere were inextricably tied to their abilities to mobilize the populations over which they claimed to rule. Military leaders played prominent roles in founding newly independent states, the best-known examples being Marshal Jozef Pilsudski in Poland and Field Marshal Karl Mannerheim in Finland. As new proto-elites experimented with techniques of mobilization in the context of revolution and civil war, national movements pressed weak governments to elevate the principle of ethnicity to greater prominence in army organization. For all the new states, the national principle was a dramatic departure from Imperial practice. Nearly everywhere, the old loyalties to tsar, dynasty, or faith were replaced by appeals to national unity against foreign tyranny and intrusion. Among these national movements, that in the Ukraine was the largest of those operating on territory not controlled by the Germans. Because Ukraine figured so prominently and in such complicated ways in the strategic and political thinking of the

---

[43] Richard Pipes argues that national movements were at their strongest among the soldiers. See his *The Formation of the Soviet Union: Communism and Nationalism, 1917–1923* (Cambridge, Mass., 1964), 52.

major belligerents during the Civil War, it merits special attention.[44] Yet Ukrainization was but one of several parallel movements that had as their goal and consequence the creation of military units made up predominantly of one, non-Russian national group, using a non-Russian language for command and administration.

By the time the Bolsheviks seized power in Petrograd in October 1917 and sent their commissars to assume command over the various fronts, they faced heavily Ukrainized Southwest and Romanian fronts. While the newly constituted Central Council, or Rada, did little to win the loyalties of Ukrainian soldiers for Kiev, its appeal was nevertheless ethnic in

FIGURE 12. Dimitri Moore, *To the Peoples of the Caucasus* (1920). Colored lithograph for the Political Directorate of the Revolutionary Military Council of the USSR. Hoover Institution Archives.

The Russian Revolution complicated the attitude of European socialists to war and introduced a major new variant of the relationship between revolutionary political legitimacy and military mobilization. European socialist parties had adamantly opposed war in any form for at least a generation before 1914 and acquiesced grudgingly in the national mobilizations sparked by the July Crisis. In turn, war had created revolutionary conditions in Russia – the opposite of the pattern that had prevailed in the 1790s – conditions the Bolsheviks had exploited by adopting a policy of "revolutionary defeatism," which elevated an ideological rejection of war over the claims of national self-defense as usually understood. Having once seized power, however, the need to ward off counterrevolutionary forces within and outside the fledgling Soviet state, and to regain control of the peripheral nationalities of the former tsarist empire, became pressing concerns.

The problem was not simply to increase the size of the Red Army through enforced conscription but to create armed forces galvanized by revolutionary energy, like those that were believed to have saved France in the Year II. In the Russian case, however, the appeal could not be to *la patrie en danger* – at least not directly – but rather to a revolutionary class consciousness that transcended national identities without obliterating them.

Dimitri Moore's striking poster was created to aid such mobilization in the Caucasus, a region of hard fighting at the time Moore's poster appeared, and not fully under Bolshevik control until 1921, when the independent Menshevik Republic of Georgia was finally suppressed. Moore's work adapts what had by then become a standardized image of the revolutionary crowd – in which town and country, worker and peasant, stand side by side – in order to show the diverse ethnicities and confessions of the region, all answering the call to arms (reproduced in the poster's lower margin in five languages). The galvanizing figure at right bears a flag with a hammer and plough superimposed upon a red star, and is dressed in a costume reminiscent of that worn by Cossacks. That Moore places the bearer of the revolutionary appeal on a bridling white horse is a concession to traditional expectations about how military leadership will present itself, and perhaps also to the region's historic role as a provider of cavalry for the tsar's armies – a traditionalism that contrasts with the highly stylized rendering of the image as a whole.

[44] The best account of the revolution and civil war in Ukraine remains John S. Reshetar, Jr., *The Ukranian Revolution, 1917–1920: A Study in Nationalism* (Princeton, N.J., 1952).

character, in response to pressure from soldiers, among others. The Rada was chased out of Ukraine by the Bolsheviks, restored by the invading Germans and Austrians, and then overthrown, with Austrian connivance, by a former Imperial general, Pavlo Skoropads'kyi. His rule was proclaimed as a "Hetmanate," a populist recasting of a seventeenth-century form of state that fused military and political leadership. The Hetmanate, established in those parts of Ukraine controlled by Germany and Austria-Hungary, actually raised the small army it was permitted under the terms of Brest-Litovsk, albeit on nonethnic principles. It employed thousands of Imperial officers who had taken refuge on Ukrainian soil from the Red terror. Still, Skoropads'kyi's government continued and extended the experiment in Ukrainization of the armed forces begun during the war, which meant at a minimum the use of the Ukrainian language and some attention to local lore in educational programs. Inevitably, however, the Hetman's state- and nation-building projects were compromised by his dependence on the predatory German occupation forces. His reign ended in widespread peasant insurgency and his unceremonious flight into German exile.[45]

All the parties that claimed authority over the lands of the former Russian empire assumed that their regime would rally the population and, most importantly, that the soldiers would back them because they advanced the claims of popular sovereignty against the class or national oppression of the enemy, however defined. During the Civil War all sides continued to appeal to national symbols, but with variations designed to take into account specific constituencies and the enemies' counterclaims (figure 12). The major legatee of the Provisional Goverment's vision of a united Russia as the bulwark against internal and external enemies was the White movement, which led its armies into battle against Bolsheviks and Ukrainians alike under the slogan "Great Russia, one and indivisible."

Characteristically, the name that the anti-Bolshevik forces adopted for their military forces was the Volunteer Army.[46] At first the White leaders appealed to all "healthy elements" in Russian society, to defend the territorial integrity of the empire and the social and political achievements of the Provisional Government. Gradually, however, their ideological appeals were transformed into a more authoritarian vision of Russian national greatness, backed by policies that were intolerant of any concessions to the constituencies that brought down the Provisional Government. Because White military and political leaders came to view the Bolshevik coup as a consequence of the betrayal of Russia by democrats, socialists, and anti-Russian nationalists,

---

[45] See Pavlo Skoropads'kyi, *Spohady* (Kiev, 1999).

[46] For more on the White movement(s), see Peter Kenez, *Civil War in South Russia, 1918* (Berkeley, Calif., 1971); and his *Civil War in South Russia, 1919–1920* (Berkeley, Calif., 1977).

they increasingly saw the answer to Russia's trials as a new, authoritarian political system that nonetheless was cloaked in patriotic rhetoric about the Russian nation.[47]

The Red Army as an Army of a New Type

Even the Bolsheviks deployed the rhetoric of revolutionary self-defense and national liberation from foreign conquerors whenever possible. With the regathering of the lands under the Bolsheviks, a party that had given primacy to class was compelled to reconsider its short- and long-term strategies with regard to the national question. The Bolsheviks came to power with a very rudimentary program on military affairs, in part because they expected that their Revolution was only a prelude to a much greater one on a global scale, after which they would not really need an army at all, but also because the writings of Marx, Engels, and Jean Jaurès did not offer clear instructions to revolutionaries-turned-leaders.

The socialist program was generally hostile to the maintenance of standing armies and the preservation of officer prerogatives, and presumed that the Revolution would produce its own *levée en masse* with all the spontaneity that legend demanded. Jaurès's *armée nouvelle* was to be a militia based on the armed urban population. It would elect its own commanders, pursue exclusively defensive aims, and only minimally disrupt the production process by restricting training to off-hours at the factories.[48] Army Commissar Nikolai Podvoiskii proposed to the Congress on Demobilization that convened in December 1917 that a future socialist army be made up of "the laboring classes, workers and peasants, with a firm proletarian core." He appealed to all socialists to take part in the creation of an army in order to wage "a sacred war for socialism." All citizens who volunteered to serve in the Socialist Guard were required to obtain recommendations from the "revolutionary-socialist parties or workers', soldiers', or peasants' organizations."[49]

The other Revolutionary institution that resonated with the experience of the *levée en masse* was the Red Guards. These were militias of armed factory

---

[47] For the evolution of the White leaders' views on power, authority, and nation, see Anna Procyk, *Russian Nationalism and Ukraine: The Nationality Policy of the Volunteer Army during the Civil War* (Edmonton and Toronto, 1995).

[48] For more on socialist writings on military organization, see Martin Berger, *Engels, Armies and Revolution* (Hamden, Conn. 1977); and Sigmund Neumann and Mark von Hagen, "Engels and Marx on Revolution, War, and the Army in Society," in Peter Paret (ed.), *Makers of Modern Strategy from Machiavelli to the Nuclear Age* (Princeton, N.J., 1986), 262–80.

[49] For an excellent account of the Bolshevik debates about demobilization and the future Socialist Guard, see E. N. Gorodetskii, "Demobilizatsiia armii v 1917–1918 gg.," *Istoriia SSSR* 1 (1958), 3–31.

workers, who served in rotation and elected their commanders from among
their own members. By the end of 1917 their numbers reached 200,000, and
they were being dispatched from Petrograd, Moscow, and other revolutionary cities to aid beleaguered soviets in provincial cities.[50] The leaders of the
Red Guards, most notably Valentin Trifonov, were among the most ardent
advocates of basing a new people's militia on the Red Guard core. In mid-
January 1918, the Third Congress of Soviets proclaimed the "Declaration of
the Rights of the Laboring and Exploited," which sanctioned the arming of
all laborers, the formation of a socialist Red Army of workers and peasants,
and the complete disarming of the property-holding classes. The congress
defined citizenship in the new republic in two articles: first, only people
engaged in productive and socially useful labor could claim the rights of citizens; second, citizens had the exclusive and honorable right to bear arms for
the new state. Thus the new state made army service integral to its policies
of class discrimination.[51]

When the Bolsheviks' hopes for a rapid end to the war were dashed by a
renewed German offensive in the winter of 1917–18, which was accompanied by the outbreak of armed domestic resistance to Bolshevik rule, the new
leadership reconsidered its opposition to a standing army and postponed the
transition to a militia until more propitious conditions would appear. Still,
the commitment to a revolutionary *levée* persisted in the Bolsheviks' discriminatory policies in favor of the urban proletariat, which they viewed as the
most "class-conscious" part of the population, and therefore the most reliable fighting force. The longer the fighting continued, the more compromises
the new leadership had to make between the realities of Russian society and
its desire to promote class purity and revolutionary *élan*. By the end of the
Bolsheviks' first year in power, the new Workers–Peasants Red Army was
overwhelmingly peasant in composition and no longer recruited even nominal volunteers, but directly conscripted them. Its leadership included a large
number of former tsarist officers, who were singled out as "military specialists," to distinguish them from those Red commanders who rose from
the ranks or graduated from crash courses in military command. As a sur-
rogate for its compromised principles, however, the new regime markedly
strengthened the institution of the political commissar, which had actually
been initiated under the Provisional Government to represent the new Revolutionary authority. Under the Bolsheviks the commissar's functions, like
those of the Committee of Public Safety's Representatives on Mission in
the Year II, included keeping watch over unreliable officers and sustaining

---

[50] For more on the Red Guards in 1917, see Rex Wade, *Red Guards and Workers' Militias in
the Russian Revolution* (Stanford, 1984).
[51] *S"ezdy sovetov Soiuza SSR: soiuznykh i avtonomnykh sovetskikh sotsialisticheskikh respub-
lik: Sbornik dokumentov, 1917–1939 gg.*, 7 volumes (Moscow, 1959), 1: 28.

troop morale and fighting spirit.[52] The commissars became synonymous with the new regime in the eyes of its enemies, who often referred to it as the commissarocracy.[53]

The debate over the future of the military in the Soviet state broke out even before the Civil War was over. Political hostilities frequently came to the fore in military units and in national forums like the Eighth Congress of the Communist Party in 1919, where a group called the Military Opposition defended the principles of partisan warfare against the politically suspect military specialists, who preferred traditional military methods. Social and professional differences were accentuated by differences in recent military experience. Those who had served in the military since at least 1914 had seen two very different types of warfare, and they tried to draw the correct lessons from both for future generations. The Red commanders, partly out of a sense of their collective *élan*, pointed to the highly mobile, dispersed operations of the Civil War as the way of the future, with heavy emphasis on political propaganda and popular morale. Generally the military specialists downplayed the significance of the Civil War and warned that future wars would more likely be variants of the trench warfare fought by modern mass armies, such as those that faced one another during the recent Great War. The protagonists were – to a large extent – replaying the debate between the advocates of the original *levée en masse* and those who insisted on the more conservative vision of the nation in arms that was institutionalized by the Prussian military reforms.

This debate, continuing into early 1921, was the immediate context for Mikhail Frunze's first statements on military doctrine and strategy. He and a wartime colleague, Sergei Gusev, who was then director of the Political Administration of the Red Army, presented a set of theses to the military delegates attending the Tenth Party Congress in 1921.[54] The theses were an attempt to synthesize the views of an influential majority of the political staff, Red commanders, and military specialists. They also represented one of the

---

[52] For more on the early history of the Red Army, see S. M. Kliatskin, *Na zashchite Oktiabria: Organizatsiia reguliarnoi armii i militsionnoe stroitel'stvo v sovetskoi respublike, 1917–1920* (Moscow, 1965); John Erickson, *The Soviet High Command: A Military-Political History, 1918–1941* (New York, 1962); and Francesco Benvenuti, *The Bolsheviks and the Red Army, 1918–1922* (Cambridge, 1988).

[53] See Gerhard Ritter, *Das Kommunemodell und die Begründung der Roten Armee im Jahre 1918* (Berlin, 1965), 196–209.

[54] For this and the quotations in the next five paragraphs see [Sergei Gusev and Mikhail Frunze], "Reorganizatsiia Raboche-Krest'ianskoi Krasnoi Armii (Materialy k X s"ezdu RKP)," *Desiatyi s"ezd* (1963), 710–14. Podvoiskii, as the head of the Universal Military Training Administration [*Vsevobuch*], defended the militia model over any permanent accommodation of standing armies. See his "Rezoliutsiia X s"ezda partii po voprosu o reorganizatsii vooruzhennykh sil Respubliki," *Desiatyi s"ezd* (1963), 708–9.

first attempts to present the "lessons of the Civil War." When political and military authorities discussed the lessons of the Civil War, their arguments centered on which factors had been most crucial to the Bolshevik victory, and on the nature of future warfare. Underneath, however, it was clear to all that the real debate had to do with the future of the army in Soviet society, the relationship of the Communist Party to armed force, and the shape of the socialist order to come.

Gusev's sober and often unflattering analysis of the recent performance of the Red Army characterized the Civil War as a conflict shaped by the wavering loyalties of the peasant masses, torn between the dictatorship of the bourgeoisie and the dictatorship of the proletariat. But he did not dwell long on the Civil War because, in his opinion, wars of the future would be different. Never again would the Soviet Republic face an army like that of the Whites', that was "shaky, hostile or neutral to the proletarian dictatorship, poorly trained and armed, hastily formed and not united (because of the hostile attitude of soldiers toward the officers)." Instead, the Red Army would confront an aggressive, well-armed imperialist foe. During the recent war, the Red Army had been trained and armed less well than the Whites, had a weakly prepared command staff, and was hastily organized in conditions of incessant fighting. Still, the Reds won by virtue of their numerical superiority and greater internal cohesion, achieved by the unceasing efforts of the political departments, commissars, and Communist cells, in an atmosphere of "the toiling masses' broad sympathies for the Soviet regime and their revolutionary enthusiasm." In other words, more than anything else, political work and the improvised form of Bolshevik civil–military relations won the war. Gusev believed that the Red Army had captured the revolutionary *élan* and mobilizing power of the *levée en masse*.

Gusev's characterization of the Civil War as a conflict between two shaky and improvised peasant armies, and his prediction that future wars would be waged against traditional European standing armies, supported a series of theses about the future army that also appealed to the military specialists. Gusev concluded that the Red Army, "in the form that it has currently taken, is altogether powerless against mighty imperialist armies." Therefore, the Soviet state must undertake to make the Red Army equal to its future opponents. This goal ruled out any wholesale resort to a militia army. Gusev repeated many of the arguments that pre-Revolutionary military thinkers had employed in seeking to rebut the German orientation of Russian military theory. Gusev argued that Russia was unlike Prussia in that it lacked an industrial proletariat and a well-developed railroad network to move troops speedily from one region to another in the event of war. Furthermore, he feared that militia armies would form the bulwark for "local particularistic strivings to the detriment of the interests of the Workers'-Peasants' Republic." The currently existing, centralized army organization was the only one, in Gusev's view, that could effectively defend state interests as opposed to the regional loyalties that a militia would foster. In other words, Gusev here argued that the *levée en masse* was inappropriate for future wars. If the party and government insisted on making an initial transition to a militia system, Gusev demanded that it be strictly limited to proletarian and semiproletarian cities and villages, and that the new units maintain close ties with the special assignment detachments and with trade unions. In primarily agricultural areas, Gusev concluded, the "particularistic strivings" of the peasantry would reinforce the local authorities in their inclinations toward autonomy.

The agrarian character of the Russian economy and society had other implications for military planners. Gusev warned that the persistence of an overwhelmingly "petit-bourgeois peasant" majority, fully capable of reviving capitalism in the Soviet Republic, combined with the failure of revolution to spread in the West, and the economic devastation of the country overall, created a situation particularly ripe for "Bonapartist attempts to overthrow Soviet power."[55] Gusev argued that only by preserving the political apparatus of the Red Army could the counterrevolutionary political energies of the peasantry be managed successfully. The commissar would continue to inculcate revolutionary *élan*. But commissars were no longer enough to guarantee that cohesion and spirit.

Third, Gusev argued for the training of a highly qualified officer corps, beginning with the reeducation of the Red commanders who had learned their trade on the battlefield but lacked formal preparation. Although the formation of an adequate officer corps would require a long period of training, "a workers'-peasants' government" required military leadership that was not only tactically competent but "politically conscious." Such an officer corps would present a clear threat to any "bourgeois" government that kept its soldiers in a state of ignorance, "barely conscious unskilled workers of war, who were only capable of marching, shooting, and digging trenches." In order to assure the state a steady supply of "conscious" Red Army men, Gusev called for transforming the barracks into a military and political school, as well as a "labor school," which would tie the Red Army man to the general "working life of the nation." Soldiers would participate in the economic recovery in ways that would not detract from their military training. In particular, soldiers could help repair, rebuild, and expand the network of barracks or assist peasants in agricultural work, in such a way as to "accommodate the tasks of political, military, and labor training."

In all, Gusev outlined a new form of civil–military relations derived from the experience of both the Civil War and the Great War. The army of the

---

[55] Here Gusev was following an analysis that Marx had made of the Revolutions of 1848 in *The Eighteenth Brumaire of Louis Bonaparte* (New York, 1852). Marx located the social support for the "bourgeois monarchy" of Louis Philippe in the conservative small peasantry, who resemble "a sackful of potatoes." Marx attributed many of the worst features of the Napoleonic despotism to the preponderance of the army, the *point d'honneur* of the peasants.

future would have far closer ties to the civilian economy, while the population and economy would be fully mobilized in time of war, so that the distinctions between worker and soldier, soldier and citizen, would dissolve. In Gusev's version of the *levée en masse*, the Red Army's advantages over any hostile capitalist foe arose chiefly from the peculiar character of the proletariat, which substituted for the revolutionary masses of 1917 or, for that matter, 1793.

Frunze, in his portion of the theses, and in an important article he wrote in July 1921 entitled "A Unified Military Doctrine,"[56] attempted to create a doctrine that addressed the concerns of the Imperial reformers, while reflecting the scientific approach to politics and society that he believed Marxism offered. Proletarian military doctrine started from the assumption that any future war would be a mass war and that the state would have to mobilize all its resources to fight it. The Soviet state would never initiate a war but would fight only in defense. However, once war was underway, Red Army strategy would be offensive in ways that more resembled the highly mobile fighting of the Civil War than the positional trench fighting of the Great War. Still, even a war of maneuver would be won in the end by the side with the superior political system – meaning the system that could best coordinate economic and political matters with military needs. Frunze was confident that the socialist state would triumph in such a war because it could rely on its working class far more than could the ruling bourgeoisie of the capitalist states. The burden of fighting, however, would have to fall largely on the proletariat, for it alone had the capacity to wage offensive warfare. In the proletarian dictatorship, a peasant army, as the recent experience with the partisan units and in the Polish war had demonstrated, was suitable only for narrowly defensive purposes.

Finally, Frunze conceded that a mass army alone, even with a high degree of proletarian solidarity, was not strong enough to defeat world capitalism. He insisted that the army of the future would have to attain a level of technological superiority over its imperialist rivals. To achieve the technological revolution that Frunze deemed crucial for success, the nation's political elite would have to be won over to a program of industrialization, with a high priority assigned to defense industry. Finally, the military system Frunze was proposing required an ambitious program of civic education, coupled with structural changes in the national economy, that would transform the peasant soldiers of the present into something closer to a well-disciplined proletariat. Both Frunze and Gusev were acknowledging that the current Red Army, and by extension contemporary Soviet society, had to be thoroughly remade in order to recapture the energies of the *levée en masse* for the socialist revolution.

---

[56] M. V. Frunze, "Edinaia voennaia doktrina i Krasnaia armiia," *Armiia i revoliutsiia* 1 (1921), reprinted in M. V. Frunze, *Izbrannye proizvedeniia*, 2 volumes (Moscow, 1957), 2: 4–22.

The Frunze Reforms (1924–1926)

In 1924, Frunze stepped in as Trotsky's deputy and initiated a thorough-going set of reforms intended to professionalize the Red Army under the catchword "militarization."[57] Institutional reform of the army, however, was only one aspect of Frunze's ambitious scheme. Ultimately, the army's leaders were not content to confine their militarization campaign to the military alone. In 1924, Frunze and his allies in the army went on the road to persuade political leaders and the civilian populace that they too had essential roles in aiding the army to defend the nation – the latter by learning basic military skills, the former by developing an organizational network capable of mobilizing large numbers of men and women rapidly in the event of war. Frunze justified what he called "the militarization of the civilian populace" by the small size and budget of the standing army, and because the territorial militia system failed to ensure the level of combat readiness demanded by modern warfare. "We cannot prepare the country for defense," he warned, "if we rely solely on our military resources."[58] In one speech after another, the reform team at the top of the army argued that only a society permeated with military values could successfully defend the country in future wars, which would be fought not just between armies, but between entire mobilized populations. Many of these ideas originated in the theses that Frunze and Gusev had defended earlier at the Tenth and Eleventh Party Congresses. Moreover, the recent world war had offered a foretaste of life in fully mobilized societies. But now the "militarizers" demanded a restructured peacetime civil–military relationship, one that approximated wartime conditions.[59] The militarization campaign was in an important sense an effort to erase the boundaries between civilian and military life, in order to prepare for an eventual defensive war.

Frunze's "militarization" drive sowed the seeds for a reorientation of Soviet economic policies toward defense needs.[60] It also legitimized a greater weight for military and patriotic elements in the Soviet political culture of the late 1920s and early 1930s. The measures contemplated and implemented under the catchword "militarization" emerged from the confluence of several trends in Russian and European society since the beginning of the twentieth century. Even before the Great War, Russian officers, impressed by

---

[57] For a detailed account of the 1924–5 reforms by a Soviet historian, see I. B. Berkhin, *Voennaia reforma v SSSR (1924–1925)* (Moscow, 1958).

[58] Frunze, "Ob itogakh reorganizatsii Krasnoi Armii," *Voenno-istoricheskii zhurnal* 6 (1966), 73–4.

[59] Ibid., 74.

[60] For the success of Frunze's campaign to militarize the national economy, see David R. Stone, *Hammer and Rifle: The Militarization of the Soviet Union, 1926–1933* (Lawrence, Kan., 2000).

the patriotism, enthusiasm, and self-sacrifice of Japanese soldiers during the 1904–5 war, proposed programs to improve Russian troop motivation by militarizing the entire population, including schoolchildren.[61] The militarizers' first target was the national school system. "All the efforts of the Commissariat of Enlightenment should be planned with an eye to serving the needs of defense," Frunze wrote in an essay devoted to the role of "the rear" in future wars. He pointed to the example of the United States, where universities trained officers in a "reserve officers' training corps."[62]

In every speech that Frunze and his colleagues made before civilian forums, appealing for larger budgets and for support of the militarization drive, they underscored the record of the army in transforming raw peasant recruits into Red Army men and Soviet citizens.[63] In a nation that was desperately short of qualified schoolteachers, the army offered itself as a second Commissariat of Enlightenment. Formerly illiterate peasants returned home from military service with the rudiments of a general education and a taste of urban culture. Their gratitude bolstered their loyalty to the state that the army defended. Furthermore, the army's leaders promised that military service prepared administrative cadres for the great task of "building socialism," in a country that was desperately wanting in loyal agents who knew the ropes of local administration, especially so in the rural areas to which the soldiers would return after they completed their service. Indeed, the army was a respectable, if not the best, "school of socialism" in the Soviet Republic.

The Dilemmas of Nation Building and the Soviet Army

A centerpiece of the Frunze reforms was a new law on universal military service. Just as Miliutin before him had a vision of universal service for all the Empire's ethnic and social communities, so too Frunze's vision, as laid out in his and Gusev's theses and elsewhere, saw obligatory military service gradually extended to the entire Soviet population. But in the meantime, both reformers had to compromise their vision in accord with both budgetary constraints and the uneven level of development that left some ethnic groups more integrated into national institutions and cultures than others. Frunze had to countenance large categories of deferments for conscription-age males, and continued expansion of the experiment in "national" military formations begun during World War I.[64]

---

[61] See William C. Fuller, *Civil-Military Conflict in Imperial Russia, 1881–1914*, (Princeton, 1985) 195–6, 207.

[62] M. V. Frunze, "Front i tyl v voine budushchego," in *Izbrannye proizvedeniia* (1957), 2: 133–43.

[63] Many of Frunze's speeches are compiled and translated by Walter Jacobs in his *Frunze: The Soviet Clausewitz* (The Hague, 1969).

[64] The most complete discussion of nation building in the Red Army is Berkhin, *Voennaia reforma*, 116–45; see also Sanborn, *Drafting the Russian Nation*, Chapters 2 and 3, for a

These non-Russian units were also justified with reference to the Bolshevik party-state's commitment to overcoming the legacy of tsarist oppression of national minorities. Military service in "national" Red Army units would help integrate non-Russians into Soviet institutions and train native elites to help govern the multinational Soviet state. Still, most Bolsheviks harbored few illusions about the reliability of non-Russian military units in actual combat. When Gusev argued against extending the militia model to the peasant majority because peasants were prone to local chauvinisms and autonomist behavior, he partly had in mind the Civil War experience of national military units and national armies composed mainly of conscripted peasants, who had proven unreliable in their loyalty to the Bolshevik cause. Stalin declared that the national question was in essence a peasant question, by which he meant that most of the non-Russian peoples were even more rural, hence backward, than even the Russians themselves, and could not necessarily be counted on to identify their own social and ethnic interests with those of the Russian proletariat and the Communist Party. There also remained strong voices in the party elite who opposed any policies that appeared to reinforce national differences.

It is thus not surprising that the Bolsheviks remained ambivalent about ethnicity as a political and organizational principle, despite Lenin's having won the party over to the platform of national self-determination, and the common front that the Bolsheviks forged with anti-Imperial national forces in 1917. At times, for instance, they organized Ukrainian and Lithuanian–Belorussian fronts and Tatar, Latvian, and Ukrainian armies, and even schools of Red sergeants and commanders to lead them; however, at other times they disbanded these units and schools and merged them into more ethnically neutral or internationalist, multiethnic formations. In some instances, the Red Army accepted into its own ranks those Tatarized or Ukrainized units that still survived on contemporary Soviet territory. Thus the nation-building experiments of the Red Army that were proclaimed in the policy of *korenizatsiia* by the Twelfth Party Congress in 1923, and introduced more systematically with the Frunze reforms in 1924–25, had clear precedents and significant roots in previous military practice.

From then on, military statisticians became virtually obsessed with tallying not only the class but the national breakdown of units, districts, and the Red Army as a whole. Non-Russians were separated out first into territorial infantry divisions, some cavalry divisions, and even some regular divisions (which were converted territorial divisions). The army, like the party itself, had many senior leaders who considered experiments in national differentiation to be mistaken at best, and counterrevolutionary at worst. They could

discussion of the ethnic and other exemptions in the 1925 law on conscription. Sanborn discovered a 1923 conscription measure that was not adopted. Its Mobilization Department authors envisioned the Red Army as an international revolutionary force "to preserve and expand the conquests of the October Worker-Peasant Revolution."

mask their antagonisms to Ukrainization, the largest of the nation-building experiments in the new Soviet Union, behind a doctrinal internationalism. But at least for the time being, the central military leadership and most of the Ukrainian party leadership was committed to undoing the legacy of Imperial nationality policies, promoting a Ukrainian officer corps to positions of authority, and persuading the local Ukrainian population that the Red Army was their fighting force as well, and not just another institution for Russification.

Nevertheless, the memories of the Civil War did not fade so easily. Resistance to the new policies continued to mount and was expressed more and more boldly after Frunze's death. With the launching of the revolution from above that created the Stalinist system, the bureaucracies of state and party expanded to immense sizes and claimed powers of virtually unlimited scope. All this contributed to a further reconfiguration of the relationship of citizens to the state. Ethnicity, and even class, began to be considered irrelevant, or as obstacles to the creation of a new Soviet man. Sometime during the First Five-Year Plan (1928–32), the national question was determined to have been solved. One very concrete manifestation of this "solution" was the discontinuation of counting soldiers by ethnicity, or at least the widespread reporting of such information.

The ever-expanding state gradually retreated from the principle of both national formations and territorial militia divisions. By 1938 ethnicity was abandoned entirely as an organizing principle of the Red Army. Even class appeared to be less salient, as Soviet citizenship was elevated to the primary category in the new constitution of 1936. This was followed by a new law on universal military service, which extended obligatory service to nearly all national groups that had been previously excluded, and to all social categories, even those deprived of voting rights in previous legislation. The Soviet state, its single party, and its watchdog state police force, the NKVD, were intended to be the principal foci of loyalty and identity.

The Worker–Peasant Red Army initially chose to compromise with the principle of ethnicity because it was deemed to be in accord with the Communist Party's proclaimed policy of *korenizatsiia* and allowed for the recruitment and training of national formations and territorial militia divisions. Beginning in the mid-1930s, at the same time that political loyalties were being forcibly reconfigured around new "traditions" of state and party power, these "concessions" to the national principle were withdrawn, in favor of a multiethnic army, deployed without regard to the origins of its troops and with Russian restored as the language of command. This was the Stalinist solution to the national question in the military sphere. The salience of ethnicity (and to a lesser degree class and gender) in the early postrevolutionary period had hinged on the relative retreat of state power from society and the insecurity of the new regime as it sought and created constituencies under itself. As the new bureaucratic and party elites gained their confidence, they became less tolerant of alternative forms of group solidarity that were not focused on the state and party, and succeeded in demoting them, frequently through violent means. By the mid-1930s, the process of state consolidation had taken on many of the symbols of the Imperial and Muscovite past, in an effort to restore the universalist nation-building project embarked upon by the reformist modernizers of the nineteenth century, which had been interrupted by the Revolution and Civil War.

Afterword: The Second World War and the Legacy of *Levée en masse*

When Hitler launched Operation Barbarossa against the Soviet Union on June 22, 1941, the Red Army suffered catastrophic initial losses. The magnitude of the calamity prompted several surprising responses from the Soviet leadership. Both Prime Minister Viacheslav Molotov, in his immediate postinvasion announcement, and later Joseph Stalin himself, addressed the nation in uncharacteristic language, as "brothers and sisters" rather than comrade-citizens. But perhaps more important was the rapid call for the nation to rise against the fascist invader and the summoning up of the tradition of 1812. What was known as the Second World War in most of the world became the Great Fatherland War in the Soviet Union, further embellished as a "sacred people's war" in newspapers and mass culture.[65] The military high command, reeling from the first six months of defeat, sanctioned the formation of partisan units in the occupied territories.[66] Around major unoccupied cities, citizens and local leaders created people's home guards [*narodnoe opolchenie*] with a degree of spontaneity unheard of since the Civil War itself. The extent to which the regime tried to establish its integral unity with the people of the Soviet Union was unprecedented, but it was also relatively short-lived. Once the Battle of Stalingrad suggested that the Allies might indeed emerge victorious, the older rhetoric and practice of centralized control returned, as can be seen, for instance, in the way official reporting of war news highlighted the contributions of the regular army troops to the war effort, at the expense of partisan and home guard units. In one important sense, however, Frunze's dream of militarizing society in preparation for total war was realized as never before. Nearly all inhabitants of the country, from teenagers to the elderly, were put on call for either labor or military duty, and the distinctions between military and civilian life were once again

[65] The best account of the Second World War, which captures the rhetoric and adaptations of officialdom to the crisis conditions, remains Alexander Werth, *Russia at War, 1941–1945* (New York, 1964).

[66] This occurred after disbanding the partisan units that had survived the Civil War in the early 1930s, plus the purge and arrest of nearly every commander who served in the disbanded divisions. On the changing attitude toward partisan warfare, see Il'ia Grigor'evich Starinov, "Granitsa dolzhna byt' na zamke," in P. I. Iakir and Iu. A. Geller (eds.), *Komandarm Iakir: Vospominaniia druzei i soratnikov* (Moscow, 1963), 192–7.

erased. This new version of the *levée en masse* survived as a central element of the postwar Soviet Union's legitimizing myth and continues to resonate even in the post-Soviet political imagination.[67] But, as in 1917 and the Civil War, the gestures toward the *levée en masse* that helped the Soviet Union survive its initial encounter with German arms came at a time of impending state breakdown. Once the emergency was lifted and the regime was confident about its survival, the people's war receded into the realm of myth and historical memory, to be replaced by the reality of routinized subordination of the individual to the power of the state.

[67] The most recent study of the place of the Second World War in Soviet political memory is Nina Tumarkin, *The Living and the Dead: The Rise and Fall of the Cult of World War II in Russia* (New York, 1994).

9

From Jaurès to Mao

The Levée en masse *in China*

Arthur Waldron

In China, 1793 was the fifty-eighth year of the reign of the Qing emperor Gaozong Qianlong (r. 1736–95). France was far away. Word of the Revolution itself scarcely reached China before 1800, while the extraordinary measures of social and military mobilization to which it gave rise were of course unappreciated, if not unknown. But as information gradually came through over the course of the next century or so, the commonality of military and political issues faced by France and China elicited considerable resonance. One important bearer of the Revolutionary message was Jean Jaurès's *L'Armée nouvelle*, published in France in 1910 and translated into Chinese in 1922.

By the end of the nineteenth century, China was beginning to grapple with problems comparable to those France had faced at the end of the eighteenth. In both, attempts to reconstruct the political system and economic relations, and to recast culture, language, and even religion, produced revolutionary results, which left scarcely any aspect of society untouched. Of these initiatives, none was more fraught with difficulty than the reform of the military, entailing as it did a change in the connection between military service and citizenship; and here the parallels between France and China were surprisingly close.

At the turn of the twentieth century China was still a monarchy, governed politically, and dominated socially, by a non-Chinese elite: the Manchus, descendents of the northeast-Asian warriors who had conquered China some three hundred years earlier. Its armies, by no means exclusively Chinese in composition, could never have been mistaken for the "nation in arms." They served the interests and enforced the will not of the people, but of an alien dynasty. Such conditions were not exceptional. Foreign rule had been the norm for more than a third of the preceding thousand years. That fact, plus the Confucian condemnation of the use of force, meant that the Chinese military rarely approached the degree of popular participation found even in a European feudal host.

China's history had made the military an alien part of the body politic and a most unlikely bearer of popular will and national legitimacy. Its institutional alienation is analogous in certain respects to the gulf that separated the king and nobility from their subjects, and the noble officer corps from the soldiers and sailors they commanded, some of whom were foreign mercenaries, while nearly all the rest were recruited, by force, from the lowest strata of society.

In time, however, both the French and the Chinese learned to imagine their armies as, in effect, emanations of the aroused population and direct manifestations of citizenship. The French did this with the concept of the *levée en masse*. A similar concept of social mobilization arose in China, which owed something to Chinese tradition and something to intellectual imports, among them the ideas of Jean Jaurès.

I

Knowledge of the French Revolution entered China from Japan, where the first Asian-language history was published in 1900. Subsequently Chinese activists and writers regularly spoke of the events in France, usually in ways that reflected the particular political exigencies of the time in China.[1] In the course of the next half century, at least four academic histories would also be published, the first two by Chinese in 1924 and 1930, followed by translations of the standard works of Louis Madelin and Albert Mathiez in 1936 and 1958, respectively.[2]

Each of these texts reflects, to some extent, the preoccupations of the period in which it was written (or translated): the 1920s were a period of disunity and political ferment; the 1930s, a time of centralization and, toward the end, foreign challenge; and the 1950s marked the high tide of Marxist orthodoxy. However, none of these books pays much attention to military issues. The same is true for the numerous papers presented on the two-hundredth anniversary of the Revolution, in the volumes edited by Michel Vovelle, selections from which have also been translated into Chinese.

Distinctly French ideas about military organization, of undoubted Revolutionary lineage, reached China early in the twentieth century through a somewhat different route: the translation of *L'Armée nouvelle* by the celebrated French socialist Jean Jaurès (1859–1914).[3] Today this episode seems almost entirely forgotten. Connections between the Chinese and the French

---

[1] See Zhang Zhilian (ed.), *China and the French Revolution: Proceedings of the International Conference, Shanghai, 18–21 March 1989* (Oxford, n.d.).

[2] Xu Shouling, *Faguo geming shi* (1924); Zongrong Ma, *Faguo geming shi* (1930); [Louis Madelin], *Faguo da geming shi* (1936); [Albert Mathiez], *Faguo geming shi* (1958).

[3] Jean Jaurès, *L'Armée nouvelle* (Paris, 1910; reprinted with an introduction by Dennis Sherman [New York and London, 1972]).

Revolutions were explored extensively at a series of international conferences in honor of the latter's bicentennial, but Jaurès received scarcely any notice.[4]

In the early years of the twentieth century, however, *L'Armée nouvelle* achieved considerable influence in China, for reasons that are not difficult to understand. The French original was an attempt to apply, to conditions of modern war, the fundamental approaches of the Revolutionary era – an attempt that proved as difficult and revealing in the putatively revolutionary China of the first half of the twentieth century as it had in the Third Republic. The second part of this essay will trace that process. Finally, we will turn to perhaps the most fundamental aspect of the kinship: how France and China have attempted to fuse ideas of citizenship, political participation, and democratic legitimacy, with those of nationalism and military strength, by means of a particular set of military structures.

The radical tradition of Chinese politics and thought is connected more closely to France than to any other country. And perhaps nowhere is this kinship clearer than in their shared admiration for the idea of spontaneous mobilization and mass action, both as a tool of military organization, and as an instrument for overturning old states and building new ones. In China, as in France, the overthrow of an Old Regime by mass violence, first in 1911–12 and again in 1949, disappointed those who hoped temporary upheaval would usher in an era of peace and socialism. The result instead was chaos and dictatorship, in which order, if not peace, was finally purchased at the price of militarism and renewed domination by a small elite. The post-1949 enactment of this particular tragedy remains forbidden territory for Chinese scholars, but the disappointment of the hopes invested in the 1911 revolution has long been a major focus of interest, and it is in connection with those hopes and that period, roughly 1911–49, that Jaurès' work played the role to be discussed here.[5]

Chinese thinkers looked to Jaurès because he had wrestled with the same issues they faced: what was the relationship between war and socialism? and between patriotism and internationalism? These were live issues in France at the turn of the twentieth century, where the threats of war that rumbled across Europe after the first Moroccan crisis (1905) threatened to split the socialist movement. On these questions, writes Harvey Goldberg, "the eclectic realism of Jaurès clashed with the heroics of Hervé and the dogmatics of Guesde." At the 1906 Socialist Congress in Limoges, Hervé "carried anti-patriotism to its most uncompromising limits: 'For the poor, nations are not

---

4 Two articles by Ma Shengli of Beijing University: "Jiao-le-si de shixue" [Jean Jaurès's Historical Writing], *Lishi yanjiu* (1988), 152–65 and "Jiao-le-si yu Zhongguo" [Jaurès and China], *Guoji gongyunshi yanjiu ziliao* (Beijing, 1982).

5 Zou Rong, *The Revolutionary Army: A Chinese Nationalist Tract of 1903*, translated by John Lust (The Hague, 1968), 1, 5; cited in Jerome B. Grieder, *Intellectuals and the State in Modern China: A Narrative History* (New York, 1981), 156–7.

loving mothers; they are harsh step-mothers.... Our nation can only be our class." Guesde stuck to Marxist fundamentals: "He smelled anarchists. Hervé and his friends were preaching futile and romantic insurrection." By contrast Jaurès affirmed "that the proletariat would defend the nation against unprovoked attacks," and committed the Socialist Party to "parliamentary action, public agitation, popular protest meetings, even the general strike and insurrection," in order to prevent wars of aggression.[6]

II

The translation of Jaurès into Chinese – the only language other than French in which a complete edition has appeared[7] – came about as an indirect result of China's participation in the Paris Peace Conference. By then Jaurès was dead, having been murdered at the height of the July Crisis in a restaurant not far from the offices of *L'Humanité*, which he edited. The war that followed burnished his personal reputation: French socialists (like those everywhere in Europe) supported the war, as he said they would, while its cataclysmic nature vindicated his apprehensions about what industrialized warfare would be like. Yet the war did little to further the ideas he had proposed in *L'Armée nouvelle* (1910), his last major work. In it he advocated a system of militia defense for France, basing himself in part upon Revolutionary precedents. Such a system, he argued, would combine social justice with military effectiveness. Jaurès was a member of the French Chamber of Deputies and put his ideas before the National Assembly as draft legislation. But he failed to persuade many people to take his plan seriously, and the proposal never came up for discussion or a vote. Most army officers, political leaders, and newspaper editors viewed his work as naïve fantasy.[8]

That Jaurès's text should have eventually made its way into Chinese was, as might be expected, to some extent a matter of chance. The translation was done over a period of two years by Liu Wendao and his wife, Liao Shizao, who were then studying in France (both received doctorates from the University of Paris in 1924). Liu had been born in Hubei in 1893 and educated in military schools since primary years. He had already made a name for himself in political intellectual circles in China – which, as in Germany, included a number of thoughtful military officers. In later life, Liu directed the general political department of the Kuomintang, served as minister to Germany and Austria, then as minister and ambassador to Italy, and finally held a seat on the Central Executive Committee of the Kuomintang and the Supreme National Defense Council.

---

[6] Harvey Goldberg, *The Life of Jean Jaurès* (Madison, Wisc., 1962), 378, 380.
[7] An abridged English edition of Juarès's *L'Armée nouvelle* appeared in London in 1916, entitled *Democracy and Military Service* and edited by G. G. Coulton.
[8] Goldberg, *Jean Jaurès*, 388, 12.

Liu ended up in Paris partly thanks to an essay on democratic party politics that he wrote in 1916, which had been passed on to Liang Qichao, China's preeminent political thinker at the time, by Liu's friend Jiang Fangzhen, then commandant of the Baoding Military Academy. Liang had been so delighted that he sent money to support Liu's study in Japan. When Liang set off for France at the end of 1918, Liu was part of his entourage.

Liang was not actually a delegate to the peace conference. That task was handled by professional diplomats. His status as unofficial delegate, exalted as it might seem, was in part intended to paper over the failures of China's political reformers, of whom he was a leading example. Since the turn of the century, Liang, along with many others, had been seeking to strengthen China by promoting national renewal. Like their French counterparts a century earlier, they saw this as a matter of awakening the people.

By the time Liang Qichao departed for Europe, however, it was clear enough that he and his ilk no longer held China's destiny in their hands. The trip was an opportunity to contemplate the wreckage of Chinese reform from the vantage point of the wreckage of European civilization. With Liang went some very distinguished friends. There was Zhang Jiasen or Zhang Junmai, better known as Carsun Chang (1886–1969), a philosopher and political thinker trained in Berlin but best known in the West as the leader of the "Third Force" between communists and nationalists in the 1940s; Jiang Fangzhen (1882–1938), who trained in Japan and in Germany and was already recognized as China's premier military thinker; V. K. Ting (Ding Wenjiang, 1887–1936), a geologist trained in Glasgow, whose distinguished career would include service as head of the Academia Sinica in Nanjing; and Xu Xinliu (1890–1938), a banker who had studied metallurgy in Birmingham and public finance at the Ecole des Sciences Politiques in Paris.

These people were neither pillars of the establishment nor completely marginal. They were intentionally absenting themselves from China at a time when their own prospects for office had been stymied by the rise to power of Duan Qirui (1865–1936), a protégé of China's autocratic President Yuan Shikai; yet they retained authority and public visibility. Like the traditional scholar-officials of the past, they took the affairs of the state as their own responsibility, whether in office or out, and they applied to those questions all the intellectual power they could muster.

The degree to which they looked to France and Germany for enlightenment is striking. Much of the story of nineteenth-century European political reform, particularly after Napoleon, pivoted on military issues: not only how to increase effectiveness but also more broadly on such questions as what should be the relationships among people, state, and army and between military service and citizenship. The people accompanying Liang were all wide-ranging intellectuals who wrote on many topics and combined thought with action – signing manifestos, sponsoring research, serving the state.

With the exception of the banker Xu, moreover, all at one time or another took a specific interest in military questions, which they viewed not in isolation but as part of a more general set of social and political issues. Jiang Fangzhen published a plan for military demobilization and reorganization, the *Caibing jihuashu*, in 1922. Zhang Jiasen presented a series of lectures on the origins and cures for civil war in 1924, the *Guonei zhanzheng liujiang*. Ding Wenjiang wrote a history of the military affairs of the Republic in 1926, the *Minguo junshi jinji*. The culmination of these considerations of military questions, which bears comparison to European developments in the decades preceding World War I, was Jiang Fangzhen's final work, the *Guofanglun*, or "Treatise on National Defense." It argues that national strength depends upon the congruence between social structures and military requirements, and must be considered as much a work of social science as of military analysis.[9]

These people understood that the military issues they confronted had no narrow military solutions. The whole society was the issue, and therefore their investigations ranged broadly across the whole sweep of politics, sociology, and culture – although, like their contemporary European socialists, they paid careful and thoughtful attention to war. War was proving to be the test for China's reform and development, as it had proved to be the test for European socialism. It is against this background that we should consider the translation of Jaurès, whose central concerns, like those of his Chinese admirers, were broadly social, rather than strictly military.

II

The dissemination of Jaurès's ideas in China was the work of some remarkable military intellectuals. Liu Wendao, the principal translator, was one of thousands of Chinese who chose to be trained for the still-novel career of professional military officer. As a teenager, in 1910, he had enrolled in the infantry course at the Baoding Military Academy in Hebei, just south of Beijing, an institution founded by late-Qing military reformers looking to strengthen the monarchy by improving the armed forces. When military mutinies against the Qing began, eventually leading to the forced abdication of the dynasty in the so-called *Xinhai geming*, or 1911 revolution, the academy closed, and many cadets departed to join the fight. Liu was one. He went south to Shanghai, where he served in the revolutionary forces raised by Chen Qimei (1876–1916), the man who, in 1906 in Tokyo, introduced Chiang Kai-shek to Sun Yat-sen's *Tongmenghui* party, the forerunner of the

---

[9] Zhang Jiasen, *Guonei zhanzheng liujiang* (Shanghai, 1924); Ding Wenjiang, *Minguo junshi jinji* (1926; reprinted Taipei, n.d.); Jiang Fangzhen, *Caibing jihuashu* (Shanghai, 1922); Jiang Fangzhen, *Guofanglun* (1937), in Jiang Fucong and Xue Guangqian (eds.), *Jiang Baili Xiansheng Quanji*, 2 volumes (Taipei, 1971), 2: 131–354.

Kuomintang. When Liu returned, the situation had changed dramatically. Sun Yat-sen's brief presidency, and the accompanying rule of a democratically elected parliament, were abruptly halted by the military coup of Yuan Shikai, the leading military figure of the Old Regime. These developments, along with the practical experience of fighting, left many students profoundly dissatisfied with the old-school officers then in charge of the academy.

Liu Wendao was elected as one of the student representatives to present grievances. The result was the appointment of a new commandant, Jiang Fangzhen, twentieth-century China's greatest military intellectual (he is discussed in greater detail later). But when Jiang in turn was forced to leave, Liu resigned as well and went to Japan, where he enrolled in the Department of Political Economy at Waseda University. At this time, he wrote the essay on party politics that attracted Liang Qichao's attention, and this in turn brought him into the group that accompanied Liang to France. Unlike the others, however, Liu settled down to study, entering the University of Paris on the strength of his degree from Waseda.[10] To support Liu, Jiang Fangshen commissioned him to translate Jaurès's book.

III

Like most men of the left, Jean Jaurès was suspicious of the professional military and its possible political ambitions; but unlike most of his political colleagues he also took seriously the need for national defense. *L'Armée nouvelle* was his attempt to reconcile the two concerns. It presented a series of technical proposals for reforming the French armed forces by reducing the period of active service for conscripts from two years to a few months, and placing the stress instead on the maintenance of a vast citizen reserve like that maintained by the Swiss. Jaurès admitted that such an army would lack any offensive capability, but justified it by pointing to the tremendous advantages, both moral and military, associated with the defensive in modern warfare.

Socially, such a reform would sharply reduce the influence of the professional officer corps, which Jaurès regarded as a bastion of reaction out of step with the rest of society. Finally, Jaurès argued that the concepts of national defense that he offered could reconcile the seemingly conflicting imperatives of nationalism and internationalism.

Liu completed the translation in November 1920 and sent it to Liang and Jiang for publication in a series sponsored by their Cooperative Study Society [*Gongxuehui*]. It was produced by the Commercial Press in Shanghai, China's foremost publisher. The series in which it appeared was impressive and eclectic. More than eighty titles had been published by the time Liu's

---

[10] See "Liu Wendao neijiao waiwu," *Hubei Wenxian* 38 (October 1976), 29–32. I am indebted to Dr. Jui-te Chang of the Academia Sinica for bringing this article to my attention.

book appeared, including translations of Tolstoy, Turgenev, and Spencer, histories of the Russian Revolution and the Battle of Verdun, and a history of the European Renaissance by Liu's patron Jiang Fangzhen (a true polymath). The first edition of Jaurès, titled *Xinjunlun* [Treatise on the New Army], appeared in October 1922 and was eventually reprinted three times.[11]

Jaurès's work acquired its apparently considerable influence because it provided answers to questions about the connection between national strength and social order that were then preoccupying many Chinese thinkers. In 1925, when Liu joined Chiang Kai-shek's insurgent headquarters in Canton, the general proudly showed Liu the copy he kept on his shelf. Chiang's interest in Liu's book meant that one of the most important intellectual products of the French Revolutionary tradition had joined the Chinese revolutionary stream, part of a pattern of mixing that has not ceased since.

One says "Liu's" book because, like many other so-called translations then popular in China, the *Xinjunlun* would more accurately be termed a paraphrase and summary of Jaurès. The Chinese text is 394 pages in all; the French original runs to 557. Certain sections are drastically truncated or left out altogether. This was by no means a straightforward process of compression. In some places, for instance, Liu avoids using Chinese words that might be thought to parallel the French meanings quite closely. His reason seems to have been to maintain the newness of the French text and to avoid creating unintended linguistic linkages that would suggest continuity with earlier Chinese writings. A good example is the title of the first chapter, which in French is "Force militaire et Force morale." For "Force morale" one might use the Chinese word *dao* or some compound or variation of it: the word, after all, is used in a very similar sense at the beginning of Sun-Tzu's *Art of War*: "The first of these factors is moral influence" [*dao*], which, as General Samuel B. Griffith notes in his translation, is usually rendered as 'The Way' or 'The Right Way.' Here *dao* refers to the morality of government, particularly to that of the sovereign. "If the sovereign governs justly, benevolently, and righteously, he follows the Right Path or the Right Way, and thus exerts a superior degree of moral influence."[12] This is admittedly not exactly the same as the French meaning, but there is a clear overlap. Yet Liu chose instead to entitle the first chapter of his translation "Armed Force and Formless [*wuxing*] Force," presumably because he wanted to avoid any such antique linkage. He did not want the pronouncements of scientific European socialism to resound with unintended echoes of ancient Chinese philosophy.

Such echoes and associations were a persistent problem in rendering European ideas into Chinese. The danger was always that, like the proverbial invader who was Sinicized, a sharp-edged modern European idea would dissolve into the already vast sea of Chinese thought. Hence the tendency to

---

[11] Zhuo-lai [Jaurès], *Xinjunlun*, translated by Liu Wendao and Liao Shizhao (Shanghai, 1922).
[12] Samuel B. Griffith (ed. and trans.), *Sun Tzu: The Art of War* (New York, 1963), 63.

coin new words, sometimes phonetic equivalents, sometimes calques (which were generally created first in Japanese and then imported), and sometimes revivals of obsolete ancient usages. To be recognized as modern, the words had to look different.[13]

There are also times when one is surprised that Liu does not choose more evocative translations, most especially of the key French term *levée en masse*. References to the "masses" [*qunzhong*, another modern coinage] become ubiquitous in Chinese revolutionary rhetoric a bit later in the twentieth century, and the idea of "rising" is of course virtually a cliché of revolutionary language. "Arise! Arise! [*Qilai*! *Qilai*!] All people who will not be slaves," is the opening line of Tian Han's "March of the Volunteers," a song first heard in a left-wing film of the Second World War, and later adopted as the national anthem of the People's Republic of China.[14] Yet one looks in vain for an linguistic equivalent to the dynamism of revolutionary military organization. Compare, for instance, two passages, first the French:

C'est un grand esprit révolutionnaire, très hardi tout à la fois et très sense, qui anime cette loi de l'amalgame du 21 février 1793 qui est, avec la loi du 23 août de la même année sur la réquisition universelle et la levée en masse, le statut organique de l'Armée de la Révolution.[15]

Now the Chinese "translation":

I have already spoken of the motivation to reorganize the military and remove the sources of its problems. As for the implementation of the reorganization, it began with the promulgation of the amalgamation law of February 21, 1793. The law of amalgamation was one of the laws of the great Revolution. The proposing and establishing of this law were at once very brave and very reasonable. Along with the law of general conscription and recruitment [*yiban zhenmufa*], it formed the foundation of the post-reform Revolutionary army.[16]

Levée en masse is rendered as *yiban zhenmufa*. The import of *yiban* is not so much "en masse" as "in general" – it is used, for instance, in the titles of textbooks on subjects like "general economics." The dictionary defines it as "general, ordinary, common."[17] As for *levée*, it is rendered by two words that simply mean conscription and recruitment, a distinctly pallid rendition of a potentially electric concept. But overall the paraphrase is competent and

[13] This is the case with many key terms in modern Chinese thought: revolution [*geming*] and society [*shehui*], for instance, enter Chinese from Japanese [*kakumei* and *shakai*, which read differently in the two languages, though the characters are the same]. See Gao Mingkai and Liu Zhengtan, *Xiandai Hanyu Wailaici Yanjiu* (Beijing, 1958), 85, 87.

[14] Howard L. Boorman (ed.), *Biographical Dictionary of Republican China*, 5 volumes (New York, 1967–79), 3: 266–7.

[15] Jaurès, *Democracy and Military Service*, 162.

[16] Liu, *Xinjunlun*, 142.

[17] See Wu Jingrong (ed.), *The Pinyin Chinese–English Dictionary* (Beijing, 1979), 808.

conveys Jaurès's ideas with substantial accuracy. Those ideas turned out to
have a very powerful relevance to the China in which Liu's book appeared.

IV

Already in traditional times China manifested political violence on a scale
scarcely matched in the world, and in the twentieth century it has only sur-
passed itself. What was new in the twentieth century was the way wars
and bloody power struggles were given intellectual structure and meaning
by invoking a foreign vocabulary and foreign parallels, both of which were
often drawn from France. Chinese history was explained by applying what
J. L. Talmon has called the myth of "people's revolutionary war," in which
mass participation is a standard ingredient very much along the lines bequeathed to the world by the French. In this kind of struggle "patriotism
and ideological revolutionary ardour become fused. The defence of the native
land [becomes] identified with the struggle for a political-social ideal against
a counter-revolutionary league of selfish traitors and foreign reactionary
powers."[18]

Certainly much Chinese historical writing has adopted such a framework.
The question is whether it has any more solidity when applied to China than
it does anywhere else. Peter Paret identified the difficulties in assessing the
original French *levée en masse* with his observation that "the historical legend . . . interprets the *levée* as expressing the people's enthusiastic defense of
the Revolution and the nation," even though it was in fact "less a measure of popular enthusiasm than of the political acumen of the Montagnard
leaders."[19]

Much the same may be said of the idea of the people in Chinese reformist
thought of the late Qing period. Chinese revolutionaries imagined that, once
aroused, the people could spontaneously overthrow the dynasty and create a
new and legitimate order to replace it. Among sources for this idea, they drew
on some of the most ancient moral concepts of Chinese philosophy. Thus, in
a famous essay of 1902 entitled "The Renovation of the People" [*Xin min*]
Liang Qichao echoed the classical injunction to "renew the people" [*xin min*]
found in the *Great Learning* [*Da xue*]: "What the Great Learning teaches
is – to illustrate illustrious virtue; to renovate the people; and to rest in the
highest excellence."[20] Liang's eloquent essay inspired a powerful intellectual
and social movement for reform, even as its idiom defined a new prose style.

---

[18] J. L. Talmon, *The Myth of the Nation and the Vision of Revolution: The Origins of Ideological Polarisation in the Twentieth Century* (London, 1980), 5.

[19] "Conscription and the end of the *ancien régime* in France and Prussia," in Peter Paret,
Understanding War: Essays on Clausewitz and the History of Military Power (Princeton,
1992), 63.

[20] Liang Qichao, "The Renovation of the People," in *The Chinese Classics*, 2nd ed., translated
by James Legge, 5 volumes (Taipei, 1971), 1: 356.

More "revolutionary" thinkers such as Zhang Bingling (1868–1936) took a somewhat different approach, calling for an end to the "foreign" Manchu dynasty and an assertion of Chinese racial nationalism. Still others called specifically for violence. A year after Liang's "The Renovation of the People," a powerful essay titled "The Revolutionary Army" [*Gemingjun*] was published by Zou Rong (1885–1905), with a preface by Zhang Bingling. Zou was a young Chinese then studying in Japan. He envisioned a vast and self-actualizing uprising:

To sweep away the despotism of these thousands of years, to cast off the servile nature bred in us over these thousands of years, to exterminate the five million and more hairy and horned Manchus, to expunge the pain and anguish of our two-hundred-and-sixty-year humiliation [under Manchu rule], to cleanse the great land of China... this most exalted and incomparable aim is revolution! How imposing a thing is revolution! How magnificent a thing is revolution![21]

When it came unexpectedly in 1911, however, the revolution proved disappointing. Military mutinies in central China precipitated the crisis that forced the Manchus to abdicate, but the new regime was quickly taken over by the military. Sun Yat-sen stepped down as president, the newly elected parliament was dissolved, and Yuan Shikai, the greatest military commander of the Qing, ran an autocratic, modernizing regime. Military contention for the succession, at his death in 1916, ushered in the era of so-called warlordism. Chinese reformers reacted to this disappointment by renewing their criticism of their own inheritance and increasing their attention to the West.

As Jerome Grieder has suggested, "the image of a self-reliant people responsive to the challenges and the opportunities of history, animated by a unifying sense of its own political and cultural identity, able and anxious to assume the responsibilities of citizenship," was not a description of fact, but a political mythology.

It was a mythology that appealed to, and in part described, the young audience of activists whose education, both in and out of school, was informed by these ideas. But it was a work of invention, or of autobiographical fiction, not a political program. As substantial as were their accomplishments as civic educators in the years between 1898 and 1911, the radical intellectuals, whether revolutionary or reformist in political persuasion, had failed in the effort to create a Chinese nation.... The political community remained for them an intellectual construct. All spoke one way or another of a popular community: Liang Qichao of "the new people" [*xinmin*]; Zhang Bingling and Zou Rong of "the Chinese [Han] people" [*hanmin*]; others more generally of "the citizenry" [*gongmin*], of the "common people" [*pingmin*], or simply "the people" [*renmin*] – the term now used in communist rhetoric.[22]

[21] Zou Rong, "The Revolutionary Army," in *The Revolutionary Army*, 1, 5.
[22] Grieder, *Intellectuals and the State in Modern China*, 198.

Hence the particular receptivity, among chastened Chinese thinkers and would-be revolutionaries, to thinking about more than the revolutionary spirit: to look instead at structures, and military structures in particular.

This background suggests that the seeming practicality of Jaurès was one of the things that recommended his work. Far from being intoxicated by fantasies of revolution drawn from France, Chinese reformers and intellectuals in the mid-1920s were well immunized against the wilder constructions of the *levée en masse*. The group who commissioned and received the translation understood that there were no easy answers to the problems of military effectiveness and control of the military class. That much was clear both from the Chinese past and from the European experience that had produced Jaurès.

The whole failure of the 1911 revolution had been, broadly speaking, a failure of the Chinese people to play their assigned role. As the earlier quotation from Grieder indicates, the quick resurgence of the military, the reconstruction of an autocratic regime, and the return of the mass of the people to passivity and apathy revealed just how delusory had been the hopes of a Zou Rong or a Sun Yat-sen or a Liang Qichao. The popular rising, such as it was in 1911–12, had been rather disappointing. Progressive Chinese thinkers at this time had their illusions about the masses shattered. What they faced in the years following, while the heirs to the generals who had overthrown the Qing struggled for power among themselves, was not a "self-reliant people... able and anxious to assume the responsibilities of citizenship," but what European thinkers termed "militarism," and what in China would be called "warlordism."[23]

V

How Jaurès's thought related to these issues can be seen in the work of Jiang Fangzhen (Bai-li, also transliterated as Chiang Fangchen or Chiang Pai-li, 1882–38). As has been mentioned, Jiang was, by general agreement, the most important military thinker of twentieth-century China, as well as the commandant Liu Wendao followed away from Baoding, and the patron who commissioned the translation as a means of supporting the impoverished Liu in Paris.[24]

Jiang was that *rara avis*, a soldier's soldier who was also an intellectual's intellectual. Born into a long line of scholars in Zhejiang province, he had

---

[23] For these developments see Arthur Waldron, "The Warlord: Twentieth Century Chinese Understandings of Violence, Militarism, and Imperialism," *American Historical Review* 96/4 (October 1991), 1073–1100.

[24] For Jiang, see Jan-chih Wang, "General Chiang Pai-li and his Military Thought," Ph.D. dissertation, St. John's University, 1972; also Stephen Mackinnon, "Jiang Baili (1882–1938): Military Intellectual" (Paper presented at the International Conference on Chinese Military Thought, Cambridge University, 1997).

turned against the dynasty after Japan defeated China in 1895. He was expelled for political reasons from one school in Hangzhou, and in 1901 went to Japan, where his mentor, Liang Qichao, got him into the Shikan Gakko, Japan's elite school for officers. He graduated at the head of his class in 1905, for which achievement he received a ceremonial sword from the hands of the Japanese emperor himself. After leaving the Baoding Military Academy he adopted the traditional role that both Confucius and Sun-Tzu had played in their day – that of the itinerant intellectual and adviser, a figure of rare knowledge and skill, searching for the political patron whose power will permit his ideas to be put into practice.

Jiang was of course a close student of Sun-Tzu, having published an extensive annotation of the latter's *Art of War*.[25] But even if their places in society were somewhat parallel, their approaches to warfare could scarcely have been more different, as Jiang's interest in the *levée en masse* makes clear. That interest marked something new in Chinese military thought. Jiang identified the pursuit of a strategic decision by means of protracted fighting as a key element of modern warfare – which meant taking into consideration the overall capacity of society, including its economic and social strength, when assessing its military power. Sun-Tzu had spoken chiefly about the need to achieve rapid decision by means of operations designed to shatter at a stroke the cohesion of the enemy's forces, thus creating a form of chaos [*luan*] that will permit those forces to be reorganized under new political auspices.

Operations that can do this are above all those that throw the enemy off psychologically: they involve surprise, deception, and clever stratagems, and they have long been staples of Chinese military thought. Although these processes involve the shattering and reconstruction of mass armies, as traditionally understood they have nothing in common with the basic concept of the *levée en masse*. Remember, first of all, that Sun-Tzu is speaking about wars within the Chinese cultural realm, not wars of nations. Under such circumstances, political differences matter mostly to the elite and can scarcely be discerned by ordinary soldiers. Second, the processes of cohesion and dissolution on which Sun-Tzu focuses operate from the top down. A successful general will seek to conduct an operation whose success will have a powerful psychological effect on all participants. Any wavering soldiers or allies on his side will rally to him; his opponents will defect. The result will be an army – or an alliance – having a single leader and marching in a single direction.

It is only a slight exaggeration to say that most traditional Chinese military thought – indeed most modern and even contemporary Chinese military thought – is concerned with how to use such stratagems to cause the defection

---

[25] Jiang Fangzhen and Liu Bangji, *Sun Zi Qian Shuo* (1930), in *Jiang Baili Xiansheng Quanji* 2:5–130.

of enemy forces in order to reconstitute them into a new and dominant coalition.[26] Jiang Fangzhen is the great exception. Jiang knew a great deal about military technology. He was deeply involved in China's attempt, during the first half of the twentieth century, to stay abreast of technological developments that might assist in the achievement of the kind of disruptive victory classical theory admired above all. He was a close student of armored tactics, a reader of Heinz Guderian's *Achtung! Panzer* (1935), and arguably about as knowledgeable on the subject as any European. He also knew the air power theories so popular in the interwar period. His protégé Liu Wendao was minister in Rome during this period and very active in attempting to purchase Italian aircraft for the fledgling Chinese air force.[27] But unlike many other Chinese of the time, Chiang Kai-shek included, Jiang saw beyond the traditional fascination with weapons and stratagems, to the question of where the military fits in the social fabric, drawing upon his command of European history to do so.

Chinese military thought is not unique in seeking quick decision [*sujue*]. In Europe this approach had been adopted by aristocratic and hierarchical states, following patterns that Europeans at the time, and Jiang as well, called militarism. The result, in 1914–18, had been ultimate failure. In Jiang's view, the ability to achieve swift results on the battlefield had been Prussia's strength in the nineteenth century; and in the twentieth, he pointed out, it was what Japan was seeking in China, by dint of overwhelming superiority in weapons and tactics.

To counter this, Jiang argued, one must use the strengths not simply of the military in isolation, but of the whole society. Jiang recognized that Napoleon's success had been based on the social changes brought about by the French Revolution, at least as much as on his own tactical and strategic skills, and that the Prussian ability to match the French had depended as much on social reforms as on the creation of the General Staff and associated measures. He saw in the First World War an enormously expanded example of the sort of disaster that befell China whenever a general or would-be political leader attempted to bypass the long and difficult business of social reform in favor of some bold, overreaching stratagem. Armed forces genuinely based on the masses, in other words, were not only the key to effective defense. They were also the bulwark against warlordism and Japanese- or Prussian-style militarism.

---

[26] See Avery Goldstein, *From Bandwagon to Balance of Power Politics: Structural Constraints and Politics in China 1949–1978* (Stanford, 1991). These concepts are usually applied internationally. See also Robert Jervis and Jack Snyder (eds.), *Dominoes and Bandwagons: Strategic Beliefs and Great Power Competition in the Eurasian Rimland* (New York, 1991).

[27] Michael R. Godley, "Lessons from an Italian Connection," in David Pong and Edmund S. K. Fung (eds.), *Ideal and Reality: Social and Political Change in Modern China* (New York, 1985), 93–123.

Therefore, confronted with the Japanese threat in the 1930s, China, like France in 1871 or 1914, would have to offer a prolonged defense based on mass support:

To be the antithesis of the enemy is everything – if a quick decision is beneficial for them, we must *rely on protracted sustainment* so as to make them exhausted; while their forces are on the first line, we must put our forces on the second line of battle, so that they will have difficulty in finding places to exert their force.[28]

This, of course, was exactly the defensive strategy, relying on deep popular mobilization, that Jaurès had proposed against Germany. To explain it, Jiang turned to the translation he had commissioned. Unlike nearly every other Chinese military theorist of modern times, Jiang understood that successful military institutions had social foundations. China was not an aristocratic monarchy, as Germany had been before 1918. It was more like France, without a single leader or even a cohesive ruling class, but possessing nevertheless a vast mass of patriotic and stubborn peasants who could and would defend the country – provided the way of fighting could be connected to the way they lived. It was no good to create a specialized military force that had no commonalities with society. The point was to take the already existing shape of society and create a military that would grow from it organically, and then to capitalize on its strengths.

A long tradition of doing just this existed in Chinese thought. Dynasty after dynasty had attempted to make farmers into soldiers and vice versa (*yu bing yu nong*); local defense organizations (*tuan lian*) had long been a feature of traditional warfare. Jiang argued that, if China were to be confronted militarily by another country in the near future, it would be better for it to adopt the tactics of protracted resistance (he mentions the Boers) rather than risk everything on bolder, more aggressive strategies. China should primarily adopt a retrograde defensive and delaying strategy, in order to preserve its own forces while luring the enemy in deep. When the enemy was exhausted and did not have enough force to support itself, China could then wipe it out with one stroke. The experience of the Russians in defeating Napoleon's army could be adapted by China to deal with foreign aggressors – an idea proposed in the 1910s by Jiang's close friend, the revolutionary Cai O.[29]

Jiang's own masterpiece, the *Treatise on National Defense [Guofanglun]*, is a study of social institutions and social reforms as well as military needs. His comprehensive approach to the problem remains unique and remarkable in China, but paralleled elsewhere in the careers of the genuine transformers of national strength, for such transformation inevitably had a vast social dimension. Jiang had seized upon Jaurès's fundamental understanding of

[28] *Jiang Baili Xiansheng Quanji*, 2: 269–77.
[29] *Cai Songpo xiansheng yiji* (Taipei, 1962), 52.

the interrelationship between society and military effectiveness, and it was this rather realistic and sober version of the *levée en masse* that he attempted, without success, to apply to China.

At this point we encounter the basic difference between Jiang's thought and what might seem to be a reflection of French Revolutionary ideas in the Chinese communist movement. Jiang, like Jaurès, and unlike those who see military mobilization as an opportunity for social transformation, saw the organization of national self-defense as an extension of the basic relationships of civil society that already exist. It is this that makes military institutions, as both men conceived them, bulwarks against militarism. Both sought a sober and practical approach to issues of defense. Much may be wrong with their prescriptions, but the error is not the result of intoxication with the mythology of the *levée en masse*.

VI

The myth of the *levée* would stir again, a few years after Liu's translation of Jaurès was published, in the wake of the May Thirtieth Movement of 1925. This was a tide of protest that began with some shootings by British police in Shanghai and soon spread to many of China's most important cities. Chiang Kai-shek's Northern Expedition seemed to ride that tide to military victory a few years later.[30] The nineteenth century had brought forth a powerful romanticization of the masses, one that was impossible to falsify entirely, and with the "goings to the people" of the next several decades, and most importantly with the rise of the communist movement, it took on new life.

In this, of course, Mao Zedong (1893–1976) played a critical role. His military thought was fundamentally muddled. At its best it drew (without acknowledgment) on Jiang Fangzhen. At its worst, it caricatured even the myth of the *levée en masse*. But owing to his political importance, it became sacred text.

Most characteristic of Mao was a belief in spontaneous revolution. His celebrated "investigation" of the peasant movement in Hunan disclosed to him a social movement about to explode. As he put it in one of his most frequently quoted writings:

In a very short time, in China's central, southern, and northern provinces, several hundred million peasants will rise like a mighty storm, like a hurricane, a force so swift and violent that no power, however great, will be able to hold it back. They will smash all the trammels that bind them and rush forward along the road to liberation. They will sweep all the imperialists, warlords, corrupt officials, local tyrants, and evil gentry into their graves.[31]

---

[30] For this history, see Arthur Waldron, *From War to Nationalism: China's Turning Point, 1924–1925* (Cambridge, 1995).

[31] Mao Tse-tung, "Report on an Investigation of the Peasant Movement in Hunan" (March 1927) in *Selected Works of Mao Tse-tung*, 4 volumes (Peking, 1967), 1: 23–4.

This rush of people is, for Mao as for so many thinkers in the revolutionary tradition, in effect the "nation" untrammeled, simply forming itself. It could be summoned up in China just as it had been in France. Mao, however, understood neither Hunan nor China. The nascent revolution he imagined in Hunan was, as Edward McCord has demonstrated, not a consequence of the sorts of social factors to which Mao attributed it – landlordism, economic change, and so forth. Rather, society in that province was in turmoil because it had been a battleground, over and over again, in civil wars. People were impoverished, displaced, desperate, and angry – and thus ripe for the kind of political exploitation that had, in 1917, brought mutiny to the French army and the Bolshevik *coup d'état* to Russia.[32]

Neither of these explosive developments should be mistaken for the sort of spontaneous bottom-up construction of citizenship that the myth of the *levée* asserts. Furthermore, the attempts by Mao and other revolutionary romantics to trigger such risings repeatedly failed, eliciting harsh criticism from those communists who actually knew something about war, such as Liu Bocheng (1892–1986). Liu had studied at the Frunze Military Academy in the Soviet Union and would later command the communist First Field Army and establish the Military Academy of the People's Republic of China. As he put it, in slightly Aesopian language:

Many comrades have failed to use modern strategy and tactics flexibly . . . . They have insisted on using the ancient classic *Romance of the Three Kingdoms* and Sun-Tzu's *Art of War* as a strategic guide in modern times. Some comrades, conceited in being erudite, treat the half-century old *Collected Works* of Zeng Guofan [leader of the Qing's successful anti-Taiping mass armies] as a typical military code. . . . Certain units of the Red Army still show the weakness of "fearing casualties" and "fighting tricky battles."[33]

The tactic of attempting to trigger instant revolution had not worked, even against the Chinese nationalists.[34] It did even worse against the Japanese, and even Mao was forced to fall back on the idea of protracted warfare, a concept he found fundamentally uncongenial. Here again he was drawing on ideas to which Jiang Fangzhen had given shape, drawing on both Chinese history and European socialism.[35]

To the extent that Mao's thought contains something like the idea of a nation unleashed, it is in the form of a carefully indoctrinated and "mobilized" army and populace. He distrusted spontaneity. As Shu Guang Zhang notes, "even a national revolutionary war . . . cannot be won without extensive and

---

[32] Edward A. McCord, *The Power of the Gun: The Emergence of Modern Chinese Warlordism* (Berkeley, Calif., 1993).

[33] Quoted in James Pinckney Harrison, *The Long March to Power: A History of the Chinese Communist Party, 1921–1972* (New York, 1972), 230.

[34] For a sense of how communist insurgency worked in reality, see Gregor Benton, *Mountain Fires: The Red Army's Three Year War in South China, 1934–1938* (Berkeley, Calif., 1992).

[35] Mao Zedong, "On Protracted War" (May 1938) in *Selected Works*, 2: 113–94.

thoroughgoing political mobilization," which he defined as "telling the army and the people about the political aim of the war...why the war must be fought and how it concerns him...[and] the steps and policies for its attainment."[36] But even this concept of orchestrated mobilization occupies, in Mao's thought, a place secondary to a very traditional fascination with stratagem. For Sun-Tzu "all warfare is deception." Chinese history is filled with tales of clever generals like Zhuge Liang, who triumphed through trickery and tactical brilliance. In fact, such measures rarely worked as well in reality as they did in retelling; yet they dominated Mao's own approach to war.[37] He operated as if he genuinely believed in the sort of popular and national rising depicted in the legendary version of the *levée*, and because he succeeded, some have imagined that at least in China, the myth was reality.

VII

What we find in China is not confirmation of the myth of spontaneous, self-organizing popular violence, but rather its inversion. In France, at the time Jaurès was writing, the distrust between society and military was real and understandable, given the betrayals of democracy that had begun almost simultaneously with the Revolution itself. Jaurès was trying to fix this problem with his argument that democracy and national security could be reconciled through a military system based on universal citizen participation. It would be strong enough to defend the nation, but equally incapable of foreign conquests and domestic *coups d'état*.

If anything, the bloodletting of the First World War seemed to confirm the wisdom of Jaurès's outlook. Certainly French interwar planning, with its stress on the defensive, on mobilization of reserves, and on the methodical battle, had something in common with the evolution of the idea of the *levée en masse* – shorn, however, of its Revolutionary *élan*. In the interwar period, despite much political turmoil, the French succeeded in limiting and shaping their military institutions to meet the requirements of citizenship as they understood them.

Quite the opposite has been the case in China. The generation of intellectuals who read Jaurès and took the French experience seriously, men like Liu Wendao, Jiang Fangzhen, and Liang Qichao, recognized that, before it could be awakened, Chinese citizenship had to come into existence. But their initial attempt to create genuine citizenship in the decade or so following the fall of the Manchus proved a failure and has not been repeated. Instead, as Professor Michael Godley has pointed out, military models have increasingly become templates for the reform of Chinese society – and even substitutes

---

[36] Shu Guang Zhang, *Mao's Military Romanticism: China and the Korean War, 1950–1953* (Lawrence, Kan., 1995), 13.
[37] Liu Jikun, *Mao Zedong's Art of War* (Hong Kong, 1993), 223–8.

for the attempt.[38] This was true during the "Self Strengthening" [*yangwu*] movement of the late Qing period, which sought to build modern forces with the latest artillery and battleships, but without political change. The "warlords" of the 1920s, as well as Chiang Kai-shek, tried to use the military organizations they controlled as the armature for an entire society. Above all, this has been true for the Communists, whose movement began as a party army and has never really transcended the role. In China, in other words, we don't find the idea of the "citizen-soldier," with the first role defining the second; instead we find the idea of the soldier as the model for citizenship.

Chinese thinkers quickly adopted the European nationalist mythology according to which, beneath the surface chaos of the twentieth century, real nations lay fully formed, waiting only for the right leader or moment to awaken. In China, as elsewhere, that myth proved deeply misleading.[39] The endless public ceremonials organized to this day by China's elites have little to do with citizenship or genuine popular participation. They are simply one more manifestation of that country's long history of what one Australian sinologist has aptly termed "contentless politics."[40] Indeed, even the challenge of the Second World War, when vast Japanese armies ravaged China, was not enough to summon up such a nation. For many Chinese that war was simply an opportunity to continue score-settling or self-aggrandizement under new conditions.

The relationship between citizenship and military service, not to mention military effectiveness, is far more complex than most twentieth-century Chinese military thinkers (Jiang apart) have recognized. The history of the *levée en masse* demonstrates that the roles of citizen and soldier rarely overlap, and reinforce each other more rarely still – and even then only in certain sorts of wars and under specific conditions of political participation and legitimacy. Otherwise they coexist only very uneasily or in opposition. The idea that a multitude of patriotic heroes, of one heart and one mind, lurks under the surface of even the most turbulent society, waiting to be unleashed, has been shown to be false in both the French and the Chinese cases. What the French case has shown, however, is that in the right circumstances ordinary people will make great sacrifices for a country they believe to be their own. But that country cannot be defined, military style, from the top down, by enforced identity. It can only emerge, as the French tradition at its best understands, through a free, fair, and pluralistic political process that weaves together the various strands of nationhood. This is a truth that China is still far from facing.

---

[38] Michael R. Godley, "Politics from History: Lei Haizong and the *Zhanguo* Clique," *Papers on Far Eastern History* 40 (September 1989): 95–122.

[39] See John Fitzgerald, *Awakening China: Politics, Culture, and Class in the Nationalist Revolution* (Stanford, Calif., 1996).

[40] John Byron [pseudonym], *The Claws of the Dragon* (New York, 1992).

10

In Lieu of the *Levée en masse*

Mass Mobilization in Modern Vietnam

Greg Lockhart

It would be unsafe to assume that Vietnamese terms for raising armies have ever corresponded with those of the *levée en masse*. *Mo binh* means "to recruit soldiers." *Huy dong* and *dong vien* mean "to mobilize" them. Certain old insurrectionary terms that were used to sanction revolts against decadent courts or foreign invaders may share some of the ideological character of the *levée* of 1793: *khoi nghia* and *nghia quan*, which are usually rendered "righteous uprising" and "righteous army," for instance. Yet the foundations for state power in Vietnam were far more fragmented than those in modern France, and so were the means of recruiting armies. In premodern Vietnam even the strongest courts only raised regular regiments [*linh ve*] from loyal clans in provinces around the capital. Auxiliary forces [*linh co*] from less loyal clans in more remote regions were recruited by military secretaries, who did not deal with individuals, but negotiated with village councils about the number of men a village might release from work in the fields.[1]

In modern Vietnam, regional autonomy has continued to have a strong effect on military recruiting. The strike battalions of the colonial army and the draftees who went to World War One tended to be recruited from particular regions. Moreover, in the war of national independence between 1945 and 1975, regional forces [*dia phuong quan*] recruited by local committees were fundamental to the formation of the People's Army. What I want to show in this chapter, however, is that since the French conquest of 1859–84, there has been a fundamental shift in the basis for recruiting armies, one that placed the process of regional recruitment in a new, national context.

It will be seen how the destruction of the monarchy by the forces of French imperialism gave rise to "the people" as the political–military category of

---

[1] Greg Lockhart, *Nation in Arms: The Origins of the People's Army of Vietnam* (Sydney, 1989), 13–23.

fundamental importance in modern Vietnam. The best way to understand the mass mobilization of the postcolonial era, therefore, is to place it alongside the radically new construction of military affairs that had already taken shape in the colonial period. This construction may be described as a *general* one – that is, its novelty lay in its abstract universality – which was necessary to place the old dynastic foundations for recruiting armies in the new national context.

The End of the Ancient Order

Although the destruction of the Vietnamese monarchy was not complete until the emperor Bao Dai abdicated in 1945, its fall was foreshadowed by its reaction to the gradual French conquest of the country in the nine-teenth century. As the French presence expanded, the military response of the Vietnamese court was largely one of "passive defense" [*giu de hoa*]. This was partly because internal conflict between the Nguyen court and various regional clans tended to weaken its capacity to resist the French. But this weakness was also created and exploited by the overwhelming impact of modern weapons and military organization on an ancient order.

Various memorials written for the emperor Tu Duc in the 1860s and 1870s capture the Vietnamese court's assessment of its position in the face of French power:

The enemy's ships are as fast as the wind, their guns can fire through stone walls, and have a range of over ten miles. Since the enemy has weapons like that fighting them is not feasible... during the last three or four years our soldiers have not been dependable, our guns not good, and our fortresses not strong... with the exception of a peace policy I am at a loss to say what we should do.[2]

Or,

Our country is long and not wide. Apart from the extreme north and south, the area from Thanh Hoa to Binh Thuan is long and narrow. In front of our country is a vast ocean and at the back of it are great mountains and jungles. When the country is broken up the work of supplying the army must break down and the inner and outer regions cannot save each other. Also from the north all the way to the south our country is bordered by the ocean and an external enemy is able to land wherever he likes. Because of this the task of defending the coast is most pressing.[3]

---

[2] Dang Huy Van, "Cuoc dau tranh giua phai Chu chien va nhung phai Chu Hoa trong cuoc khang chien chong Phap o cuoi the ky XIX" [The Struggle Between the "War Faction" and the "Peace Factions" in the Resistance War Against the French at the End of the Nineteenth Century], *Nghien Cuu Lich Su* [Historical Studies] 94 (Hanoi, 1962), quoting *Thuc luc ky thu* 4 quyen 24.

[3] Ibid., quoting Vo Duy Thanh, "Ban dieu tran gui Tu Duc" [Memorials Sent to Tu Duc], extracted from Doan Ke Thien, *Danh Nhan Viet Nam* [Famous People of Vietnam](Hanoi, 1943).

Or,

Our provincial capitals are built on exposed plains and near rivers and the coast for ease of communications. But today the truth is that for the enemy the provincial capitals are vital, while for us attempts to hold them are very dangerous. Why is this? This is because the enemy have very mobile ships and guns. Once they have created a pretext for hostilities they bring their large ships close [to our provincial towns] in order to fire their big guns. Our army jealously guarding the town walls has no way of avoiding the danger, and so, being frightened out of its wits, disintegrates. All the more reason for this is that our fortresses are no higher than twenty feet and no more than two feet thick, and the enemy use ladders to climb the walls and tunnels to attack them. This is why they could not help winning.[4]

When coalitions of royal and regional regiments were actually mustered to fight pitched battles with the French, as at Ky Hoa near Saigon in 1861, and at Son Tay in the north in 1883,[5] they were quickly dispersed. With the fall of the independent monarchy and the installation of a puppet court by the French in 1884, this left the colonialists to campaign against the "righteous uprisings" of regional guerrilla resistance groups, which sought to reestablish the monarchy until they were finally suppressed around the turn of the century.[6]

The impact of modern weapons was fundamental to the French victory. But so too were the inefficiency and looseness of premodern Vietnamese military organization. Even though the basic notion of political obligation in the old order was "loyalty to the monarch" [*trung quan*], the decentralized recruitment of both regular and regional regiments meant that local leaders retained great influence in military affairs. Even after the Nguyen dynasty was well established in the early nineteenth century, the evidence suggests that no high command was appointed. When the court sent an army to exterminate rebels and bandits, civil mandarins in the central and regional bureaucracies gave instructions to military commanders as fighting contingents moved through their regions. Also, because large contingents usually combined regular and regional elements, which kept their own leaders, the resulting force might be commanded by two or more mandarins.[7] Thus, while the foundation for political–military service in old Vietnam was a hierarchical sense of "loyalty to the monarch," this was mediated by a strong sense of obligation to local clan leaders, even when it was in the interests of the clans to remain loyal to the court.

---

4 Ibid., quoting *Tho Van Nguyen Xuan On* [The Poetry of Nguyen Xuan On], translated by Nguyen Du Van and Ha Van Dai (Hanoi, 1961), 167.

5 Lockhart, *Nation in Arms*, 24–5, 33.

6 A. Thomazi, *La conquete de l'Indochine* (Paris, 1934); on pacification after 1884, Général Gallieni, *Gallieni au Tonkin (1892–1896)* (Paris, 1948). Two recent studies are David G. Marr, *Vietnamese Anticolonialism* (Berkeley, Calif., 1971), and Charles Fourniau, *Annan-Tonkin 1885–1896: Lettrés et paysans vietnamiens face à la conquete coloniale* (Paris, 1989).

7 A. L. M. Bonifacy, "La révolte de Nong Van Van," *Revue Indochinoise* (July 1914), 25–57; Lockhart, *Nation in Arms*, 21–2.

Some idea of the speed with which the conquest revealed tensions in the old order, and then changed the foundations of Vietnamese military organization, may be gained from the history of the Vietnamese colonial army. Vietnamese combat companies recruited from villages that were hostile to the royal court were attached to French forces from the beginning of the conquest. In the 1860s a *Garde Civile* was established in the south to police the new colony of Cochinchina. In 1879 the first regular regiment of Vietnamese *tirailleurs* was recruited to complement the French expeditionary force in its campaigns in the north.[8] The creation of the *Garde Indigène* as a colonial militia was also related to these campaigns. Formed in 1886 to assist with the repression of regional resistance groups in Tonkin, it drew on the model of the Bengal Police in British India but was recruited by canton chiefs who retained the same responsibility for recruiting under the French as they had in precolonial times.[9] The formation of a second regular regiment of Vietnamese *tirailleurs* in 1903 may then be taken to mark the end of serious regional resistance to the French occupation. It was recruited in Tonkin to replace French and French African troops that were being withdrawn from Indochina for service in other parts of the French empire.[10]

By around 1900, therefore, the recruiting of Vietnamese soldiers was being affected by global influences. This new globalism did not necessarily change the regional nature of recruiting. Yet it did place the old procedures in an unprecedented political context, as certain semantic shifts that began to occur in Vietnamese during the early colonial period demonstrate.[11]

New World, New Nation: The Semantics
of Modern Vietnamese Globalism

The new globalism involved nothing less than a changing conception of "the world." Far from suggesting a "round" earth or "globe," *thien ha*, the old term for "world," conveyed a sense of "all beneath heaven," a realm in which people lived on a flat earth surmounted by a curved sky.[12] Since

---

[8] Lockhart, *Nation in Arms*, 31.

[9] E. Daufès, *La Garde Indigène d'Indochine de sa création à nos jours* (Avignon, 1933–4), introduction to volume 1.

[10] Lockhart, *Nation in Arms*, 38.

[11] The discussion that follows is based on ibid., 41–64.

[12] The first modern Vietnamese geography was Truong Vinh Ky's *Du Do Thuyet Luoc* [Elementary Geography] of 1887. Even though it still used the term *thien ha*, it presented modern maps of all the continents and lessons on modern historical and administrative geography. These lessons located and described "Annam" and "Basse Cochinchine" in relation to the other countries of Asia and the world and were prefaced with an explanation of why the "earth" [*trai dat*] was a "globe" [*dia cau*] – and how, with "1,200 million people" on its surface, the globe rotated around its own axis every twenty-four hours. A new sense of global "movement" – leading to other new historical constructions such as "progress," "revolution," "world revolution," "mass movements," and many others – had clearly begun to change the Vietnamese conception of "the world."

this was the realm of the semidivine monarch, it was fitting that with the destruction of the monarchy a new term for "world" came into circulation. This was *the gioi*, in which *the* [time] plus *gioi* [the directions – north, south, east, west, up, and down] encompassed the modern globe.[13] This semantic revolution was then accompanied by the construction of "the people" as the fundamental category of political and social significance in the twentieth century.

The transfer of sovereignty from the monarch to "the people" in modern Vietnamese political thinking was approached in many works by turn-of-the-century literati. One work that marks this shift most clearly is Phan Boi Chau's 1905 *History of the Loss of the Country*, when it makes a striking observation: "The country of Vietnam has people" [*Nuoc Viet Nam co dan*].[14] This sentence prefaced an explanation of the nineteen onerous French taxes that had replaced the two taxes imposed by the old royal court.[15] But what is so interesting about it is that, in ancient times, the fundamental political question was whether or not the country had a good king. There was no doubt it had people. If the country had a good king, human affairs would be regulated because of *his* moral virtue and benevolence, and not because of any intrinsic virtue of "the people." With the French conquest, however, this old Confucian sense of righteous order had become meaningless, as Phan demonstrated in another text, written in exile in 1906.

This was his *Letter Written in Blood*,[16] which presents us with a series of fascinating, radical constructions that isolate "the people" [*dan*] as an independent political category. These constructions include the following: "[the people] establish the foundation for the wealth of our country," "the people are of the country, and the country is of the people," and "if we do not have people, then we do not have anything."[17] One sees here a shift from the people as subjects to the people as the source of political legitimacy, the foundation of the modern idea of "nation."

---

[13] The term *the gioi* had been revived from medieval Buddhist sutras. It is thus most accurate to describe it as one of the many old/new terms that reflected the reorganization of ancient categories that occurred under the impact of modern change.

[14] Phan Boi Chau, "Viet Nam vong quoc su" [History of the Loss of the Country], translated (from Chinese to Vietnamese) by Chu Thien and Chuong Thau (Hanoi, 1957), 55. Chinese scholars tell me this sentence is odd in Chinese. However, while line 7 of the tenth page of the Chinese text in *Dai Hoc Van Khoa*, 1959–1960 edition, shows that this is indeed what Phan wrote, I do not think his construction can be explained simply in terms of his "bad Chinese." He could write good Chinese poetry. I would thus argue that his construction reflects particular Vietnamese perceptions and conditions, as well as a desire to popularize his message.

[15] Ibid., 55.

[16] Phan Boi Chau, *Hai Ngoai Huyet Thu* in Van Hoc, *Hop Tuyen Tho Van Yeu Nuoc va Cach Mang Dau The Ky XX, 1900–1930* [Collected Patriotic and Revolutionary Poetry at the Beginning of the Twentieth Century, 1900–1930] (Hanoi, 1972), 50–72.

[17] Ibid., 56, 58, 539n, and 551. These ideas were circulating widely in Vietnam by around 1906.

From the 1900s on, "nation" was rendered in Vietnamese by a number of new terms – *quoc gia, dan toc,* and *quoc dan* – that were based on a sense of the sovereignty of the "the people," as opposed to "loyalty to the monarch."[18] As I have discussed elsewhere, there are special problems with interpreting the term *quoc gia.* It had meant "kingdom" for many centuries, and so until at least the 1920s we can not always be sure what the literati meant when they used it.[19] Nevertheless, the term *quoc gia* was often used interchangeably with the other new ones just mentioned, all of which came to mean "nation" from the 1900s: *quoc dan,* which may be rendered "a country of people," and *dan toc,* "a people of clans." These terms, which placed an unprecedented stress on "the people" [*dan*], could be used interchangeably as late as the 1950s to mean "people," "citizen," "nation," or "nation-state."[20] The fact that these new terms became more or less synonymous with an old expression like *quoc gia* shows that a modern mutation in Vietnamese perceptions of their collectivity was already taking place by the 1910s. The primary impact of the French regime had been to topple the monarchy and bring "the people" and "the nation" into existence as political categories of fundamental importance.

"The people" constituted the foundation for what might be described as a horizontal or popular construction of the new nation's military affairs. This horizontal construction tended to conflict with the vertical or autocratic one, which shaped the fragmented regional/dynastic foundations for recruiting armies in the old monarchical order. Its gradual emergence, along with the national perspective to which it was linked, helps clarify the new *general,* as opposed to the old *piecemeal,* approach to military mobilization that first crystallized in Vietnam during World War One.

World War One and the General Construction of Vietnamese Military Affairs

In July 1917, the first number of a monthly journal called *Nam Phong* [Southern Wind – hereafter *NP*] was published in Hanoi, with the aim of developing a Vietnamese "national" culture. Since the journal was also committed to supporting "France in its role at the forefront of the war of

---

[18] Huynh Kim Khanh, *Vietnamese Communism 1925–1945* (Ithaca, N.Y., and London, 1982), 29, and passim, rightly stresses that "patriotism" (*chu nghia ai quoc*) was a motive force of Vietnamese group solidarity or nationalism in the twentieth century. However, this does not show how the old communal groupings took on a new political significance at the same time.

[19] Ibid. The term *quoc gia,* literally a "country of families," was an ancient one. For further discussion see Lockhart, *Nation in Arms,* 44.

[20] For example, Diep Van Ky's use of the term *dan toc* in *Su Cach Mang* [A History of Revolutions] (Saigon, 1927), 34, clearly means "nation" and "nationalism" [*chu nghia dan toc*]. Also see Khanh, *Vietnamese Communism,* 27, especially n. 9.

nations,"[21] it was clear that the development of a national culture was related both to Vietnam's colonial status within the French Empire and to its participation in global war: by 1917, 86,000 Vietnamese soldiers and workers would be recruited for service in France.[22] *NP* itself was a product of this unprecedented mobilization of people and resources and published what may be the earliest sustained war narratives in modern Vietnamese literature.[23]

These took the form of monthly commentaries on the war and began appearing in the first issue. They were appropriately grounded in "the world" [*the gioi*] rather than in "the realm beneath heaven" [*thien ha*]. The first appeared under the general heading "Major World Affairs" [*Viec Nhon The Gioi*] and contained various subheadings: "War Matters" [*Viec Chien Tranh*], "Naval War Matters," "Diplomatic and Political Matters," and "Home Affairs" – that is, Vietnamese affairs as distinct from those in other countries. *NP*'s reporting on the war thus conveyed a sense of distinctive Vietnamese national interest and identity. It also began to disseminate a range of new terms that were necessary to relate the new sense of an emerging national polity to the war of nations.

I am thinking of such expressions as: "general mobilization" [*tong dong vien*], "general offensive" [*tong cong*], "general counteroffensive" [*tong phan cong*], "general staff" [*tong tham muu*], "general munitions board" [*dan duoc tong cuc*], and "general strategy and tactics" [*chien luoc va chien thuat chung*].[24] This new vocabulary clearly embodied a level of conceptual and organizational abstraction that, though incipient from the time of the French conquest and the establishment of the *Gouverneur Général*, was still new in Vietnam and was fundamental to the development of the

---

[21] The French translation appeared above the Vietnamese text. This was not so odd because *NP* was published in Vietnamese, with French and Chinese language supplements.

[22] A total of 91,747 were actually mobilized, but only 86,000 actually went overseas.

[23] By contrast with these, an outstanding feature of the old memorials quoted earlier was their matter-of-fact defeatism, or the clarity with which they explain how, in the face of French power, fighting the French was "not feasible." Given such clear vision in the face of disaster, it could be argued that we are dealing with an unflinching kind of fatalism, which assumes that, whatever the outcome of an event, there is no point in contesting it because "heaven's" will is always fulfilled. A major difference in the modern texts is the way they fit into a highly rationalized discourse that is rooted in "the world."

[24] Also see, for example, "general munitions board," *NP* 5 (November 1917), 337; "general strategy and tactics," *NP* 16 (October 1918), 194. Many other terms further reinforced this generalizing inference of the *NP* commentaries: "Aircraft Production Board" [*phi co che tao cuc*], *NP* 5 (November 1917), 337; "national defense bonds [*bang ve quoc phong trai phieu*], *NP* 5 (November 1917), 347; "territorial integrity" [*linh tho hoan toan*], *NP* 6 (December 1917), 404. Later in the 1920s and 1930s, related terms such as "general manager," "general strike," and "general uprising" could be added to the list. Insofar as these terms were subversive in the colonial context, it may be added that *NP* also covered the Russian Revolution from July 1917.

modern Vietnamese sense of nation. The modern administrative, weapons, communications, and transportation systems that displaced the Vietnamese monarchy helped engender a change in consciousness that in turn gave rise to a modern sense of nationhood. These nation-making systems embodied a mode of thought that entailed a new level of abstraction, one that was also necessary to imagine the new categories of national discourse: those of "the people" and "the world."

The recent doctoral thesis by Mireille Favre illustrates how a modern sense of nation began to crystallize out of the general mobilization (of mainly 1916) in Vietnam.[25] Although Favre is not explicitly concerned with the general construction of civil or military affairs, she nevertheless shows how a modern system of incentives – the rewards of food, pay, and clothing, which the colonial administration offered in exchange for military service – tended to override wide regional differences in the recruiting base. Both the 1915 and 1916 intakes, which raised 65,000 of the 86,000 men who eventually went to France,[26] came overwhelmingly from the villages of Tonkin and northern Annam, rather than from Cochinchina in the south.[27] One reason for this was that the southern commune did not have the relatively tight control over its people that the northern one did, so that southern leaders were not in the same position as northern notables, who often ingratiated themselves with the French by providing recruits.

By 1916, when some antirecruiting tracts appeared in the Saigon press, resistance to recruiting was quite strong in the south. This resistance included disturbances around Saigon and farther afield in Cochinchina and Cambodia.[28] However, just as support for recruiting in some regions contributed to the development of the state administrative apparatus, resistance to recruiting in other regions did so too. The main response of the colonial administration to the resistance in Cochinchina and Cambodia was to establish the *Sureté Générale* throughout all of Indochina.[29]

Tonkin and northern Annam provided a strong regional base for recruiting in 1916, despite conditions that in earlier times would have made such a response unlikely: 1916 was a year of drought and floods. Indeed, one reason

---

[25] John Horne reminded me of Favre's thesis, "Un Milieu Porteur de Modernisation: travailleurs et tirailleurs Vietnamiens en France pendant la première guerre mondiale," Ecole Nationale des Chartes, 1986.

[26] Ibid., 183, 258–267.

[27] Ibid., 51–2. The authorities did have some early success in recruiting tradesmen and soldiers in the south. For example, some 700 workers and artisans (fitters and metalworkers) and some 500 riflemen were recruited in Saigon after June 1915. The artisans went to France, and the riflemen mainly reinforced *L'Armée d'Orient* in Djibouti in November. A small number joined a largely Tonkinese battalion that was sent to China.

[28] Ibid., 125, 201–230.

[29] Ibid., 303. The *Sureté* was established in 1915. The reorganization of 1917 led to the formation of the *Sureté Générale*. See Patrice Morlat, *La répression coloniale au Vietnam (1908–1940)* (Paris, 1990).

to raise an army in premodern Vietnam might have been to help a flood-stricken province. It would not have been to take its men away. The difference in 1916, however, was that while natural disasters dangerously threatened a region's livelihood, the food, pay, and clothing that the government offered provided powerful incentives to enlist. As Favre shows, the most famine-stricken provinces – especially Ninh Binh and Thanh Hoa – produced the largest number of volunteers.[30]

In the liberal mythology of the nation, the volunteer soldier is thought to fight freely for democracy and citizenship, and for freedom itself. In modern Vietnam, however, the idea of the volunteer freedom fighter had little social traction. Many were volunteers in name only, having been forced to enlist by ambitious village officials. Available evidence also suggests that many who enlisted of their own volition did so because of a combination of ignorance and a yearning to escape the asphyxiating poverty and conformity of their present circumstances.[31] In any case, the struggle for "independence" [*doc lap*] in various forms is central. Some young people wanted to break free of communal values that had reinforced collective conformity for millennia. Others longed to be free of the hunger and poverty that was so common in the old peasant commune. Only later, when the political struggle against imperialism became more polarized, would a desire for "national independence" come into sharp focus. During the First World War, however, the reality of Vietnamese voluntary recruitment fell far short of the liberal ideal. It was largely about seizing personal opportunities.

Given the rudimentary state of the colonial administration in 1915, those opportunities were still very limited. Since communal budgets financed recruiting centers,[32] conditions at these centers were worst in the poorest

---

[30] Favre, "Un Milieu Porteur," 196.

[31] One draftee who published a memoir of his experience of the war in 1983 spoke for many other Vietnamese who were mobilized for the First World War: "It was the spring of 1916, a time when the First World War had entered its bloodiest period. Quang Tri was a very poor province, the earth was rough [*rabougrie*], full of stones, and the landowners had left to make their living elsewhere. I was then a healthy twenty-six-year-old student, but I could not live on this land. Despite the great efforts of my parents to work it, poverty was forever the rule for everyone. A group of village notables also existed who taxed and exploited the peasants.

One day, I left for Hue to find work because it was a big town with many factories. After I reached Hue I learnt that the Mother Country [i.e., France] was then recruiting soldier-workers and combatants to go to France and work in the factories there or in the colonial army. At that time my only aim was to find work, I did not realize that to be a soldier-worker or combatant meant to go and work in the arms factories or serve on the front. I was thus led to leave voluntarily." This "Témoignage de M. T. P." originally appeared in Vietnamese in *Doan Ket* 349 (June 1983), 12, a monthly publication of the Union of Vietnamese in France. Because I have not been able to see the original, my translation is made from the French version presented in Favre's thesis.

[32] Favre, "Un Milieu Porteur," 131.

provinces – which also tended to provide the largest number of recruits. Doctors and technical personnel were rare. Barracks facilities and equipment were very inadequate. Many recruits had to be turned back, either because they could not be processed, or because they were not fit. On January 29, 1916, at Thanh Hoa, for example, 1,756 candidate *tirailleurs* presented themselves to authorities, but only 52, or 3 percent, were accepted. The other 97 percent either failed to meet the basic physical requirements (which were a height of 1.5 meters and a weight of 45 kilograms)[33] or were suffering from various illnesses.[34] In 1916 recruiting could only proceed by fits and starts because of a widespread cholera epidemic. Perpetual transport delays encouraged desertion, and shipboard conditions on the way to France were so bad that they are known to have led some to suicide.

Miraculously, however, 65,000 men, plus 100,000 tons of grain, actually reached France in 1916 – plus another 21,000 men from later recruiting drives. This kind of mobilization was as unprecedented in Vietnam as the system of incentives and administrative imperatives on which it depended. So too was the experience of war and a wider world to which it gave rise. Two of the four Vietnamese combat battalions, the 7th and 21st, were deployed around the Chemin des Dames in France, while the 1st and 27th fought the Germans in Macedonia and Albania. For the troops in these units, the modern world would be a suitably unsympathetic place. When some Vietnamese survivors were withdrawn from the line in April 1917, for example, hospital authorities at Nice noted their "very advanced exhaustion" and "deep demoralization."[35] Some of the militarized workers who were sent to France gained training in apprenticeships and developed skills as drivers or mechanics. The great majority, however, were employed in the ammunition factories of southern France, where conditions were bad.

The bullying of factory foremen, long hours, strange food, unaccustomed illness, frequent explosions, and suicides were common features of working life. Vietnamese workers also became guinea pigs in developing assembly line production techniques in French factories. Previously, French unions had inhibited experiments in what was then called "Fordism." With the arrival of a vulnerable conscript workforce like the Vietnamese, however, factory owners were able to resume their experiments, with such success that they led, for example, to the adoption of the new methods in Renault's factories.[36]

---

[33] Ibid., 133.

[34] Ibid, 140. Trachoma and tuberculosis were common. Many also suffered from serious indigestion after overeating at the reception centers. Some ate themselves to death.

[35] Quoted in Favre, "Un Milieu Porteur," Chapter 3.

[36] Ibid., 75, 351–61.

Whether they were being bombarded at Verdun or servicing the treadmills of the factories of the future, Vietnamese draftees were participating in the more or less universal experience of modern machine culture and machine-age war. For the Vietnamese, such participation helped to transform their sense of political and social order. Because the new construction of military affairs rested upon a foundation of mass participation, it tended to stimulate democratic political and social change that ran counter to the interests of the colonial government in the postwar period. Some idea of the extent to which World War One undermined the basis for colonial rule in the 1920s and 1930s is thus necessary if we are to appreciate how, by the 1940s, it was possible to imagine a "people's army" in Vietnam.

Old Soldiers, Subversion, and the Impetus for Change

People often noticed that those who had been to the war came home as "changed men." Violent quarrels around the ports of disembarkation were one sign of this. So was the trouble in the towns that sprang from unem-ployment. Social menace and isolation are built into the stories about old soldiers that we find in the dominant liberal-humanist strand of Vietnamese literature in the 1920s and 1930s.

In one story by The Lu, for instance, some veterans pose an undefined but pervasive threat to people on a ship running between Hai Phong and Saigon. In another story by Nhat Linh there is a joke about how Annamese soldiers had black teeth, which made French people think they were cannibals.[37] The tone of Thach Lam's short story, "The Old Soldier," is somewhat different. Because he has become a beggar, the old soldier in this story is incapable of much overt menace. But as he lies destitute on the floor of an inn, the story he tells two passersby of his happy (postwar) years in France creates a romantic global backdrop against which his present destitution stands out as a dark indictment of the colonial order in Vietnam.[38]

It was not necessarily the overtly discontented or destitute veteran who posed the most serious threat to the colonial order. Those veterans who seemed to reintegrate themselves successfully into postwar society would actually present a deeper threat to the colonial regime. Many returned to their villages, found work in public and private enterprises, or served in the colonial army. Some, like Thach Lam's old soldier, could speak French. A few expressed opinions on public affairs and acquired state scholarships for

---

[37] See "Broken Journey: Nhat Linh's *Going to France*," translated by Greg and Monique Lockhart, with an introduction and commentary by Greg Lockhart, *East Asian History* 8 (December 1994), 110. I am unable to find again the story by The Lu and so I am relying on my recollection of it here.

[38] *Tuyen tap Thach Lam* [Selected Works of Thach Lam] (Hanoi, 1988), 75–79.

their children to attend school. After their experience of what was often referred to in Vietnam as "machine civilization,"[39] many had also acquired a taste for consumer goods – for eating canned food and for wearing shoes, watches, and modern clothes.[40] One former mechanic in France even enjoyed transitory fame by becoming the first Vietnamese to build an aircraft.[41] Such assertive modernism was often regarded as a "social danger" by the authorities[42] because it encouraged the natives to take their destiny into their own hands. For World War One veterans, social engagement led to political isolation because Vietnamese independence was anathema to the colonial regime.

The "changed men" thus became implicated in various forms of social disturbances, which tended to radicalize Vietnamese politics and align the course of mid-twentieth-century Vietnamese history with what one historian has aptly called "the revolutionary path."[43] This was especially so from around 1930, when the global experience of the veterans can be related to certain actions that some of them took against the colonial state.

With the formation of the National Party in 1927, for example, reliable historical accounts refer to the organization of suicide squads that worked in concert with "comrades in the French army" to lead uprisings in the towns.[44] Here the "French army" meant the colonial one, which contained a proportion of European veterans from the war, sprinkled through a largely Vietnamese force. By 1930–1, 20,000 of its 30,000 regular soldiers were Vietnamese. In addition, there was the *Garde Indigène*, which in 1931 numbered 15,220, plus 388 French officers and NCOs.[45]

---

[39] See ibid., 91.

[40] Favre, "Un Milieu Porteur," 625.

[41] See Nguyen Thi Kim, "Chiec may bay dau tien cua nguoi Annam va nguoi da lap ra no" [The First Aeroplane Made by an Annamese and the Person Who Made It], *Dan Ba Moi* [New Woman] (23 and 25 May 1935), 6.

[42] Favre, "Un Milieu Porteur," 300.

[43] Thomas Hodgkin, *Vietnam: The Revolutionary Path* (London, 1981). This path was also generally related to the Russian Revolution of 1917. It is well known that around the time he became a founding father of the French Communist Party in 1920, the young Vietnamese patriot, Ho Chi Minh, spent some time spreading the message of the Russian Revolution among Vietnamese soldiers and workers who were waiting for repatriation in France. The historian Tran Van Giau notes that, as Vietnamese in France began to take a more serious interest in proletarian politics, they often sent news about the Russian Revolution home. "Among the tradesmen and interpreters who returned to Vietnam [after World War One]," he writes, "many still maintained correspondence with people in France and read communist newspapers that arrived from France by many means." See Tran Van Giau, *Tu Cach Mang Thang Muoi Den Cach Mang Thang Tam* [From the October Revolution to the August Revolution] (Hanoi, 1957), 104.

[44] Tran Huy Lieu, *Tai lieu tham khao lich su cach mang can dai Viet Nam* [Historical Research Documents on Vietnam's Modern Revolution] (hereafter *CMCD*) (Hanoi, 1957), 10: 33.

[45] Lockhart, *Nation in Arms*, 38.

Not all the National Party's comrades had necessarily returned from the Great War. However, National Party policy stated that "returned military cadres would command the righteous uprising."[46] When Vietnamese troops in the garrison at Yen Bai mutinied in February 1930 and initiated the widespread uprisings that would soon involve cadres of the newly formed Communist Party in the provinces of Nghe An and Ha Tinh, it is reasonable to assume that some of the ringleaders were, or had been influenced by, veterans of the First World War.

Some veterans disturbed the Old Regime in other ways. On one occasion in the Nghe An village of Vo Liet, for example, the commune had made some customary sacrifices to the village genie. These consisted of a buffalo, two pigs, and some glutinous rice, of which selected morsels were normally reserved for the mandarins and village notables. However, on this day a villager named Nong appeared at the head of a group of fifty or sixty people and, confronting the mandarins, said: "The rice belongs to the villagers, therefore, the ritual feast is also theirs. You gentlemen do not have the right to feast apart, taking all for yourselves." With this, Nong proceeded to sound the village tocsin and call the inhabitants to come and take their parts of the feast. Seeing the crowd grow, the mandarins fled.

Nong was a peasant who had been a *tirailleur* for three years during World War One.[47] Whatever his motives, the kind of transformation he helped to precipitate in his village was consistent with the structural change that the mobilization of 1915–16 necessitated in Vietnam. By usurping the village ritual and causing the mandarins to flee, he was challenging and undermining the foundations for monarchical rule in Vo Liet. To that extent, he was promoting the idea of "the people."

Nong, like all the other veterans, was still a relatively isolated agent of historical change. This is consistent with the image of the dislocated veteran that occurs in so much postwar Vietnamese (and European) literature. It would also be consistent with rash, uncoordinated mutinies in the colonial army, which the authorities quickly isolated and crushed. With the formation of the Indochinese Communist Party (ICP) in 1930 and the uprisings of that year, however, a new and less alienated image of the old soldier began to emerge, as part of a radical critique of colonial society.

As a rule, communist writings depicted Vietnamese soldiers in the colonial army as misguided pawns of imperialism, who were estranged from society, but who could nevertheless be redeemed. In 1930, for example, some of the earliest *Military Documents of the Party* assume the need to "organize in the enemy army" and "proselytize [*van dong*] in the enemy army" in order to "transform native soldiers into a revolutionary force" – or, at least, one that

---

[46] Ibid., 53.
[47] Favre, "Un Milieu Porteur," 629–30, drawing on "Il n'y a qu'une voie," *Nghe An* (1972), 24, cited in P. Brocheux, "Vietnam, le grande tournant de 1930," *L'Histoire* 69 (1984), 109–11.

would not shoot Vietnamese people during strikes and demonstrations.[48] Meanwhile, the primary image of the socialist soldier was of an individual who acted in "self-defense" [*tu ve*] against the vicissitudes of imperialist repression.

Indeed, the need to establish "self-defense forces" [*doi tu ve*] in the villages lies at the origins of Vietnam's revolutionary military history.[49] It also lies at the heart of the socialist notion of the volunteer. Insofar as self-defense fighters were thought to epitomize independence, they were also regarded as both products and precipitators of the political–social change that would lead to social justice and "national independence." Before we can fully appreciate this image of the socialist soldier, however, it is necessary to consider the mass mobilization process in which it came to be embedded by the early 1940s.

The General Construction of Revolutionary War

One of the most striking features of ICP ideology in the 1930s was the way it aligned the ancient terminology of the "righteous uprising" with the abstract and generalized vocabulary of the First World War. The notion of a "general righteous uprising" [*tong khoi nghïa*] and of a "general rebellion" [*tong bao dong*] had come into circulation during the disturbances at Yen Bai and in Nghe An in 1930. As compared to the "righteous uprising" of the past, the new formulations no longer assumed the possibility of restoring a good king. Yet the genius of the new construction was that, just as the general mobilization of 1916–17 tended to place Vietnamese regionalism in an entirely new context, so the ancient language of the clan-based insurrection became married to the rhetoric of modern revolutionary change.

In the decade before World War Two many other new terms contributed to the development of new conceptions of political and military action in Vietnam. I am thinking of such expressions as "general strike," "mass struggle," "mass movement," "soviet movement," "class struggle," "demonstration," "general insurrection," "boycott," "world revolution," "general secretary" (of the Communist Party), "revolutionary army" and "worker–peasant army," and a "soldier–worker–peasant government." These terms were derived largely from the experience of the Russian revolution, which emphasized the organization of the urban proletariat and the subversion of the standing army. However, toward the end of the decade, when the Japanese invasion of China presaged the Japanese occupation of Indochina

---

[48] *Van Kien Quan Su Cua dang 1930–1945* [Military Documents of the Party 1930–1945] (Hanoi, 1969), 15, 33, 45, and 50.
[49] Ibid., 45, offers one of the earliest references to "self-defense forces" in Vietnam. In Lockhart, *Nation in Arms*, 60, n. 67, I relate this to Engels' conception of "the self-acting armed organization of the population."

in September 1940, the new language of insurrection began to reflect the interest that radical Vietnamese strategists were then taking in the Chinese communist models for mobilizing the peasantry in a guerrilla war.

As early as 1938, the writings of various Chinese revolutionary strategists, which emphasized the motive force of "the people" or "the masses" [*quan chung*], were in circulation in Vietnamese translation and compilation. As the writings put it: "our victory must depend on the participation of the masses in the resistance war," and "the way of guerrilla war is the highest form of resistance war of the masses."[50] Also outlined, therefore, were the essential elements of what would become Mao's famous three-stage model for a guerrilla war of "national liberation."[51]

Here we briefly recapitulate this well-known model. In the "defense stage," revolutionary cadres would build their bases among the masses and resist the onslaught of the enemy's regular army. In the "holding" stage, the guerrilla units would gradually gain ascendancy in a region through hit-and-run tactics and the mobilization of quasi-regular battalions and regiments. Then, finally, when guerrilla tactics and mass mobilization in many regions had tired the enemy and permitted the concentration of regular "main force" [*chu luc*] units, it was envisaged that the regular army would lead the masses in a "general counteroffensive" [*tong phan cong*]. The overarching theme was the integration of small-scale guerrilla actions within a broadly progressive scheme of military activity that would lead to the creation of a mass army.

The relevance of this approach to "national liberation" and "independence" in Vietnam was confirmed by the formation of Ho Chi Minh's Vietnam Independence League [Viet Minh] in the mountains of the Viet Bac in 1942. This guerrilla activity was part of a process of mass mobilization. At the center was a system of "armed propaganda" modeled on Chinese methods, with which Ho became familiar during a visit there in 1942. It was designed to construct a new, socially engaged image of the guerrilla fighter, and also to develop a nationwide network of links between the army and the people. In its basic form, Viet Minh cadres simply arrived in remote highland villages offering to work in the fields. As time passed, they would explain their mission to sympathetic supporters and gradually begin recruiting. A Viet Minh training manual, written close to the August 1945 seizure of power, explains the technique: "Propaganda teams must work hard. Sometimes they must help our people in their work or work their way

---

[50] The first quote comes from a passage by Chou En Lai; the second, from a passage by Zhu De. Both appear in Nguyen Duc Thuy, *Phuong phap khang Nhat cua Hong Quan Tau* [The Method of Anti-Japanese Resistance of the Chinese Red Army] (Hanoi, January 1938), 10 (emphasis in the original). For a more detailed discussion see Lockhart, *Nation in Arms*, 66–70.

[51] See for example Mao Tse Tung and Che Guevara, *Guerrilla Warfare* (London, 1965).

into a crowd of people who are harvesting or transplanting in the fields and propagandize them." The next step was

> to explain to them clearly that joining the revolutionary army is a responsibility of the people and a glorious honor. Clearly outline the long term gains if all the people are liberated and the short term gains if the revolutionary army becomes stronger every day and wins wherever it fights.... [Also] use pamphlets, cartoons, and slogans to carry out propaganda. But the most important means is verbal communication so that the propaganda teams organize meetings and lectures and use theatrical performances and songs (with accompaniment if possible).[52]

The implantation of "people's committees" [*uy ban nhan dan*] and "national salvation organizations" [*hoi cuu quoc*] was crucial to the early stage of the mobilization process. As these groups spread throughout sympathetic villages, they became constituents of a mass organization designed to focus the support of different groups in society – peasants, women, youth, artisans, intellectuals, religious groups, and others. Even though they were not widespread to begin with, these organizations were central both to the Viet Minh's general construction of the popular interest and to their military organization. Because the organizational structure suggested links with similar groups everywhere, it provided a conceptual foundation for the integration of the people into a network that would harness the military energy of the nation.

The resulting network did not instantly become a nationwide institution. Until quite close to the end of World War Two, its development did not extend far beyond the Viet Bac, and even in that region there was resistance to it. There is, for example, evidence that the burning of a few houses in the northern highlands in 1944 was necessary to help draw people to the revolutionary side.[53] For an *armed* propaganda campaign, coercion was clearly acceptable as a means of ensuring that "the revolutionary army becomes stronger every day and wins wherever it fights." Nevertheless, there is no foundation for thinking that the Viet Minh came to power in August 1945 on the strength of a reign of terror, as much Western writing on the subject has assumed.[54]

Given the conditions of famine that prevailed in northern Vietnam in late 1944 and early 1945, the primary task of any party seeking national power was to suppress widespread banditry and anarchy; it was to *recreate* political and social order. In the central and southern parts of the country, where there

---

[52] Viet Nam Doc Lap Dong Minh [Vietnam Independence League], *Chinh Tri Vien Trong Quan Doi* [Political Cadres in the Army] (Hanoi, 1945), 13–14. Hoang Van Hoan also describes the participation of cadres in weddings and other village rituals. See *Giot nuoc trong bien ca (Hoi ky cach mang)* [A Drop in the Ocean (Revolutionary Memoirs)] (Peking, 1986), 210–11.

[53] Général Yves Gras, *Histoire de la guerre d'Indochine* (Paris, 1979), 27.

[54] On terror in the Vietnamese revolution, see Lockhart, *Nation in Arms*, 104, 113–15, 170.

was no famine, but where the Viet Minh presence extended no farther than a relatively small number of agents and sympathizers in key places (such as in the Advance Youth Guard Units that the Japanese had been developing for use in the event of an Allied landing), the problem was also to create national organizations where virtually none existed. Since a new order would have to be established in the face of at least some resistance, the use of armed forces to support national (salvation) committees and similar organizations was inevitable. This required that the new forces be identified with a national ethos, rather than with the self-interest of a faction. Accordingly, Viet Minh propaganda always insisted that the primary task of freedom fighters was to identify themselves with "the people."

Nowhere is this more clearly reflected than in the image of the new Viet Minh freedom fighter that began to take shape in the earliest days of the anti-imperialist guerrilla resistance. Because guerrilla forces depended on the villagers for their survival, it was vital that their image and conduct reflect their political and social integration with the general population. A typical artefact of the new resistance culture was a song celebrating "The Ten Viet Minh Policies," as follows:

1. Absolute obedience to orders from above.
2. Do not take as much as a needle and thread from the people.
3. Buying and selling must be carried out fairly.
4. It is absolutely forbidden to take public property.
5. Speak politely.
6. Wherever you stay, the house and garden must be kept clean for the people.
7. Whatever is borrowed must be returned.
8. Whatever is broken must be replaced.
9. No bathing in front of women.
10. No alcohol, gambling, or opium.[55]

A strictly well-behaved, egalitarian image of the soldier is what we see. Officially, he/she was assumed to be a volunteer. In practice, the issue of voluntarism hardly mattered in the early days of the revolution, because those who did not serve it were considered to be its enemies, or at least legitimate objects of armed propaganda.[56] As it was disseminated in the training courses of the first local village squads and platoons, however, the

---

[55] Ibid., 99–100, quoting *Lich su quan doi nhan dan Viet Nam* [History of the People's Army of Vietnam] (hereafter *LSQD*) (Hanoi, 1974), 82. The policies are close to the code of behavior of the Chinese Liberation Army.

[56] This is consistent with what Vo Nguyen Giap says in *People's War, People's Army* (Hanoi, 1974), 71: "For many years [between the mid-1940s and mid-1950s], the Vietnam People's Army was based on voluntary service: all officers and men voluntarily enlisted for an undetermined period." Referring to the period after the defeat of the French in 1954, he adds, "Since the return to peace, it has become necessary to replace voluntary service by *compulsory military service*. This substitution has met with a warm response from the population." Emphasis in original.

new military ideal was soon reinforced by two major developments that also worked to link the army to its social base.

One of these was the terrible famine of the winter of 1944–5, which led to the deaths of some two million people. Viet Minh propaganda had been highlighting food issues since at least 1943. By early 1945, when Viet Minh cadres were leading attacks on grain stores set aside for the Japanese army of occupation, there is no doubt that the famine had inspired what Woodside describes as "broad support for the Viet Minh in northern and northern central villages."[57] The second general factor was the Japanese *coup d'état* of March 9, 1945, which was a result of Japanese fears that, with the deterioration of their position in the Pacific, their nominal Vichy French allies would become hostile to them.

When the Japanese overthrew the French colonial administration, the colonial army and *Garde Indigène* simply disintegrated.[58] A considerable amount of more or less spontaneous mobilization followed in the northern provinces, as units of the Viet Minh's new-styled "Liberation Army" made great propaganda from a number of small skirmishes with Japanese forces. As one history of the revolution puts it: "Cadres of the propaganda units were deployed with regional armed units to organize new Liberation Army platoons and prepare to continue the fight with the Japanese."[59] However, at a time when the northern region had hardly recovered from the effects of the famine, the questions that now faced the revolutionary leadership went beyond those of shaping the new image of the freedom fighter. The basic problem for the expanding Liberation Army was how society was going to feed, clothe, equip, and generally support it. From around May 1945, therefore, the resistance leadership began a detailed formulation of the economic and general community assistance that would be necessary to ensure the success of their plans for military expansion.

One Vietnamese military manual that deals in some depth with economic as well as political and other issues is *Anti-Japanese Resistance Work in Rear Areas: Questions and Answers*,[60] which was probably printed around May 1945. After establishing that "rear area work is very important" because "the rear area is our base area, the origin of our vanguard," the manual presents a series of questions and answers having to do with electing people's committees in the villages and with raising mass organizations. It then goes on to explain the concrete ways in which community support would be organized for the army. For example:

---

[57] Alexander Woodside, *Community and Revolution in Modern Vietnam* (Boston, 1976), 232.
[58] Lockhart, *Nation in Arms*, 179, offers an assessment of the numbers who defected to the revolutionary side.
[59] *CMCD*, 11: 33.
[60] *Cong Tac Khang Nhat Hau Phuong: Van Dap* (Viet Bac, [April/May?] 1945).

Q. What is the People's Government's position with respect to the people who work
   for it?
A. At the beginning when the Government does not yet have finances it can only
   help officials and army men to a limited extent and order the people to help their
   families. For example, a family with a person in the ranks of the revolutionary
   army will receive help in ploughing, transplanting, collecting firewood, and car-
   rying water from the other people in the village. When a soldier's parents are sick,
   the village committee looks after them, etc.
Q. What can the people in rear areas do to help the Liberation Army?
A.

   a) Establish Liberation Army supply stores that are stocked with the help of
      the people or the confiscated paddy of Vietnamese traitors that support the
      Japanese.
   b) Help with clothing, medicinal herbs, food, shoes, etc.
   c) Help by guiding the army along the road. When the Liberation Army is
      launched into battle then the self-defense forces help by carrying their equip-
      ment, preparing the battlefield, and rescuing the wounded.
   d) Mobilize even greater numbers of youth, men, and women to join the ranks
      of the Liberation Army.[61]

Later, after the anti-Japanese resistance effort merge into an anti-French
resistance war, and the anti-French resistance war eventually merged into
an anti-American one, the economic aspects of the Viet Minh's war effort
became increasingly complex.[62] Even in late 1945 it already had an international dimension. By this time, the new army was not only drawing on
leftover Japanese stockpiles of weapons and equipment. Its agents were also
at work in Hai Nan, in Bangkok, and in other parts of Southeast Asia organizing war supplies. Yet no matter how extensive the international dimension of the logistics battle became, the army was never able to outgrow the
kind of community self-help that the resistance manuals already emphasized
by mid-1945. This was because, to survive and expand, the army had to
be integrated – through armed propaganda and mass mobilization – with
the society's capacity to support it with people, food, and resources at the
village level. Nevertheless, this realization could not prevent the army's capacity for orderly political, social, and economic development from being
overwhelmed by the popular upheaval of the August Revolution, and the
mass enthusiasm for military action that followed it.

The "General Righteous Uprising"

By May 1945, the Liberation Army had mobilized about thirteen more
or less regular companies, roughly 1,000 soldiers, who were active in the

---

[61] Ibid., 10–11.
[62] Christopher E. Goscha, "Le contexte asiatique de la guerre franco-vietnamienne: réseaux,
   relations et économie (d'août 1945 à mai 1954)," Ph.D. dissertation, Sorbonne, 2000, places
   the First Indochina War in a regional context and deals extensively with its economic aspects.

ring of provinces around Hanoi. By early August, when the Japanese surrender created a sudden power vacuum in Vietnam, armed propaganda
teams had begun arriving on the outskirts of that city. From this point
to mid-August, mass mobilization consisted of a series of political–military
manifestations, including "meetings" [*mit tinh*], and then the increasingly
spectacular "demonstrations" [*bieu tinh*] and "armed demonstrations" [*bieu
tinh vu trang*], in which some people could be armed with bird guns and agricultural implements.[63] These episodes swamped the Liberation Army's own
capacity for integrated development, just as it swamped the development of
national salvation committees and organizations between May and August
1945. But the point to stress here is that the manifestations were integrated
into the "general righteous uprising" that Vietnamese sources describe in
this period[64] because they would either follow the lead of, or encourage the
development of, self-defense units and the national (salvation) organizations,
or both.

   Some good examples of how these manifestations linked the army and
the people may be taken from the northern and north-central provinces in
mid-August, before the Viet Minh seized power in Hanoi on the 19th, Hué
on the 23rd, and Saigon on the 25th.[65] In Bac Giang, for instance, months of
mobilization in the countryside saw around 1,000 self-defense and guerrilla
fighters ready to seize power. The province chief and the *Garde Indigène*
then handed the capital over to a ten-man self-defense squad that entered
the public buildings as crowds gathered on the 18th. In Ha Tinh, a large
meeting was organized by the Viet Minh on the 15th to tell people about
the situation inside and outside the country. On the 17th, several truckloads
of self-defense fighters arrived in the capital and marched into the bank
and provincial administrative buildings. On the 18th, armed demonstrations
accompanied the seizure of power in Ha Tinh and Hai Duong, as they did
in Hanoi the following day.

   In some places, the armed propaganda squads encouraged mobilization
by executing alleged spies and traitors. In most, the seizure of power was
soon legitimized by the formation of a committee. But the general theme
is one of unregimented revolutionary action, as illustrated, for instance, by
the efforts of one propaganda team to spread the word of a mass meeting
in Ba Dinh Square on Sunday the 19th. The meeting had been organized

---

[63] There is of course no doubt that large numbers of people gathered during peasant uprisings
    in old Vietnam. But what makes the "meeting" and the "demonstration" new in twentieth-
    century Vietnam is that it was thought to be a manifestation of the will of "the people," part
    of a "mass movement," and thus of the new, general construction of the nation's political
    and military affairs.

[64] Lockhart, *Nation in Arms*, 133–6, offers a discussion of the "general" insurrection that I still
    think contains a number of useful points. As indicated by the present discussion, however,
    I would now reorient my original one to some extent.

[65] The following account of the August revolution is largely extracted from *LSQD*, 157–74.
    See also Lockhart, *Nation in Arms*, Chapter 4.

by functionaries of the existing Tran Trong Kim administration, but the
Viet Minh were planning to take it over to mark their seizure of power. The
description in David Marr's history of the revolution conveys an atmosphere
of mass expectation and popular participation in a major political event:

> On the morning of the 18th, an automobile festooned with Viet Minh flags, with
> youths standing on the running boards yelling through megaphones, moved slowly
> through the city streets, followed by a pack of cyclists passing out leaflets announcing
> the Sunday morning meeting. Other flag-carrying teams spread the word on foot,
> passing out leaflets, shouting slogans, and drawing noisy excited crowds at each in-
> tersection. Tailor shops busily turned out flags, while families sought scarce pieces of
> red and yellow cloth to sew their own. At some factories and shops, workers took
> control of the premises on the 18th, prepared banners, and guarded machinery and
> supply inventories against looting and sabotage.[66]

The seizure of power in Hué, on the 20th, involved the famous Ba To
guerrilla units and armed propaganda teams who mobilized large crowds to
march into the city. Likewise in Saigon, the armed Vanguard Youth Units,
which the Japanese had organized, and which came over to the Viet Minh
on the 22nd, played an important role in the seizure of power as tens of
thousands poured into the city for a vast demonstration, over which the ICP's
Southern People's Committee presided on the 25th. The stage was then set
for rapid military developments, once the first unit of the Liberation Army
arrived in Hanoi to a warm welcome around the 28th.[67] Bao Dai, the last
Vietnamese emperor, abdicated on the 30th, and Ho Chi Minh proclaimed
national independence on September 2.

By August 1945, the Viet Minh's military units were clearly able to stimulate, to follow, and to flourish within an atmosphere of mass political and
social upheaval. In this they were decisively aided by their self-presentation
as instruments of the people's general will and interest, by their emerging
network of local organizations linked at the national level, and by the conditions created by the northern famine and the rapid collapse of Japanese
power. The "general righteous uprising" of August was largely their doing.

---

[66] David G. Marr, *Vietnam 1945: The Quest for Power* (Berkeley, 1995), 389.
[67] Lockhart, *Nation in Arms*, 142, says that 1,000 members of the Liberation Army arrived in
Hanoi on the 19th. However, even though there is considerable confusion in the sources on
the date of this event, the 19th is a mistake. The number may also be an exaggeration. The
caption to one of the photos in Archimedes L. A. Patti, *Why Vietnam? Prelude to America's
Albatross* (Berkeley, Calif., 1980), which shows some 90 troops without catching either the
head or the tail of the column (see the eighth photo in the selection following page 236), says
that the Liberation Army entered Hanoi on 25 August and that "the procession continued
for several days." *LSQD*, 173, gives the date as the 28th. Marr, *Vietnam 1945*, 514, says that
100 soldiers of the Liberation Army arrived on the 28th. One other important Vietnamese
source on the revolution, Tran Huy Lieu, *Cach Mang Thang Tam: Tong khoi nghia o Ha
Noi va cac dia phuong* [August Revolution: The General Righteous Uprising in Hanoi and
the Regions], 2 volumes (Hanoi, 1960), 1: 59, n. 1, says the 29th.

Yet it would not take long before the vulnerability of the links to their social base would be exposed.

1945–1946: The Failure of the *Levée en masse*

Vietnam's Thirty Years War of national independence began on September 22, when elements of a French expeditionary force landed in Saigon and began to reoccupy the southern half of the country. On the 23rd, the Southern People's Committee responded by declaring a guerrilla war. In the north, Ho Chi Minh's new government did what it could to support the southern guerrillas. At the same time, it bargained with the French in the hope that a negotiated settlement of Vietnamese independence might still be possible. In any case, talks would buy time to organize the National Army in the north. As it happened, negotiations eventually broke down and Franco-Vietnamese clashes around Hanoi in December 1946 finally initiated full-scale hostilities.[68] It was probably in the sixteen-month period between the August Revolution and the outbreak of full-scale war that the process of mass mobilization in Vietnam came closest to resembling a *levée en masse*.

Almost from the outset, the French army was aware of the "universal hostility" that confronted its mission to reoccupy Vietnam. In such conditions, armed propaganda was no longer needed to mobilize people. Village self-defense forces and guerrilla units multiplied at such a rate that the government had difficulty controlling them. By late 1946, Vietnamese sources claim that, in the north alone, "almost a million" people had become involved in the irregular militias,[69] and, although this claim is perhaps exaggerated, its basic import is confirmed by the most authoritative French account of the period. Also referring to the north, Philippe Devillers says:

Each street and village had its self-defense groups comprising all the young people eligible to carry arms, as well as selected former soldiers. In the minds of the government the self-defense groups placed under the authority of the People's Committees would become guerrillas in the case of a French invasion.[70]

In the south, where Tran Van Giau, the head of the regional People's Committee, was well acquainted with French Revolutionary history, the main response to the French attacks in September 1945 was to form a "Republican Guard" [*Cong hoa ve binh*] with a paper strength of some 17,000 men.[71]

---

[68] Lockhart, *Nation in Arms*, 146–53, 180–2. Stein Tonnesson, *1946: le déclenchement de la guerre d'indochine* (Paris, 1987) offers an excellent discussion.

[69] Vo Nguyen Giap, *Unforgettable Days* (Hanoi, 1978), 86.

[70] Philippe Devillers, *Histoire du Viet Nam de 1940 à 1952* (Paris, 1952), 184. Even in French accounts, the popular image of the self-defense fighter comes through. He/she is young and, emerging from the people, eager to fight the French. He/she represents the army *and* the people.

[71] *LSQD*, 187–8; Lockhart, *Nation in Arms*, 150.

Likewise in the north, when the French attacked in December 1946, their intelligence calculated that Vo Nguyen Giap, another Viet Minh leader with a taste for French Revolutionary history, had massed some 35,000 men in thirty battalions around Hanoi.[72] Many Vietnamese officers and soldiers from the former colonial army joined the new revolutionary forces. The official history of the People's Army mentions the contribution of "former soldiers who loved the country,"[73] and it is clear from other sources that numerous former junior officers and adjutants of *tirailleurs* were commanding companies and battalions in the new National Army in late 1945 and 1946.[74]

Still, in marked contrast to the French Revolutionary experience, this upsurge of popular military energy contained the seeds of the Viet Minh's first strategic disaster. In the south, the Republican Guard simply disintegrated with the first touch of French forces in late 1945. In the north, Giap's thirty battalions were dispersed by a combination of river and airborne operations launched by the French in late 1946 and early 1947. Afterward, Communist press critiques identified the weaknesses in the initial battle array: "a plan was slow in coming out"; "orders and instructions were not concrete"; and

The organization of our units was still slapdash. It can be said that from the form of organization to the system of administration nothing was clear. Units were not quite regular units and not quite guerrilla units. Each zone simply followed its own developments concerning tactics and organization.[75]

The plan to stop the French had failed because spontaneous and uncoordinated action led to such hasty and unbalanced military development that the French were able to divide the army and the people.

As the Viet Minh strategists came to understand this, however, they were able to recreate the political–military links that were necessary to develop the people's army. In fact, the most important aspect of the critique of 1947–8 was its identification of the need to break large units down into many smaller ones. This meant that the people's army no longer presented a significant target to a technologically superior enemy, and it made armed propaganda and guerrilla units available to return to the villages and mobilize people and resources there.

A recent Vietnamese study explains how, in early 1947, the Viet Minh leadership "made guerrilla strategies the principle ones" so as to "advance to people's war." By November the leadership had ordered numerous regiments

---

[72] Tonnesson, 1946, 169.

[73] Lockhart, *Nation in Arms*, 175–6, quoting *LSQD*, 210.

[74] Ngo Van Chieu, *Journal d'un combattant Viet Minh*, translated by Jacques Despuech (Paris, 1955), 47–8, 54. Bernard B. Fall, *The Viet Minh Regime: Government and Administration in the Democratic Republic of Vietnam*, Data Paper Number 14, Southeast Asian Program, Cornell University (April 1954), 12, says the disbanded colonial army provided the "hard core of the Viet Minh's nascent army."

[75] *Cuoc khang chien than thanh cua nhan dan Viet Nam* [The Sacred Resistance War of the Vietnamese People], 4 volumes (Hanoi, 1958–60), 2: 40–1.

to dissolve one or two of their battalions. These were then formed into hundreds of small units: independent companies [*dai doi doc lap*], armed propaganda units, and armed propaganda assault units. Many suicide squads [*quyet tu quan*] were also formed. The function of the independent companies was to assist guerrilla units with cadres, weapons, training, and organization; that of the suicide squads was "to create a movement" among the people. In other words, all these units would provide good "propaganda to mobilize the masses and create infrastructure."[76]

Such a strategy assumed its own cyclical nature. Clearly, the purpose of a guerrilla presence and propaganda in the villages was to reestablish infrastructure for the reformation of large units once the stronger enemy had left an area, or been weakened by protracted guerrilla warfare.[77] In these terms, the small-scale guerrilla war tended to regenerate the earlier process of mass mobilization, until it culminated in either a successful general counteroffensive or a new cycle of unbalanced development that led to strategic failure. Still, once Viet Minh strategists understood the failure of the general uprising against the French, they led the resistance into a strategic upturn, which showed that they had identified the strategy of disciplined mass mobilization that would finally produce victory in a protracted people's war.

Epilogue: Strategic Cycles in the Process of Mass Mobilization

Just as the popular uprising of 1945–6 led to a downturn in the strategic cycle, its upturn between 1948 and early 1950 led to another downturn. In fact, once the armed propaganda revival of 1948 and 1949, and the opening of international support from China in early 1950, created the conditions for the remarkable border victories of late 1950, these were soon followed by the debacle of the "general counteroffensive" on the Red River Delta. It is well understood that the reason for this failure was essentially the same as the one in 1946–7: the excessive development of large regular forces that tended to follow a major victory because of the unrealistic expectations it generated.[78] For much the same reasons, similar cycles of success and failure also characterize Vietnamese strategy in the 1960s and 1970s.

---

[76] Nguyen Manh Ha, "Dai doi doc lap voi viec gay dung va phat trien chien tranh du kich" [The Independent Companies and the Task of Stimulating and Developing Guerrilla War], in *Thong Tin Lich Su Quan Su* [The Journal of Military History] (hereafter *TTLSQS*) 15 (March 1987), 14–15.

[77] For a full discussion see Lockhart, *Nation in Arms*, Chapter 6.

[78] James Pinckney Harrison, *The Endless War: Fifty Years of Struggle in Vietnam* (London, 1982), 123, gets at the existence of strategic cycles when he describes the effects of support from China after the Communist victory there in October 1949: "The final phase in the war was not long in coming. Viet Minh units, following victories along the northern border in 1950 and temporary setbacks in 1951, began moving into northwestern mountain areas, especially after October 1952" – from which time the Viet Minh suffered no major strategic reversals before the division of the country after the Geneva accords.

Because that strategy was meant to culminate in a "general counteroffensive," it could also be argued that a major structural weakness of the Maoist model for guerrilla war in Vietnam was that, as in 1945–6 and beyond, it tended to create a situation in which there was no easy way to control the rate of mobilization and military organization after it was unleashed by a major victory. As in late 1946 and early 1947, only a significant setback could be sure to do that. As a corrective to this inherent strategic instability, however, we have seen that the People's Army had the technique of armed propaganda to help integrate the development of small and large unit war.[79]

Another way of highlighting the importance of armed propaganda is to realize that as the war developed into a contest between zones that were occupied by the revolutionary and the counterrevolutionary forces, victory would tend to go to the side that had the greatest capacity to mobilize people in the other's occupied areas. In this context, one Vietnamese authority comments:

> To facilitate the task of mass mobilization in enemy controlled areas, the independent companies usually designated an armed propaganda squad to go in advance of it and establish the initial infrastructure for the remainder of the unit to advance into. This was a very important [strategic] development. Later it had a big influence on the operations of independent companies.[80]

It would not be difficult to show that this was indeed the case in the mass mobilization of people and resources for the most important regular offensives of the war.[81] This is another reason why the history of mass mobilization in Vietnam's Thirty Years War is best constructed as a gloss on armed propaganda.

---

[79] This integration took place at various levels. For example, the integration of quasi-regular regional forces and village guerrillas can be found in the south in the buildup to the "general uprising" [*dong khoi*] of 1960. See Nguyen Huy Thuc, "Phong trao dong khoi cua nhan dan mien nam" [The General Uprising Movement of the Southern People], *TTLSQS* 2 (1990), 30–1. Then, as in the major regular main force offensive in Quang Tri in 1972, there were cases where tank and infantry columns were guided into position on the battlefield by local village guerrillas. See Nguyen Giang, "Chien dich tien cang Quang Tri nam 1972" [The 1972 Quang Tri Offensive], *TTLSQS* 15 (March 1987), 7. A good work, written from the American perspective, which understands this interaction, is Eric M. Bergerud, *The Dynamics of Defeat: The Vietnam War in Hau Nghia Province* (Boulder, Colo., 1991), Chapters 4 and 5.

[80] Nguyen Manh Ha, "Dai doi doc lap," *TTLSQS* 15 (March 1987), 15.

[81] I have discussed the armed propaganda that was necessary to support such campaigns as Le Loi, Hoa Binh, and Dien Bien Phu against the French in Lockhart, *Nation in Arms*, 217–19, 250, 253. Nguyen Huy Thuc, "Phong trao dong khoi," *TTLSQS* 2 (1990), 31, mentions the use of "armed propaganda" in the south in 1960. Although it does not stress "armed propaganda," I would assume it was behind the "mass mobilization" referred to in Nguyen De, "Dong bang Song Cuu Long trong tong tien cong va noi day xuan 1974" [The Mekong Delta in the 1974 Spring General Offensive and Uprisings], *TTLSQS* 3 (1990), 6–13. Another function that Independent Companies could have as they prepared a region for a forthcoming offensive was to go into an area and cultivate gardens that would be used to feed the troops.

Consider, then, the strategic formulation that Vo Nguyen Giap made in 1961, at a time when the People's Army was beginning to apply the lessons it had learned in the anti-French war to the war against the American-backed Ngo Dinh Diem regime in the South:

> If you do not have guerrilla war then you are unable to have a war of movement; but if you have guerrilla war and do not advance to a war of movement then not only will the strategic responsibility to destroy the enemy's main force be unrealised but you will not be able to maintain and develop the original guerrilla war.[82]

Note the global grasp of this circular strategic conception. It assumes the dissolution and concentration of regular forces on a bed of guerrilla resistance. This further assumes the central role of armed propaganda in the process of integrating the complex cycles of small and large unit war.

What was fundamental to Giap's concept, however, were the regional variations in political–military and other circumstances that led to different rates of political–military development in different times and places. Insofar as its aim was one of mass mobilization for people's war, Giap's formulation may indeed be regarded as an analogue of the general mobilization that the colonial authorities conducted under the different circumstances of 1915–17.

The obvious difference between the colonial mobilization of 1915–17 and the revolutionary one after 1942 was that the latter could not override the lack of support for its cause in some regions with a general system of modern incentives. Rather than offer pay, food, and clothing for service on a far-flung campaign, the post-1942 resistance had to cast the complex political, military, social, and economic goals of the struggle for national liberation in a global strategic form.

Central to this, as Giap emphasizes, was the integration of the small-scale guerrilla campaigns and the large-scale war of movement. Clearly, such integration would be very uneven in a territorial sense for much of the war. But as long as the development of regular forces was maintained in a certain number of regions, while the development of guerrilla forces was in others, the overall effect would be progressively to weaken and divide the stronger enemy forces as they were forced to disperse in an attempt to deal with the various regular and irregular tactical configurations they faced. In other words, different kinds of war in many places were necessary to tire the enemy, at the same time that they mobilized the population in them. We may conclude, therefore, that Giap's 1961 formulation assumed that the enemy's defeat was implicit in the mass mobilization of the people because nothing less would suffice to express the unity of the nation in the military sphere.

---

[82] Vo Nguyen Giap, *Nhung kinh nghiem lon cua Dang ve lanh dao dau tranh vu trang va xay dung vu trang cach mang* [Major Experiences of the Party in Leading the Armed Struggle and Building Armed Forces] (Hanoi, 1961), 41. For more on this see Lockhart, *Nation in Arms*, 217.

11

The Algerian War (1954–1962)

The Inversion of the Levée en masse

Douglas Porch

The influence of the *levée en masse* on all sides of the Algerian Civil War of 1954–62 came from two directions: directly from the French Revolutionary example and filtered through theories and images of third-world revolution. The *Front de libération nationale* (FLN) insurgency drew inspiration from French history, as did its most zealous opponents, the *Organisation armée secrète* (OAS). The FLN also closely studied, and attempted to imitate, the Viet Minh revolt against France in Indochina, while FLN success encouraged the OAS to launch a campaign of terrorism against the French government. The French army in Algeria was influenced in its methods of repression by the belief that the FLN had indeed succeeded in producing a Muslim *levée*. For its part, the government of Charles de Gaulle was obliged to muster a popular *levée* to thwart the rebellions of partisans of *Algérie française*.

The eighteenth-century example of the *levée en masse* did not transfer to twentieth-century Algeria free of contamination, however. Both the FLN and the OAS inverted the classical paradigm in two important ways: in the hands of the FLN, the *levée* ceased to be an expression of state power but rather was invoked to attack the state. For its part, the OAS not only sought to separate the *levée en masse* from the authority of the state. It tried to separate the *levée* from the notion of revolution itself, to impress the *levée* into the service of counterrevolution.

How did the *levée* in this amended version influence the outcome of the Algerian War? The most successful application of the *levée* came in its classical form associated with and reinforcing state power – French President Charles de Gaulle's call for the citizens and soldiers of France to rally against those elements of the *pied noir* community and the French army that had rebelled against the Fifth Republic. Within Algeria, however, the *levée* failed utterly, both as a theory of revolution and as a strategy, and equally so for both the FLN and the OAS. When the *levée en masse* was divorced from the authority, the legality, and the coercive power of the state, its ability to mobilize armies of revolutionaries against the authority of the state proved a disappointment, for the reality of state power proved stronger than the theory of the *levée*. Indeed, reliance on the *levée* to whip up popular enthusiasm to challenge state authority generally produced only apathy and neutrality, at best reluctant compliance, among the very people most expected to respond to its call. The failure of the OAS "revolution" demonstrated that the *levée* could be divorced from the coercive power of the state only with difficulty, and, furthermore, that the *levée* could not be separated from the idea of revolution itself. In short, the ideal of the people in arms worked badly as a theory of counterrevolution.

On another level, however, the myth of the *levée en masse* was responsible in great part for the ultimate victory of the FLN. Even though the *levée en masse* failed to legitimize the revolutionary movement among the "people," such was the power of the *levée* in the public mind that it invariably helped to legitimize the revolutionary movement beyond the theater of conflict. The myth of the *levée* provided the margin of victory for the FLN because it was influential in three crucial arenas: among the French forces fighting the FLN, in France itself, and finally internationally.

France's Revolutionary past was frequently invoked by all sides during Algeria's war for independence. The direct influence of France was most obvious on the French side of the conflict. The formation of Committees of Public Safety and the sacking of Algiers's *Hôtel de Ville* by *pied noir* militants in May 1958, as well as their January 1960 erection of barricades in the streets of Algiers, offer the most self-conscious examples of attempts to resurrect the imagery, reproduce the slogans, and summon up the ghosts of the Great Revolution to justify defiance of state authority. But the evocation of France's Revolutionary past during the Algerian War was something more than extravagant rhetoric manufactured by frightened Europeans marooned in Africa. It is no exaggeration to say that the *levée en masse* provided a theory of victory both for Muslim insurgents who initiated a revolution against seemingly hopeless odds, and for *pied noir ultras* who, in the war's closing months, sought to breath faint life into the dying embers of *Algérie française*. In this way, each side became the mirror image of the other: each inverted the classical paradigm and invoked the *levée en masse* to challenge state authority.

In its original 1793 version, the *levée en masse* was a state-sponsored mobilization of the popular will in response to a national crisis. The fundamental assumption of this classical paradigm is that the state is the embodiment of revolutionary legitimacy. Therefore, the state supplies the impulse and in turn becomes the vehicle through which the popular will can be expressed. The *levée en masse* reinforces state power because the popular response to the call to arms legitimizes the authority of the state. The state blesses the *levée en masse* and is in turn blessed by it. The legality of state power, and the legitimacy that the "people" bestow upon the state by rising to its defense, form the twin underpinnings of the *levée en masse*.

A problem that confronts those who attempt to adapt the *levée en masse* to revolutionary theory in a non-European situation is that this classical paradigm is back-to-front. The Revolution of 1789 preceded and legitimized the *levée* of 1793. While the 1793 example implicitly acknowledges, indeed insists upon, the Revolutionary foundations of the *levée en masse*, the Revolution by then controlled the levers of state power. The French government of 1793 defined the crisis and possessed the authority to mobilize French citizens to defend the state. The "danger" to which *la patrie* was subjected was the direct consequence of the state's revolutionary origins, because a revolutionary regime by its very nature challenges the order of the international system. "The Republic is in a state of siege," Lazar Carnot declared on August 23, 1793. "Republican unity" was henceforth compulsory.[1]

FLN revolutionaries who sought to fashion the *levée en masse* into a vehicle for insurrection had to reverse the experience of the French Revolution. Because they did not control the reigns of state power, Algerian revolutionaries, like those of other non-European countries, were forced to place the cart of 1793 before the horse of 1789. A "spontaneous uprising of the people" occurred, not only without the state, but against the state. Rather than being rooted in legality, the *levée en masse* became a vehicle to contest the legitimacy of state power. As a theory of revolution, this inverted version of the *levée* sought to enfranchise and legitimize those who contested legal authority.

The Algerian experience also deviated from the classical paradigm in a second way: the 1793 *levée* began as a pragmatic response to the failure of earlier call-ups to produce soldiers in sufficient numbers. Only gradually did the myth of the *levée en masse* as an overwhelming demonstration of popular support for the Revolution develop to dwarf the original reality. The process was reversed in Algeria. The *levée en masse* began as a mythical faith in the spontaneous nature of popular revolution. Only gradually did the *levée* evolve into a pragmatic response to the failure of Algerian Muslims to rally to the FLN-sponsored revolution.

Both FLN and OAS insurgents shared the assumption that a sympathetic community imbued with a high level of political awareness already existed. All the revolutionaries needed to do was mobilize and militarize it. "We did not have any precise concept of what should be the revolutionary program," admitted Mohammed Boudiaf, one of the "*neuf historiques*," the nine "historic" founders of the FLN, in the summer of 1954. "Nothing precise beyond national independence and the desire to have the masses participate in the insurrection." Given the assumption that Algeria was a tinderbox of Muslim anger, a few explosives would detonate an insurrectional *levée*. The proclamation of independence that accompanied the bomb attacks of November 1, 1954, called for nothing less than the "mobilization

---

[1] J. M. Thompson, *The French Revolution* (Oxford, 1966), 424.

of all the energies [of the Algerian people] and all national resources.... Sure of your anti-imperialist sentiments, we will give the best of ourselves to the Fatherland."[2] Likewise, the founders of the OAS envisioned the creation of "a true apparatus of revolutionary combat, essentially [made up of] civilians." In concert with their supporters in the army, their goals sprang from "a desire to remake France." Propaganda posters sought to revivify the cause of French Algeria by speaking the idiom of the *levée en masse* – "Aux Armes Citoyens" (Figure 13).[3]

Both groups sought inspiration in the success of other revolutions. The progress of the Viet Minh revolt in Indochina was closely monitored by Algerian militants. The news of the fall of Dien Bien Phu, which arrived in Algeria on May 8, 1954, the ninth anniversary of the unsuccessful, if inspirational, Sétif rebellion against French rule, was taken as an omen that portended the success of their revolutionary enterprise.[4] Likewise, the leaders of the OAS were encouraged in their aims and methods in part by the very success that their FLN rivals, as well as the Viet Minh, had enjoyed.[5] But the decision to rebel, and the conviction that success was possible, reflected a process of direct cultural transfer from the French historical experience to a situation of non-European revolution, even counterrevolution.

The historical precedent that came closest to what both camps saw as the most obviously applicable model of a successful *levée en masse* against state authority was the French Resistance. The guerrilla leaders were inspired to launch their insurgency "thanks to the famous books about the Resistance."[6] For the OAS, the links between the Resistance to the Germans and their rebellion against de Gaulle were more direct. Ex-Prime Minister Georges Bidault enthusiastically threw himself into the work of the OAS,

---

[2] Yves Courrière, *La Guerre d'Algérie*, 4 volumes (Paris, 1968–71), 1: 171, 445–6. This naïve faith in the revolutionary potential of the Muslim population was seriously at odds with the theorists of French counterinsurgency warfare, who assumed that revolution only occurred after revolutionary militants had thoroughly infiltrated the population. See Peter Paret, *French Revolutionary Warfare from Indochina to Algeria: The Analysis of a Political and Military Doctrine* (Princeton, 1964), 12–13, 16.

[3] Courrière, *La Guerre d'Algérie*, picture at 4: 384; Paret, *French Revolutionary Warfare*, 29. The desire to regenerate the homeland had a long tradition in French colonial military circles. See Hubert Lyautey, "Du rôle coloniale de l'armée," *Revue des deux mondes* 157 (January 15, 1900), 238; Douglas Porch, "Bugeaud, Galliéni, Lyautey: The Development of French Colonial Warfare," in Peter Paret (ed.), *The Makers of Modern Strategy from Machiavelli to the Nuclear Age* (Princeton, 1986), 376–407; Douglas Porch, *The Conquest of Morocco* (New York, 1982), chapter 6 and passim.

[4] In May 1945, an insurrection occurred at Sétif, a town in the Constantinois, during the celebration to mark the end of World War II. Some Algerian nationalists saw the Sétif uprising and the subsequent savage repression by the French as the first act in the Algerian War.

[5] Courrière, *La Guerre d'Algérie*, 4: 398; Paret, *French Revolutionary Warfare*, 12–16 and passim. Roger Trinquier, *La guerre modern* (Paris, 1961) illustrates how the Indochinese experience influenced French military thinking in Algeria.

[6] Courrière, *La Guerre d'Algérie*, 1: 173, 188.

FIGURE 13. "Aux armes citoyens." OAS Poster, Algeria (1961). Musée d'Histoire Contemporaine, Paris.

Both the OAS and their FLN opponents drew inspiration from the legend of the *levée en masse*, particularly as embodied in the equally mythologized French Resistance of the Second World War. The somewhat crude poster reproduced here illustrates the perverse and inverted meanings that historical memory could acquire in the Algerian context. The poster consciously echoes countless images of popular uprising in the past to suggest that the (counterrevolutionary) OAS was the true bearer of the French revolutionary tradition in the present. It also seizes upon the idea of the nation – symbolized by the French flag held aloft by the two OAS fighters – and of citizenship, as additional, legitimizing props for a program whose highest aspiration was to overthrow the French government, in order to retain millions of Algerian Muslims as subjects of a rump French imperium, within which they had never been citizens.

which he championed as "the army of the New Resistance." Bidault insisted that "a grand *maquis* army is organizing."[7] Indeed, when Bidault succeeded Raoul Salan as the leader of the OAS, he renamed it, with more than a touch of nostalgia, the Comité National de la Résistance.[8]

---

[7] Ibid., 4: 387, 483.
[8] Douglas Porch, *The French Secret Services: A History of French Intelligence from the Dreyfus Affair to the Gulf War* (New York, 1995), 402.

The fact that the example of the French Resistance supplied inspiration to the revolutionaries underscores the second inversion of the classical paradigm: the extent to which the myth of the *levée* shaped the approach of both groups to revolution. Of course, every myth has a foundation in reality. The actual contribution of the French Resistance to the liberation of France is a matter for legitimate debate. What is certain, however, is that for de Gaulle, the primary value of the Resistance was political. The Resistance was promoted by the Gaullists as an expression of the French "people," a *levée* designed to give legitimacy to de Gaulle's government in exile. In May 1943, Jean Moulin, "president" of the "parliament" of the Resistance, declared that group's total allegiance to the principles of Fighting France, and acknowledged de Gaulle as "the only head of the French Resistance."[9] Only in this way could they answer Roosevelt's objections that the Free French had no legitimacy because they had never been voted into office.

Nevertheless, even those who argue that the Resistance enjoyed success as a military and intelligence organization against the Germans – or, more broadly, that some contribution to the anti-Nazi struggle, however minor, was necessary to restore French dignity – must concede at least two points: first, that an infinitesimal percentage of the French people ever belonged to any Resistance group; and second, that France could never have liberated herself. The belief that the Resistance had made an important contribution to the liberation of France must count as a "necessary myth," a psychological remittance that repaid in small measure the humiliation of French defeat and occupation in World War II.[10] Therefore, to take the Resistance model as an inspiration for revolution suggests how far the myth of the Resistance *levée* had outdistanced its slim basis in reality. The FLN leaders were young and uneducated, and might be forgiven for failing to notice that when de Gaulle praised Paris for "liberating herself" in August 1944, he was surrounded by scores of U.S., Canadian, and British divisions. That Bidault and Colonel Yves Godard, an Indochina veteran and advocate of "*la guerre révolutionnaire*" in the forefront of the OAS revolt, appear to have been seduced by their own propaganda is even more astonishing.[11]

---

[9] Philippe Buton, *Les Lendemains qui déchantent: Le Parti communiste français à la Libération* (Paris, 1994), 25–6, 29.

[10] For a discussion of the political role of the French Resistance in World War II and its effectiveness as a military and intelligence organization, see Porch, *The French Secret Services*, Chapters 9 and 10.

[11] This is especially true for Godard, who had witnessed firsthand the suppression of the *maquis* uprising on the Vercors Plateau near Grenoble in 1944. The Free French had hoped to establish a "National Redoubt" from which the Resistance could sally forth to harass German supply routes. On June 10, 1944, in response to news of the Normandy landings, the Resistance closed off the passes into the Vercors Plateau and announced the creation of the Free Republic of the Vercors. On July 19, German troops and the Vichy *Milice* assaulted the plateau and occupied it after three days of fighting, killing or dispersing the Resistance.

For either the FLN or the OAS to base a revolutionary enterprise on the legend of the French Resistance indicated, at the very least, a level of self-deception, perhaps even of desperation or a lack of clear thinking, which offered an open invitation to disaster. The myth of the Resistance as a successful *levée en masse*, directed against the authority of the Vichy state and the German occupiers, substituted for a clear conception of how either revolutionary movement was to succeed. On the other hand, the myth of the *levée en masse* was important for at least four reasons. First, without it, neither group would have found the inspiration or the courage to attempt an uprising at all. Second, by invoking the *levée en masse*, both groups sought to gain legitimacy, even "legality," in their own eyes, in the eyes of their respective populations, and in those of world opinion. Third, the assumption that the *levée en masse* formed the basis for a successful revolution suggested, if not a strategy, at least a theory of victory, a vision of how their respective struggles would be guided to a successful outcome. Finally, the *levée en masse* was linked to the concept of total war, one whose objective was the unconditional surrender of the adversary.

The myth of successful popular mobilization against "tyranny" proved to be so inspirational for both groups of Algerian revolutionaries that it drew them into an overly optimistic assessment of the situation in the country. At the very least, reliance on the power of the *levée* papered over what amounted to a dangerous leap of faith. The success of either "revolution" was a long shot, both for the FLN in 1954 and the OAS seven years later. In the summer of 1954, the French state was well entrenched in Algeria, backed by almost 60,000 troops. The moderate nationalists in Ferhat Abbas's *Union Démocratique du Manifeste Algérien* (UDMA) and in the *Mouvement pour le Triomphe des Libertés Démocratiques* (MTLD) led by Messali Hadj, not the extremists, were drawing crowds of up to 6,000 supporters to their political rallies. Messali Hadj was venerated as "El-Zaim," "The Unique," because he believed himself the unique "nationalist symbol." His movement, he insisted, was the only "gathering place of the Muslim opposition." Messali's moderate rival, Hocine Lahouel, greeted claims by Muslim hard-liners that Algeria was ripe for revolution as "frankly ridiculous," a plan whose only result would be to "send the people to the abattoir." In Cairo, Gamal Abdel Nasser listened to schemes for an Algerian *levée* put forward by Ahmed Ben Bella with polite disbelief. Optimistic assessments placed the numbers of dedicated revolutionaries in Algeria at around 800, in a population of nine million Muslims.[12] The OAS in 1961 was a motley of army deserters, failed politicians, jumped-up street agitators, and thugs. What they shared with the FLN was the belief that the intensity of popular anger and disgust against the established government matched their own

---

[12] Courrière, *La Guerre d'Algérie*, 1: 82–4, 129, 254; Alistair Horne, *A Savage War of Peace: Algeria 1954–1962* (London, 1977), 73–4.

and required only a spark to ignite a spontaneous mobilization against the Gaullist state.

By invoking the *levée en masse*, both groups sought to gain legitimacy, even legality, for their movements. This was no easy task, given their insistence that their respective *levées* were not only assembled without the state, but also directed against legal authority. "No one has the right to forget that the people are the stake in this war," FLN propaganda proclaimed. "Our revolution is made by the people for the people."[13] The FLN held an advantage in resolving this obvious conflict because they could add North African resonances to a French phenomenon. Their appeal blended the example of the French and Algerian Resistance movements, a *maquis* in *djellabas*. They conjured up images of epic struggle against the French in the 1830s and 1840s under the legendary guerilla Abd el-Kader, the uprising of the Kabylia following France's defeat by Germany in 1871, and the Sétif rebellion of May 1945. They appealed to Maghrebian unity[14] and the revolutionary legitimacy of the anticolonial struggle. They also reinforced an Islamic discipline. The reference to sweeping principles and a common heritage was necessary in part to overcome the distrust between Berber and Arab within the FLN, a distrust which meant that the two groups often preferred to communicate in French. Indeed, when Ben Bella first appealed for aid in Cairo, he shocked his Egyptian hosts by addressing them in French because he was afraid they would not understand his Arabic.[15] The FLN was aided also by factors of negative integration: a history of poor Muslim/*pied noir* relations, including elections stolen by the *pieds noirs*, and incomprehension and blatant racism in France and Algeria. Their first choice of targets were symbols of French presence and power in society – power stations, telephone exchanges, oil storage facilities, and radio stations. Gradually, they reinforced their claim to legitimacy by creating shadow government structures to recruit, collect funds and intelligence, and dispense justice in the name of the revolution.

Not surprisingly given its character, described by one author as an "uncooked pudding of conflicting freakish ideas, aspirations, and principles,"[16] the OAS's grope toward legitimacy and "legality" was destined to be a tortured one. Separating the *levée en masse* from state power produced

---

[13] Charles-Robert Ageron, "La 'guerre psychologique' de l'Armée de libération nationale algérienne," in Charles-Robert Ageron (ed.), *La guerre d'Algérie et les Algériens 1954–1962* (Paris, 1997), 224.

[14] "We are all united in a single hand. From Morocco to Tunisia we all see ourselves as brothers without distinction." Ibid.

[15] Algerian unity was a constant propaganda theme: "The Algerians belong to the same Arab–Berber race, which has remained pure because it has refused to combine with Roman, Byzantine, and French invaders. That is why they have preserved the pure character of their ancestors, loyal warriors, courageous and dignified." Ageron, "La 'guerre psychologique,' " 224.

[16] Quoted in Horne, *A Savage War of Peace*, 485.

something like a split personality among *pied noir* militants and within the OAS. On one hand, the organization carried out a brutal offensive against the state. On the other, some of its more prominent members seemed to believe that they were simply the political party of *Algérie française*. General Raoul Salan, a man of the left, saw the OAS as a rallying point for all of France's anti-Gaullists, "an inverse Popular Front," while Christian Democrat Georges Bidault insisted that the OAS was "a legal movement supported by the totality of *pieds noirs*." The OAS sought respectability and legitimacy by advancing a kebab of *ancien régime* politicians and *émigré* generals, led by Salan, against a "dictatorial prince–president" – an implied comparison between de Gaulle and Louis-Napoleon Bonaparte, who replaced the Second Republic with the Second Empire in 1851.[17]

A final advantage of the *levée en masse* was that it suggested, if not a strategy, at least a vision of how their revolutions would evolve toward victory. Their challenge was to stimulate a *levée en masse* in the absence of state coercion, while overcoming serious divisions within their own ranks and in those of their potential supporters. The obvious, the only, answer was to employ violence. The FLN was so convinced that Algeria was ripe for revolution that it eschewed the thorough preparation of the population for revolution advocated by Mao. Well-directed violence against symbolic targets would "detonate" the revolution by "striking a psychological blow against French power."[18]

The spontaneous *levée* that was expected to follow would also resolve the FLN's second problem – the threat of reformism. The desire to put an end to attempts by the UDMA and the MTLD to work within the system, to demonstrate that reform was impossible in a colonial setting, revealed a contradiction in the FLN's strategic assessment. On one hand, they insisted that Muslim Algeria was ripe for revolution. On the other, they sensed that, given the choice, Muslims were happy to remain part of the French system so long as it gave them greater economic opportunity and a political voice. Through violence, the FLN would instantly discredit the moderate nationalists by moving the revolution to the next stage, showing that "the FLN is powerful and afraid of nothing."[19] Moderate Muslim nationalists would have the choice of joining the *levée* or being left behind.[20] "The word 'revolution,'" as Boudiaf explained, "designated above all the way in which we hoped to conquer independence, on one hand, against the colonial apparatus through violence, on the other, against the bureaucratic and reformist methods of the nationalist movement by exploding its outdated structures."[21]

---

[17] Courrière, *La Guerre d'Algérie*, 4: 482–3.
[18] Ibid., 1: 37, 82.
[19] Ibid., 1: 299.
[20] Alf Andrew Heggoy, *Insurgency and Counterinsurgency in Algeria* (Bloomington, Ind., 1972), 66, 88.
[21] Courrière, *La Guerre d'Algérie*, 1: 91, 254, 171.

Violence would supply incremental success, galvanize the will of the Muslim population for independence, and stimulate an "oil spot" of revolution that would spread across the country from east to west. Finally, violence and the Muslim *levée en masse* that it was supposed to touch off would "create a psychosis of fear and general insecurity" that would discourage the French and cause them to give up Algeria.[22]

Given their diverse origins and degree of desperation, how the *levée* would play out as a theory of victory was at least as vague and myth-dependent for the OAS as it had been for the FLN. Violence was expected to discredit de Gaulle, rally the *pieds noirs* and the army, and demonstrate that the OAS was "the only real power in Algeria."[23] The theory of victory that the *levée* suggested for the Hungarian Legionnaire Roger Degueldre was that a *pied noir* uprising would transform Algiers into another Budapest 1956 and force the Gaullists into a house-by-house *reconquista* of Algeria's capital city. Several leaders appear to have believed that the OAS's declaration of war would rally the *pied noir* population of Algeria's major towns, sweep up Muslims loyal to France, and "at least" seize power in Algeria, if not, indeed, in France. Only Yves Godard appears to have entertained the more rational belief that the army might be enticed to overthrow de Gaulle in a putsch, thus bringing to power a government willing to take a harder line toward the FLN. But in the event, even this limited and indirect theory of victory proved overly optimistic.[24]

The idea of the *levée en masse* worked even less well for the OAS than for the FLN. The most obvious reason for this was that the inspirational value of their goal, *Algérie française*, was simply not potent enough to "detonate" a spontaneous call to arms among the *pied noir* population, much less the people of France. Without the coercive authority of the state behind it, the OAS had no power to compel. "When it was a question of a dangerous mission," one OAS militant complained,

we didn't get many volunteers. Unfortunately, that night they had to stay home because the wife or the father-in-law was sick. Even in Bab El-Oeud [the working-class district of Algiers where many *pied noir* militants lived] where 'they were tough,' there were few volunteers for difficult jobs. Put up posters, pass out tracts, rough someone up, ok. But the rest – look, even to shoot an Arab – no one wanted to do it. They were OAS and proud of it, proud to say it. But OAS *tranquilles*! Without risks.[25]

Clearly, by 1961, many *pieds noirs* had taken the FLN choice of "the suitcase or the coffin" very much to heart and had begun to pack their bags, at least psychologically. Even in the army, where officials feared the OAS counted enough sympathizers seriously to compromise discipline, terrorism

[22] Ibid., 1: 174, 254.
[23] Ibid., 4: 483.
[24] Ibid., 4: 396, 481; Horne, *A Savage War of Peace*, 485.
[25] Courrière, *La Guerre d'Algérie*, 4: 455

produced only neutrality or a "wait-and-see" attitude. The best OAS strategists could hope for was not a military *levée en masse* against de Gaulle, but
a level of "inaction [on the part of the army]...[which] gives the impression
that the OAS is in control of events."[26]

Few rallied to the OAS cry of *la patrie en danger*. The most obvious
reason was that the majority of French people judged the OAS to be a far
greater danger to the Fatherland than was the policy of Charles de Gaulle.
Unable to stimulate a *pied noir* uprising, the OAS fell victim to a Gaullist
levée en masse instead. In the competition to mobilize the population behind
their respective causes, the Gaullists enjoyed several advantages over their
OAS rival: they were backed by the full authority of the state and supported
by French public opinion, which, by 1960, was war weary and desperate
to disengage from Algeria. OAS activism confirmed the French people in
their view that Algeria was simply not worth the price of a civil war. In
January 1961, a referendum approved negotiations between the government
and the FLN.

Because he controlled the levers of state power, de Gaulle also commanded
the technical and bureaucratic power to intimidate and disorient those who
would oppose his policies. On assuming power in 1958, he had begun to
purge the army in Algeria of its most aggressively *Algérie française* elements.
During "Barricades Week" in January 1960, when *pied noir* militants briefly
seized the streets of Algiers, and again during the failed coup in April 1961,[27]
de Gaulle masterfully employed television and radio to isolate militant nationalists, to delegitimize them in the eyes of the French public and the army,
and to summon up a groundswell of support to defend the government. OAS
efforts to appropriate the Republican symbolism of the military uniform,
evoked by rebellious soldiers and some *pied noir* militants, also played into
de Gaulle's hands. During the January 1960 crisis, the French president appeared on national television in uniform, "in order to show that it is General
de Gaulle who speaks, as well as the Head of State." Without the legitimizing
structure of the state, de Gaulle insisted, the French army would be nothing
but "an anarchic and absurd conglomeration of military feudalisms." The
"Generals' Putsch" of April 1961 produced a repeat performance, this time
to expressly "forbid every Frenchman, and above all every soldier," to exe-
cute the directives of "a coterie of generals in retirement."[28]

Like the FLN, the OAS was an expression of desperation. But unlike the
FLN, the OAS materialized at the end of a long and bitter struggle, which had

---

[26] Ibid., 4: 461–2, 489.
[27] "Barricades Week," a *pied noir* rebellion in Algiers, was touched off by the recall of the
popular parachute general Jacques Massu, credited with winning the "Battle of Algiers" in
1957–8, after he publicly criticized de Gaulle. The April 1961 putsch was led by four generals
upset by negotiations between the FLN and the French government.
[28] Horne, *A Savage War of Peace*, 368–9 (and photographs), 455

witnessed the failure of an *Algérie française levée*. The OAS was a reaction to defeat, not a movement whose purpose was to jump-start a stalled nationalist movement. As such, the OAS *levée* attacked not just the state but also the idea of the Revolution itself. It was a beleaguered remnant in search of an insurgency, Mensheviks stripped of their workers' revolution, whose only fate could be detection, arrest, death, or exile. The OAS failed because, to paraphrase Clausewitz, it tried to turn the *levée en masse* into something it could not be – a counterrevolution. Conversely, de Gaulle succeeded because he stole the revolutionary ground from the OAS. His appeal to a French *levée* against *Algérie française* evoked not defeat, as the OAS believed, but the same promise of French renewal as had been embodied in the "Appeal of 18 June 1940," by which the French Resistance against the Nazis was first proclaimed.

A final advantage of the *levée* for the FLN was that it summoned a vision of total war, an ultimate struggle for existence that eschewed compromise and rejected out of hand a strategy of limited objectives. The *levée* conjured up an attitude of "victory or death," a mentality that steeled the FLN against seductive appeals by de Gaulle for a *paix des braves*, partition, or "dual nationality," objectives short of total victory that would have divided rebel ranks, imperiled the goals of the revolution, and bequeathed a fifth column of *ci-devant pieds noirs* to the revolutionary Islamic state.

On the other hand, for the OAS and its military supporters to declare "total war" against the state they served, and upon which the very success of their battle to keep Algeria French depended, was nothing short of self-defeating. How could they hope to succeed when they had first to defeat their own government, before they could confront their real enemy, the FLN? In the end, it proved impossible to pursue "total war" against the FLN after the government and population of France calculated that *Algérie française* was simply not worth the effort. For the OAS then to declare a *levée* against their own government was a sure indication that, for the partisans of *Algérie française*, the game was truly over.

For the FLN, the *levée* was both a failure and a success. The reasons for each could be traced to the original strategic assessment carried out by the *neuf historiques* in the summer of 1954 and to the unintended consequences of their strategy. The failure stemmed from the fact that, in their desire to summon up a Muslim rebellion against the French regime in Algeria, the FLN's founders desperately overestimated the revolutionary inclinations of Algerian Muslims. To be sure, there was residual support for rebellion in some regions: for instance, in the Aurès Mountains a tradition of "dissidence," reverence for "bandits," and the fact that the area was lightly policed combined to make it especially fertile ground for FLN calls to revolution. Likewise, the Kabylia, the mountainous region east of Algiers, was open to contagion. Like the Aurès, the Kabylia had a strong sense of regional and ethnic Berber identity, which historically had made it a center of resistance to French rule. Kabyle villages – fiercely independent, democratically run, linguistically distinct, and overpopulated – exported their excess male populations to Algiers and France, from which they returned with the politicized vocabulary of the trade unions. A nationalist insurgency under Belkacem Krim, who rallied to the FLN, had simmered there since 1947, long before the FLN had even existed. The survival of Krim's insurgency gave proof in itself that rebellion was possible in Algeria. In Western Algeria, FLN activity centered around Tlemcen, a city close to the Moroccan border, whose strong religious tradition had long made it a center of resistance to French rule. But the sad fact for the FLN was that isolated regional traditions of armed dissent, even when added to the chronic disenfranchisement, poverty, and exploitation of Algerian Muslims, did not add up to revolution.

However, the FLN soon discovered that terror could turn its chief liability – an inability to produce a spontaneous, popular *levée* – into an asset. If the FLN could not gain the whole-hearted support of Algerian Muslims, at least terror allowed them to deny Muslim support to the French and to subvert government attempts to organize a Muslim *levée* against the revolution. Of course, one's perspective on the role played by FLN terror in the Algerian War depends largely on the camp one supported. Mouloud Feraoun, a schoolteacher in the Kabylia, insisted that FLN terrorism actually produced a Muslim *levée en masse* because it succeeded in driving a wedge between Muslims and French in Algeria, where "there never was a marriage" between the two communities. Terrorism forced Kabyles to "reflect," according to Feraoun, and pointed up the fact that the French were "strangers in our land." European apprehension mounted as they saw Westernized Algerians return to traditional dress. French cafés suddenly emptied of their Muslim clientele, who avoided any practices that contravened FLN dictates about proper Muslim behavior. "It is clear that everyone participates in his heart in the combat," Feraoun enthused. "The French believe that we are afraid and excuse us for obeying the FLN dictates. Out of friendship, they seem to believe that we are playing a double game to avoid the worst: When they see a colleague cease to drink, to smoke, suddenly put on a tarboosh, even a burnous, they shrug their shoulders and say: 'Yes, I don't blame you. I'd do the same in your place'."[29]

For their part, the French insisted that FLN terror had silenced Muslim opposition to the FLN. "Brutality pays," wrote Lieutenant Jean-Jacques Servan-Schreiber:

[Violence] promotes among their troops the feeling of a holy and therefore justifiable fury that, striking blindly, disgusts the Muslims not yet sure which side they are on. For these rebels, the worst crimes are the most effective. If they have to choose between liquidating a police officer who everyone knows is a monster and a Marcus

[29] Mouloud Feraoun, *Journal, 1955–1962* (Paris, 1962), 45, 47–8.

who is trying to make contact, they will pick Marcus without a moment's hesitation. They want to do the most possible harm, to destroy any attempt at reconciliation or compromise. They must root out from Algerian soil, by terror if necessary, the slightest sentiment that might lead to a desire for understanding. They are the Stalinists of the rebellion. They have staked their money on a complete smash-up.[30]

More importantly, the FLN campaign of terror, by chance or by design, had the effect of creating the illusion of a Muslim *levée*. By forcing Muslims to adopt traditional dress and follow Islamic customs on pain of death, the FLN sent the message that the Muslim community was solidly pro-FLN. French *Section Administrative Spécialisé* (SAS) officer Serge Bromberger insisted that this was far from the case. The well-publicized September 26, 1955, vote by sixty-one Algerian Muslim deputies in the Algerian Assembly repudiating Algerian "integration" with France and calling on the French government to recognize "the Algerian national idea," Bromberger claimed, came as the result of death threats by FLN "night visitors."[31] Bromberger's contention is supported, up to a point, by Ahmed Ben Bella, who claimed that the Algerian deputies were "opportunists" who contacted the FLN to "cover themselves. For our part, we lost no time in telling them in plain terms that their political game would only be tolerated by us in so far as it could further our own activities."[32]

Terror meant that Muslims dared defy neither the FLN-dictated boycott of French schools, nor their call for general strikes like the one that closed down Algiers in January 1957. Requests by SAS officers for Muslims to serve on tribal councils produced panic. Even the Muslim demonstrations of December 11, 1960, in Algiers, Bromberger argued, should not be taken as evidence of an FLN *levée*. They had actually begun as an attempt by French psychological-action officers to produce a pro–de Gaulle demonstration to counter those of the *pieds noirs*. But the rallies had been hijacked by the FLN, who passed out FLN flags and urged the crowd to shout FLN slogans.[33]

The truth was doubtless less categorical than either the FLN or their opponents hoped. There were undoubtedly those who rallied to the FLN out of conviction. In the first year of the rebellion, the French presence in many areas of Algeria was so discreet that joining the FLN was virtually a risk-free option. With time heavy on their hands because of an FLN-enforced boycott

[30] J.-J. Servan-Schreiber, *Lieutenant in Algeria* (New York, 1957), 70–1.
[31] Serge Bromberger, *Les rebelles Algériens* (Paris, 1958), 70–2, 142.
[32] Robert Merle, *Ahmed Ben Bella* (New York, 1967), 97. Ben Bella's claims must be taken with a grain of salt, because he has a tendency to assert that spontaneous events that worked to FLN advantage were really the result of strategic foresight.
[33] Courrière, *La Guerre d'Algérie*, 4: 188–92, argues that the demonstrations were actually organized by French SAU (*Section Administrative Urbaine*) officers to counter anti–de Gaulle *pied noir* demonstrations. Horne, *A Savage War of Peace*, 431, calls the December 11, 1960, demonstrations "one of those inexplicable explosions caused by long-pent-up forces," but gives credit to the FLN for preparing the ground for it.

of French schools, some Muslim students joined the FLN *faut de mieux*. The brutality of French counterinsurgency methods also produced some recruits for the FLN. But this did not a *levée en masse* make. One historian has estimated that no more than 20 percent of the Muslim population of Algeria actively supported the FLN.[34] Even at the height of the Battle of Algiers in 1957, French experts calculated that the FLN counted only 200 active terrorists and perhaps 4,500 part-time operatives and sympathizers in a city whose population had been swelled by war to 800,000 people.[35]

So, if FLN terror could not produce a *levée*, what was its effect on Algerian Muslims? The assassination, exile, or silencing of Muslims who actively supported the French denied critical Muslim support to the policy of "integration." Terror allowed the FLN to extend their influence, especially as the French could not be strong everywhere. From 1955, a new breed of leader emerged in the FLN – fanatical, remorseless, convinced that terror could reap benefits where an attempt to raise a popular insurrection had failed. Ait Hamouda, alias Amirouche, "dreaded for his remorseless cruelty," according to British historian Alistair Horne, was able to extend FLN control over the Soummam region of eastern Kabylia by instituting a reign of terror enforced by barely 800 men. Moderates, meaning any Muslim who might serve as a bridge between Muslims and Europeans, were targeted. In the first two and one-half years of the war, an estimated 6,352 Muslims were assassinated by the FLN, compared to only 1,035 Europeans. Silence descended on the villages, as Muslims realized that even a casual conversation with a French person might sentence them, or members of their family, to death.[36] On assuming the post of Governor General of Algeria in 1955, Jacques Soustelle noted that "terror had taken hold. No one spoke. The population as a whole, without throwing in its lot with the rebels, remained frightened and noncommittal."[37] This probably sums up Muslim opinion for the remainder of the war. Bromberger complained that, by the time the French began a serious campaign to reclaim the Kabylia from the FLN in 1956, it was simply too late. Every pro-French village leader, teacher, policeman, or forest ranger had been assassinated. There was simply no one left around whom the French could rebuild a base of support.[38] Deprived of pro-French Muslim leadership, even of security, the remainder of the population had been intimidated and only sought to survive the war. FLN terrorism against Muslims produced, not support for the Revolution, only fear and apathy. The Muslim population was neither pro-French, nor pro-FLN. Many fled to Algiers, even to France, Morocco, or Tunisia to escape the war. Most of those who remained in the

[34] Heggoy, *Insurgency and Counterinsurgency*, 100.
[35] Bromberger, *Les rebelles Algériens*, 23–4, 35, 80–1, 93, 156–7.
[36] Horne, *A Savage War of Peace*, 131–5.
[37] Quoted in Horne, *A Savage War of Peace*, 107.
[38] Bromberger, *Les rebelles Algériens*, 84.

war zones carried out, as best they could, their own "internal emigration" into neutrality, a neutrality that favored the revolution because it denied the government Muslim support that was vital to its war effort.

The intellectual journey of Mouloud Feraoun was probably typical of many Algerian Muslims. Early in the rebellion, he was attracted to the FLN who "behave like Kabyles, and take the trouble not to offend us. According to the case, they flatter our fanaticism, our pride, our hopes, or share our ideas, our democratic social concepts, our humanist sentiments." Their idealism encouraged the concept of the *levée en masse*: "There is an imperative desired by all, an ideal to reach, and that is to be free. Feel liberated, the equal of all men. They have already achieved this ideal in the *maquis*." Soon, however, his initial sympathy for the FLN subsided into fear as he witnessed the systematic FLN slaughter of those who defied their edicts: fifteen-year-old Muslim girls shot for speaking to French soldiers; men assassinated for smoking cigarettes, drinking wine, or wearing trousers instead of the *djellaba*; and so on. The FLN even ordered all dogs in Feraoun's village to be killed, lest they bark at the approach of "patriots." Those appointed by SAS officers to serve on tribal *djemmas* (councils) accepted office like the death sentence it was: "The *maquisards* wait tranquilly as the Captain designates their victims." "Everyone understands that 'the brothers' are not infallible, not courageous, not heroes," Feraoun concluded in the spring of 1958:

But everyone also knows that they are cruel and hypocritical. They demand everything, but they give only death in return. They continue to ransom, to requisition, to destroy. They continue to speak of religion, to forbid everything that they are in the habit of forbidding and whatever new it pleases them to forbid. We must call them 'brothers' and venerate them as Gods.[39]

Frightened and disgusted, Feraoun joined the Kabyle emigration to Algiers to escape the war.

Terrorism, therefore, offered the FLN tactical victory, at least in some regions. By eliminating pro-French Muslims and driving many of the rest of the population into neutrality, it denied Muslim support to the French. When the French moved in strength into an area, the FLN simply went to ground, or shifted to a less well-policed region. However, by itself, terrorism could not produce an FLN victory. It was a Fabian strategy designed to deny success to the French and buy time for the FLN. But the time purchased worked for the FLN only if the French ultimately calculated that the price of victory exceeded the value of the objective. This, indeed, had been the original FLN theory of victory – that the French, seeing they could not win, would simply leave Algeria.[40] The problem with FLN terrorism as a strategy was that it inflicted pain on Muslims, not on the French. However, it was only the French

[39] Feraoun, *Journal*, 44, 88, 210, 269.
[40] Courrière, *La Guerre d'Algérie*, 1: 174.

who could give the FLN their political objective – independence. With no direct incentive to disengage, the French would gradually track down and eliminate FLN operatives and restore equilibrium in a Muslim population terrorized into silence. Over time, the FLN would become yet another of the "bandit" gangs that had traditionally roamed the Algerian *bled*.

To win their revolution, the FLN needed to add an offensive component to their strategy, one that increased the cost of the war to the French. That offensive component was supplied by the myth of the *levée en masse* and was largely psychological. Although the FLN had failed to produce a Muslim *levée* against the French, the important thing was to convince French soldiers, French people, and the international community that they had done precisely that: an illusion that was the more powerful for being addressed, in the first instance, to a nation convinced by its own history that the people, once truly in arms, would prevail in the end.

French soldiers and administrators in Algeria were the first to fall victim to the myth of the Muslim *levée*. In truth, it was an easy sell among men whose profession and mentality conditioned them to think in terms of worst-case scenarios. They also carried with them into Algeria the heavy burden of history – the belief that the indigenous peoples of France's vast empire had accepted France's "civilizing mission" only at the point of a bayonet. Indeed, a sullen spirit of rebellion, which had always composed the subtext of France's imperium, had been brought to the surface everywhere by France's humiliation in 1940. The fact that France appeared weak had emboldened revolutionaries who, with the aid of the Communist Bloc eager to challenge Western values the world over, had launched an attack on the French empire, first in Indochina and now in North Africa. 1954 was not only the year of Dien Bien Phu but also the year that Morocco and Tunisia slithered into turmoil. That a revolution had now broken out in Algeria confirmed the worst nightmares of France's praetorians.

Faced with what they believed to be a Muslim population unified in iron determination to expel the French back across the Mediterranean, French soldiers and administrators in Algeria became convinced that they did indeed confront an FLN *levée*. Predictably, they behaved in ways calculated to provoke precisely the sort of widespread popular resistance they hoped to avoid. The ill-advised French reaction to the November 1, 1954 bombings gave the FLN no end of help early on. Reacting as they had following the Sétif rebellion nine years earlier, they cracked down on the very moderates who might have facilitated a peaceful dialogue between France and the Muslim community. The government immediately dissolved the MTLD and arrested many Muslim reformers, who were tortured to sign "confessions." When the "confessions" were later repudiated before examining magistrates, news of the torture was leaked to the press and convinced some who had hoped to avoid violence to join the FLN.[41] "The government thereby relieved us of the

---

[41] Heggoy, *Insurgency and Counterinsurgency*, 83.

presence of a lot of political meddlers who were assumed to be our accomplices but who, in fact, were a terrible hindrance to our movement because of the confusion which they created in the minds of the republic," remembered Ahmed Ben Bella. "Now, thanks to the enemy, [the FLN] became the only political force in Algeria."[42]

The French military reacted to the outbreak of the rebellion with the same slash-and-burn mentality that afflicted the French police. In the minds of French soldiers, every shepherd boy became an FLN lookout, and every Muslim male, a potential assassin. French troops answered FLN attacks, especially those in which the bodies of French soldiers were left mutilated, their heads turned toward Mecca, with a policy of "collective responsibility" – shooting large numbers of people in a village on the assumption that the village had known about, and cooperated in, the attack. "With the increase of rebel atrocities," writes Alistair Horne, "the time was approaching when the army would regard almost every Muslim as a potential killer."[43] The French army reacted to demonstrations that culminated in the horrible "Philippeville massacres" of August 1955, by going on a rampage of slaughter and village burning. Their actions recalled the harsh repression of the Sétif uprising ten years before, which had included the naval bombardment of Algerian coastal villages hundreds of miles from Sétif. Not surprisingly, Muslims began to flee at the sight of French troops, or of French planes, which strafed and bombed their miserable *mechtas* indiscriminately, on the principle that whatever couldn't be defended should be destroyed. The sight of Muslims fleeing at the approach of government soldiers in turn confirmed the French in their suspicions that the Muslims were at one with the FLN.

Soon, burning houses and butchering livestock became "the normal course of events in these villages which are supporting the *fellagha*," according to Legionnaire Simon Murray. In this way, the belief in an FLN *levée* became a self-fulfilling prophesy, as each French tactical success brought them closer to strategic defeat:

With all the good results...[there] was a steady build-up of hatred against the French – a hatred that comes from living in fear and terror. And this antagonism drew the Arabs, so often before divided among themselves, into a common cause: it made them feel the necessity of combining for survival and it made them finally aware of their own strength. The French became the foreign intruder and the concept of nationalism was born in the Arabs, which was never there before. I wonder how many more crosses must be struck before the end comes – the end of the French, when a new nation will be born, conceived entirely through French misunderstanding.[44]

Murray undoubtedly overstates his case. Certainly, French brutality, torture, and "collective responsibility" made excellent recruiting sergeants for

---

[42] Merle, *Ahmed Ben Bella*, 94.
[43] Horne, *A Savage War of Peace*, 115.
[44] Simon Murray, *Legionnaire: My Five Years in the French Foreign Legion* (New York, 1978), 158–9, 67–8.

the FLN. The brutal French repression following the Philippeville massacres went a modest way toward reviving the fortunes of the FLN in the North Constantine.[45] It was reckoned that roughly 40 percent of the male population of the Casbah was tortured during the 1957 Battle of Algiers, some of whom subsequently joined the FLN. But French inability to distinguish friend from foe, and more importantly to distinguish either from the vast majority of neutral Muslims, did not automatically make Muslims pro-FLN, as Murray believed. As has been seen, the FLN could see the French home in the brutality game any day of the week. What it did was to remove any burning desire on the part of many Muslims to rally to the French cause, because the French did not bring security. On the contrary, they were actually more dangerous than the FLN because their terror was likely to be totally indiscriminate, while that of the FLN at least was targeted and had a rationale. French counterterror, based on the belief that they did indeed face a Muslim *levée en masse*, deprived the French of an opportunity to turn FLN brutality against the insurgency. The most important effect of French methods, when combined with those of the FLN, was to drive Muslims deeper into quietism and despair, which worked to the advantage of the FLN if only because it denied vital Muslim support to the French.

Not surprisingly, the belief of the French soldiers in Algeria that they faced an FLN-induced Muslim *levée* soon transmitted itself to France, where it had a particularly demoralizing effect because the French associated it with their own experience of the German Occupation. As suggested earlier, the French Resistance had hardly been a *levée en masse*. Nevertheless, in the postwar world, the myth that the French had actively participated in their own liberation had helped ease the humiliation of 1940. Careers had been built in postwar France on the strength of Resistance records, real and invented, and resisters spoke with great moral authority. And the full weight of that authority was felt when several of them began to criticize the torture of Muslims by French soldiers.

Torture became an issue during the Battle of Algiers in 1957, brought to public notice by conscience-struck soldiers, Catholics, and the Left. Captain Pierre-Henri Simon was inspired to write his *Contre la Torture* to save France from the "moral degradation" he believed he had encountered among Germans who refused to accept moral responsibility for the death camps. Simon compared the policy of "collective responsibility" adopted in Algeria with the SS mentality that had led to the massacre of 643 French men, women, and children in the village of Oradour in June 1944. French administrator Paul Teitgen and the writer Vercors (Jean Bruller) used their status as resisters to denounce a practice that had been inflicted on them by the Germans. French General Jacques de la Bollardière was given thirty days house arrest after he publicly compared methods used by 10th Paratroop Division

---

[45] Horne, *A Savage War of Peace*, 119.

commander General Jacques Massu in Algeria with those of the Germans in occupied France. These were small protests that did not end French support of the war, but their effect was cumulative. Protest against French methods tickled a French conscience sensitized by the Resistance myth of the French *levée* against the Germans. It introduced an element of doubt about the morality of France's role in Algeria, forfeited the moral high ground, and made the French vulnerable to the pressure of international opinion, which increasingly sided with the FLN.[46]

From the beginning, the FLN had staked their hopes for success on the support of outsiders. In fact, their calculation that Western opinion was especially receptive to a belief in the *levée en masse* of the Algerian people was undoubtedly the most accurate part of the original strategic assessment of the *neuf historiques*. The declaration of the self-determination of subject peoples had been built into the United Nations Charter precisely because it was assumed that these peoples longed to throw off the yoke of colonialism.

1955 was a critical year for the FLN, because it was then that Algeria became an international issue. The French reaction to the Philippeville massacres was largely responsible for this because it reinforced the belief that the FLN was the authentic spokesman for an Algerian Muslim *levée*. From then on, the French fought a losing battle to convince international opinion that the FLN was a minority movement, not a *levée*. The irony was that the Philippeville massacres were an act of desperation on the part of the FLN, at a time when its actual support among the Muslim population was at a very low ebb. On the eve of Philippeville, the FLN in North Constantine was reduced to barely 200 men with seventy weapons among them. Its leaders determined that an act of exemplary violence was required to unleash a "people's revolt."[47] They pursued a deliberate tactic of forcing Muslims to demonstrate in front of barracks and police stations and then firing on soldiers and police, who inevitably lashed out at the demonstrators.

The "people's revolt" did not materialize in the North Constantine. However, French repression paid dividends on the international level far beyond the FLN's calculations: Governor General Jacques Soustelle placed the military defeat of the rebellion above the need to pass reforms to enfranchise the Muslim population. The "motion of the sixty-one" and the subsequent suspension of the Algerian Assembly that followed the Philippeville massacres increased the gulf between the two communities. Finally, through the support of the emerging Third World movement, the Algerian problem was taken up by the UN General Assembly. Soustelle complained that this was "worth a convoy of arms."[48] He was wrong. It was worth far more than that.

---

[46] On the issue of torture, see ibid., 115, 194–207, 232–4; on the antiwar movement, see ibid., 234–6 and 416–17.

[47] Ibid., 119.

[48] Ibid., 123–4.

Events in Algeria helped the FLN to exploit the new international environment. First, it acquired a better class of recruit as French arrests of
moderate Muslims and the suspension of the Soustelle plan (and with it
hopes for reform of the system) convinced many young Algerian intellectuals that the future of Algeria must be severed from that of France.[49] As both
the UDMA and the MTLD were dissolved, many of their members rallied to
the FLN, while young, politically engaged Muslims now had no place to go
but the FLN. In this way, Soustelle helped the FLN to acquire a more educated and sophisticated pool of technicians and specialists to staff ministries,
embassies, and FLN interest groups.[50] The Provisional Government of the
Algerian Republic (GPRA), set up in Tunis, gave authority and respectability
to the independence movement. Their forceful message was that they alone
spoke for the Algerian people. It was a message the French were powerless
to counter. Gradually, by posing as the legitimate vanguard of the Muslim
levée in Algeria, the FLN was able to strip away reluctance to oppose France
over Algeria, in the Arab world, among France's NATO allies, and finally in
the Communist Bloc.

The second development was a military one. As has been seen, so confident
were the *neuf historiques* that Algeria was ripe for revolution, that they
believed a few acts of terrorism would spark a Muslim *levée*. In doing this,
they had ignored Mao's prescription that a popular uprising confronting the
power of the state must be protected by a revolutionary army possessing the
same sort of discipline, resilience, and institutional integrity as its opponent
(albeit in different tactical forms). Such a force had to be built up gradually
by careful political preparation of the population. It would then provide the
basis for constructing a revolutionary state.

By 1957, it was clear that the "general insurrection" on which the *neuf
historiques* had counted would not occur. Only in the Kabylia, where the
FLN had concentrated on eliminating Muslim opponents, while strengthening its hold over the population through the creation of cell networks in the
villages, had a solid political foundation been established. In other areas, like
the Aurès, where enthusiastic revolutionaries had attacked French soldiers

---

[49] The Soustelle program, presented to the assembly in Algiers in February 1955, sought to
integrate Muslims into the political life of Algeria, while retaining Algeria as a department
of France. It called for the decentralization of the administration, the creation of several
new departments, and the recruitment of more Muslims into positions of responsibility. The
two-tiered electoral college system that disenfranchised many Muslims was to be abolished.
The *communes mixtes*, dominated by the *pieds noirs*, were to be broken into elected rural
communes. The SAS were created to place representatives of France in distant villages that
seldom saw a French administrator. Arabic was to become the official language in Muslim
schools. The school-building program would be doubled. A beginning was to be made on
land reform. Finally, the equivalent of $148 million was placed toward poverty eradication.
See Horne, *A Savage War of Peace*, 108–9.
[50] William B. Quant, *Revolution and Political Leadership: Algeria 1954–1968* (Cambridge,
Mass., 1969), 110.

and been rapidly defeated, the revolution sputtered. Nor could the *Armée de Libération Nationale* (ALN), based in Tunisia, give much help. In Mao's theory, the army created the state because it supplied the protection behind which the structures of government could be organized to allow for the mobilization of "the people." In Algeria, however, the Morice Line, which ran along the Algeria–Tunisia border from the Mediterranean to the Sahara, effectively cut off the FLN from its nascent military arm, while French counterinsurgency forces put increasing pressure on revolutionary cadres in Algeria itself. The ALN could never become powerful enough to offer a secure base for the revolution. All it could do within Algeria was to keep the French off balance and terrorize those who cooperated with them.

The adaptation to this situation by a new generation of young ALN leaders, led by Houari Boumedienne, was brilliant. They created an army in Tunis not to fight, but to exist as a symbol of the revolution, an armed force that embodied the *levée* of the Algerian people, even if the power of French arms temporarily prevented that popular uprising. Like George Washington during the American Revolution, they dared not risk their army against a superior force. Unlike Washington, however, and indeed unlike Giap, they got neither a Yorktown nor a Dien Bien Phu. They did not have to – the myth of the *levée* supplied the offensive component of their strategy which, over time, helped to break the French will to continue the war.

The *levée en masse* shaped the outcome of the Algerian war in a way neither the FLN nor the OAS had envisaged. Neither the French Revolutionary model, nor the FLN's assessment of the revolutionary potential of Algerian Muslims, prepared the FLN for the fact that a popular uprising might not be possible absent the coercive power of the state. The FLN quickly discovered, however, that the myth of the *levée* was more powerful than its disappointing reality. They learned to manipulate the myth so that it would work to their advantage by creating, in the minds of French soldiers, the French nation, and international opinion the illusion that their movement was indeed the expression of a universal desire among Algerian Muslims for independence from France. For its part, the OAS discovered that the *levée* worked not at all as a theory of counterrevolution.

12

Looking Backward

The People in Arms and the Transformation of War

Arthur Waldron

The army created by the *levée en masse* of 1793 was perceived by its architects and opponents alike not simply as an instrument of French national power, but, as Daniel Moran has noted, as a force of nature – indeed, as a "natural" army, expressive of every participant's inherent instinct for citizenship. Its putatively organic character was supposed to make it incomparably more powerful than the "unnatural," state-concocted armies that opposed it. The main reason this concept took root was that experience seemed to bear it out. The armies of Revolutionary France, even before Napoleon took them in hand, proved themselves more than a match for the best the Old Regime could bring against them. Later on the German people proved themselves equal to the French challenge by seizing upon its methods. Within a few decades, they had come to dominate Europe.

So much, at least, was apparent even from the periphery of the European world system. In China, a handful of military thinkers realized that what European history demonstrated was not so much the preeminence of technology – the main inference drawn by the Vietnamese royal court (as well as many in China and elsewhere), who accordingly concluded that resistance would be futile – but rather that social change, set in motion by the French Revolution, had endowed Europeans with natural armies, as military expressions of the natural nation-state. Both depended upon the idea of the "mass," of universally shared identity independent of, indeed defiant of, traditional social distinctions; an identity that bound citizens together, even while affirming their individual (but also identical) rights. As the Chinese rendering of identity – *rentong*, literally "recognizing sameness" – reminds us, the search for modern identity is not just about finding what one is in one's self alone, but above all about finding who else is like you. In the post-Revolutionary world, not simply armies, but states, would be freed from the distortions of imposed authority, and so express their true nature.

The new army and the new state were indeed connected. The rising of the people would sweep away old political structures and call into being new ones, based upon the powerful affinity of citizens, rather than the artificial, draconian discipline of the Old Regime. Add all this together, and you have a phenomenon that, for the last two centuries, has provided a believable avatar for that most resonant of all nineteenth- and twentieth-century social science terms: revolution.

The *levée en masse*, as the chapters in this volume have demonstrated in a variety of contexts, embodied, in the realm of war, both the imaginative power, and the kernel of truth embedded in the idea of revolution. Yet our authors have nonetheless approached their subject with a sympathetic skepticism. That the *levée* was not what many believed was already clear in the 1790s. Young men did not stream unbidden to the defense of *la patrie en danger*, not in France, not anywhere, however real the danger. The passionately nationalistic and populist Chinese writers of the early twentieth century were not notable for the numbers of them that actually joined armies – a reflection of the traditionally low status accorded military service in China, which has persisted right down to the present, despite all intervening national and revolutionary ferment.

In its legendary form, in other words, the *levée en masse* did not occur in any of the cases our authors have surveyed. If anything, the armies thought best to exemplify the "people in arms" approached their peaks of performance in proportion to the extent to which the state organizations they served provided a firm basis for action. The people, in other words, even when armed, are not self-rising dough. Napoleon's army became the best in Europe not least because it was the best organized – a tribute to the bureaucratic efficiency of the French state. Germany's subsequent military transformation was as much the result of professionally motivated military reform as of the changing temper of German public opinion, real though the latter was. The Vietnamese army that drove the United States from Indochina was likewise the product of a long evolution, involving shifts in how the Vietnamese thought of themselves – in how much more broadly they "recognized sameness" – but also of purely military changes inspired by European examples, not to mention close alliances with China and the USSR. China got a national army (to the extent that it has one, the People's Liberation Army being an instrument not of the state, but of the Communist Party) only when state institutions were reconstructed after the defeat of Japan.

Strong states can have any sort of army they choose. They can enforce a uniform draft – the dominant military expedient of the twentieth century – or they can foster elite, professional forces, drawn from social groups deemed reliable as instruments for the suppression of popular movements. The appeal of the *levée en masse*, however, is not chiefly to strong states but to imaginative nationalists on the one hand, and to soldiers and bureaucrats struggling to find men to stem the tide of military defeat, on the other. For both, its singular virtue has been its putatively self-actualizing quality.

The people in arms was, again, a natural phenomenon. It was what society would do if freed from artificial, inorganic constraints. But of course no army emerges *ex nihilo*. To speculate what a natural army – or a natural state – would be is a bit like wondering what language people would speak if left to themselves.

Recourse to the *levée en masse* has been characteristic of those moments in a people's history when regular armies and state institutions have been in crisis, or in the throes of reconstruction. Under such conditions, those in authority – officially constituted, or merely nascent – have sought to use the loyalties and volition of the individual to substitute for the purposes and the organizational powers of the state. Recurring historical experience has revealed the people in arms to be an interim expedient, not a first glimpse of a new and stable form of military organization.

What is perhaps less apparent is that a similar interim quality attaches the *levée*'s intellectual partner, nationalism. It too dominates the political stage only at times when more familiar characters – state, bureaucracy, legally defined rights, and so forth – are for whatever reason *hors de combat*, usually because the state that has hitherto provided them has divided within itself and unleashed civil conflict, or been overthrown by an invader, or (rarely) overthrown by its own people. Under such circumstances the state guarantees of personal status and security shift under our feet, and primal questions arise. Who is friend or kin? Who is enemy? Whom can we trust? To which the "natural" answer, tragically, has proven to be: people who look like us, believe like us, talk like us. Those to whom we are the same.

Most historians have long ago concluded that this recognized sameness is delusory: that it exists in the imagination, perhaps, but not in reality. Even the most homogenous social groups enclose all sorts of readily identifiable differences. These indubitable facts, however, have not prevented the nationalist principle from becoming the default mechanism for building states and choosing sides in a conflict; any more than the comparably illusory qualities of the *levée en masse* have prevented it from being seized upon when all else has failed.

When, in 1870, the French army was smashed by the Prussians, the emperor imprisoned, and Paris invested, the head of the self-proclaimed French Republic, Léon Gambetta, escaped dramatically by balloon and invoked the *levée en masse*. Brave talk, one might say. Yet it proved to be a gesture capable of giving pause to the best army in the world. For German soldiers, the prospect of unmanageable hordes of extemporaneously militarized Frenchmen was a force to conjure with, against which neither Bismarck's diplomacy nor Moltke's tactical proficiency were thought to be of much use. Much of this was a figment of the German imagination, a nightmare oppressing an army caught short by the scale of its own victory. Yet they proved sufficient to persuade Bismarck of the need for an immediate settlement, lest the Franco-Prussian War become "people's war."

Something of the same hall-of-mirrors process occurs in Algeria, where all parties are sufficiently convinced by the legend of the *levée en masse* that victory is largely determined by which group can present the best impersonation of it. Similar imaginative processes have conditioned political outcomes in China, Vietnam, and elsewhere.

Nevertheless, viewed against a longer historical perspective, the *levée en masse* appears to have more military than political significance. It is the harbinger of the mass armies that slaughtered each other in the twentieth century. Under conditions of industrialized warfare, numbers counted in a way they had not before, when trained manpower had to be jealously conserved. And, indeed, as they may not in the future, as the claims of skill and technological excellence have so forcefully asserted themselves against those of the big battalions, not to mention the "human wave."

The *levée en masse* contributed to the transformation of European warfare in the nineteenth century and of world warfare in the twentieth. But in neither case was it the sole or even the decisive factor. It provided the idea of a popular mass army and a rationale and set of powerful slogans for raising it. But it alone could not have carried the day, absent the professionalization of the world's officer corps, the development of weapons that could be handled effectively by an imperfectly trained force, and the emergence of state institutions that could provide the financial, legal, and administrative resources required to sustain mass military effort.

At the intellectual and imaginative level, however, as this volume has made clear, the mythology of the *levée en masse* had a palpable impact on the conduct of European wars, and, as it entangled itself with indigenous traditions, on anticolonial wars and other extra-European conflicts as well.

It is chiefly in the historiography of these non-European states that we continue to encounter characters that were once the mainstays of European national history but that have now been shooed from the stage by generations of critical historians: the aroused masses, the national hero, the uncanny success of popular forces arrayed against praetorian outsiders, and so forth. Here the impact on how historians have come to conceive of their subject has been particularly marked. As is well known, historians until perhaps a century ago concerned themselves disproportionately with dynasties and battles. That at any rate is the caricature, and like most caricatures we recognize its element of truth. But another way of thinking about the same issue is to observe that historians before the last few generations were concerned above all with the vertical, or hierarchical, organization of society; with the authority of one man or group over another; and with the periodic displacements in that hierarchy that have repeatedly led to social disorder, killing, and war.

What sorts of events were these with which those historians long concerned themselves? They were matters that today scarcely receive attention at all: the failure of a queen to produce a male heir; the struggles among brothers or cousins for a throne once the father has died; the rivalries and clashes between local hierarchies – noble, religious, social, occupational, and so forth – that formed the fiber of premodern societies. In such situations, it was accepted, events as insignificant as the tactical mistakes that lose a battle, or a poorly judged marriage, or the premature death of the heir to a throne, could prove as consequential for the historical trajectory of society as a misaligned railway switch can for the passengers on a train.

Since the early 1900s this approach to history has been greatly complicated, if not superseded, by the introduction of broad economic, demographic, and cultural factors of such sweeping integrative power that the quarrels within and between hierarchies of status and dominance have attracted a diminishing share of historical attention. They have been marginalized as variables dependent upon putatively larger historical forces, whose existence and pervasive effects are inferred by analogy with the natural sciences. The result is fascinating: in place of what might be called a *vertical* approach to history, which treats society as a matter of linkages from top to bottom, king through serf, and in which conflict chiefly arises between these various pyramids, a *horizontal* view has arisen, with markedly different concerns and explanatory methods.

This horizontal view is the one with which we have all grown up. It conceives society like a section cut through the earth's surface, revealing layer upon layer of geological sediment. The most imposing feature thus revealed is that of class structure, imaginatively adumbrated in Plato's *Republic*, but fully worked out by Marx and his cohort, and by the social historians: with proletarians and the underclass, the working class, the various degrees of middle class, the elites, the dominant classes, and so forth, all assigned their places by their relationship to the "means of production," which is to say, in practice, to technology. To the extent that such a view incorporated a dynamic element, it was thought to culminate with socialism, a perfectly horizontal society in which a homogenous population shares a single set of interests, and without any vertical structure of dominance at all. That, as Leszek Kolakowski puts it, was "the greatest fantasy of our [twentieth] century."[1] Though of course the fact that the horizontal approach should become absurd at the limit is not surprising; so too does the vertical, with its concepts of Divine Right, history on horseback, and so forth.

This evolution of modern historical thinking has not, of course, proved a futile exercise, nor one without great value. We historians require both an x and a y axis. But the horizontal approach encounters real difficulties when it comes to explaining war. For the more closely we examine human conflicts, the fewer examples we find, if indeed we find any at all, where the tension along the horizontal boundaries – between one class and another – actually causes, or even drives, the conflict, and the more we find that the

---

[1] Leszek Kolakowski, *Main Currents of Marxism: Its Origin, Growth, and Dissolution*, translated by P. S. Falla, 3 volumes (Oxford, 1978), 3: 523.

old hierarchical categories are to blame, however much their roles may be obscured by the ideologically charged language of the protagonists. Thus the great revolutions – American, French, Russian, Chinese, Vietnamese, and the others – that were once put forward as validating the horizontal approach, now seem to render it problematical. In every case, we find elite struggle for dominance preceding the mobilization of the masses, and the mobilized masses not aligning according to their shared, horizontal interests (e.g., class) but rather dividing among themselves along the same lines as the contenders at the top. The instability begins at the summit of the pyramid, and not at the base (earthquakes being, evidently, far more common in geology than in history).

Both the *levée en masse* and the vast aureole of popular and academic mythology that have come to surround it partake of the real and imaginary processes of history, while lying at the intersection of the horizontal and vertical forces that shape human affairs. By grappling with both sets of dimensions – real and imaginary, horizontal and vertical – our contributors have disentangled and clarified a great deal and presented something like a believable biography of one of the most ubiquitous characters in mankind's historical drama: the "people in arms." Chapter after chapter has demonstrated how unexpected and fraught with irony and paradox have been this character's recurring appearances on the historical stage.

Nor has he made his final bow. As these words are written, the Western imagination (and perhaps the Muslim as well) is transfixed by the vision of something like a *levée en masse* in the Land of Islam – a force that purports to sweep away all opposition before a great rush of aroused, passionate, religiously inspired warriors. One suspects that real and imaginative components are compounded today in roughly the same proportions we have found in the original *levée* and its sequels, thoroughly mixed with all the particularities of local and hierarchical rivalry that plagued the original. Indeed, building on the lessons of the chapters in this volume, one can perhaps argue that successful state structures will in the end prove more important to the Muslim world than the zeal of the masses, or the charisma of their leaders. But at a certain level none of that matters. Appearance, myth, and historical memory – these are real forces today, as they have always been.

We are left with a few concluding questions, of which perhaps the most fundamental is the future of the *masse*. Students of humanity's horizontal structures have, on the whole, envisioned a historical process by which social complexity diminished over time. The myriad local loyalties of medieval times, the profusion of duchies, kingdoms, electorates, languages, confessions, guilds, coats of arms, and what have you – all were destined to be fused and refined by the universal logic of economic and political rationality, into structures whose contradictions would diminish with each forward turn of the historical wheel. As history progressed, society would grow ever more simple.

This of course has proved entirely wrong. Today's world is incomparably more complex and differentiated, and more interpenetrated by conflicting interests of every sort, than was that of the nineteenth and twentieth centuries. They were in turn decidedly more complex than those that preceded them – which were themselves by no means simple; otherwise, Marx would never have located in them the great, unrefined mass of diversity that he expected the future to fuse into a uniform social substance. As historians have recognized this fact, they have had not only to set aside the Western version of what the Chinese call *datong*, or "great harmony," coming in the future, but also to turn their attention back to those supposedly epiphenomenal clashes of political and other interests by which social stability has always been, and continues to be, threatened.

This is a challenging task, not least for the student of how military and social institutions connect to one another. What commonalities will bind the armies of the future together – whether of nations, coalitions, or pan-national communities? What will lead the soldier to lay down his life? *Pro patria*? If not, *pro* what? And what about weaponry? As it grows more complex, only the career specialist can control and manage it. What are the implications of this for the citizen army?

And finally, what about political institutions? War, we may pessimistically expect, will continue to be a dominant feature of human society. The change in the nature of war between the eighteenth and nineteenth centuries, of which the *levée en masse*, real and imagined, was a crucial part, left its most powerful legacy in the consolidation of the European state system, a structure whose pacification, to the extent that this has been achieved, entailed a scale of violence few could have imagined before they had seen it for themselves. What effects will future changes in the nature of war impose on our current political and international arrangements? For considering questions of this kind, the story of the *levée* is not a bad point of departure.

Index

Lightning Source UK Ltd.
Milton Keynes UK
UKOW07f0434251114

242134UK00007B/261/P